ITALIAN
Vocabulary

Second Edition

Marcel Danesi, Ph.D.

BARRON'S

BARRON'S EDUCATIONAL SERIES, INC.

All inquiries should be addressed to:
Barron's Educational Series, Inc.
250 Wireless Boulevard
Hauppauge, New York 11788
http://www.barronseduc.com

International Standard Book No. 0-7641-2190-1

Library of Congress Catalog Card No. 2002028316

Library of Congress Cataloging-in-Publication Data

Danesi, Marcel, 1946–.
    Italian vocabulary / by Marcel Danesi.—2nd ed.
      p.   cm.
    ISBN 0-7641-2190-1 (alk. paper)
  · 1. Italian language—Conversation and phrase books—English.
  2. Italian language—Glossaries, vocabularies, etc. I. Title.

PC1121 .D355 2003
458.3'421—dc21   2002028316

PRINTED IN CHINA
9 8 7 6 5 4 3 2

CONTENTS

CONTENTS

CONTENTS

CONTENTS

PREFACE TO THE SECOND EDITION

This second edition of *Italian Vocabulary* has been modified and expanded in various ways. First and foremost, the list of entries has been updated to reflect the changes that have occurred in Italy (and the world) since the first edition came out in 1990—to mention just one example, Italy has replaced its *lira* currency with the *euro*. Specifically, in this second edition you will find that:

- more "call-outs" explaining points of form and meaning, or providing further vocabulary information (such as idiomatic expressions), have been added;
- a number of sections have been renamed or reorganized to provide more clarity and information on their content;
- new sections have been added (e.g. Internet vocabulary, telecommunications vocabulary, etc.) reflecting the many changes in the world that have come to pass since 1990.

All in all, the number of vocabulary items has almost doubled since the first edition, making this book a contemporary and comprehensive study guide to the learning of Italian vocabulary.

Marcel Danesi
University of Toronto, 2003

HOW TO USE THIS BOOK

THIS IS NOT JUST ANOTHER DICTIONARY!

When you learn another language, there comes a time when you will feel the need to fill in the vocabulary gaps left by the learning process, so that you can truly speak about any topic in your new language. But an ordinary dictionary, which simply lists words in alphabetical order, is of no use to you in helping you fill in the gaps in a systematic fashion.

This book will help you do exactly *that* in Italian. It is not a dictionary, although it can be used as one. It is a comprehensive and structured study guide to over 10,000 Italian words, all of which you will need to be able to speak about virtually anything, from the weather to controversial issues such as the environment and drugs. The book guides you systematically through the ways in which the Italian language organizes its vocabulary into categories of thought and communication. These form the knowledge base upon which you will be able to acquire a comprehensive control of the kind of vocabulary you will need to carry out everyday communicative tasks.

OVERALL DESIGN

This book consists of a pronunciation guide, nine main thematic sections (*Basic Information, People,* etc.), an appendix of the irregular verbs that are found in it, and an English-Italian *Wordfinder*. The pronunciation guide gives you the essential details of how to pronounce Italian words, phrases, and sentences.

Each thematic section is divided into subcategories (44 in all). For example, the section dealing with *People* sets up the study of this topic in terms of three subcategories: *Family and Friends, Describing People,* and *The Body*. Each of these is then subdivided into more specific themes (e.g. *Family Members, Age Concepts,* etc.). This section is thus designed to provide you with a structured access to the kind of vocabulary you will invariably need when talking about people in Italian.

USING THIS BOOK FOR DIFFERENT LEARNING GOALS

If you are attempting to learn Italian from scratch, you will find that this book provides you with an effective framework for acquiring the basic vocabulary tools of the Italian language. If you already have some knowledge of the language, you will find the way in which it has organized vocabulary items to be extremely useful for helping you increase or reinforce your control of vocabulary. If you are a student of Italian, enrolled in some program of study, you will find this book to be an effective aid in helping you prepare for oral classroom tasks and for written assignments on specific topics.

FEATURES

The English concept is given to you on the left-hand side of the page; the Italian equivalent or equivalents appear in the middle of the page; and a pronunciation guide appears on the right-hand side. Complete phonetic transcriptions are given mainly for difficult items. Frequently occurring items, easily pronounceable words, and many one-syllable items (such as prepositions) are not transcribed.

ENGLISH CONCEPT	ITALIAN EQUIVALENT	PRONUNCIATION
↓	↓	↓
five	cinque	*'čin-kwe*

The English concepts are arranged in alphabetical order, unless the nature of the category requires some other logical system of organization (e.g. numbers). Related items, concepts, or specific uses are indented under the main item.

ENGLISH CONCEPT	ITALIAN EQUIVALENT	PRONUNCIATION
birth	nascita	*'na-ši-ta*
• **birth certificate**	certificato di nascita	*čer-ti-fi-'ka-to*
• **birth pain**	doglie	*'do-lye*
• **birth rate**	tasso di natalità	*'tas-so*
• **(to) give birth**	partorire	*par-to-'ri-re*
• **premature birth**	parto prematuro	*'par-to pre-ma-'tu-ro*

Each noun is given in its singular form, unless it does not occur in this form within a specific category.

Regular Italian Nouns

> • A masculine noun ends in *-o* (*ragazzo* "boy") or in *-e* (*padre* "father")
> • A feminine noun ends in *-a* (*ragazza* "girl") or in *-e* (*madre* "mother")
>
> *The gender of nouns ending in –e will thus be marked throughout the book as either masculine (m) or feminine (f)*

Nouns that have a different masculine and feminine form will be indicated accordingly. For example, the concept "nurse" is rendered as *infermiere* in reference to male nurses and as *infermiera* in reference to female ones. This will be shown in the following way:

infermiere (-a)

Adjectives will be given in their masculine singular form (*alto* "tall", *grande* "big"). Invariable adjectives (i.e. those having only one form, singular and plural) are identified with (inv).

Verbs will be listed in their infinitive form as follows:

(to) eat   mangiare   *man-'ja-re*

If a verb has an irregular conjugation, it will be marked with an asterisk (*). All such verbs are found in the *Irregular Verbs* section at the back. Verbs conjugated with *essere* in compound tenses are indicated with (ess). And third conjugation verbs that are conjugated with *–isc* in present tenses (e.g. *finisco* "I finish") are also identified for your convenience with (isc).

ABBREVIATIONS

FOR NOUNS

m   =   masculine

f   =   feminine

s   =   singular

pl   =   plural

fam   =   familiar

inv   =   invariable

pol   =   polite

FOR VERBS

*   =   irregular

ess   =   conjugated with *essere* in compound tenses (since *essere* itself is conjugated with *essere*, this will not be indicated in its own case)

isc   =   a third-conjugation verb conjugated with *–isc* in present tenses

IN GENERAL

subj   =   subject

obj   =   object

inv   =   invariable

pol   =   polite form

fam   =   familiar form

PRONUNCIATION GUIDE

Figuring out how to pronounce written Italian words is a fairly easy task. The following charts summarize the symbols used in this book to help you pronounce them.

VOWELS

Alphabet Letters	English Equivalents	Examples	Symbols Used
a	f<u>a</u>ther "ah"	*casa* / house *acqua* / water	*a*
e	b<u>e</u>t "eh"	*bene* / well *esame* / exam	*e*
i	mach<u>i</u>ne "eeh"	*vini* / wines *indirizzi* / addresses	*i*
o	s<u>o</u>rry "oh"	*otto* / eight *oro* / gold	*o*
u	b<u>oo</u>t "ooh"	*uva* / grapes *gusto* / taste	*u*

Speakers in various parts of Italy pronounce *e* and *o* differently. In some parts, these vowels are pronounced with the mouth relatively more open. In others, they are pronounced with the mouth relatively more closed. In many areas, however, *both* pronunciations are used.

To get an idea of what this means, consider how the *a* in "tomato" is pronounced in North America. In some areas, it is pronounced like the *a* in "father." In other areas, it is pronounced like the *a* in "pay." However, whether it is pronounced one way or the other, no one will have much difficulty understanding that the word is "tomato." This is exactly what happens in the case of Italian *e* and *o*.

The letters *i* and *u* can also stand in some words for semivowel sounds.

SEMIVOWELS

Alphabet Letters	English Equivalents	Examples	Symbols Used
i	say yes	*ieri* / yesterday *poi* / then	*y*
u	way how	*uomo* / man *causa* / cause	*w*

CONSONANTS: I

The following Italian consonants should cause you few problems:

Alphabet Letters	English Equivalents	Examples	Symbols Used
b	boy	*bello* / beautiful *bravo* / good	*b*
d	day	*dopo* / after *ladro* / thief	*d*
f	fun	*forte* / strong *frutta* / fruit	*f*
l	love	*latte* / milk *alto* / tall	*l*
m	more	*matita* / pencil *mondo* / world	*m*
n	nice	*naso* / nose *nono* / ninth	*n*
p	price	*porta* / door *prezzo* / price	*p*
q	quick	*quanto* / how much *quinto* / fifth	*k*
r	Like a "rolled" *r* sound (as in some Scottish dialects).	*rosso* / red *raro* / rare	*r*
t	too	*tardi* / late *tu* / you	*t*
v	vine	*vino* / wine *vero* / true	*v*

Note that the letter *h* does not represent any sound. It is like the silent *h* of "hour": *ho* ("I have"), *hai* ("you have").

CONSONANTS: II

The following letters are pronounced in different ways, as indicated in the chart:

Alphabet Letters	English Equivalents	Examples	Symbols Used
c	<u>c</u>at	Used in front of *a, o, u,* and any consonant. *cane* / dog *come* / how *cuore* / heart *classe* / class *cravatta* / tie	*k*
ch	<u>ch</u>emistry	Used in front of *e* and *i.* *che* / what *chi* / who *chiesa* / church	*k*
c	<u>ch</u>in	Used in front of *e* and *i.* *cena* / dinner *cinema* / movies	*č*
ci	<u>ch</u>at	Used in front of *a, o, u.* *ciao* / hi, bye *cioccolata* / chocolate	*č*
g	good	Used in front of *a, o, u,* and any consonant. *gatto* / cat *gola* / throat *guanto* / glove *gloria* / glory *grande* / big, large	*g*
gh	get	Used in front of *e* and *i.* *spaghetti* / spaghetti *ghiaccio* / ice	*g*

Alphabet Letters	English Equivalents	Examples	Symbols Used
g	<u>j</u>ust	Used in front of *e* and *i*.	*j*
		gente / people *giro* / turn, tour	
gi	Bel<u>gi</u>an	Used in front of *a, o, u*.	*j*
		giacca / jacket *giorno* / day *giugno* / June	
sc	<u>sc</u>ale	Used in front of *a, o, u*, or any consonant.	*sk*
		scala / staircase *scopa* / broom *scuola* / school *scrivere* / to write	
sch	<u>sch</u>ool	Used in front of *e* and *i*.	*sk*
		scherzo / prank *schifo* / disgust	
sc	<u>sh</u>ine	Used in front of *e* and *i*.	*š*
		scena / scene *sciocco* / unsalted, flavorless	
sci	<u>sh</u>uffle	Used in front of *a, o, u*.	*š*
		sciopero / labor strike *sciupare* / to waste	
s	<u>s</u>oul	*sapone* / soap *specchio* / mirror	*s*
s	pre<u>s</u>ent	Used in front of *b, d, g, l, m, n, r, v*; and between vowels.	*z*
		sbaglio / mistake *casa* / house	

Alphabet Letters	English Equivalents	Examples	Symbols Used
gn	ca<u>ny</u>on	*sogno* / dream *giugno* / June	*ny*
gli	mi<u>lli</u>on	*figlio* / son *luglio* / July	*ly*
z	ca<u>ts</u> do<u>gs</u>	*zio* / uncle *zucchero* / sugar	*ts* *dz*

CONSONANTS: III

Most of the above consonants can have a corresponding double articulation. The pronunciation of double consonants lasts twice as long as that of the corresponding single consonant. In this book, double consonants will be indicated with double symbols, belonging to separate syllables:

fato ("fate")   =   *'fa-to*   *fatto* ("fact")   =   *'fat-to*
caro ("dear")   =   *'ca-ro*   *carro* ("cart")   =   *'kar-ro*

SYLLABICATION

Syllables will be separated by hyphens, and the stressed syllable will be indicated with a preceding mark.

amico ("friend")   =   *a-'mi-ko*

BASIC INFORMATION

1. MATHEMATICS

A. CARDINAL NUMBERS

zero	zero	ʹdze-ro
one	uno	ʹu-no
two	due	ʹdu-e
three	tre	tre
four	quattro	ʹkwat-tro
five	cinque	ʹčin-kwe
six	sei	ʹse-i
seven	sette	ʹset-te
eight	otto	ʹot-to
nine	nove	ʹno-ve
ten	dieci	ʹdye-či
eleven	undici	ʹun-di-či
twelve	dodici	ʹdo-di-či
thirteen	tredici	ʹtre-di-či
fourteen	quattordici	ʹkwat-ʹtor-di-či
fifteen	quindici	ʹkwin-di-či
sixteen	sedici	ʹse-di-či
seventeen	diciassette	di-čas-ʹset-te
eighteen	diciotto	di-čot-to
nineteen	diciannove	di-čan-ʹno-ve
twenty	venti	ʹven-ti
twenty-one	ventuno	ven-ʹtu-no
twenty-two	ventidue	ven-ti-ʹdu-e
twenty-three	ventitré	ven-ti-ʹtre
twenty-four	ventiquattro	ven-ti-ʹkwat-tro
twenty-five	venticinque	ven-ti-čin-kwe
twenty-six	ventisei	ven-ti-ʹse-i
twenty-seven	ventisette	ven-ti-ʹset-te
twenty-eight	ventotto	ven-ʹtot-to
twenty-nine	ventinove	ven-ti-ʹno-ve
thirty	trenta	ʹtren-ta
thirty-one	trentuno	tren-ʹtu-no
thirty-two	trentadue	tren-ta-ʹdu-e
thirty-three	trentatré	tren-ta-ʹtre
...		

forty	quaranta	*kwa-'ran-ta*
forty-one	quarantuno	*kwa-ran-'tu-no*
forty-two	quarantadue	*kwa-ran-ta-'du-e*
forty-three	quarantatré	*kwa-ran-ta-'tre*
...		
fifty	cinquanta	*čin-'kwan-ta*
fifty-one	cinquantuno	*čin-kwan-'tu-no*
fifty-two	cinquantadue	*čin-kwan-ta-'du-e*
fifty-three	cinquantatré	*čin-kwan-ta-'tre*
...		
sixty	sessanta	*ses-'san-ta*
...		
seventy	settanta	*set-'tan-ta*
...		
eighty	ottanta	*ot-'tan-ta*
...		
ninety	novanta	*no-'van-ta*
...		
one hundred	cento	*'čen-to*
one hundred and one	centouno	*čen-'to-u-no*
one hundred and two	centodue	*čen-to-'du-e*
...		
two hundred	duecento	*du-e-'čen-to*
two hundred and one	duecentouno, duecentuno	*du-e-čen-'to-u-no*
...		
three hundred	trecento	*tre-'čen-to*
...		
one thousand	mille	*'mil-le*
one thousand and one	milleuno	*mil-le'u-no*
...		
two thousand	duemila	*du-e-'mi-la*
two thousand and one	duemilauno	*du-e-mi-la'u-no*
...		
three thousand	tremila	*tre-'mi-la*
...		
four thousand	quattromila	*kwat-tro-'mi-la*
...		
five thousand	cinquemila	*čin-kwe-'mi-la*
...		
one hundred thousand	centomila	*čen-to-'mi-la*
...		
two hundred thousand	duecentomila	*du-e-čen-to-'mi-la*
...		
one million	un milione	*un mi-'lyo-ne*
...		
two million	due milioni	*'du-e mi-'lyo-ni*
...		

three million	tre milioni	'tre mi-'lyo-ni
...		
one hundred million	cento milioni	'čen-to mi-'lyo-ni
...		
one billion	un miliardo	un mi-'lyar-do
...		
two billion	due miliardi	du-e mi-'lyar-di

Formation Rule

In front of *uno* and *otto* (the two numbers that start with a vowel), drop the final vowel of the tens number:

| 21 | *venti* | → | *vent- + uno* | → | *ventuno* |
| 38 | *trenta* | → | *trent- + otto* | → | *trentotto* |

When *tre* is added on, it must be written with an accent (to show that the stress is on the final vowel):

| 23 | *venti + tre* | → | *ventitré* |
| 33 | *trenta + tre* | → | *trentatré* |

B. ORDINAL NUMBERS

first	primo	'pri-mo
second	secondo	se-'kon-do
third	terzo	'ter-tso
fourth	quarto	'kwar-to
fifth	quinto	'kwin-to
sixth	sesto	'ses-to
seventh	settimo	'set-ti-mo
eighth	ottavo	ot-'ta-vo
ninth	nono	'no-no
tenth	decimo	'de-či-mo
eleventh	undicesimo	un-di-'če-zi-mo
twelfth	dodicesimo	do-di-'če-zi-mo
thirteenth	tredicesimo	tre-di-'če-zi-mo
...		
twenty-third	ventitreesimo	ven-ti-tre-'e-zi-mo
thirty-third	trentatreesimo	tren-ta-tre-'e-zi-mo
forty-third	quarantatreesimo	kwa-ran-ta-tre-'e-zi-mo
...		
hundredth	centesimo	čen-'te-zi-mo
...		

thousandth	millesimo	*mil-'le-zi-mo*
...		
millionth	milionesimo	*mi-lyo-'ne-zi-mo*
...		
billionth	miliardesimo	*mi-lyar-'de-zi-mo*

Formation Rule

The ordinals greater than *decimo* are formed by adding
the suffix *-esimo* to the corresponding cardinal number.
The final vowel of the cardinal is dropped in the process:

e.g. *undici* + *-esimo* = *undicesimo* (= eleventh).

Exception: the *-e* in cardinal numbers ending in *-tré* is
retained without the accent mark: *ventitré* + *-esimo* =
ventitreesimo (= twenty-third)

Useful Expressions

double	=	il doppio
two by two	=	a due a due
three by three	=	a tre a tre
...		
a dozen	=	una dozzina
about twenty	=	una ventina
about thirty	=	una trentina
...		
about a hundred	=	un centinaio
about two hundred	=	due centinaia
about three hundred	=	tre centinaia
...		
about one thousand	=	un migliaio
about two thousand	=	due migliaia
about three thousand	=	tre migliaia
...		

C. FRACTIONS

General Rule

$$\frac{2}{3} \quad \to \quad \text{due (= cardinal number)}$$
$$\phantom{\frac{2}{3}} \quad \to \quad \text{terzi (= ordinal number)}$$

two thirds = due terzi

one-half	metà (f)	*mę-'ta*
	mezzo	*'met-tso*
one-third	un terzo	*un 'ter-tso*
one-quarter	un quarto	*un 'kwar-to*
...		
two-thirds	due terzi	*du-e 'ter-tsi*
two-fifths	due quinti	*du-e 'kwin-ti*
...		
three-elevenths	tre undicesimi	*tre un-di-če-zi-mi*
three-twenty-fifths	tre venticinquesimi	*tre ven-ti-čin-'kwe-zi-mi*

D. TYPES OF NUMBERS

Arabic	arabo	*'a-ra-bo*
cardinal	cardinale	*car-di-'na-le*
complex	complesso	*com-'ples-so*
decimal	decimale	*de-či-'ma-le*
digit	cifra	*'či-fra*
even	pari (inv)	*'pa-ri*
fraction	frazione (f)	*fra-'tsyo-ne*
• **fractional**	frazionario	*fra-tsyo-'na-ri-o*
imaginary	immaginario	*im-ma-ji-'na-ri-o*
integer	intero	*in-'te-ro*
irrational	irrazionale	*ir-ra-tsyo-'na-le*
negative	negativo	*ne-ga-'ti-vo*
number	numero	*'nu-me-ro*
• **(to) number**	numerare	*nu-me-'ra-re*
• **numeral**	numerale (m)	*nu-me-'ra-le*
• **numerical**	numerico	*nu-'me-ri-ko*
odd	dispari (inv)	*'dis-pa-ri*
ordinal	ordinale	*or-di-'na-le*
positive	positivo	*po-zi-'ti-vo*
prime	primo	*'pri-mo*
rational	razionale	*ra-tsyo-'na-le*
real	reale	*re-'a-le*
reciprocal	reciproco	*re-'či-pro-ko*
Roman	romano	*ro-'ma-no*
square	quadrato	*kwa-'dra-to*

E. BASIC OPERATIONS

arithmetical operations	operazioni aritmetiche	o-per-a-'tsyo-ni a-rit-'me-ti-ke
(to) add	addizionare	ad-di-tsyo-'na-re
• **(to) add on**	aggiungere*	aj-'jun-je-re
• **addition**	addizione (f)	ad-di-'tsyo-ne
• **plus**	più	pyu
• **two plus two equals four**	due più due è uguale a quattro	—
(to) subtract	sottrarre*	sot-'trar-re
• **subtraction**	sottrazione (f)	sot-tra-'tsyo-ne
• **minus**	meno	—
• **three minus two equals one**	tre meno due è uguale a uno	—
(to) multiply	moltiplicare	mol-ti-pli-'ka-re
• **multiplication**	moltiplicazione (f)	mol-ti-pli-ka-'tsyo-ne
• **multiplication table**	tavola pitagorica	'ta-vo-la pi-ta-'go-ri-ka
• **multiplied by**	moltiplicato per	mol-ti-pli-'ka-to per
• **three times two equals six**	tre per due è uguale a sei	—
(to) divide	dividere*	di-'vi-de-re
• **division**	divisione (f)	di-vi-'zyo-ne
• **divided by**	diviso (per)	di-'vi-zo
• **six divided by three equals two**	sei diviso (per) tre è uguale a due	—
(to) raise to a power	elevare alla potenza di	e-le-'va-re 'al-la po-'ten-dza di
• **power**	potenza	po-'ten-dza
• **squared**	al quadrato	al kwa-'dra-to
• **cubed**	al cubo	—
• **to the fourth power**	alla quarta potenza	al-la 'kwar-ta po-'ten-dza
• **to the nth power**	all'ennesima potenza	al-len-'ne-zi-ma po-'ten-dza
• **two squared equals four**	due al quadrato è uguale a quattro	—
(to) extract the root	estrarre* la radice	es-'trar-re la ra-'di-če
• **root**	radice (f)	ra-'di-če
• **square root**	radice quadrata	ra-'di-če kwa-'dra-ta
• **cube root**	radice cubica	ra-'di-če 'ku-bi-ka
• **nth root**	ennesima radice	en-'ne-zi-ma ra-'di-če
• **the square root of nine equals three**	la radice quadrata di nove è uguale a tre	—
ratio, proportion	proporzione (f)	pro-por-'tsyo-ne
• **twelve is to four as nine is to three**	dodici sta a quattro come nove sta a tre	—

Summary of Arithmetical Operations

Addition
2 + 3 = 5 → due più tre è uguale a cinque
or
due più tre fa cinque

Subtraction
9 − 3 = 6 → nove meno tre è uguale a sei
or
nove meno tre fa sei

Multiplication
4 × 2 = 8 → quattro per due è uguale a otto
or
quattro per due fa otto
or
quattro moltiplicato due è uguale a otto
or
quattro moltiplicato due fa otto

Division
10 ÷ 2 = 5 → dieci diviso (per) due è uguale a cinque
or
dieci diviso (per) due fa cinque

Raising to a power
$3^2 = 9$ → tre al quadrato è uguale a nove
$2^3 = 8$ → due al cubo è uguale a otto
$5^4 = 625$ → cinque alla quarta potenza è uguale a seicentoventicinque

Extraction of a root
$^2\sqrt{4} = 2$ → la radice quadrata di quattro è uguale a due
$^3\sqrt{27} = 3$ → la radice cubica di ventisette è uguale a tre

Ratio
12:4 = 6:2 → dodici sta a quattro come sei sta a due

F. GENERAL MATHEMATICAL CONCEPTS

algebra	algebra	'al-je-bra
• **algebraic**	algebrico	al-'je-bri-ko
algorithm	algoritmo	al-go-'rit-mo
arithmetic	aritmetica	a-rit-'me-ti-ka
• **arithmetical**	aritmetico	a-rit-'me-ti-ko

average	media	*'me-di-a*
(to) calculate	calcolare	*kal-ko-'la-re*
• calculation	calcolo	*kal-'ko-lo*
constant	costante (f)	*kos-'tan-te*
(to) count	contare	*kon-'ta-re*
decimal	decimale (m)	*de-či-ma-le*
difference	differenza	*dif-fe-'ren-tsa*
equality	uguaglianza	*u-gwa-'lyan-tsa*
equation	equazione (f)	*e-kwa-'tsyo-ne*
• (to) be equal to	essere* uguale a	*'es-se-re u-'gwa-le a*
• (to) be equivalent to	essere* equivalente a	*e-kwi-va-'len-te*
• (to) be greater than	essere* maggiore di	*maj-'jo-re*
• (to) be less than	essere* minore di	*mi-'no-re*
• (to) be similar to	essere* simile a	*'si-mi-le*
• equation in one unknown	equazione (f) a una incognita	*in-'ko-nyi-ta*
• equation in two unknowns	equazione (f) a due incognite	*in-'ko-nyi-te*
exponent	esponente (m)	*es-po-'nen-te*
factor	fattore (m)	*fat-'to-re*
• (to) factor	fattorizzare	*fat-to-ri-'dza-re*
• factorization	fattorizzazione (f)	*fat-to-ri-dza-'tsyo-ne*
function	funzione (f)	*fun-'tsyo-ne*
logarithm	logaritmo	*lo-ga-'rit-mo*
• logarithmic	logaritmico	*lo-ga-'rit-mi-ko*
mathematician	matematico (-a)	*ma-te-'ma-ti-ko*
minus	meno	—
multiple	multiplo	*'mul-ti-plo*
percent	percento	*per 'čen-to*
• percentage	percentuale (f)	*per-čen-tu-'a-le*
plus	più	*pyu*
problem	problema (m) (problemi, pl)	*pro-'ble-ma*
• problem to solve	problema da risolvere	*ri-'zol-ve-re*
product	prodotto	*pro-'dot-to*
proposition	proposizione (f)	*pro-po-zi-'tsyo-ne*
quotient	quoziente (m)	*kwo-'styen-te*
set	insieme (m)	*in-'sye-me*
solution	soluzione (f)	*so-lu-'tsyo-ne*
• (to) solve	risolvere*	*ri-'zol-ve-re*
statistical	statistico	*sta-'tis-ti-ko*
sum	somma	*'som-ma*
• (to) sum up	sommare	*som-'ma-re*
symbol	simbolo	*'sim-bo-lo*
theorem	teorema (m) (teoremi, pl)	*te-o-'re-ma*
unknown	incognita	*in-'ko-nyi-ta*
variable	variabile (f)	*va-'rya-bi-le*

G. BRANCHES OF MATHEMATICS

accounting, bookkeeping	contabilità (f, inv)	*kon-ta-bi-li-'ta*
	ragioneria	*ra-jo-ne-'ri-a*
algebra	algebra	*'al-je-bra*
• **set algebra**	algebra degli insiemi	*in-'sye-mi*
• **linear algebra**	algebra lineare	*li-ne-'a-re*
arithmetic	aritmetica	*a-rit-'me-ti-ka*
calculus	calcolo	*'kal-ko-lo*
• **differential calculus**	calcolo differenziale	*dif-fe-ren-'tsya-le*
• **integral calculus**	calcolo integrale	*in-te-'gra-le*
geometry	geometria	*je-o-me-'tri-a*
• **analytical geometry**	geometria analitica	*a-na-'li-ti-ka*
• **descriptive geometry**	geometria descrittiva	*des-krit-'ti-va*
• **Euclidean geometry**	geometria euclidea	*eu-kli-'de-a*
• **non-Euclidean geometry**	geometria non euclidea	—
• **projective geometry**	geometria proiettiva	*pro-yet-'ti-va*
• **solid geometry**	geometria solida	*'so-li-da*
mathematics	matematica	*ma-te-'ma-ti-ka*
statistics	statistica	*sta-'tis-ti-ka*
topology	topologia	*to-po-lo-'ji-a*
trigonometry	trigonometria	*tri-go-no-me-'tri-a*

2. GEOMETRY

A. FIGURES

circle	cerchio	*'čer-kyo*
• **arc**	arco	*'ar-ko*
• **center**	centro	*'čen-tro*
• **circumference**	circonferenza	*čir-kon-fe-'ren-tsa*
• **diameter**	diametro	*di-'a-me-tro*
• **radius**	raggio	*'raj-jo*
• **tangent**	tangente (f)	*tan-'jen-te*
cone	cono	—
cube	cubo	—
cylinder	cilindro	*či-'lin-dro*
decagon	decagono	*de-'ka-go-no*
dodecahedron	dodecaedro	*do-de-ka-'e-dro*
figure	figura	*fi-'gu-ra*
• **plane figure**	figura piana	*'pya-na*
• **four-sided figure**	figura a quattro lati	—
• **solid figure**	figura solida	*'so-li-da*
heptagon	ettagono	*et-'ta-go-no*
hexagon	esagono	*e-'za-go-no*
icosahedron	icosaedro	*i-ko-za-'e-dro*
octagon	ottagono	*ot-'ta-gono*

octahedron	ottaedro	*ot-ta-'e-dro*
parabola	parabola	*pa-'ra-bo-la*
parallelepiped	parallelepipedo	*pa-ral-le-le-'pi-pe-do*
parallelogram	parallelogramma (m)	*pa-ral-le-lo-'gram-ma*
	(parallelogrammi, pl)	
pentagon	pentagono	*pen-'ta-go-no*
polygon	poligono	*po-'li-go-no*
polyhedron	poliedro	*po-li-'e-dro*
prism	prisma (m) (prismi, pl)	*'priz-ma*
• **right prism**	prisma retto	—
pyramid	piramide (f)	*pi-'ra-mi-de*
quadrilateral	quadrilatero	*kwa-dri-'la-te-ro*
rectangle	rettangolo	*ret-'tan-go-lo*
rhombus	rombo	*'rom-bo*
solid	solido	*'so-li-do*
sphere	sfera	*'sfe-ra*
square	quadrato	*kwa-'dra-to*
tetrahedron	tetraedro	*te-tra-'e-dro*
trapezium	trapezio	*tra-'pe-zi-o*
triangle	triangolo	*tri-'an-go-lo*
• **acute-angled**	acutangolo	*a-ku-'tan-go-lo*
• **equilateral**	equilatero	*e-kwi-'la-te-ro*
• **isosceles**	isoscele	*i-'zo-še-le*
• **obtuse-angled**	ottusangolo	*ot-tu-'zan-go-lo*
• **right-angled**	rettangolo	*ret-'tan-go-lo*
• **scalene**	scaleno	*ska-'le-no*

B. CONCEPTS

angle	angolo	*'an-go-lo*
• **acute**	acuto	*a-'ku-to*
• **adjacent**	adiacente	*a-dya-'čen-te*
• **bisector**	bisettrice (f)	*bi-set-'tri-če*
• **complementary**	complementare	*kom-ple-men-'ta-re*
• **concave**	concavo	*kon-'ka-vo*
• **consecutive**	consecutivo	*kon-se-ku-'ti-vo*
• **convex**	convesso	*kon-'ves-so*
• **obtuse**	ottuso	*ot-'tu-zo*
• **opposite**	opposto	*op-'pos-to*
• **right**	retto	—
• **side**	lato	—
• **straight**	piatto	*'pyat-to*
• **supplementary**	supplementare	*sup-ple-men-'ta-re*
• **vertex**	vertice (m)	*'ver-ti-če*
axis	asse (m)	*'as-se*
coordinate	coordinata	*ko-or-di-'na-ta*
• **abscissa**	ascissa	*a-'šis-sa*
• **ordinate**	ordinata	*or-di-'na-ta*

Plane Figures

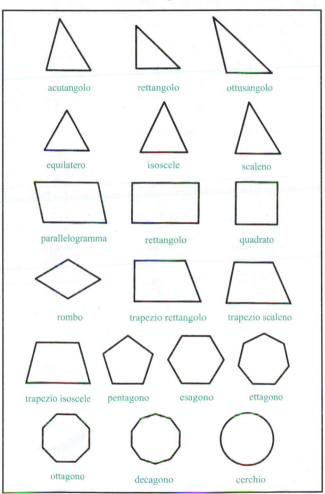

acutangolo   rettangolo   ottusangolo

equilatero   isoscele   scaleno

parallelogramma   rettangolo   quadrato

rombo   trapezio rettangolo   trapezio scaleno

trapezio isoscele   pentagono   esagono   ettagono

ottagono   decagono   cerchio

Solid Figures

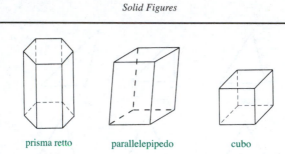

prisma retto   parallelepipedo   cubo

piramide regolare   tetraedro   ottaedro

dodecaedro   icosaedro regolare   cilindro retto

cono retto   cono obliquo   sfera

degree	grado	—
diagonal	diagonale	*di-a-go-'na-le*
drawing instruments	strumenti del disegno	*stru-'men-ti di-'ze-nyo*
• compass	compasso	*kom-'pas-so*
• (to) draw	disegnare	*di-ze-'nya-re*
• eraser	gomma	*'gom-ma*
• pen	penna	*'pen-na*
• pencil	matita	*ma-'ti-ta*
• protractor	goniometro	*go-ni-'o-me-tro*
• ruler	riga	*'ri-ga*
• template	sagoma	*'sa-go-ma*
geometry	geometria	*je-o-me-'tri-a*
• geometrical	geometrico	*je-o-'me-tri-ko*
hypotenuse	ipotenusa	*i-po-te-'nu-za*
line	linea	*'li-ne-a*
• broken	spezzata	*spe-'tsa-ta*
• curved	curva	*'kur-va*
• horizontal	orizzontale	*o-ri-dzon-'ta-le*
• parallel	parallela	*pa-ral-'le-la*
• perpendicular	perpendicolare	*per-pen-di-ko-'la-re*
• straight	retta	*'ret-ta*
• vertical	verticale	*ver-ti-'ka-le*
perimeter	perimetro	*pe-'ri-me-tro*
point	punto	—

Lines

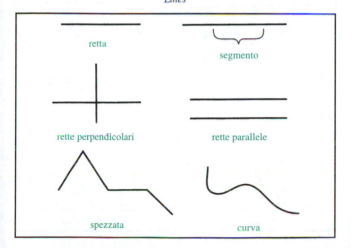

Angles

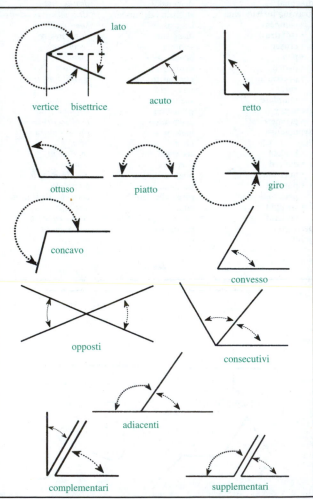

Pythagorean theorem	teorema di Pitagora	*te-o-'re-ma pi-'ta-go-ra*
segment	segmento	*seg-'men-to*
space	spazio	*'spa-tsyo*
trigonometry	trigonometria	*tri-go-no-me-'tri-a*
• **cosecant**	cosecante (f)	*ko-se-'can-te*
• **cosine**	coseno	*ko-'se-no*
• **cotangent**	cotangente (f)	*ko-tan-'jen-te*
• **secant**	secante (f)	*se-'kan-te*
• **sine**	seno	—
• **tangent**	tangente (f)	*tan-'jen-te*
• **trigonometric**	trigonometrico	*tri-go-no-'me-tri-ko*
vector	vettore (m)	*vet-'to-re*

3. QUANTITY, SPACE, SHAPE, AND MOVEMENT

A. WEIGHTS AND MEASURES

area	area	*'a-re-a*
	superficie (f)	*su-per-'fi-ce*
• **hectare**	ettaro	*'et-ta-ro*
• **square centimeter**	centimetro quadrato	*čen-'ti-me-tro kwa-'dra-to*
• **square kilometer**	chilometro quadrato	*ki-'lo-me-tro*
• **square meter**	metro quadrato	*'me-tro*
• **square millimeter**	millimetro quadrato	*mil-'li-me-tro kwa-'dra-to*
height	altezza	*al-'te-tsa*
• **centimeter**	centimetro	*čen-'ti-me-tro*
• **foot**	piede (m)	*'pye-de*
• **inch**	pollice (m)	*'pol-li-če*
• **meter**	metro	—
length	lunghezza	*lun-'ge-tsa*
• **centimeter**	centimetro	*čen-'ti-me-tro*
• **kilometer**	chilometro	*ki-'lo-me-tro*
• **meter**	metro	—
• **millimeter**	millimetro	*mil-'li-me-tro*
speed, velocity	velocità (f)	*ve-lo-či-'ta*
• **per hour**	all'ora	—
• **per minute**	al minuto	—
• **per second**	al secondo	—
volume	volume (m)	*vo-'lu-me*
• **cubic centimeter**	centimetro cubico	*čen-'ti-me-tro 'ku-bi-ko*
• **cubic kilometer**	chilometro cubico	*ki-'lo-me-tro*
• **cubic meter**	metro cubico	—
• **cubic millimeter**	millimetro cubico	*mil-'li-me-tro*
• **liter**	litro	—
• **quart**	quarto	*'kwar-to*

weight	peso	*'pe-zo*
• **gram**	grammo	*'gram-mo*
• **hectogram**	ettogrammo	
	etto	*et-to-'gram-mo*
• **kilogram**	chilogrammo	*ki-lo-'gram-mo*
	chilo	
• **pound**	libbra	
width	larghezza	*lar-'ge-tsa*
• **centimeter**	centimetro	*čen-'ti-me-tro*
• **kilometer**	chilometro	*ki-'lo-me-tro*
• **meter**	metro	—
• **millimeter**	millimetro	*mil-'li-me-tro*

B. BASIC CONCEPTS OF QUANTITY, SIZE, AND MEASUREMENT

a lot, much	molto	—
	tanto	
all, everything	tutto	*'tut-to*
• **everyone**	tutti	*'tut-ti*
	ciascuno	*čas-'ku-no*
	ognuno	*o-'nyu-no*
almost, nearly	circa	*'čir-ka*
	quasi	*'kwa-zi*
approximately	approssimativamente	*ap-pros-si-ma-ti-va-'men-te*
as much as	tanto…quanto	—
balance/scale	bilancia	*bi-'lan-ča*
big	grande	—
• **(to) become big**	ingrandire (isc, ess)	*in-gran-'di-re*
• **(to) make bigger**	aggrandire (isc)	*ag-gran-'di-re*
both	ambedue	*am-be-'du-e*
	tutti e due	—
capacity	capienza	*ka-'pyen-tsa*
	capacità (f, inv)	*ka-pa-či-'ta*
compact	compatto	*kom-'pat-to*
decrease	diminuzione (f)	*di-mi-nu-'tsyo-ne*
• **(to) decrease, diminish**	diminuire (isc)	*di-mi-nu-'i-re*
• **(to) reduce**	ridurre*	*ri-'dur-re*
dense	denso	*'den-so*
• **density**	densità (f, inv)	*den-si-'ta*
dimension	dimensione (f)	*di-men-'syo-ne*
double	doppio	*'dop-pyo*
• **(to) double**	raddoppiare	*rad-dop-'pya-re*
each, every	ogni	*'o-nyi*
empty	vuoto	*'vwo-to*
enough	abbastanza	*ab-bas-'tan-dza*
• **(to) be enough**	bastare (ess)	*bas-'ta-re*
	essere* abbastanza	*'es-se-re ab-bas-'tan'dza*

entire	intero	in-'te-ro
expansion	espansione (f)	es-pan-'syo-ne
• (to) expand	espandere* (ess)	es-'pan-de-re
extension	estensione (f)	es-ten-'syo-ne
full	pieno	'pye-no
• (to) fill	riempire	ri-em-'pi-re
• fullness	ampiezza	am-'pye-tsa
growth	crescita	'kre-ši-ta
• (to) grow	crescere* (ess)	'kre-še-re
half	metà (f, inv)	me-'ta
	mezzo	'me-dzo
handful	manciata	man-ča-ta
heavy	pesante	pe-'zan-te
high, tall	alto	—
how much	quanto	'kwan-to
increase	aumento	au-'men-to
	incremento	in-kre-'men-to
• (to) increase	aumentare	au-men-'ta-re
	incrementare	in-kre-men-'ta-re
large	grande	'gran-de
	grosso	'gros-so
less	meno	'me-no
level	livello	li-'vel-lo
light	leggero	lej-'je-ro
little, small	piccolo	'pik-ko-lo
• a little	un po'	un po
long	lungo	'lun-go
mass	massa	'mas-sa
massive	massivo	mas-'si-vo
maximum	massimo	'mas-si-mo
measure, size	misura	mi-'zu-ra
• (to) measure	misurare	mi-zu-'ra-re
• measuring tape	metro	'me-tro
medium	medio	'me-dyo
minimum	minimo	'mi-ni-mo
more	più	pyu
	di più	di pyu
narrow	stretto	'stret-to
no one	nessuno	nes-'su-no
nothing	nulla	'nul-la
	niente	'nyen'te
pair	paio (paia, f, pl)	'pa-yo ('pa-ya)
part	parte (f)	—
partial	parziale	par-'tsya-le
piece	pezzo	'pet-tso
pile	mucchio	'muk-kyo
	catasta	ka-'tas-ta

portion	porzione (f)	por-'tsyo-ne
quantity	quantità (f, inv)	kwan-ti-'ta
reduction	riduzione (f)	ri-du-'tsyo-ne
several	parecchio	pa-'rek-kyo
short	corto	—
• (to) shorten	accorciare	ak-kor-'ča-re
size	misura	mi-'zu-ra
small	piccolo	'pik-ko-lo
• (to) become small	impiccolire (isc)	im-pik-ko-'li-re
	rimpiccolire (isc)	rim—pik-ko-'li-re
some	alcuni (m)	al-'ku-ni
	alcune (f)	al-'ku-ne
	qualche	'kwal-ke
• some of it	ne	—
• I want some	ne voglio	've-lyo
sufficient	sufficiente	suf-fi-čen-te
• (to) be sufficient	essere* sufficiente	—
supplement	supplemento	sup-ple-'men-to
thickness	spessore (m)	spes-'so-re
• thick	spesso	'spes-so
	fitto	'fit-to
• thin, fine	fino	'fi-no
ton	tonnellata	ton-nel-'la-ta
too much	troppo	'trop-po
total	totale (m)	to-'ta-le
triple	triplo	'tri-plo
weight	peso	'pe-zo
• (to) weigh	pesare	pe-'za-re
wide	largo	'lar-go

C. BASIC CONCEPTS OF LOCATION, SPACE, AND DISTANCE

above	sopra	'so-pra
across	attraverso	at-tra-'ver-so
ahead, forward	avanti	a-'van-ti
among, between	fra	—
	tra	—
away	via	'vi-a
back	dietro	'dye-tro
• backward	indietro	in-'dye-tro
behind	dietro	'dye-tro
beside, next to	accanto a	ak-'kan-to
beyond	oltre	'ol-tre
bottom	fondo	'fon-do
• at the bottom	in fondo	—
compass	bussola	'bus-so-la
depth	profondità (f, inv)	pro-fon-di-'ta
• deep	profondo	pro-fon-do

diffusion, spread	diffusione (f)	dif-fu-'zyo-ne
• (to) spread	diffondere*	dif-'fon-de-re
• (to) spread out	spargere*	'spar-je-re
dimension	dimensione (f)	di-men-'syo-ne
direction	direzione (f)	di-re-'tsyo-ne
distance	distanza	dis-'tan-dza
down	giù	ju
east	est	—
• eastern	orientale	o-ryen-'ta-le
• north-east	nord-est	—
• south-east	sud-est	—
• to the east	ad est	—
edge	orlo	'or-lo
	margine (m)	'mar-ji-ne
extension	estensione (f)	es-ten-'syo-ne
far	lontano	lon-'ta-no
from	da	—
front	fronte (f)	'fron-te
	facciata	fač-'ča-ta
• in front	di fronte	—
	davanti	—
here	qui	—
horizontal	orizzontale	o-ri-dzon-'ta-le
in	in	—
inside	dentro	'den-tro
left	sinistra	si-'nis-tra
• to the left	a sinistra	—
length	lunghezza	lun-'ge-tsa
• (to) lengthen	allungare	al-lun-'ga-re
level	livello	li-'vel-lo
mile	miglio (miglia, f, pl)	'mi-lyo
middle	mezzo	'me-dzo
• in the middle	in mezzo (nel mezzo)	—
narrow	stretto	'stret-to
near	vicino	vi-'či-no
	presso	'pres-so
nearly	quasi	'kwa-zi
north	nord	—
• northern	settentrionale	set-ten-tryo-'na-le
• to the north	a nord	—
nowhere	da nessuna parte	—
on	su	—
outside	fuori	'fwo-ri
place	posto	'pos-to
	luogo	'lwo-go
position	posizione (f)	po-zi-'tsyo-ne
right	destra	'des-tra
• to the right	a destra	—

section	sezione (f)	se-'tsyo-ne
somewhere	da qualche parte	'kwal-ke
south	sud	—
• **southern**	meridionale	me-ri-dyo-'na-le
• **to the south**	a sud	—
space	spazio	'spa-tsyo
• **spacious**	spazioso	spa-'tsyo-zo
surface	superficie (f)	su-per-'fi-če
there	là	
	lì	—
through	per	—
	attraverso	at-tra-'ver-so
to, at	a	—
• **to someone's place**	da	—
• **to Sarah's place**	da Sara	—
top	cima	'či-ma
• **on top**	in cima	—
toward	verso	'ver-so
under	sotto	'sot-to
up	su	—
vertical	verticale	ver-ti-'ka-le
west	ovest	—
• **western**	occidentale	oč-či-den-'ta-le
• **north-west**	nord-ovest	—
• **south-west**	sud-ovest	—
• **to the west**	ad ovest	—
where	dove	—
wide, broad	largo	'lar-go
zone	zona	'dzo-ona

Compass Points

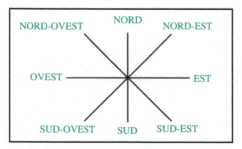

D. SHAPES AND PATTERNS

boundary	confine (m)	kon-'fi-ne
check	quadretto	kwa-'dret-to
• checkered	a quadretti	—
circuit	circuito	čir-ku-'i-to
circular, round	circolare	čir-ko-'la-re
	rotondo	ro-'ton-do
column	colonna	ko-'lon-na
conical	conico	'ko-ni-ko
cross	croce (f)	'kro-če
cylindrical	cilindrico	či-'lin-dri-ko
design	disegno	di-'ze-nyo
disk	disco	'dis-ko
dot	punto	'pun-to
emblem	emblema (m)	em-'ble-ma
	(emblemi, pl)	
enclosed, surrounded	circoscritto	čir-ko-'skrit-to
	racchiuso	rak-'kyu-zo
enclosure	recinto	re-čin-to
even	uguale	u-'gwa-le
form	forma	'for-ma
frame	cornice (f)	kor-'ni-če
furrow	solco	'sol-ko
graph	grafico	'gra-fi-co
irregular	irregolare	ir-re-go-'la-re
labyrinth, maze	labirinto	la-bi-'rin-to
layout	stesura	ste-'zu-ra
lined	a righe	'ri-ge
marbled	marmorizzato	mar-mo-ri-'dza-to
margin	margine (m)	'mar-ji-ne
orbit	orbita	'or-bi-ta
outline, profile	profilo	pro-'fi-lo
	contorno	kon-'tor-no
pattern	modello	mo-'del-lo
• (to) pattern	modellare	mo-del-'la-re
• patterned	modellato	mo-del-'la-to
periphery, outskirts	periferia	pe-ri-fe-'ri-a
pyramidal	piramidale	pi-ra-mi-'da-le
rectangular	rettangolare	ret-tan-go-'la-re
relief	rilievo	ri-'lye-vo
ring	anello	a-'nel-lo
row	fila	'fi-la
schema	schema (m)	
	(schemi, pl)	'ske-ma
silhouette	sagoma	'sa-go-ma
slice	fetta	'fet-ta
spherical	sferico	'sfe-ri-ko

spiral	spirale (f)	*spi-'ra-le*
spotted	macchiato	*mak-'kya-to*
	chiazzato	*kya-'tsa-to*
square	quadrato	*kwa-'dra-to*
star	stella	*'stel-la*
streaked	vergato	*ver'ga-to*
stripe, streak	striscia	*'stri-ša*
• striped	a strisce	*a stri-'še*
stroke	tratto	*'trat-to*
surveying	topografia	*to-po-gra-'fi-a*
tortuous	tortuoso	*tor-'two-zo*
triangular	triangolare	*tri-an-go-'la-re*
twisting, winding	avvolgente, serpeggiante	*av-vol-'jen-te —*
uneven	disuguale	*diz-u-'gwa-le*
veined, grainy	venato	*ve-'na-to*
wavy, undulating	ondulato	*on-du-'la-to*
zigzag	zigzag (inv)	*dzig-'dzag*

E. CONTAINERS

bag, sack	sacco	*'sak-ko*
barrel	botte (f)	*'bot-te*
basket	cesto	*'čes-to*
	cestino	*'čes-'ti-no*
• flower basket	canestro di fiori	*'fyo-ri*
• fruit basket	canestro di frutta	—
box	scatola	*'ska-to-la*
• cardboard box	scatola di cartone	*kar-'to-ne*
• round box	scatola rotonda	*ro-'ton-da*
• square box	scatola quadrata	*kwa-dra-ta*
• tin box	scatola di latta	*'lat-ta*
• wood box	scatola di legno	*'le-nyo*
bucket	secchio	*'sek-kyo*
case	cassa	*'kas-sa*
cask	barile (m)	*ba-'ri-le*
container	contenitore (m)	*kon-te-ni-'to-re*
• (to) contain	contenere*	*kon-te-'ne-re*
• contents	contenuto	*kon-te-'nu-to*
handbag	borsa	*bor-sa*
jar, tin	barattolo	*ba-'rat-to-lo*
packing crate	cassa d'imballaggio	*'kas-sa dim-bal-'laj-jo*
receptacle	recipiente (m)	*re-či-'pyen-te*
reservoir	cisterna	*čis-'ter-na*
safe, strongbox	cassaforte (f)	*kas-sa-'for-te*
tank	serbatoio	*ser-ba-'to-yo*
toolbox	cassetta degli arnesi	*kas-'set-ta 'de-lyi ar-'ne-zi*
toy box	scatola dei balocchi	*'ska-to-la dei ba-'lok-ki*

trunk	baule (m)	*ba-'u-le*
tub	vasca	*'vas-ka*
water tank	cisterna dell' acqua	*čis-'ter-na*

F. MOVEMENT

(to) accelerate	accelerare	*ač-če-le-'ra-re*
(to) approach	avvicinarsi a	*av-vi-či-'nar-si*
ascent	salita	*sa-'li-ta*
	ascesa	*a-'še-za*
(to) arrive	arrivare (ess)	*ar-ri-'va-re*
(to) avoid	evitare	*e-vi-'ta-re*
back and forth	avanti e indietro	*a-'van-ti e in-'dye-tro*
(to) bend	piegare	*pye-'ga-re*
(to) blink	battere le palpebre	*'bat-te-re le 'pal-pe-bre*
bow	inchino	*in-'ki-no*
• (to) bow	inchinarsi	*in-ki-'nar-si*
(to) brush against	sfiorare	*sfyo-'ra-re*
(to) bump into	imbattersi in	*im-'bat-ter-si*
(to) bustle about	darsi* da fare	*'dar-si da 'fa-re*
(to) catch	afferrare	*af-fer-'ra-re*
(to) chase	inseguire	*in-se-'gwi-re*
circulation	circolazione (f)	*čir-ko-la-'tsyo-ne*
• (to) circulate	circolare	*čir-ko-'la-re*
(to) clap	applaudire (isc)	*ap-plau-'di-re*
(to) climb, (to) go up	salire* (ess)	*sa-'li-re*
(to) cling on	appiccicarsi	*ap-pi-či-'kar-si*
	stringersi*	*'strin-jer-si*
(to) collapse	crollare	*krol-'la-re*
(to) come	venire* (ess)	*ve-'ni-re*
(to) crash	fracassare	*fra-kas-'sa-re*
(to) crawl	strisciare carponi	*stri-'ša-re kar-'po-ni*
descent	discesa	*di-'še-za*
• (to) descend	scendere* (ess)	*'šen-de-re*
(to) dodge	schivare	*ski-'va-re*
(to) drive	guidare	*gwi-'da-re*
(to) embrace, hug	abbracciare	*ab-brač-'ča-re*
(to) enter	entrare (ess)	*en-'tra-re*
fall	caduta	*ka-'du-ta*
• (to) fall	cadere* (ess)	*ka-'de-re*
• (to) fall down	cadere* per terra	—
fast	veloce	*ve-'lo-če*
(to) fling	lanciare	*lan-'ča-re*
(to) follow	seguire	*se-'gwi-re*
gesture	gesto	*'jes-to*
(to) get going	cominciare	*kom-in-'ča-re*
(to) get up, rise	alzarsi	*al-'tsar-si*
(to) go	andare* (ess)	*an-'da-re*

• (to) go across	attraversare	*at-tra-ver-'sa-re*
• (to) go around	andare* (ess) in giro	*an-'da-re in 'ji-ro*
• (to) go away	andare* (ess) via	—
	andarsene*	*an-'dar-se-ne*
• (to) go backwards	andare* (ess) indietro	*in-'dye-tro*
• (to) go forward	andare* (ess) avanti	—
• (to) go on foot	andare* (ess) a piedi	—
• (to) go out, exit	uscire* (ess)	*u-'ši-re*
• (to) go toward	andare* (ess) verso	—
(to) grab	afferrare	*af-fer-'ra-re*
(to) greet	salutare	*sa-lu-'ta-re*
(to) handle	maneggiare	*ma-nej-'ja-re*
(to) hit	colpire (isc)	*kol-'pi-re*
	picchiare	*pik-'kya-re*
(to) hold hands	tenersi* per mano	*te-'ner-si*
(to) hurry	affrettarsi	*af-fret-'tar-si*
	sbrigarsi	*sbri-'gar-si*
(to) jump	saltare	*sal-'ta-re*
(to) kick	dare* un calcio	*'da-re un 'kal-čo*
	prendere* a calci	*'pren-de-re a 'kal-či*
(to) kneel	inginocchiarsi	*in-ji-nok-'kya-rsi*
(to) knock	bussare	*bus-'sa-re*
(to) lean against	appoggiarsi a	*ap-poj-'jar-si*
(to) leap	balzare	*bal-'tsa-re*
(to) leave, (to) depart	partire (ess)	*par-'ti-re*
(to) lie down	sdraiarsi	*zdra-'yar-si*
(to) lift	alzare	*al-'za-re*
(to) march	marciare	*mar-'ča-re*
movement	movimento	*mo-vi-'men-to*
• (to) move	muovere*	*'mwo-ve-re*
	muoversi*	*'mwo-ver-si*
(to) nod	fare* un cenno	*'fa-re un 'čen-no*
(to) pass by	passare davanti	*pas-'sa-re da-'van-ti*
(to) pass near	passare vicino	*pas-'sa-re vi-'či-no*
(to) pinch	pizzicare	*pi-tsi-'ka-re*
(to) precede	precedere	*pre-'če-de-re*
(to) pull	tirare	*ti-'ra-re*
(to) push	spingere*	*'spin-je-re*
(to) put	mettere*	*'met-te-re*
• (to) put down	posare	*po-'za-re*
quickly	velocemente	*ve-lo-če-'men-te*
(to) raise	sollevare	*sol-le-'va-re*
(to) reach	raggiungere*	*raj-'jun-jere*
(to) return	tornare (ess)	*tor-'na-re*
(to) rub	strofinare	*stro-fi-'na-re*
(to) run	correre*	*'kor-re-re*
• (to) run away	scappare (ess)	*skap-'pa-re*
(to) send	inviare	*in-vi-'a-re*

(to) shake	agitare	*a-ji-'ta-re*
(to) shake hands	dare* la mano	—
(to) shake one's head	scuotere* la testa	*'skwo-te-re*
(to) sit down	sedersi*	*se-'der-si*
(to) slide, slip	scivolare	*ši-vo-'la-re*
slow	lento	*'len-to*
• (to) slow down	rallentare	*ral-len-'tar-e*
• slowly	lentamente	*len-ta-'men-te*
(to) squat	rannicchiarsi	*ran-nik-'kyar-si*
(to) stand up, get up	alzarsi	*al-'tsar-si*
(to) step forward	fare* un passo avanti	—
(to) stop	fermare	*fer-'ma-re*
(to) stretch	stirare	*sti-'ra-re*
(to) stroke	lisciare	*li-'ša-re*
(to) stroll	passeggiare	*pas-sej-'ja-re*
	fare* una passeggiata	*pas-sej-'ja-ta*
(to) stumble	inciampare	*in-čam-'pa-re*
(to) throw	gettare	*jet-'ta-re*
(to) tiptoe	camminare in punta	*kam-mi-'na-re*
	di piedi	
(to) touch	toccare	*tok-'ka-re*
(to) turn	girare	*ji-'ra-re*
• (to) turn around	girarsi	*ji-'rar-si*
• (to) turn left	girare, voltare a sinistra	—
• (to) turn right	girare, voltare a destra	—
(to) twist	torcere*	*'tor-če-re*
walk	camminata	*kam-mi-'na-ta*
• (to) walk	camminare	*kam-mi-'na-re*
(to) wander	girovagare	*ji-ro-va-'ga-re*

4. TIME

A. TELLING TIME

What time is it?	Che ora è?	*ke 'o-ra e*
	Che ore sono?	*ke 'ore so-no*
• It's 1:00.	È l'una.	—
• It's 2:00.	Sono le due.	—
• It's 3:00.	Sono le tre.	—
• It's 3:00 on the dot.	Sono le tre in punto.	—
• It's 1:10.	È l'una e dieci.	*'dye-či*
• It's 4:25.	Sono le quattro e	
	venticinque.	*ven-ti-'čin-kwe*
• It's 3:15.	Sono le tre e quindici.	*'kwin-di-či*
	Sono le tre e un quarto.	
• It's 3:30.	Sono le tre e trenta.	
	Sono le tre e mezzo	
	(mezza).	*'me-dzo*

The 24-Hour Clock

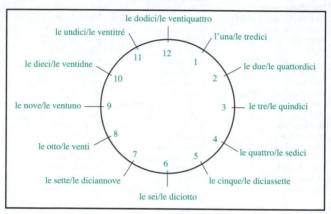

• It's 2:45.	Sono le due e quarantacinque.	*kwa-ran-ta-'čin-kwe*
	Sono le due e tre quarti.	
	Sono le tre meno un quarto.	
• It's 5:50.	Sono le cinque e cinquanta.	*cin-'kwan-ta*
	Sono le sei meno dieci.	*'dye-či*
• It's 5:00 A.M.	Sono le cinque.	*'čin-kwe*
• It's 5:00 P.M.	Sono le diciassette.	*di-čas-'set-te*
• It's 10:00 A.M.	Sono le dieci.	*'dye-či*
• It's 10:00 P.M.	Sono le ventidue.	*ven-ti-'du-e*
At what time?	A che ora?	*a ke 'o-ra*
• At 1:00.	All'una.	—
• At 2:00.	Alle due.	—
• At 3:00.	Alle tre.	—

B. CLASSIFYING AND MEASURING TIME

afternoon	pomeriggio	*po-me-'rij-jo*
• **in the afternoon**	nel pomeriggio	—
	di pomeriggio	
• **this afternoon**	questo pomeriggio	—
	oggi pomeriggio	*'oj-ji*
• **tomorrow afternoon**	domani pomeriggio	—
century	secolo	*'se-ko-lo*

Alternatives

As the next hour approaches, an alternative way of expressing the minutes is (as shown above), the next hour minus (*meno*) the number of minutes left to go.

8:58 = *le otto e cinquantotto* or *le nove meno due*
10:50 = *le dieci e cinquanta* or *le undici meno dieci*

The expressions *un quarto* (a quarter), and *mezzo (mezza)* (half) can be used for the quarter and the half hour.

3:15 = *le tre e quindici* or *le tre e un quarto*
4:30 = *le quattro e trenta* or *le quattro e mezzo (mezza)*
5:45 = *le cinque e quarantacinque* or *le sei meno un quarto* or *le cinque e tre quarti* (three quarters)

dawn, sunrise	alba	'*al-ba*
day	giorno	'*jor-no*
• **all day**	tutta la giornata	*jor-'na-ta*
• **daily**	quotidianamente	*kwo-ti-dya-na-'men-te*
decade	decennio	*de-'čen-nyo*
evening	sera	'*se-ra*
• **in the evening**	di sera	—
• **last evening**	ieri sera	*ye-ri 'se-ra*
• **this evening**	questa sera	—
• **tomorrow evening**	domani sera	—
hour	ora	—
instant	istante (m)	*is-'tan-te*
midnight	mezzanotte (f)	*me-dza-'not-te*
• **at midnight**	a mezzanotte	—
millennium	millennio	*mil-'len-ni-o*
minute	minuto	*mi-'nu-to*
moment	momento	*mo-'men-to*
month	mese (m)	'*me-ze*
• **monthly**	mensile	*men-'si-le*
morning	mattina	*mat-'ti-na*
	mattino	
• **in the morning**	di mattina	—
• **this morning**	questa mattina	—
• **tomorrow morning**	domani mattina	—
night	notte (f)	'*not-te*
• **at night**	di notte	—
• **last night**	ieri notte	'*ye-ri*
• **this night**	questa notte	—
• **tomorrow night**	domani notte	—

noon	mezzogiorno	*me-dzo-'jor-no*
• at noon	a mezzogiorno	—
second	secondo	*se-'kon-do*
sunrise	alba	*'al-ba*
sunset, twilight	tramonto	*tra-'mon-to*
time (in general)	tempo	*'tem-po*
• time (hour)	ora	—
• time (occurrence)	volta	—
today	oggi	*'oj-ji*
tomorrow	domani	*do-'ma-ni*
• day after tomorrow	dopodomani	*do-po-do-'ma-ni*
tonight	stasera (*evening*)	*sta-'se-ra*
	stanotte (*night*)	*sta-'not-te*
week	settimana	*set-ti-'ma-na*
• weekly	settimanalmente	*set-ti-ma-nal-'men-te*
year	anno	*'an-no*
• yearly	annuo	*'an-nu-o*
	annuale	*an-'nwa-le*
yesterday	ieri	*'ye-ri*
• day before yesterday	l'altro ieri	*lal-tro 'ye-ri*
• yesterday morning, afternoon, etc.	ieri mattina	*mat-'ti-na*
	ieri pomeriggio	*po-me-'rij-jo*
	ecc.	

C. GENERAL TIME CONCEPTS AND EXPRESSIONS

after	dopo	*'do-po*
again	ancora (una volta)	*an-'ko-ra*
	di nuovo	*di 'nwo-vo*
ago	fa	—
• two years ago	due anni fa	—
almost always	quasi sempre	*kwa-zi 'sem-pre*
almost never	quasi mai	*kwa-zi 'ma-i*
already	già	*ja*
always	sempre	*'sem-pre*
anterior, before	anteriore	*an-te-'ryo-re*
as soon as	appena	*ap-'pe-na*
at the same time	allo stesso tempo	*'stes-so*
(to) be about to	stare* (ess) per	*'sta-re*
(to) be on the point, verge of	essere* sul punto di	*'es-se-re*
(to) be on time	essere* in orario	*o-'ra-ryo*
(to) be punctual	essere* puntuale	*pun-tu-'a-le*
before	prima	—
brief	breve	*'bre-ve*
• briefly	brevemente	*bre-ve-'men-te*
by now	ormai	*or-'ma-i*

duration	durata	du-'ra-ta
during	durante	du-'ran-te
early	presto	'pres-to
• **(to) be early**	essere* in anticipo	'es-se-re in an-'ti-ci-po
end	fine (f)	'fi-ne
• **(to) end, finish**	finire (isc)	fi-'ni-re
equinox	equinozio	e-kwi-'no-tsyo
every once in a while	di tanto in tanto	—
frequent	frequente	fre-'kwen-te
from now on	d'ora in poi	dora in 'po-i
future	futuro	fu-'tu-ro
(to) happen, occur	accadere* (ess)	ak-ka-'de-re
	avvenire* (ess)	av-ve-'ni-re
in an hour's time (in two	tra un'ora	—
hours time, etc.)	tra due ore	
	ecc.	
in the long run, term	a lungo andare	a lun-go an-'da-re
	a lungo termine	'ter-mi-ne
in the meanwhile	intanto	in-'tan-to
	nel frattempo	frat-'tem-po
in the short term	a breve termine	'ter-mi-ne
in time	in orario	o-'ra-ryo
just, as soon as	appena	ap-'pe-na
last	scorso	'skor-so
• **last month**	il mese scorso	—
• **last year**	l'anno scorso	—
(to) last	durare (ess)	du-'ra-re
• **(to) last a long time**	durare (ess) a lungo	—
• **(to) last a short time**	durare (ess) poco	'po-ko
late	tardi	'tar-di
• **(to) be late**	essere* in ritardo	'es-se-re in ri-'tar-do
long-term	a lunga scadenza	lun-ga ska-'den-tsa
(to) look forward to	non vedere* l'ora di	ve-'de-re
never	mai	'ma-i
now	ora	—
	adesso	a-'des-so
• **from now on**	d'ora in poi	—
• **nowadays**	oggigiorno	oj-ji-'jor-no
occasionally	di tanto in tanto	—
	ogni tanto	
often	spesso	'spes-so
once	una volta	—
• **once in a while**	ogni tanto	o-nyi 'tan-to
past	passato	pas-'sa-to
posterior	posteriore	pos-te-'ryo-re
present	presente (m)	pre-'zen-te
• **presently**	attualmente	at-twal-'men-te
rare	raro	—
• **rarely**	raramente	ra-ra-'men-te

recent	recente	*re-'čen-te*
• recently	recentemente	*re-čen-te-'men-te*
regular	regolare	*re-go-'la-re*
• regularly	regolarmente	*re-go-lar-'men-te*
right away	subito	*'su-bi-to*
short-term	a breve scadenza	*ska-'den-tsa*
simultaneous	simultaneo	*si-mul-'ta-ne-o*
• simultaneously	simultaneamente	*si-mul-ta-ne-a-'men-te*
since, for	da	—
• since Monday	da lunedì	*lu-ne-'di*
• since yesterday	da ieri	*'ye-ri*
• for three days	da tre giorni	*'jor-ni*
soon	tra poco	*'po-ko*
• as soon as	appena	*ap-'pe-na*
• sooner or later	prima o poi	*pri-ma o 'po-i*
(to) spend (time)	passare	*pas-'sa-re*
	trascorrere*	*tras-'kor-re-re*
sporadic	sporadico	*spo-'ra-di-ko*
• sporadically	sporadicamente	*spo-ra-di-ka-'men-te*
still	ancora	*an-'ko-ra*
(to) take place	avere* luogo	*a-'ve're 'lwo-go*
	svolgersi*	*'zvol-jer-si*
temporary	temporaneo	*tem-po-'ra-ne-o*
• temporarily	temporaneamente	*tem-po-ra-ne-a-'men-te*
then	allora	*al-'lo-ra*
	poi	*'po-i*
timetable, schedule	orario	*o-'ra-ryo*
to this day, till now	tutt'oggi	*tut-'toj-ji*
until	fino a	—
	finché (*conjunction*)	*fin-'ke*
usually	di solito	*di 'so-li-to*
(to) wait (for)	aspettare	*as-pet-'ta-re*
when	quando	*'kwan-do*
while	mentre	*'men-tre*
within	entro	*'en-tro*
• within two days	entro due giorni	*'jor-ni*
yet	ancora	*an-'ko-ra*

Idiomatic Expressions

Time is money!	=	Il tempo è denaro!
Time flies!	=	Il tempo vola!
Time is short!	=	Il tempo stringe!
Once upon a time	=	C'era una volta
It was high time!	=	Era ora!
Better late than never!	=	Meglio tardi che mai!

D. TIMEPIECES

alarm clock	sveglia	'sve-lya
clock	orologio	o-ro-'lo-jo
dial	quadrante (m)	kwa-'dran-te
grandfather clock	orologio a pendolo	o-ro-'lo-jo a 'pen-do-lo
hand (of a clock, watch)	lancetta	lan-'čet-ta
watch	orologio	o-ro-'lo-jo `
• **digital watch**	orologio digitale	di-ji-'ta-le
• **The watch is fast.**	L'orologio va avanti.	a-'van-ti
• **The watch is slow.**	L'orologio va indietro.	in-'dye-tro
• **wristwatch**	orologio da polso	'pol-so
(to) wind	caricare	ka-ri-'ka-re

5. DAYS, MONTHS, AND SEASONS

A. DAYS OF THE WEEK

day of the week	giorno della settimana	'jor-no set-ti-'ma-na
• **Monday**	lunedì (m, inv)	lu-ne-'di
• **Tuesday**	martedì (m, inv)	mar-te-'di
• **Wednesday**	mercoledì (m, inv)	mer-ko-le-'di
• **Thursday**	giovedì (m, inv)	jo-ve-'di
• **Friday**	venerdì (m, inv)	ve-ner-'di
• **Saturday**	sabato	'sa-ba-to
• **Sunday**	domenica	do-'me-ni-ka
holiday	giorno festivo, feriale	—
weekend	fine (m) settimana	'fi-ne set-ti-'ma-na
What day is it?	Che giorno è?	ke 'jor-no
workday	giorno lavorativo	'jor-no la-vo-ra-'ti-vo

B. MONTHS OF THE YEAR

calendar	calendario	ka-len-'da-ryo
leap year	anno bisestile	an-no bi-ses-'ti-le
month	mese	'me-ze
• **January**	gennaio	jen-'na-yo
• **February**	febbraio	feb-'bra-yo
• **March**	marzo	'mar-tso
• **April**	aprile	a-'pri-le
• **May**	maggio	'maj-jo
• **June**	giugno	'ju-nyo
• **July**	luglio	'lu-lyo
• **August**	agosto	a-'gos-to
• **September**	settembre	set-'tem-bre
• **October**	ottobre	ot-'to-bre
• **November**	novembre	no-'vem-bre
• **December**	dicembre	di-'čem-bre

monthly	mensile	*men-si-le*
	mensilmente	*men-sil-men-te*
school year	anno scolastico	*χan-no sko-ʃas-ti-ko*
What month is it?	Che mese è?	—

Jingle

> **Trenta giorni ha novembre,**
> **con aprile, giugno e settembre,**
> **di ventotto ce n'è uno,**
> **tutti gli altri ne han(no) trentuno**
>
> Thirty days has November,
> as does April, June, and September,
> there is only one with twenty-eight
> all the others have thirty-one

C. SEASONS

season	stagione (f)	*sta-jo-ne*
• **autumn**	autunno	*au-tun-no*
• **winter**	inverno	*in-ver-no*
• **spring**	primavera	*pri-ma-ve-ra*
• **summer**	estate (f)	*es-ta-te*

The Seasons

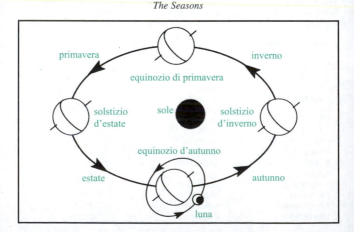

Earth	Terra	*'ter-ra*
moon	luna	*'lu-na*
planet	pianeta (m) (pianeti, pl)	*pya-'ne-ta*
solstice	solstizio	*sol-'sti-tsyo*
star	stella	*'stel-la*
sun	sole (m)	*'so-le*

D. THE ZODIAC

horoscope	oroscopo	*o-'ros-ko-po*
zodiac	zodiaco	*dzo-'di-a-ko*
• **signs of the zodiac**	segni dello zodiaco	*'se-nyi*
• **Aquarius**	Acquario	*ak-'kwa-ryo*
	(21 gennaio-18 febbraio)	
• **Aries**	Ariete (m)	*a-'rye-te*
	(21 marzo-20 aprile)	
• **Cancer**	Cancro	*'kan-kro*
	(22 giugno-22 luglio)	
• **Capricorn**	Capricorno	*ka-pri-'kor-no*
	(22 dicembre-20 gennaio)	
• **Gemini**	Gemelli (pl)	*je-'mel-li*
	(22 maggio-21 giugno)	
• **Leo**	Leone	*le-'o-ne*
	(23 luglio-23 agosto)	
• **Libra**	Bilancia	*bi-'lan-ča*
	(24 settembre-23 ottobre)	
• **Pisces**	Pesci (pl)	*'pe-ši*
	(19 febbraio-20 marzo)	
• **Sagittarius**	Sagittario	*sa-jit-'ta-ri-o*
	(23 novembre-21 dicembre)	
• **Scorpio**	Scorpione (m)	*skor-'pyo-ne*
	(24 ottobre-22 novembre)	
• **Taurus**	Toro	*'to-ro*
	(21 aprile-21 maggio)	
• **Virgo**	Vergine (f)	*'ver-ji-ne*
	(24 agosto-23 settembre)	

For the planets, see §13a

E. EXPRESSING THE DATE

What's the date?	Quanti ne abbiamo oggi?	*'oj-ji*
• **October first**	il primo ottobre	*ot-'to-bre*
• **September 15**	il quindici settembre	*'kwin-di-či set-'tem-bre*
• **June 23**	il ventitré giugno	*'ju-nyo*

Useful Expressions

prossimo	next
la settimana prossima	next week
il mese prossimo	next month
scorso	last
la settimana scorsa	last week
il mese scorso	last month
a domani, a giovedì, ecc.	till tomorrow, till Thursday, etc.
il giorno	the day
la giornata	the whole day (long)
la sera	the evening
la serata	the whole evening (long)
oggi	today
ieri	yesterday
domani	tomorrow
avantieri	the day before yesterday
dopodomani	the day after tomorrow

What year is it?	Che anno è?	—
• **It's 2005.**	È il duemila cinque	—
When were you born?	Quando è nato (m, pol)?	—
	Quando sei nato (m, fam)?	
	Quando è nata (f, pol)?	
	Quando sei nata (f, fam)?	
• **I was born in 1994**	Sono nato (-a) nel	—
	mille novecento novantaquattro	

Distinctions and Patterns

Use the ordinal **primo** for the first of each month, and cardinal numbers for the other days

il primo gennaio = January first
il due gennaio = January second

Use **Quanti ne abbiamo?** when the complete date is not required:

Quanti ne abbiamo?	What's the date?
Ne abbiamo quindici	It's the fifteenth
Ne abbiamo ventuno	It's the twenty-first

F. IMPORTANT DATES

Christmas	Natale	*na-ta-le*
• **Merry Christmas!**	Buon Natale!	*bwon na-'ta-le*
Easter	Pasqua	*'pas-kwa*
• **Happy Easter!**	Buona Pasqua!	*'bwo-na 'pas-kwa*
Feast of the Assumption	Ferragosto	*fer-ra-'gos-to*
holiday	giorno festivo	*'jor-no fes-'ti-vo*
holidays	ferie (f, pl)	*'fe-rye*
New Year	Anno Nuovo	*'an-no 'nwo-vo*
• **Happy New Year!**	Felice Anno Nuovo!	*fe-'li-če*
New Year's	Capodanno	*ka-po-'dan-no*
New Year's Eve	Vigilia di Capodanno	*vi-'ji-li-a*
vacation	vacanza	*va-'kan-dza*

6. TALKING ABOUT THE WEATHER

A. GENERAL WEATHER VOCABULARY

air	aria	*'a-rya*
atmosphere	atmosfera	*at-mos-'fe-ra*
• **atmospheric**	condizioni	*kon-di-'tsyo-ni*
conditions	atmosferiche	*at-mos-'fe-ri-ke*
(to) be bad (awful)	fare* brutto, cattivo	*'fa-re 'brut-to*
weather	tempo	*kat-'ti-vo 'tem-po*
(to) be good (beautiful)	fare* bel tempo	—
weather		
(to) be windy, blow wind	tirare vento	*ti-'ra-re 'ven-to*
clear	sereno	*se-'re-no*
• **The sky is clear.**	Il cielo è sereno.	*'če-lo*
climate	clima (m)	*'kli-ma*
• **continental**	continentale	*kon-ti-nen-'ta-le*
• **dry**	asciutto	*a-'šut-to*
• **humid**	umido	*'u-mi-do*
• **Mediterranean**	Mediterraneo	*me-di-ter-'ra-ne-o*
• **tropical**	tropicale	*tro-pi-'ka-le*
cloud	nuvola	*'nu-vo-la*
• **cloudy**	nuvoloso	*nu-vo-'lo-zo*
• **cloudburst**	nubifragio	*nu-bi-'fra-jo*
cold	freddo	*'fred-do*
• **(to) be cold**	fare* freddo	—
cool	fresco	*'fres-ko*
• **(to) be cool**	fare* fresco	—
dark	buio	*'bu-yo*
• **It's dark today.**	Oggi è buio.	*'oj-ji e 'bu-yo*
dew	rugiada	*ru-'ja-da*
drizzle	pioggerellina	*pyoj-je-rel-'li-na*

• drizzly	piovigginoso	pyo-vij-ji-'no-zo
drop	goccia	'goč-ča
dry	asciutto	a-'šut-to
	secco	'sek-ko
flash of lightning	fulmine (m)	'ful-mi-ne
• (to) flash	lampeggiare	lam-pej-'ja-re
fog	nebbia	'neb-'bya
• foggy	nebbioso	neb-'byo-zo
foul weather	tempaccio	tem-'pač-čo
frost	gelo	'je-lo
• (to) freeze	gelare	je-'la-re
• frozen	gelato	je-'la-to
	ghiacciato	gyač-'ča-to
hail	grandine (f)	'gran-di-ne
• (to) hail	grandinare	gran-di-'na-re
• hailstorm	tempesta di grandine	tem-'pes-ta
hoarfrost	brina	'bri-na
hot	caldo	'kal-do
• (to) be hot	fare* caldo	—
humidity	umidità (f, inv)	u-'mi-di-'ta
• humid, damp	umido	'u-mido
hurricane	uragano	u-ra-'ga-no
ice	ghiaccio	'gyač-čo
light	luce (f)	'lu-če
lightning (bolt of)	lampo	'lam-po
	fulmine (m)	'ful-mi-ne
• There's lightning	Sta lampeggiando.	lam-pej-'jan-do
mild	mite	'mi-te
• (to) be mild	essere* mite	—
mist, haze	foschia	fos-'ki-a
moon	luna	'lu-na
• moonbeam	raggio della luna	'raj-jo
mugginess	afa	'a-fa
• muggy	afoso	a-'fo-zo
rain	pioggia	'pyoj-ja
• (to) rain	piovere	'pyo-ve-re
• (to) rain heavily	piovere a dirotto	di-'rot-to
• rainy	piovoso	'pyo-vo-zo
• pouring rain	pioggia torrenziale	'pyoj-ja tor-ren-'tsya-le
sea	mare (m)	'ma-re
shadow, shade	ombra	'om-bra
shower	acquazzone (m)	a-kwa-'tso-ne
sky	cielo	'če-lo
sleet	nevischio	ne-'vis-kyo
slippery	scivoloso	ši-vo-'lo-zo
snow	neve (f)	'ne-ve
• (to) snow	nevicare	ne-vi-'ka-re
• snowball	palla di neve	'pal-la

Idiomatic Expressions

(to) have one's head in the clouds	=	avere la testa fra le nuvole
The weather is foul.	=	Fa un tempo da cani.
It's raining cats and dogs.	=	Piove a catinelle.
		Piove a dirotto.

• **snow-capped**	coperto di neve	ko-'per-to
• **snowflake**	fiocco di neve	'fyok-ko
• **snowman**	pupazzo di neve	pu-'pa-tso
• **snowstorm**	bufera di neve	bu-'fe-ra
star	stella	'stel-la
storm	tempesta	tem-'pes-ta
sun	sole	'so-le
• **(to) sunbathe**	prendere* sole	'pren-de-re
• **sunbeam**	raggio di sole	'raj-jo
• **sunglasses**	occhiali da sole	ok-'kya-li
• **sunny**	pieno di sole	'pye-no
thaw	disgelo	diz-'je-lo
• **(to) thaw**	sgelare	zje-'la-re
thunder	tuono	'two-no
• **(to) thunder**	tuonare	two-'na-re
• **thunderstorm**	temporale (m)	tem-po-'ra-le
tornado	tornado	—
typhoon	tifone (m)	ti-'fo-ne
weather	tempo	'tem-po
wind	vento	'ven-to
• **(to) be windy**	tirare vento	ti-'ra-re
• **wind gust**	raffica di vento	'raf-fi-ka

B. REACTING TO THE WEATHER

(to) be cold	avere* freddo	a-'ve-re 'fred-do
(to) be hot	avere* caldo	a-'ve-re 'kal-do
(to) bear	sopportare	sop-por-'ta-re
• **I can't stand the cold.**	Non sopporto il freddo.	sop-'porto
• **I can't stand the heat.**	Non sopporto il caldo.	
(to) have chills	avere* i brividi	a-'ve-re i 'bri-vi-di
How's the weather?	Che tempo fa?	—
	Com'è il tempo?	—
• **It's bad (weather).**	Fa brutto (tempo).	—
• **It's cloudy**	È nuvoloso.	nu-vo-'lo-zo
• **It's cold.**	Fa freddo.	'fred-do
• **It's very cold.**	Fa molto freddo.	'fred-do
• **It's cool.**	Fa fresco.	'fres-ko
• **It's hot, warm.**	Fa caldo.	'kal-do

• It's very hot.	Fa molto caldo.	—
• It's a bit hot.	Fa un po' caldo.	—
• It's humid.	È umido.	*'u-mi-do*
• It's mild.	È mite.	*'mi-te*
• It's muggy.	È afoso.	*a-'fo-zo*
• It's nice (weather).	Fa bello.	—
	Fa bel tempo.	—
• It's pleasant.	È piacevole.	*pya-če-vo-le*
	È bello.	—
• It's raining	Piove.	*'pyo-ve*
• It's snowing	Nevica.	*'ne-vi-ka*
• It's sunny.	C'è il sole.	*ce il 'so-le*
• It's thundering.	Tuona.	*'two-na*
• It's windy.	Tira vento.	*'ti-ra 'ven-to*
• There's lightning.	Lampeggia.	*lam-'pej-ja*
(to) perspire	sudare	*su-'da-re*
(to) warm up	riscaldarsi	*ris-kal-'dar-si*

C. WEATHER-MEASURING INSTRUMENTS AND CONCEPTS

barometer	barometro	*ba-'ro-me-tro*
• barometric pressure	pressione barometrica	*pres-'syo-ne bar-o-'me-tri-ka*
boiling point	temperatura dell'acqua bollente	*tem-pe-ra-'tu-ra del-'lak-kwa bol-'len-te*
Celsius	Celsius (m, inv)	*'čel-si-us*
Centigrade	centigrado	*čen-'ti-gra-do*
degree	grado	*'gra-do*
Fahrenheit	Fahrenheit (m, inv)	—
maximum	massimo	*'mas-si-mo*
• maximum temperature	temperatura massima	*tem-pe-ra-'tu-ra*
(to) melt	sciogliere*	*'šo-lye-re*
• melting point	temperatura del ghiaccio fondente	*gyač-čo fon-'den-te*
mercury	mercurio	*mer-'ku-ri-o*
minimum	minimo	*'mi-ni-mo*
• minimum temperature	temperatura minima	—
minus	meno	—
plus	più	*pyu*
thermometer	termometro	*ter-'mo-me-tro*
thermostat	termostato	*ter-'mos-ta-to*
weather bulletin	bollettino meteorologico	*bol-let-'ti-no me-te-o-ro-'lo-ji-ko*
weather conditions	condizioni meteorologiche	*kon-di-'tsyo-ni me-te-o-ro-'lo-ji-ke*
weather forecast	previsioni del tempo	*pre-vi-'zyo-ni*

zero	zero	'dze-ro
• above zero	sopra zero	—
• below zero	sotto zero	—

7. COLORS

A. BASIC COLORS

What color is it?	Di che colore è?	di ke co-l'o-re 'e
black	nero	'ne-ro
• pitch black	nero come la pece	'pe-če
blue	azzurro	a-'dzur-ro
• dark blue	blu (inv)	—
• light blue, sky blue	celeste	če-'les-te
brown	marrone (inv)	mar-'ro-ne
gold	oro (inv)	—
gray	grigio	'gri-jo
• pearl gray	grigio perla (inv)	'per-la
green	verde	'ver-de
• military green	verde militare (inv)	mi-li-'ta-re
ivory	avorio	a-'vo-ryo
lemon	limone (inv)	li-'mo-ne
mauve	malva (inv)	'mal-va
orange	arancione (inv)	a-ran-'čo-ne
pink	rosa (inv)	'ro-za

Color Idioms

(financially) broke	al verde
1-800 number	numero verde
carte blanche	carta bianca
dark mood	umore nero
dull life	vita grigia
extremely angry	giallo dalla rabbia
help line	telefono azzurro
information radio	onda verde
mystery story	giallo
national Italian team	squadra azzurra
rare thing	mosca bianca
red light	luci rosse
sleepless night	notte bianca
Snow White	Bianca Neve
terrified	verde di paura
(to) be extremely angry	essere verde dalla rabbia
(to) become embarrassed	diventare rosso
yellow pages	le pagine gialle

plum	prugna (inv)	*'pru-nya*
pure	puro	*'pu-ro*
purple, violet	viola (inv)	*'vyo-la*
red	rosso	*'ros-so*
silver	argento (inv)	*ar'jen-to*
turquoise	turchino	*tur-'ki-no*
white	bianco	*'byan-ko*
yellow	giallo	*'jal-lo*

B. DESCRIBING COLORS AND COLORING ACTIVITIES

bright	acceso	*ač-če-zo*
	brillante	*bril-'lan-te*
color	colore (m)	*ko-'lo-re*
• (to) color	colorare	*ko-lo-'ra-re*
• colored	a colori	—
chocolate	cioccolato	*čok-ko-'la-to*
dark	scuro	*'sku-ro*
dull	cupo	*'ku-po*
	spento	*'spen-to*
light	chiaro	*'kya-ro*
lively	vivace	*vi-'va-če*
opaque	opaco	*o-'pa-ko*
painting	pittura	*pit-'tu-ra*
	dipinto	*di-'pin-to*
	quadro	*'kwa-dro*
• (to) paint	pitturare	*pit-tu-'ra-re*
	dipingere*	*di-'pin-je-re*
• painter	pittore (-trice)	*pit-'to-re*
pen	penna	*'pen-na*
• felt pen	pennarello	*pen-na-'rel-lo*
• pencil	matita	*ma-'ti-ta*
• brush	pennello	*pen-'nel-lo*
tint	tinta	*'tin-ta*
• (to) tint	tingere*	*'tin-je-re*
transparent	trasparente	*tras-pa-'ren-te*

8. BASIC GRAMMAR

A. GRAMMATICAL TERMS

adjective	aggettivo	*aj-jet-'ti-vo*
• demonstrative	dimostrativo	*di-mos-tra-'ti-vo*
• descriptive	qualificativo	*kwa-li-fi-ka-'ti-vo*
• indefinite	indefinito	*in-de-fi-'ni-to*
• interrogative	interrogativo	*in-ter-ro-ga-'ti-vo*
• possessive	possessivo	*pos-ses-'si-vo*

adverb	avverbio	av-'ver-byo
alphabet	alfabeto	al-fa-'be-to
• accent	accento	ač-'čen-to
• consonant	consonante (f)	kon-so-'nan-te
• letter	lettera	'let-te-ra
• phonetics	fonetica	fo-'ne-ti-ka
• pronunciation	pronuncia	pro-'nun-ča
• vowel	vocale (f)	vo-'ka-le
article	articolo	ar-'ti-ko-lo
• definite	determinativo	de-ter-mi-na-'ti-vo
• indefinite	indeterminativo	in-de-ter-mi-na-'ti-vo
clause	proposizione (f)	pro-po-si-'tsyo-ne
• main	principale	prin-či-'pa-le
• relative	relativa	re-la-'ti-va
• subordinate	subordinata	su-bor-di-'na-ta
conjunction	congiunzione (f)	kon-jun-'tsyo-ne
discourse	discorso	dis-'kor-so
• direct	diretto	di-'ret-to
• indirect	indiretto	in-di-'ret-to
gender	genere (m)	'je-ne-re
• feminine	femminile	fem-mi-'ni-le
• masculine	maschile	mas-'ki-le
grammar	grammatica	gram-'ma-ti-ka
interrogative	interrogativo	in-ter-ro-ga-'ti-vo
mood	modo	—
• conditional	condizionale	kon-di-tsyo-'na-le
• imperative	imperativo	im-pe-ra-'ti-vo
• indefinite	indefinito	in-de-fi-'ni-to
• indicative	indicativo	in-di-ka-'ti-vo
• subjunctive	congiuntivo	kon-jun-'ti-vo
noun	nome (m)	'no-me
• substantive	sostantivo	sos-tan-'ti-vo
number	numero	'nu-me-ro
• singular	singolare	sin-go-'la-re
• plural	plurale	plu-'ra-le
object	complemento	kom-ple-'men-to
• direct	diretto	di-'ret-to
• indirect	indiretto	in-di-'ret-to
participle	participio	par-ti-'či-pi-o
• past	passato	pas-'sa-to
• present	presente	pre-'zen-te
partitive	partitivo	par-ti-'ti-vo
person	persona	per-'so-na
• first	prima	'pri-ma
• second	seconda	se-'kon-da
• third	terza	'ter-tsa
predicate	predicato	pre-di-'ka-to
preposition	preposizione (f)	pre-po-zi-'tsyo-ne

pronoun	pronome (m)	*pro-'no-me*
• demonstrative	dimostrativo	*di-mos-tra-'ti-vo*
• interrogative	interrogativo	*in-ter-ro-ga-'ti-vo*
• object	di complemento	*kom-ple-'men-to*
• personal	personale	*per-so-'na-le*
• possessive	possessivo	*pos-ses-'si-vo*
• reflexive	riflessivo	*ri-fles-'si-vo*
• relative	relativo	*re-la-'ti-vo*
• subject	soggetto	*soj-'jet-to*
sentence	frase (f)	*'fra-ze*
• declarative	dichiarativa	*di-kya-ra-'ti-va*
• interrogative	interrogativa	*in-ter-ro-ga-'ti-va*
• exclamatory	esclamativa	*es-kla-ma-'ti-va*
subject	soggetto	*soj-'jet-to*
tense	tempo	*'tem-po*
• future	futuro	*fu-'tu-ro*
• imperfect	imperfetto	*im-per-'fet-to*
• past	passato	*pas-'sa-to*
• past absolute	passato remoto	*re-'mo-to*
• perfect	perfetto	*per-'fet-to*
• present perfect	passato prossimo	*'pros-si-mo*
• pluperfect	trapassato	*tra-pas-'sa-to*
• present	presente	*pre-'zen-te*
verb	verbo	*'ver-bo*
• active	attivo	*at-'ti-vo*
• conjugation	coniugazione (f)	*kon-yu-ga-'tsyo-ne*
• gerund	gerundio	*je-'run-di-o*
• infinitive	infinito	*in-fi-'ni-to*
• intransitive	intransitivo	*in-tran-si-'ti-vo*
• irregular	irregolare	*ir-re-go-'la-re*
• modal	modale	*mo-'da-le*
• passive	passivo	*pas-'si-vo*
• reflexive	riflessivo	*ri-fles-'si-vo*
• regular	regolare	*re-go-'la-re*
• transitive	transitivo	*tran-si-'ti-vo*

B. ARTICLES

a, an		
• a boy	un ragazzo	*ra-'ga-tso*
• a girl	una ragazza	*ra-'ga-tsa*
• an uncle	uno zio	*'dzi-o*
• a friend	un amico (m)	*a-'mi-ko*
• a friend	un'amica (f)	*a-'mi-ka*
the		
• the boy	il ragazzo	*ra-'ga-tso*
• the boys	i ragazzi	*ra-'ga-tsi*
• the uncle	lo zio	*'dzi-o*

• the uncles	gli zii	'dzi-i
• the friend	l'amico (m)	a-'mi-ko
• the friends	gli amici (m)	lyi a-'mi-či
• the girl	la ragazza	ra-'ga-tsa
• the girls	le ragazze	ra-'ga-tse
• the friend	l'amica (f)	a-'mi-ka
• the friends	le amiche (f)	a-'mi-ke

C. PARTITIVES

some

• some boys	dei ragazzi	de-i ra-'ga-tsi
	alcuni ragazzi	al-'ku-ni ra-'ga-tsi
	qualche ragazzo	'kwal-ke ra-'ga-tso
• some friends	degli amici (m)	de-lyi a-'mi-či
	alcuni amici	al-'ku-ni a-'mi-či
	qualche amico	'kwal-ke a-'mi-ko
• some uncles	degli zii	de-lyi 'dzi-i
	alcuni zii	al-'ku-ni 'dzi-i
	qualche zio	'kwal-ke 'dzi-o
• some girls	delle ragazze	'del-le ra-'ga-tse
	alcune ragazze	al-'ku-ne ra-'ga-tse
	qualche ragazza	'kwal-ke ra-'ga-tsa
• some friends	delle amiche (f)	'del-le a-'mi-ke
	alcune amiche	al-'ku-ne a-'mi-ke
	qualche amica	'kwal-ke a-'mi-ka

a bit, little, some

• some, a bit of butter	del burro	del 'bur-ro
	un po' di burro	—
• some, a bit of sugar	dello zucchero	del-lo 'dzuk-ke-ro
	un po' di zucchero	—
• some, a bit of cake	della torta	del-la 'tor-ta
	un po' di torta	—
• some, a bit of water	dell'acqua	del-'lak-kwa
	un po' di acqua	—

D. DEMONSTRATIVES

this, these

• this boy	questo ragazzo	'kwes-to ra-'ga-tso
• these boys	questi ragazzi	'kwes-ti ra-'ga-tsi
• this girl	questa ragazza	'kwes-ta ra-'ga-tsa
• these girls	queste ragazze	'kwes-te ra-'ga-tse

that, those

• that boy	quel ragazzo	kwel ra-'ga-tso
• those boys	quei ragazzi	kwe-i ra-'ga-tsi
• that uncle	quello zio	kwel-lo 'dzi-o
• those uncles	quegli zii	kwe-lyi 'dzi-i

• that friend	quell'amico (m)	*kwel-la-'mi-ko*
• those friends	quegli amici (m)	*kwel-lyi a-'mi-či*
• that girl	quella ragazza	*kwel-la ra-'ga-tsa*
• those girls	quelle ragazze	*kwel-le ra-'ga-tse*
• that friend	quell'amica (f)	*kwel-la-'mi-ka*
• those friends	quelle amiche (f)	*kwel-le a-'mi-ke*

E. POSSESSIVES

my

• my book	il mio libro	*'mi-o 'li-bro*
• my books	i miei libri	*'mye-i 'li-bri*
• my pen	la mia penna	*'mi-a 'pen-na*
• my pens	le mie penne	*'mi-e 'pen-ne*

your (s, fam)

• your book	il tuo libro	*'tu-o*
• your books	i tuoi libri	*'two-i*
• your pen	la tua penna	*'tu-a*
• your pens	le tue penne	*'tu-e*

his, her, its, your (s, pol)

• his, her, your book	il suo libro	*'su-o*
• his, her, your books	i suoi libri	*'swo-i*
• his, her, your pen	la sua penna	*'su-a*
• his, her, your pens	le sue penne	*'su-e*

our

• our book	il nostro libro	*'nos-tro*
• our books	i nostri libri	*'nos-tri*
• our pen	la nostra penna	*'nos-tra*
• our pens	le nostre penne	*'nos-tre*

your (pl, fam)

• your book	il vostro libro	*'vos-tro*
• your books	i vostri libri	*'vos-tri*
• your pen	la vostra penna	*'vos-tra*
• your pens	le vostre penne	*'vos-tre*

their, your (pl, pol)

• their, your book	il loro libro	*'lo-ro*
• their, your books	i loro libri	—
• their, your pen	la loro penna	—
• their, your pens	le loro penne	—

F. PREPOSITIONS

above	sopra	*'so-pra*
among	fra	—
	tra	—
at	a	—
	in	—
below	sotto	*'sot-to*

between	fra	—
	tra	—
for	per	—
from	da	—
in	in	—
of	di	—
on	su	—
over	sopra	'so-pra
	su	
to	a	—
with	con	—
without	senza	'sen-tsa

G. PERSONAL PRONOUNS

I	io	'i-o
• **me**	mi *(before verb)*	—
	me *(after verb)*	—
• **to me**	mi *(before verb)*	—
	a me	—
• **myself**	mi	—
you (s, fam, subj)	tu	—
• **you**	ti *(before verb)*	—
	te *(after verb)*	—
• **to you**	ti *(before verb)*	—
	a te	—
• **yourself**	ti	—
he	lui, egli	'lu-i
• **him**	lo *(before verb)*	—
	lui *(after verb)*	'lu-i
• **to him**	gli *(before verb)*	lyi
	a lui	'lu-i
• **himself**	si	—
she	lei, ella	'le-i
• **her**	la *(before verb)*	—
	lei *(after verb)*	—
• **to her**	le *(before verb)*	—
	a lei	'le-i
• **herself**	si	—
you (s, pol)	Lei	—
• **your**	Lo *(before verb)*	—
	Lei *(after verb)*	—
• **to you**	Le *(before verb)*	—
	a Lei	—
• **yourself**	si	—
we	noi	'no-i
• **us**	ci *(before verb)*	či
	noi *(after verb)*	—

• to us	ci *(before verb)*	—
	a noi	—
• ourselves	ci	*či*
you (pl, fam)	voi	*'vo-i*
• you	vi *(before verb)*	—
	voi *(after verb)*	—
• to you	vi *(before verb)*	—
	a voi	—
• yourselves	vi	—
they, you (pl, pol)	loro, Loro	*'lo-ro*
• them	li (m) *(before verb)*	—
	le (f) *(before verb)*	—
• to them	gli *(before verb)*	*lyi*
	a loro *(after verb)*	—
• themselves	si	—

H. OTHER PRONOUNS

everyone	tutti	*'tut-ti*
	ognuno	*o-nyu-no*
everything	tutto	*'tut-to*
many	molti (molte, f)	*'mol-ti*
	tanti (tante, f)	*'tan-ti*
one (in general)	si *(before verb)*	—
others	altri (altre, f)	*'al-tri*
some, of it, of them	ne *(before verb)*	—
some (people)	alcuni (alcune, f)	*'al-ku-ni*
someone	qualcuno	*kwal-'ku-no*
something	qualcosa	*kwal-'ko-za*

I. CONJUNCTIONS

also	anche	*'an-ke*
although	benché	*ben-'ke*
	sebbene	*seb-'be-ne*
and	e	—
as	come	*'ko-me*
as if	come se	—
as soon as	appena	*ap-'pe-na*
because	perché	*per-'ke*
but	ma	—
	però	*pe-'ro*
despite	malgrado	*mal-'gra-do*
	nonostante	*no-nos-'tan-te*
even though	anche se	*'an-ke*
however	comunque	*ko-'mun-kwe*
	tuttavia	*tut-ta-'vi-a*
if	se	—

in fact	infatti	*in-'fat-ti*
in the event that	nel caso che	*nel 'ka-zo ke*
on account of	a causa di	*a 'kau-za di*
provided that	purché	*pur-'ke*
since	poiché	*poy-'ke*
so that	affinché	*af-fin-'ke*
	perché	*per-'ke*
thanks to	grazie a	*'gra-tsye*
therefore	quindi	*'kwin-di*

J. COMMON ADVERBS

again	di nuovo	*'nwo-vo*
almost	quasi	*'kwa-zi*
already	già	*ja*
also, too	anche	*'an-ke*
as a matter of fact	anzi	*'an-tsi*
bad(ly)	male	*'ma-le*
	malamente	*ma-la-'men-te*
by chance	per caso	*per 'ka-zo*
by now	ormai	*or-'ma-i*
early	presto	*'pres-to*
enough	abbastanza	*ab-bas-'tan-dza*
far	lontano	*lon-'ta-no*
first	prima	*'pri-ma*
in a hurry	in fretta	*'fret-ta*
in a little while	fra (tra) poco	*'po-ko*
in the meanwhile	nel frattempo	*frat-'tem-po*
instead	invece	*in-'ve-če*
just, barely	appena	*ap-'pe-na*
late	tardi	*'tar-di*
near(by)	vicino	*vi-'či-no*
nowadays	oggigiorno	*oj-ji-'jor-no*
only	solo	*'so-lo*
rather	piuttosto	*pyut-'tos-to*
right away	subito	*'su-bi-to*
still, yet, again	ancora	*an-'ko-ra*
then	allora	*al-'lo-ra*
• then, after	poi	*'po-i*
there	lì	—
	là	—
this evening	stasera	*sta-'se-ra*
this morning	stamani	*sta-'ma-ni*
today	oggi	*'oj-ji*
together	insieme	*in-'sye-me*
tomorrow	domani	*do-'ma-ni*
unfortunately	purtroppo	*pur-'trop-po*
until now	finora	*fi-'no-ra*

K. NEGATIVES

neither...nor	non...né...né	—
never	non...mai	—
no more, no longer	non...più	*pyu*
no one	non...nessuno	*nes-'su-no*
not even	non...neanche	*ne-'an-ke*
	non...nemmeno	*nem-'me-no*
	non...neppure	*nep-'pu-re*
not really, not quite	non...mica	*'mi-ka*
nothing	non...niente	*'nyen-te*
	non...nulla	—

9. REQUESTING INFORMATION

answer	risposta	*ris-'pos-ta*
• (to) answer	rispondere*	*ris-pon-de-re*
(to) ask (for)	chiedere*	*'kye-de-re*
• (to) ask a question	fare* una domanda	*'fa-re u-na do-'man-da*
Can you tell me...?	Mi sa dire... (pol)?	—
	Mi sai dire... (fam)?	—
How?	Come?	*'ko-me*
How come?	Come mai?	—
How much?	Quanto?	*'kwan-to*
I don't understand.	Non capisco.	*ka-'pis-ko*
So?	E allora?	*al-'lo-ra*
	E con ciò?	*kon čo*
What?	Che?	*ke*
	Cosa?	*'ko-za*
	Che cosa?	*ke 'ko-za*
What does it mean?	Che significa?	*ke si-'nyi-fi-ka*
	Che vuol dire?	*ke vwol 'di-re*
When?	Quando?	*'kwan-do*
Where?	Dove?	*'do-ve*
Which (one)?	Quale?	*'kwa-le*
Who?	Chi?	*ki*
Why?	Perché?	*per-'ke*

PEOPLE

10. FAMILY AND FRIENDS

A. FAMILY MEMBERS

aunt	zia	*'dzi-a*
• great-aunt	prozia	*pro-'dzi-a*
brother	fratello	*fra-'tel-lo*
• brother-in-law	cognato	*ko-'nya-to*
• half-brother	fratellastro	*fra-tel-'las-tro*
cousin	cugino (m)	*ku-'ji-no*
	cugina (f)	—
child	bambino (-a)	*bam-'bi-no*
• godchild	figlioccio (-a)	*fi-'lyoč-čo*
dad	papà (m, inv)	*pa-'pa*
daughter	figlia	*'fi-lya*
• daughter-in-law	nuora	*'nwo-ra*
• stepdaughter	figliastra	*fi-'lyas-tra*
family	famiglia	*fa-'mi-lya*
• family relation	parentela	*pa-ren-'te-la*
father	padre (m)	*'pa-dre*
• father-in-law	suocero	*'swo-če-ro*
• godfather	padrino	*pa-'dri-no*
• stepfather	patrigno	*pa-'tri-nyo*
fraternal	fraterno	*fra-'ter-no*
grandchild	nipote (m/f)	*ni-'po-te*
• great grandchild	pronipote (m/f)	*pro-ni-'po-te*
grandfather	nonno	—
• great grandfather	bisnonno	*biz-'non-no*
grandmother	nonna	—
• great grandmother	bisnonna	*biz-'non-na*
head of the family	capofamiglia	*ka-po-fa-'mi-lya*
household	casa	*'ka-za*
	domicilio	*do-mi-'či-lyo*
	focolare	*fo-ko-'la-re*
husband	marito	*ma-'ri-to*
maternal	materno	*ma-'ter-no*
mother	madre (f)	*'ma-dre*
• godmother	madrina	*ma-'dri-na*
• mother-in-law	suocera	*'swo-če-ra*
• mom	mamma	—
• stepmother	matrigna	*ma-'tri-nya*

nephew	nipote (m)	*ni-'po-te*
niece	nipote (f)	*ni-'po-te*
parent	genitore (-trice)	*je-ni-'to-re*
paternal	paterno	*pa-'ter-no*
relative	parente (m/f)	*pa-'ren-te*
sister	sorella	*so-'rel-la*
• half-sister	sorellastra	*so-rel-'las-tra*
• sister-in-law	cognata	*ko-'nya-ta*
son	figlio	*fi-lyo*
• son-in-law	genero	*'je-ne-ro*
• stepson	figliastro	*fi-'lyas-tro*
twin	gemello (-a)	*je-'mel-lo*
uncle	zio	*'dzi-o*
• great-uncle	prozio	*pro-'dzi-o*
wife	moglie (f)	*'mo-lye*

B. FRIENDS AND SIGNIFICANT OTHERS

acquaintance	conoscenza	*ko-no-'šen-dza*
boyfriend	amico	*a-'mi-ko*
	ragazzo (*amorous*)	*ra-'ga-tso*
chum	compagno (-a)	*kom-'pa-nyo*
colleague	collega (m/f)	*kol-'le-ga*
enemy	nemico (-a)	*ne-'mi-ko*
fiancé	fidanzato	*fi-dan-'tsa-to*
fiancée	fidanzata	*fi-dan-'tsa-ta*
friend	amico (-a)	*a-'mi-ko*
• (to) become friends	diventare (ess) amici	*di-ven-'ta-re a-'mi-či*
	fare* amicizia	*'fa-re a-mi-'či-tsya*
• (to) break off a friendship	rompere* un'amicizia	*'rom-pe-re*
• close friend	amico (-a) intimo (-a)	*a-'mi-ko 'in-ti-mo*
• dear friend	caro (-a) amico (-a)	—
• family friend	amico (-a) di famiglia	*a-'mi-ko di fa-'mi-lya*
• friendship	amicizia	*a-mi-či-tsya*
girlfriend	amica	*a-'mi-ka*
	ragazza (*amorous*)	*ra-'ga-tsa*
lover	amante (m/f)	*a-'man-te*
• love affair	relazione (amorosa)	*re-la-'tsyo-ne*
people	gente (f)	*'jen-te*
person	persona	*per-'so-na*

11. DESCRIBING PEOPLE

A. GENDER AND PHYSICAL APPEARANCE

adorable	adorabile	*a-do-'ra-bi-le*
agile	agile	*'a-ji-le*

alert	sveglio	'zve-lyo
athletic	atletico	at-'le-ti-ko
attractive	attraente	at-tra-'en-te
average height	altezza media	al-'te-tsa 'me-dya
baldness	calvizie (f, inv)	kal-'vi-tsye
• bald	calvo	'kal-vo
(to) be slightly built	avere* un fisico debole	a-'ve-re un 'fi-zi-ko 'de-bo-le
(to) be strongly built	avere* un fisico forte	'for-te
beauty	bellezza	bel-'le-tsa
• beautiful, handsome	bello (-a)	—
(to) become fat	ingrassare	in-gras-'sa-re
(to) become thin	dimagrire (isc)	di-ma-'gri-re
big	grande	'gran-de
• big, huge	grosso	'gros-so
blond	biondo	'byon-do
• blonde	bionda	—
(to) blush	arrossire (isc)	ar-ros-'si-re
body	corpo	'kor-po
bow legs	gambe storte	'gam-be 'stor-te
boy	ragazzo	ra-'ga-tso
brawny	poderoso	po-de-'ro-zo
broad chin	mento largo	'men-to 'lar-go
broad forehead	fronte spaziosa	'fron-te spa-'tsyo-za
broad-shouldered	con le spalle larghe	'spal-le 'lar-ge
brown eyes	occhi castani	'ok-ki kas-'ta-ni
brown skin	pelle bruna	'pel-le 'bru-na
build	fisico	'fi-zi-ko
chapped hands	mani screpolate	skre-po-'la-te
chubby	grassottello	gras-sot-'tel-lo
clean	pulito	pu-'li-to
clear skin	pelle chiara	'pel-le 'kya-ra
(to) color one's hair	tingersi* i capelli	'tin-jer-si i ka-'pel-li
(to) comb oneself	pettinarsi	pet-ti-'nar-si
corpulent	corpulento	kor-pu-'len-to
curly	riccio	'rič-čo
cute	simpatico	sim-'pa-ti-ko
dark skin	pelle nera	'pel-le 'ne-ra
dark-haired	bruno	'bru-no
delicate, frail	delicato	de-li-'ka-to
dimple	fossetta (del mento)	fos-'set-ta
dirty	sporco	'spor-ko
double chin	doppio mento	'dop-pyo 'men-to
dry skin	pelle secca	'pel-le 'sek-ka
emaciated	emaciato	e-ma-'ča-to
energetic	energico	e-'ner-ji-ko
expression	espressione (f)	es-pres-'syo-ne
face, countenance	faccia	'fač-ča
	viso	'vi-zo

fascinating	affascinante	*af-fa-ši-'nan-te*
fat	grasso	*'gras-so*
female	femmina	*'fem-mi-na*
• feminine	femminile	*fem-mi-'ni-le*
fleshy	carnoso	*kar-'no-zo*
frail, slender	gracile	*'gra-či-le*
freckles	lentiggini (f)	*len-'tij-ji-ni*
• freckled	lentigginoso	*len-tij-ji-'no-zo*
frizzy, fuzzy hair	capelli crespi	*ka-'pel-li 'kres-pi*
gentleman	signore (m)	*si-'nyo-re*
giant	gigante	*ji-'gan-te*
good complexion	carnagione bella	*kar-na-'jo-ne 'bel-la*
good figure, shapely	bella figura	*'bel-la fi-'gu-ra*
gray hair	capelli grigi	*ka-'pel-li 'gri-ji*
haggard face	viso stravolto	*'vi-zo stra-'vol-to*
hairstyle	acconciatura (dei capelli)	*ak-kon-ča-'tu-ra*
hairy	peloso	*pe-'lo-zo*
happy face	viso allegro	*'vi-zo al-'le-gro*
(to) have a slim waistline	avere* una vita snella	*a-'ve-re u'na 'vi-ta 'znel-la*
heavy	pesante	*pe-'zan-te*
hefty	robusto	*ro-'bus-to*
height	altezza	*al-'te-tsa*
• short	basso	*'bas-so*
• tall	alto	*'al-to*
high forehead	fronte alta	—
hunched	curvo	*'kur-vo*
husky, manly	aitante	*ai-'tan-te*
lady	signora	*si-'nyo-ra*
• young lady	signorina	*si-nyo-'ri-na*
lanky, long-legged	slanciato	*zlan-'ča-to*
large	grosso	*'gros-so*
lean	magro	*'ma-gro*
(to) lose one's hair	perdere* i capelli	*'per-de-re i ka-'pel-li*
(to) lose weight	perdere* peso	*'per-de-re 'pe-zo*
low forehead	fronte bassa	*'fron-te 'bas-sa*
male	maschio	*'mas-kyo*
man	uomo (uomini, pl)	*'wo-mo ('wo-mi-ni)*
• masculine	maschile	*mas-'ki-le*
midget	nano (-a)	—
muscular	muscoloso	*mus-ko-'lo-zo*
mustache	baffi (pl)	*'baf-fi*
obese	obeso	*o-'be-zo*
olive skin	pelle olivastra	*'pel-le o-li-'vas-tra*
pale cheeks	guance pallide	*'gwan-če 'pal-li-de*
parted hair	capelli con la scriminatura	*skri-mi-na-'tu-ra*
paunch	pancia	*'pan-ča*

pimple	foruncolo	*fo-'run-ko-lo*
pleasant, friendly face	viso simpatico	*'vi-zo sim-'pa-ti-ko*
plump	pasciuto	*pa-'šu-to*
pot-bellied	panciuto	*pan-'ču-to*
pretty	carino	*ka-'ri-no*
pudgy	tozzo	*'to-tso*
puny	smunto	*'zmun-to*
red hair	capelli rossi	*ka-'pel-li 'ros-si*
robust, strong	robusto	*ro-'bus-to*
rosy cheeks	guance rosee	*'gwan-če 'ro-ze-e*
rough skin	pelle ruvida	*'pel-le 'ru-vi-da*
round face	viso rotondo	*'vi-zo ro-'ton-do*
scrawny, skin and bones	scheletrico	*ske-'le-tri-ko*
seductive	seducente	*se-du-'čen-te*
sex	sesso	*'ses-so*
short	basso	*'bas-so*
skinny	magro	*'ma-gro*
slant eyes	occhi a mandorla	*'ok-ki a 'man-dor-la*
slim, lean	snello	*'snel-lo*
small, little	piccolo	*'pik-ko-lo*
smile	sorriso	*'sor-'ri-zo*
• **(to) smile**	sorridere*	*sor-'ri-de-re*
stocky	tarchiato	*tar-'kya-to*
straight hair	capelli lisci	*ka-'pel-li 'li-ši*
streaked hair	capelli striati	*ka-'pel-li stri-'a-ti*
strength	forza	*'for-tsa*
• **strong**	forte	*'for-te*
tall	alto	—
toothless	sdentato	*zden-'ta-to*
ugly	brutto	*'brut-to*
untidy, disheveled hair	capelli sfatti	*ka-'pel-li 'sfat-ti*
vigorous	vigoroso	*vi-go-'ro-zo*
virile	virile	*vi-'ri-le*
waistline	vita	—
wavy hair	capelli ondulati	*ka-'pel-li on-du-'la-ti*
weakness	debolezza	*de-bo-'le-tsa*
• **weak**	debole	*'de-bo-le*
weight	peso	*'pe-zo*
well-built	ben fatto	—
woman	donna	—
wrinkles	rughe (f, pl)	*'ru-ge*
youthful	giovanile	*jo-va-'ni-le*

B. AGE CONCEPTS

adolescence	adolescenza	*a-do-le'-šen-tsa*
• **adolescent, teenager**	adolescente (m/f)	*a-do-le'-šen-te*
adulthood, maturity	maturità (f, inv)	*ma-tu-ri-'ta*

• adult	adulto	a-'dul-to
age	età (f, inv)	e-'ta
• (to) be…years old	avere*…anni	—
• I am 55 years old.	Ho cinquantacinque anni.	čin-kwan-ta-'cin-kwe
baby, child	bambino (-a)	bam-'bi-no
• children	bambini	—
big (in the sense of old)	grande	'gran-de
boy	ragazzo	ra-'ga-tso
childhood	fanciullezza	fan-cul-'le-tsa
girl	ragazza	ra-'ga-tsa
(to) grow up	crescere* (ess)	'kre-še-re
infancy	infanzia	in-'fan-tsya
• infantile	infantile	in-fan-'ti-le
mature person	persona matura	per-'so-na ma-'tu-ra
middle age	mezza età	'me-dza e-'ta
newly-born	neonato (-a)	ne-o-'na-to
old	vecchio	'vek-kyo
• old age	vecchiaia	vek-'kya-ya
	terza età	'ter-tsa e-'ta
• older	maggiore	maj-'jo-re
	più vecchio	pyu 'vek-kyo
	più grande	pyu 'gran-de
• older brother	fratello più grande	—
	fratello maggiore	—
• older person	vecchio (-a)	—
• senior	anziano (-a)	an-'tsya-no
• (to) become old	invecchiarsi	in-vek-'kyar-si
puberty	pubertà (f, inv)	pu-ber-'ta
• senile	senile	se-'ni-le
youth	gioventù (f, inv)	jo-ven-'tu
	giovinezza	jo-vi-'ne-tsa
• young	giovane	'jo-va-ne
• younger	minore	mi-'no-re
	più piccolo	pyu 'pik-ko-lo
• younger sister	sorella più piccola	so-'rel-la
	sorella minore	mi-'no-re
• young lady	signorina	si-nyo-'ri-na
• young man	giovanotto	jo-va-'not-to
• young person	giovane (m/f)	'jo-va-ne

C. MARRIAGE AND THE HUMAN LIFE CYCLE

abortion	aborto	a-'bor-to
• (to) abort	abortire (isc)	a-bor-'ti-re
adoption	adozione (f)	a-do-'tsyo-ne
• (to) adopt	adottare	a-dot-'ta-re
adultery	adulterio	a-dul-'te-ryo
alimony	alimenti (m, pl)	a-li-'men-ti

ancestor	antenato	*an-te-'na-to*
anniversary	anniversario	*an-ni-ver-'sa-ryo*
• diamond	di diamante	*dya-'man-te*
• golden	d'oro	—
• silver	d'argento	*dar-'jen-to*
artificial insemination	fecondazione (f)	*fe-kon-da-'tsyo-ne*
	artificiale	*ar-ti-fi-'ča-le*
baby bottle	biberon (m, inv)	*bi-be-'ron*
bachelor	scapolo (-a)	*'ska-po-lo*
(to) be born	nascere* (ess)	*'na-še-re*
(to) be in mourning	essere* in lutto	*'es-se-re in 'lut-to*
(to) be pregnant	essere* incinta	*'es-se-re in'čin-ta*
best man	testimone (dello sposo)	*tes-ti-'mo-ne 'del-lo 'spo-zo*
birth	nascita	*'na-ši-ta*
• birth certificate	certificato di nascita	*čer-ti-fi-'ka-to*
• (to) give birth	partorire (isc)	*par-to-'ri-re*
• premature birth	parto prematuro	*'par-to pre-ma-'tu-ro*
birthday	compleanno	*kom-ple-'an-no*
• Happy Birthday!	Buon compleanno!	—
(to) breast-feed	allattare	*al-lat-'ta-re*
bride	sposa	*'spo-za*
bridesmaid	damigella	*da-mi-'jel-la*
burial	sepoltura	*se-pol-'tu-ra*
• (to) bury	seppellire (isc)	*sep-pel-'li-re*
cadaver	cadavere (m)	*ka-'da-ve-re*
childbirth	parto	—
coffin	bara	—
(to) cohabit, live together	convivere*	*kon-'vi-ve-re*
cohabitation	convivenza	*kon-vi-'ven-tsa*
cremation	cremazione (f)	*kre-ma-'tsyo-ne*
death	morte (f)	*'mor-te*
• death certificate	certificato di morte	*čer-ti-fi-'ka-to*
• deceased, late	defunto	*de-'fun-to*
• (to) die	morire* (ess)	*mo-'ri-re*
dependent	persona a carico	*per-'so-na a 'ka-ri-ko*
divorce	divorzio	*di-'vor-tsyo*
• (to) divorce	divorziare	*di-vor-'tsya-re*
• divorced	divorziato (-a)	*di-vor-'tsya-to*
dowry	dote	*'do-te*
engagement	fidanzamento	*fi-dan-tsa-'men-to*
• (to) get engaged	fidanzarsi	*fi-dan-'tsar-si*
estate	successione (f)	*suc-ces-'syo-ne*
expectant mother	futura mamma	*fu-'tu-ra 'mam-ma*
family tree	albero genealogico	*'al-be-ro je-ne-a-'lo-ji-ko*
first-born	primogenito	*pri-mo-'je-ni-to*
funeral	funerale (m)	*fu-ne-'ra-le*

groom	sposo	'spo-zo
heredity	eredità (f, inv)	e-re-di-'ta
honeymoon	luna di miele	'lu-na di 'mye-le
husband	marito	ma-'ri-to
(to) inherit	ereditare	e-re-di-'ta-re
• inheritor	erede (m/f)	e-'re-de
kiss	bacio	'ba-čo
• (to) kiss	baciare	ba-'ča-re
late	fu	—
life	vita	—
• (to) live	vivere*	'vi-ve-re
love	amore (m)	a-'mo-re
• (to) love	amare	a-'ma-re
• (to) fall in love	innamorarsi	in-na-mo-'rar-si
• in love	innamorato	in-na-mo-'ra-to
maid-of-honor	damigella d'onore	da-mi-'jel-la do-'no-re
marital status	stato civile	'sta-to či-'vi-le
marriage, matrimony	matrimonio	ma-tri-'mo-ni-o
• marriage vow	promessa di matrimonio	pro-'mes-sa
• (to) marry	sposare	spo-'za-re
• matrimonial	matrimoniale	ma-tri-mo-'nya-le
• (to) get married	sposarsi	spo-'zar-si
• married	sposato (-a)	spo-'za-to
• unmarried	celibe (m)	'če-li-be
	nubile (f)	'nu-bi-le
miscarriage	aborto spontaneo	a-'bor-to spon-'ta-ne-o
newborn	neonato (-a)	ne-o-'na-to
newlyweds	novelli sposi	no-'vel-li 'spo-zi
offspring	discendenza	di-šen-'den-tsa
orphan	orfano (-a)	'or-fa-no
• orphanage	orfanotrofio	or-fa-no-'tro-fi-o
pregnancy	gravidanza	gra-vi-'dan-dza
• pregnant	incinta	in-'čin-ta
(to) remarry	risposarsi	ri-spo-'zar-si
separation	separazione (f)	se-pa-ra-'tsyo-ne
• separated	separato (-a)	se-pa-'ra-to
single	single (inv)	—
spouse	coniuge (m/f)	'kon-yu-je
	consorte (m/f)	kon-'sor-te
test-tube baby	figlio in provetta	'fi-lyo in pro-'vet-ta
tomb	tomba	—
• tombstone	lapide (f)	'la-pi-de
veil	velo	—
wedding	nozze (f, pl)	'no-tse
• wedding invitation	partecipazione (f)	par-te-ci-pa-'tsyo-ne
• wedding ring	fede (f)	'fe-de
widow	vedova	've-do-va
• widower	vedovo	—

wife	moglie	*'mo-lye*
will	testamento	*tes-ta-'men-to*
witness	testimone (m/f)	*tes-ti-'mo-ne*
wreath	ghirlanda	*gir-'lan-da*

D. RELIGION

abstinence	astinenza	*a-sti-'nen-dza*
agnostic	agnostico	*a-'nyos-ti-ko*
• altar	altare (m)	*al-'ta-re*
• altar-boy	chierichetto	*kye-ri-'ket-to*
• high altar	altare maggiore	*maj-'jo-re*
angel	angelo	*'an-je-lo*
archbishop	arcivescovo	*ar-či-'ves-ko-vo*
Ash Wednesday	Ceneri (f, pl)	*'če-'ne-ri*
atheism	ateismo	*a-te-'iz-mo*
• atheist	ateo	*'a-te-o*
(to) atone for one's sins	scontare i propri peccati	*skon-'ta-re i 'pro-pri pek-'ka-ti*
baptism	battesimo	*bat-'te-zi-mo*
• baptismal font	fonte battesimale	*'fon-te bat-te-zi-'ma-le*
baptistery	battistero	*bat-tis-'te-ro*
belief	credenza	*kre-'den-dza*
• (to) believe	credere	*'kre-de-re*
• believer	credente (m/f)	*kre-'den-te*
bell-tower	campanile (m)	*kam-pa-'ni-le*
Benedictine	Benedettino	*be-ne-det-'ti-no*
Bible	Bibbia	*'bib-bya*
bishop	vescovo	*'ves-ko-vo*
blasphemy	blasfemia	*blas-'fe-mya*
blessing	benedizione (f)	*be-ne-di-'tsyo-ne*
• (to) bless	benedire* (isc)	*be-ne-'di-re*
Buddhism	Buddismo	*bud-'diz-mo*
• Buddhist	Buddista (m/f)	*bud-'dis-ta*
cardinal	cardinale (m)	*kar-di-'na-le*
catechism	catechismo	*ka-te-'kiz-mo*
cathedral	cattedrale (f)	*kat-te-'dra-le*
Catholicism	Cattolicesimo	*kat-to-li-'če-zi-mo*
• Catholic	Cattolico (-a)	*kat-'to-li-ko*
chalice	calice (m)	*'ka-li-če*
chapel	cappella	*kap-'pel-la*
choir	coro	—
Christianity	Cristianesimo	*cris-tya-'ne-zi-mo*
• Christian	Cristiano (-a)	*cris-'tya-no*
Christmas	Natale (m)	*na-'ta-le*
church	chiesa	*'kye-za*
• church candle	cero	*'če-ro*
clergy	clero	*'kle-ro*

cloister	chiostro	*'kyos-tro*
collection	colletta	*kol-'let-ta*
Commandment	Comandamento	*ko-man-da-'men-to*
Communion	Comunione (f)	*ko-mu-'nyo-ne*
confess	confessarsi	*kon-fes-'sar-si*
Confession	Confessione (f)	*kon-fes-'syo-ne*
• confessional box	confessionale (m)	*kon-fes-syo-'na-le*
confirmation	Cresima	*'kre-zi-ma*
congregation	congregazione (f)	*kon-gre-ga-'tsyo-ne*
convent	convento	*kon-'ven-to*
cross	croce (f)	*'kro-če*
• (to) cross oneself	farsi* il segno della croce	*'far-si il 'se-nyo del-la 'kro-če*
crucifix	Crocifisso	*kro-či-'fis-so*
cult	culto	*'kul-to*
deacon, deaconess	diacono (-essa)	*di-'a-'ko-no*
deadly sin	peccato mortale	*mor-'ta-le*
denomination	confessione (f)	*kon-fes-'syo-ne*
Devil	Diavolo	*'dya-vo-lo*
devotion	devozione (f)	*de-vo-'styo-ne*
• devout	devoto	*de-'vo-to*
Dominican	Domenicano	*do-me-ni-'ka-no*
Easter	Pasqua	*'pas-kwa*
ecclesiastic	ecclesiastico	*ek-kle-zi-'as-ti-ko*
Eucharist	Eucarestia (Eucaristia)	*eu-ka-res-'ti-a*
evangelist	evangelista (m/f)	*e-van-je-'lis-ta*
Exodus	Esodo	*'e-zo-do*
faith	fede (f)	*'fe-de*
• faithful	fedele (m/f)	*fe-'de-le*
fast	digiuno	*di-'ju-no*
Franciscan	Francescano	*fran-čes-'ka-no*
God	Dio	*'di-o*
	Signore	*si-'nyo-re*
Good Friday	Venerdì Santo	*ve-ner-'di 'san-to*
Gospel	Vangelo	*van-'je-lo*
Hail Mary	Ave Maria	*a-ve ma-'ri-a*
heaven, paradise	paradiso	*pa-ra-'di-zo*
Hebrew, Jewish	Ebreo (-a)	*e-'bre-o*
hell	inferno	*in-fer-no*
Hinduism	Induismo	*in-du-'izmo*
• Hindu	Indù (m/f)	*in-'du*
Holy Ghost	Santo Spirito	*'san-to 'spi-ri-to*
Holy Trinity	Santa Trinità	*'san-ta tri-ni-'ta*
homily	omelia	*o-me-'li-a*
host	ostia	*'os-tya*
hymn	inno	*'in-no*
	cantico	*'kan-ti-ko*
incense	incenso	*in-'čen-so*

English	Italian	Pronunciation
Islam	Islam (m)	—
• **Islamic**	Islamico (-a)	*iz-'la-mi-ko*
Jesuit	Gesuita (m) (Gesuiti, pl)	*je-zu-'i-ta*
Jesus Christ	Gesù Cristo	*je-'zu 'kris-to*
Judaism	Giudaismo	*ju-da-'iz-mo*
(to) kneel	inginocchiarsi	*in-ji-nok-'kyar-si*
Koran	Corano	*ko-'ra-no*
lay person, secular	laico	*'lai-ko*
Lent	Quaresima	*kwa-'re-zi-ma*
liturgy	liturgia	*li-tur-'ji-a*
Madonna, Virgin Mary	Madonna	*ma-'don-na*
martyrdom	martirio	*mar-'ti-ryo*
• **martyr**	martire (m/f)	*'mar-ti-re*
Mass	Messa	*'mes-sa*
minister	ministro	*mi-'nis-tro*
missionary	missionario (-a)	*mis-syo-'na-ryo*
monastery	monastero	*mo-nas-'te-ro*
monk	monaco	*'mo-na-ko*
Mormon	Mormone (m/f)	*mor-'mo-ne*
mosque	moschea	*mos-'ke-a*
Muslim	Musulmano (-a)	*mu-sul-'ma-no*
mysticism	misticismo	*mis-ti-'čiz-mo*
• **mystic**	mistico	*'mis-ti-ko*
myth	mito	—
nun, sister	suora	*'swo-ra*
order	ordine (m)	*'or-di-ne*
Our Father	Paternostro	*pa-ter-'nos-tro*
paganism	paganesimo	*pa-ga-'ne-zi-mo*
• **pagan**	pagano (-a)	*pa-'ga-no*
papacy	papato	*pa-'pa-to*
parable	parabola	*pa-'ra-bo-la*
parish	parrocchia	*par-'rok-kya*
• **parish priest**	parroco	*'par-ro-ko*
• **parishioner**	parrocchiano (-a)	*par-rok-'kya-no*
penance	penitenza	*pe-ni-'ten-tsa*
pew	banco di chiesa	*'ban-ko di 'kye-za*
pilgrim	pellegrino (-a)	*pel-le-'gri-no*
pilgrimage	pellegrinaggio	*pel-le-gri-'naj-jo*
pontiff	Pontefice	*pon-'te-fi-če*
pope	Papa (m)	—
prayer	preghiera	*pre-'gye-ra*
• **(to) pray**	pregare	*pre-'ga-re*
preaching, sermon	predica	*'pre-di-ka*
• **(to) preach**	predicare	*pre-di-'ka-re*
• **preacher**	predicatore (-trice)	*pre-di-ka-'to-re*
pride	superbia	*su-'per-bya*
priest	prete (m)	*'pre-te*
Protestantism	Protestantesimo	*pro-tes-tan-'te-zi-mo*

• **Protestant**	Protestante (m/f)	*pro-tes-'tan-te*
pulpit	pulpito	*'pul-pi-to*
purgatory	purgatorio	*pur-ga-'to-ryo*
rabbi	rabbino	*rab-'bi-no*
religion	religione (f)	*re-li-'jo-ne*
• **religious**	religioso	*re-li-'jo-zo*
rite	rito	—
rosary	rosario	*ro-'za-ryo*
sacrament	sacramento	*sa-kra-'men-to*
sacred	sacro	—
Sacred Scripture	Sacra Scrittura	*'sa-kra skrit-'tu-ra*
sacrifice	sacrificio	*sa-kri-'fi-čo*
sacrilege	sacrilegio	*sa-kri-'le-jo*
sacristan	sagrestano	*sa-gres-'ta-no*
sect	setta	—
sermon	sermone (m)	*ser-'mo-ne*
shamanism	sciamanismo	*ša-ma-'niz-mo*
• **shaman**	sciamano	*ša-'ma-no*
shrine, sanctuary	santuario	*san-tu-'a-ri-o*
sin	peccato	*pek-'ka-to*
• **(to) sin**	peccare	*pek-'ka-re*
• **sinner**	peccatore (-trice)	*pek-ka-'to-re*
soul	anima	*'a-ni-ma*
synagogue	sinagoga	*si-na-'go-ga*
temple	tempio	*'tem-pyo*
theology	teologia	*te-o-lo-'ji-a*
• **theologian**	teologo (-a)	*te-'o-lo-go*
vestry	sagrestia	*sa-gres-'ti-a*
vice, bad habit	vizio	*'vi-tsyo*
virtue	virtù (f, inv)	*vir-'tu*
vow	voto	—
worship	adorazione (f)	*a-do-ra-'tsyo-ne*
Zionism	sionismo	*si-o-'niz-mo*
• **Zionist**	sionista (m/f)	*si-o-'nis-ta*

E. CHARACTER AND SOCIAL TRAITS

absent-minded	distratto	*dis-'trat-to*
active	attivo	*at-'ti-vo*
adaptable	adattabile	*a-dat-'ta-bi-le*
affable	affabile	*af-'fa-bi-le*
affectionate	affettuoso	*af-fet-'two-zo*
affluent	benestante	*be-nes-'tan-te*
aggressive	aggressivo	*ag-gres-'si-vo*
altruist	altruista	*al-tru-'is-ta*
ambitious	ambizioso	*am-bi-'tsyo-zo*
annoying, unpleasant	antipatico	*an-ti-'pa-ti-ko*
anxious	ansioso	*an-'syo-zo*

arrogant	arrogante	*ar-ro-'gan-te*
artistic	artistico	*ar-'tis-ti-ko*
astute, bright	astuto	*as-'tu-to*
attentive	attento	*at-'ten-to*
audacious, bold	audace	*au-'da-ce*
bad, mean	cattivo	*kat-'ti-vo*
bigoted	bigotto	*bi-'got-to*
bothersome, irksome	noioso	*no-'yo-zo*
brash, bold	sfacciato	*sfač-'ča-to*
brilliant	brillante	*bril-'lan-te*
broad-minded	di ampie vedute	*'am-pye ve-'du-te*
brusque	brusco	*'brus-ko*
calm	calmo	*'kal-mo*
carefree	spensierato	*spen-sye-'ra-to*
careful	cauto	*'kau-to*
careless	spericolato	*spe-ri-ko-'la-to*
character	carattere (m)	*ka-'rat-te-re*
charming, fascinating	affascinante	*af-fa-ši-'nan-te*
competent, skilled	competente	*kom-pe-'ten-te*
conformist	conformista	*kon-for-'mis-ta*
conscientious	coscienzioso	*ko-šen-'tsyo-zo*
corrupt	corrotto	*kor-'rot-to*
courageous	coraggioso	*ko-raj-'jo-zo*
courteous	cortese	*kor-'te-ze*
cowardly	codardo	*ko-'dar-do*
crazy	pazzo	*'pa-tso*
	matto	*'mat-to*
creative	creativo	*kre-a-'ti-vo*
critical	critico	*'kri-ti-ko*
cruel	crudele	*kru-'de-le*
cultured	colto	*'kol-to*
delicate	delicato	*de-li-'ka-to*
depressed	depresso	*de-'pres-so*
desperate	disperato	*dis-pe-'ra-to*
diligent	diligente	*di-li-'jen-te*
diplomatic	diplomatico	*di-plo-'ma-ti-ko*
disgusted	disgustato	*diz-gus-'ta-to*
dishonest	disonesto	*di-zo-'nes-to*
disinterested	disinteressato	*di-zin-te-res-'sa-to*
downtrodden	avvilito	*av-vi-'li-to*
dynamic	dinamico	*di-'na-mi-ko*
egoist, self-centered	egoista	*e-go-'is-ta*
elegant	elegante	*e-le-'gan-te*
eloquent	eloquente	*e-lo-'kwen-te*
energetic	energico	*e-'ner-ji-ko*
envious	invidioso	*in-vi-'dyo-zo*
erudite	erudito	*e-ru-'di-to*
extraordinary	straordinario	*stra-or-di-'na-ryo*

extroverted	estroverso	es-tro-'ver-so
faithful	fedele	fe-'de-le
fearful	timoroso	ti-mo-'ro-zo
flexible	flessibile	fles-'si-bi-le
friendly	socievole	so-'če-vo-le
frivolous	frivolo	'fri-vo-lo
funny	buffo	—
fussy	fastidioso	fas-ti-'dyo-zo
generous	generoso	je-ne-'ro-zo
gentle	gentile	jen-'ti-le
gloomy	malinconico	ma-lin-'ko-ni-ko
good (at heart)	buono	'bwo-no
graceful	grazioso	gra-'tsyo-zo
greedy	avaro	a-'va-ro
grumpy	scorbutico	skor-'bu-ti-ko
happy	felice	fe-'li-če
	allegro	al-'le-gro
hard-working	laborioso	la-bo-'ryo-zo
hateful	odioso	o-'dyo-so
honest	onesto	o-'nes-to
humanity	umanità (f, inv)	u-ma-ni-'ta
humble	umile	'u-mi-le
idealist	idealista	i-de-a-'lis-ta
ignorant	ignorante	i-nyo-'ran-te
ill-mannered	maleducato	me-le-du-'ka-to
imaginative	immaginativo	im-ma-ji-na-'ti-vo
impatient	impaziente	im-pa-'tsyen-te
impetuous	impetuoso	im-pe-'two-zo
impressionable	impressionabile	im-pres-syo-'na-bi-le
imprudent	imprudente	im-pru-'den-te
impudent	impudente	im-pu-'den-te
impulsive	impulsivo	im-pul-'si-vo
incompetent	incompetente	in-kom-pe-'ten-te
inconsiderate	incosciente	in-ko-šen-te
incorruptible	incorruttibile	in-kor-rut-'ti-bi-le
indecisive	indeciso	in-de-či-zo
independent	indipendente	in-di-pen-'den-te
indifferent	indifferente	in-dif-fe-'ren-te
indigent	indigente	in-di-'jen-te
individualist	individualista	in-di-vi-dwa-'lis-ta
inept, unfortunate	disgraziato	diz-gra-'tsya-to
infallible	infallibile	in-fal-'li-bi-le
ingenious	ingegnoso	in-je-'nyo-zo
ingenuous, naive	ingenuo	in-'je-nu-o
insensitive	insensibile	in-sen-'si-bi-le
insistent, unrelenting	insistente	in-sis-'ten-te
insolent	insolente	in-so-'len-te
intellectual	intellettuale	in-tel-let-'twa-le

intelligent	intelligente	*in-tel-li-'jen-te*
introverted	introverso	*in-tro-'ver-so*
irascible	irascibile	*i-ra-ši-bi-le*
irksome	irritante	*ir-ri-'tan-te*
ironic	ironico	*i-'ro-ni-ko*
irrational	irrazionale	*ir-ra-tsyo-'na-le*
irresponsible	irresponsabile	*ir-res-pon-'sa-bi-le*
irreverent	irriverente	*ir-ri-ve-'ren-te*
jealous	geloso	*je-'lo-zo*
jovial	gioviale	*jo-'vya-le*
joyous	gioioso	*jo-'yo-zo*
kindness	gentilezza	*jen-ti-'le-tsa*
lazy	pigro	*'pi-gro*
liar	bugiardo	*bu-'jar-do*
likable	piacevole	*pya-'če-vo-le*
lively	vivace	*vi-'va-če*
loving	amoroso	*a-mo-'ro-zo*
malicious	malizioso	*ma-li-'tsyo-zo*
merit, worth	merito	*'me-ri-to*
meritorious	meritevole	*me-ri-'te-vo-le*
meticulous	meticoloso	*me-ti-ko-'lo-zo*
mischievous	capriccioso	*ka-prič-'čo-zo*
morose	scontroso	*skon-'tro-zo*
narrow-minded	di vedute ristrette	*ve-'du-te ris-'tret-te*
neat	ordinato	*or-di-'na-to*
negligent	negligente	*ne-gli-'jen-te*
nervous	nervoso	*ner-'vo-zo*
nonconformist	anticonformista	*an-ti-kon-for-'mis-ta*
obstinate	ostinato	*os-ti-'na-to*
obtuse	ottuso	*ot-'tu-zo*
optimist	ottimista	*ot-ti-'mis-ta*
original	originale	*o-ri-ji-'na-le*
patient	paziente	*pa-'tsyen-te*
perfectionist	perfezionista	*per-fe-tsyo-'nis-ta*
personality	personalità (f, inv)	*per-so-na-li-'ta*
pessimist	pessimista	*pes-si-'mis-ta*
picky, fastidious	pignolo	*pi-'nyo-lo*
pleasant, nice	simpatico	*sim-'pa-ti-ko*
politeness, courtesy	cortesia	*kor-te-'zi-a*
poor	povero	*'po-ve-ro*
possessive	possessivo	*pos-ses-'si-vo*
precise	preciso	*pre-'či-zo*
presumptuous	presuntuoso	*pre-zun-'two-zo*
pretentious	pretenzioso	*pre-ten-'tsyo-zo*
proud, haughty	orgoglioso	*or-go-'lyo-zo*
prudent	prudente	*pru-'den-te*
prudish, prim	pudico	*'pu-di-ko*
punctilious	puntiglioso	*pun-ti-'lyo-zo*

pure	puro	—
quarrelsome	litigioso	*li-ti-'jo-zo*
quiet	quieto	*'kwye-to*
rational	razionale	*ra-tsyo-'na-le*
realistic	realista	*re-a-'lis-ta*
reasonable	ragionevole	*ra-jo-'ne-vo-le*
rebellious	ribelle	*ri-'bel-le*
reckless	temerario	*te-me-'ra-ryo*
refined	raffinato	*raf-fi-'na-to*
reserved	riservato	*ri-zer-'va-to*
rich	ricco	*'rik-ko*
romantic	romantico	*ro-'man-ti-ko*
rough	rozzo	*'ro-tso*
rude	rude	*'ru-de*
ruthless	spietato	*spye-'ta-to*
sad	triste	*'tris-te*
sarcastic	sarcastico	*sar-'kas-ti-ko*
satisfied	soddisfatto	*sod-dis-'fat-to*
scoundrel	briccone (-a)	*brik-'ko-ne*
seductive	seducente	*se-du-'čen-te*
self-confident, sure	sicuro	*si-'ku-ro*
self-sufficient	autosufficiente	*au-to-suf-fi-'čen-te*
sensible	sensato	*sen-'sa-to*
sensitive	sensibile	*sen-'si-bi-le*
sentimental	sentimentale	*sen-ti-men-'ta-le*
serene	sereno	*se-'re-no*
serious	serio	*'se-ryo*
severe	severo	*se-'ve-ro*
show-off	sfarzoso	*sfar-'tso-zo*
shrewd	perspicace	*per-spi-'ka-če*
shy, timid	timido	*'ti-mi-do*
silly	sciocco	*'šok-ko*
simple	semplice	*'sem-pli-če*
sloppy, disorganized	disorganizzato	*diz-or-ga-ni-'dza-to*
snobbish	altezzoso	*al-te-'tso-zo*
strong	forte	*'for-te*
stubborn	testardo	*tes-'tar-do*
stupid	stupido	*'stu-pi-do*
stuttering	balbuziente	*bal-bu-'tsyen-te*
sullen	cupo	*'ku-po*
superstitious	superstizioso	*su-per-sti-'tsyo-zo*
sweet	dolce	*'dol-če*
tender	tenero	*'te-ne-ro*
tired	stanco	*'stan-ko*
tough	duro	—
toughness	durezza	*du-'re-tsa*
traditional	tradizionale	*tra-di-tsyo-'na-le*
tranquil, calm, serene	tranquillo	*tran-'kwil-lo*

unhappy	scontento	*skon-'ten-to*
unsatisfied	insoddisfatto	*in-sod-dis-'fat-to*
untidy	disordinato	*diz-or-di-'na-to*
vain	vanitoso	*va-ni-'to-zo*
vengeful	vendicativo	*ven-di-ka-'ti-vo*
versatile	versatile	*ver-'sa-ti-le*
virtuous	virtuoso	*vir-'two-zo*
voluble	volubile	*vo-'lu-bi-le*
vulnerable	vulnerabile	*vul-ne-'ra-bi-le*
weak	debole	*'de-bo-le*
well-mannered	educato	*e-du-'ka-to*
whimsical	capriccioso	*ka-prič-'čo-zo*
wily, sly	furbo	—
wise	saggio	*'saj-jo*
witty, spirited	spiritoso	*spi-ri-'to-zo*
worried	preoccupato	*pre-ok-ku-'pa-to*
zealous	zelante	*dze-'lan-te*

F. BASIC PERSONAL INFORMATION

For jobs and professions, see §38a

address	indirizzo	*in-di-'ri-tso*
• avenue	corso	*'kor-so*
• square	piazza	*'pya-tsa*
• street	via	*'vi-a*
	strada	*'stra-da*
• (to) live somewhere	abitare	*a-bi-'ta-re*
	vivere*	*'vi-ve-re*
• house number	numero di casa	*'nu-me-ro di 'ka-za*
• downtown	in centro	*'čen-tro*
• in the city	in città	*čit-'ta*
• in the country(side)	in campagna	*kam-'pa-nya*
• in the suburbs	in periferia	*pe-ri-fe-'ri-a*
• on...Street, number...	in via...numero...	*'vi-a 'nu-me-ro*
• with friends	presso amici	*'pres-so a-'mi-ci*
• with one's parents	con i genitori	*je-ni-'to-ri*
• forwarding address	recapito	*re-'ka-pi-to*
(to) be of...origin	essere* d'origine...	*'es-se-re do-'ri-ji-ne*
(to) be from	essere* di	—
birth	nascita	*'na-ši-ta*
• date of birth	data di nascita	—
• place of birth	luogo di nascita	*'lwo-go*
career	carriera	*kar-'rye-ra*
citizenship	cittadinanza	*čit-ta-di-'nan-tsa*

education (level)	titolo di studio	'ti-to-lo di 'stu-dyo
• **(to) go to school**	andare* (ess) a scuola	an-'da-re a 'skwo-la
• **(to) finish school**	finire (isc) la scuola	fi-'ni-re
• **university degree**	laurea	'lau-re-a
• **diploma**	diploma	di-'plo-ma
• **high school diploma**	certificato di maturità	cer-ti-fi-'ka-to di ma-tu-ri-'ta
• **graduate**	laureato (-a) (*university*)	lau-re-'a-to
	diplomato (-a) (*high school*)	di-plo-'ma-to
employment	lavoro	la-'vo-ro
• **employer**	datore di lavoro	da-'to-re di la-'vo-ro
• **employee**	dipendente (m/f)	di-pen-'den-te
identity	identità (f, inv)	i-den-ti-'ta
• **identification**	identificazione (f)	i-den-ti-fi-ka-'tsyo-ne
interests, hobbies	interessi (m, pl)	in-te-'res-si
job	mestiere (m)	mes-'tye-re
marital status	stato civile	'sta-to či-'vi-le
• **marriage**	matrimonio	ma-tri-'mo-nyo
• **married**	sposato (-a)	spo-'za-to
• **unmarried**	celibe (m)	'če-li-be
	nubile (f)	'nu-bi-le
• **separated**	separato	se-pa-'ra-to
• **divorced**	divorziato (-a)	di-vor-'tsya-to
military service	servizio militare	ser-'vi-tsyo mi-li-'ta-re
name	nome (m)	'no-me
• **first name**	nome (m)	—
• **surname**	cognome (m)	ko-'nyo-me
• **nickname**	soprannome (m)	so-pran-'no-me
• **My name is …**	Mi chiamo …	mi 'kya-mo
• **signature**	firma	—
• **(to) sign**	firmare	fir-'ma-re
nationality	nazionalità (f, inv)	na-tsyo-na-li-'ta
• **origin**	origine (f)	o-'ri-ji-ne
personal information	dati anagrafici	'da-ti a-na-'gra-fi-či
phone number	numero di telefono	'nu-me-ro di te-'le-fo-no
• **area code**	prefisso	pre-'fis-so
profession	professione (f)	pro-fes-'syo-ne
• **professional**	professionista (m/f)	pro-fes-syo-'nis-ta
references	referenze (f, pl)	re-fe-'ren-tse
residence	residenza	re-zi-'den-tsa
	domicilio	do-mi-'či-lyo
• **(to) reside**	risiedere	ri-'sye-de-re
title	titolo	'ti-to-lo
• **Accountant**	Ragioniere (-a)	ra-jo-'nye-re
• **Doctor**	Dottore (-essa)	dot-'to-re
• **Draftsperson**	Geometra (m/f)	je-'o-me-tra
• **Engineer**	Ingegnere (m/f)	in-je-'nye-re

• **Lawyer**	Avvocato (m/f)	*av-vo-'ka-to*
• **Miss, Ms.**	Signorina	*si-nyo-'ri-na*
• **Mr.**	Signore	*si-'nyo-re*
• **Mrs., Ms.**	Signora	*si-'nyo-ra*
• **Professor**	Professore (-essa)	*pro-fes-'so-re*
• **Reverend**	Reverendo	*re-ve-'ren-do*
widower, widow	vedovo	*'ve-do-vo*
	vedova	—
work	lavoro	*la-'vo-ro*
• **(to) work**	lavorare	*la-vo-'ra-re*
• **work experience**	esperienze lavorative	*es-pe-'ryen-tse*
		la-vo-ra-'ti-ve

12. THE BODY

A. PARTS, LIMBS, ORGANS, AND SYSTEMS

Achilles tendon	tallone di Achille	*tal-'lo-ne di a-'kil-le*
adenoids	adenoidi (f, pl)	*'a-de-noy-'di*
adrenaline	adrenalina	*a-dre-na-'li-na*
alimentary canal	tubo digestivo	*'tu-bo di-jes-'ti-vo*
ankle	caviglia	*ka-'vi-lya*
anus, bottom	ano	—
arm	braccio (braccia, f, pl)	*'bra̧č-čo*
armpit	ascella	*a-šel-la*
artery	arteria	*ar-'te-rya*
back	schiena	*'skye-na*
beard	barba	—
belly	pancia	*'pan-ča*
belly button	ombelico	*om-be-'li-ko*
bladder	vescica	*ve-'ši-ka*
blood	sangue (m)	*'san-gwe*
• **blood group**	gruppo sanguigno	*'grup-po san-'gwi-nyo*
• **blood pressure**	pressione del sangue	*pres-'syo-ne*
• **blood vessel**	vaso sanguigno	*'va-zo san-'gwi-nyo*
body	corpo	—
bone	osso (ossa, f, pl)	—
brain	cervello	*cer-'vel-lo*
breast	seno	*'se-no*
brow, forehead	fronte (f)	*'fron-te*
calf	polpaccio	*pol-'pa̧č-čo*
cardiovascular system	sistema cardiovascolare	*sis-'te-ma*
		kar-dyo-vas-ko-'la-re
cartilage	cartilagine (f)	*kar-ti-'la-ji-ne*
cell	cellula	*'čel-lu-la*
cheek	guancia	*'gwan-ča*
• **cheekbone**	zigomo	*'dzi-go-mo*
chest	petto	*'pet-to*

chin	mento	'men-to
complexion	carnagione (f)	kar-na-'jo-ne
diaphragm	diaframma	di-a-'fram-ma
dimple	fossetta	fos-'set-ta
disc	disco	'dis-ko
ear	orecchio	o-'rek-kyo
• eardrum	timpano	'tim-pa-no
elbow	gomito	'go-mi-to
esophagus	esofago	e-'zo-fa-go
eye	occhio	'ok-kyo
• eyebrow	sopracciglio (sopracciglia, f, pl)	so-prač-'či-lyo
• eyelash	ciglio (ciglia, f, pl)	'či-lyo
• eyelid	palpebra	'pal-pe-bra
face	faccia	'fač-ča
finger, toe	dito (dita, f, pl)	'di-to
• fingernail	unghia	'un-gya
• little finger	(dito) mignolo	('di-to) 'mi-nyo-lo
• index finger	indice (m)	'in-di-če
• middle finger	(dito) medio	('di-to) 'me-dyo
• ring finger	(dito) anulare	('di-to) a-nu-'la-re
• thumb	pollice (m)	'pol-li-če
fist	pugno	'pu-nyo
flesh	carne (f)	'kar-ne
foot	piede (m)	'pye-de
forearm	avambraccio	a-vam-'brač-čo
frame	ossatura	os-sa-'tu-ra
gall bladder	cistifellea	cis-ti-'fel-lea
gland	ghiandola	'gyan-do-la
guts	ventre (m)	'ven-tre
hair (bodily)	peli	'pe-li
hair (head)	capelli (m, pl)	ka-'pel-li
hand	mano (f) (mani, pl)	'ma-no
head	testa	'tes-ta
heart	cuore (m)	'kwo-re
• heartbeat	battito del cuore	'bat-ti-to
heel	tallone (m)	tal-'lo-ne
hip	anca	'an-ka
immune system	sistema immunitario	sis-'te-ma im-mu-ni-'ta-ryo
intestine, bowel	intestino	in-tes-'ti-no
jaw	mandibola	man-'di-bo-la
• jawbone	mascella	ma-'šel-la
joint	articolazione (f)	ar-ti-ko-la-'tsyo-ne
kidney	rene (m)	're-ne
knee	ginocchio (ginocchia, f, pl)	ji-'nok-kyo
leg	gamba	'gam-ba

limb	arto	'ar-to
lip	labbro (labbra, f, pl)	'lab-bro
liver	fegato	'fe-ga-to
lung	polmone (m)	pol-'mo-ne
lymphatic system	sistema linfatico	sis-'te-ma lin-'fa-ti-ko
membrane	membrana	mem-'bra-na
mouth	bocca	'bok-ka
muscle	muscolo	'mus-ko-lo
nape	nuca	'nu-ka
neck	collo	'kol-lo
nerve	nervo	'ner-vo
nervous system	sistema nervoso	sis-'te-ma ner-'vo-zo
nipple	capezzolo	ka-'pe-tso-lo
nose	naso	'na-zo
• nostril	narice (f)	na-'ri-če
organ	organo	'or-ga-no
palate	palato	pa-'la-to
palm	palma	'pal-ma
pancreas	pancreas (m, inv)	—
pelvis	pelvi (f, inv)	'pel-vi
pimple	foruncolo	fo-'run-ko-lo
pore	poro	—
pupil	pupilla	pu-'pil-la
respiratory system	sistema respiratorio	sis-te-ma res-pi-ra-'to-ryo
rib	costola	'kos-to-lo
saliva	saliva	sa-'li-va
scalp	cuoio capelluto	'kwo-yo ka-pel-'lu-to
shin	stinco	'stin-ko
shoulder	spalla	'spal-la
shoulder blade	scapola	'ska-po-la
skeleton	scheletro	'ske-le-tro
skin	pelle (f)	'pel-le
skull	cranio	'kra-ni-o
sole	pianta del piede	'pyan-ta del 'pye-de
spine	spina dorsale	'spi-na dor-'sa-le
spit	sputo	'spu-to
spleen	milza	'mil-tsa
stomach	stomaco	'sto-ma-ko
tendon	tendine (m)	'ten-di-ne
thigh	coscia	'ko-ša
throat	gola	—
tissue	tessuto	tes-'su-to
tongue	lingua	'lin-gwa
tonsils	tonsille (f, pl)	ton-'sil-le
torso, trunk	torso	'tor-so
urinary tract	apparato urinario	ap-pa-'ra-to 'u-ri-'na-ryo

Main Parts of the Body

vein	vena	—
vocal cord	corda vocale	*'kor-da vo-'ka-le*
waist	vita	*'vi-ta*
windpipe	trachea	*tra-'ke-a*
wrist	polso	*'pol-so*

B. PHYSICAL STATES AND ACTIVITIES

(to) be cold	avere* freddo	*a-'ve-re 'fred-do*
(to) be hot	avere* caldo	*a-'ve-re 'kal-do*
breath	respiro	*res-'pi-ro*
• (to) breathe	respirare	*res-pi-'ra-re*
• breathing	respirazione (f)	*res-pi-ra-'tsyo-ne*
burp, belch	rutto	*'rut-to*

• (to) burp, belch	ruttare	*rut-'ta-re*
(to) choke	strozzarsi	*stro-'tsar-si*
cholesterol	colesterolo	*ko-les-te-'ro-lo*
dandruff	forfora	*'for-fo-ra*
(to) defecate	defecare	*de-fe-'ka-re*
digestion	digestione (f)	*di-jes-'tyo-ne*
digestive system	sistema digerente	*sis-'te-ma di-je-'ren-te*
(to) drink	bere*	*'be-re*
(to) eat	mangiare	*man-'ja-re*
(to) exhale	espirare	*es-pi-'ra-re*
(to) feel bad	sentirsi male	*sen-'tir-si 'ma-le*
(to) feel well	sentirsi bene	—
(to) get up	alzarsi	*al-'tsar-si*
health	salute (f)	*sa-'lu-te*
• healthy	sano	*'sa-no*
hunger	fame (f)	*'fa-me*
• (to) be hungry	avere* fame	—
(to) hurt	fare male a	—
(to) inhale	inspirare	*ins-pi-'ra-re*
lack of breath	senza fiato	*'sen-tsa 'fya-to*
(to) perceive	percepire (isc)	*per-če-'pi-re*
(to) rest, relax	riposarsi	*ri-po-'zar-si*
(to) run	correre*	*'kor-re-re*
sciatic nerve	nervo sciatico	*'ner-vo 'šya-ti-ko*
(to) sense, feel, smell	sentire	*sen-ti-re*
sick	malato	*ma-'la-to*
sleep	sonno	*'son-no*
• (to) be sleepy	avere* sonno	—
• (to) fall asleep	addormentarsi	*ad-dor-men-'tar-si*
• (to) sleep	dormire	*dor-'mi-re*
thirst	sete (f)	*'se-te*
• (to) be thirsty	avere* sete	—
tiredness, fatigue	fatica	*fa-'ti-ka*
• (to) be tired	essere* stanco	*'es-se-re 'stan-ko*
urine	urina	*u-'ri-na*
• (to) urinate	urinare	*u-ri-'na-re*
(to) wake up	svegliarsi	*sve-'lyar-si*
(to) walk	camminare	*kam-mi-'na-re*

C. HEARING

bang	colpo	*'kol-po*
(to) clash	cozzare	*ko-'tsa-re*
(to) crackle, squeak	scricchiolare	*skri-kyo-'la-re*
creak	cigolio	*či-go-'li-o*
• (to) creak	cigolare	*či-go-'la-re*
deafness	sordità (f, inv)	*sor-di-'ta*
• deaf	sordo	*'sor-do*

(to) echo	echeggiare	*e-kej-'ja-re*
(to) explode, blast	scoppiare	*skop-'pya-re*
(to) grate	grattugiare	*grat-tu-'ja-re*
(to) grind	sgretolare	*zgre-to-'la-re*
(to) hear, feel, sense	sentire	*sen-'ti-re*
• **hearing**	udito	*u-'di-to*
(to) hum	mormorare	*mor-mo-'ra-re*
(to) jingle, clink, jangle	tintinnare	*tin-tin-'na-re*
(to) listen	udire*	*u-'di-re*
• **(to) listen to**	ascoltare	*as-kol-'ta-re*
noise	rumore (m)	*ru-'mo-re*
• **noisy**	rumoroso	*ru-mo-'ro-zo*
rattle	sonaglio	*so-'na-'lyo*
(to) resonate	risuonare	*ri-'swo-'na-re*
(to) ring	suonare	*swo-'na-re*
(to) rustle	frusciare	*fru-'ša-re*
(to) shriek	squillare	*skwil-'la-re*
sound	suono	*'swo-no*
(to) splash	spruzzare	*spru-'tsa-re*
(to) squeal	strillare	*stril-'la-re*
(to) whistle	fischiare	*fis-'kya-re*

D. VISION

blindness	cecità (f, inv)	*če-či-'ta*
• **blind**	cieco	*'če-ko*
• **(to) blind**	accecare	*ač-če-'ka-re*
(to) blink	battere le palpebre	*'bat-te-re le 'pal-'pe-bre*
bright	brillante	*bril-'lan-te*
(to) cast a glance	gettare uno sguardo	*jet-'ta-re u-no 'zgwar-do*
clearness	chiarezza	*kya-'re-tsa*
• **clear**	chiaro	*'kya-ro*
contact lens	lenti a contatto	*'len-ti a kon-'tat-to*
cornea	cornea	*'kor-ne-a*
darkness	oscurità (f, inv)	*os-ku-ri-'ta*
• **dark**	scuro	*'sku-ro*
eyeglasses	occhiali (m, pl)	*ok-'kya-li*
(to) fade	sbiadire (isc)	*zbya-'di-re*
far-sighted	ipermetrope	*i-per-'me-tro-pe*
glance	sguardo	*'zgwar-do*
(to) glare at someone	fissare qualcuno	*fis-'sa-re kwal-'ku-no*
glimpse	occhiata fugace	*ok-'kya-ta fu-'ga-če*
(to) glow	risplendere	*ris-'plen-de-re*
illumination,	illuminazione (f)	*il-lu-mi-na-'styo-ne*
lens (of the eye)	lente (dell'occhio)	*'len-te*
long-sighted	presbite	*'prez-bi-te*

(to) look (at), watch	guardare	gwar-'da-re
• (to) look around	guardare in giro	'ji-ro
(to) peep, peer	sbirciare	zbir-'ča-re
reflection	riflesso	ri-'fles-so
(to) see	vedere*	ve-'de-re
(to) shine	brillare	bril-'la-re
short-sighted	miope	'mi-o-pe
sight	vista	'vis-ta
sight test	controllo della vista	kon-'trol-lo
(to) sparkle	scintillare	šin-til-'la-re
(to) stare	fissare	fis-'sa-re
(to) twinkle	luccicare	luč-či-'ka-re

E. TASTE, TOUCH, AND SMELL

acrid	acro	'a-kro
aroma	aroma	a-'ro-ma
bitter	aspro	'as-pro
delicate	delicato	de-li-'ka-to
delicious	squisito	skwi-'zito
fetid	fetido	'fe-ti-do
flavor	sapore (m)	sa-'po-re
	gusto	—
fragrance	fragranza	fra-'gran-tsa
fresh	fresco	'fres-ko
insipid	insipido	in-'si-pi-do
(to) itch	prudere	'pru-de-re
• itchy	pruriginoso	pru-ri-ji-'no-zo
knobby	nodoso	no-'do-zo
olfactory	olfattivo	ol-fat-'ti-vo
prickly	pungente	pun-'jen-te
putrid	putrido	'pu-tri-do
rough	ruvido	'ru-vi-do
salty	salato	sa-'la-to
scented	profumato	pro-fu-'ma-to
sense of smell	olfatto	ol-'fat-to
slippery	scivoloso	ši-vo-'lo-zo
smell, odor	odore (m)	o-'do-re
• (to) smell	odorare	o-do-'ra-re
smooth	liscio	'li-šo
soft	soffice	'sof-fi-če
sour	amaro	a-'ma-ro
spicy	piccante	pik-'kan-te
sticky	appiccicoso	ap-pi-či-'ko-zo
stiff	rigido	'ri-ji-do
stink	puzzo	'pu-tso
• (to) stink	puzzare	pu'-tsa-re
• stinky	puzzolente	pu-tso-'len-te

sweet	dolce	*'dol-ce*
taste	gusto	*'gus-to*
	sapore (m)	*sa-'po-re*
tasteless	sciocco	*'šok-ko*
touch	tatto	*'tat-to*
• (to) touch	toccare	*tok-'ka-re*

F. PERSONAL CARE

barber	barbiere (m)	*bar-'bye-re*
beautician	estetista (m/f)	*es-te-'tis-ta*
brush	spazzola	*'spa-tso-la*
• (to) brush oneself	spazzolarsi	*spa-tso-'lar-si*
clean	pulito	*pu-'li-to*
• (to) clean oneself	pulirsi	*pu-'lir-si*
comb	pettine (m)	*'pet-ti-ne*
• (to) comb oneself	pettinarsi	*pet-ti-'nar-si*
cosmetic	cosmetico	*kos-'me-ti-ko*
curls	ricci (m, pl)	*'rič-či*
• curlers	bigodini (m, pl)	*bi-go-'di-ni*
dirty	sporco	*'spor-ko*
(to) dry oneself	asciugarsi	*a-šu-'gar-si*
hairdresser	parrucchiere (-a)	*par-ruk-'kye-re*
hairdryer	asciugacapelli (inv)	*a-šu-ga-ka-'pel-li*
hygiene	igiene (f)	*i-'jye-ne*
• hygienic	igienico	*i-'jye-ni-ko*
makeup	trucco	*'truk-ko*
• (to) put on makeup	truccarsi	*truk-'kar-si*
manicure	manicure (f)	*ma-ni-'ku-re*
mascara	mascara (m, inv)	*mas-'ka-ra*
nail polish	smalto	*'zmal-to*
perfume	profumo	*pro-'fu-mo*
• (to) put on perfume	profumarsi	*pro-fu-'mar-si*
razor	rasoio	*ra-'zo-yo*
• electric razor	rasoio elettrico	*ra-'zo-yo e-'let-tri-ko*
scissors	forbici (f, pl)	*'for-bi-či*
shampoo	shampoo (m, inv)	—
(to) shave	farsi* la barba	—
soap	sapone (m)	*sa-'po-ne*
toothbrush	spazzolino da denti	*spa-tso-'li-no*
toothpaste	dentifricio	*den-ti-'fri-čo*
towel, handcloth	asciugamano	*a-šu-ga-'ma-no*
(to) wash oneself	lavarsi	*la-'var-si*
(to) wash one's hair	lavarsi i capelli	*la-'var-si i ka-'pel-li*

THE PHYSICAL, PLANT, AND ANIMAL WORLDS

13. THE PHYSICAL WORLD

A. THE UNIVERSE

astronomy	astronomia	*as-tro-no-'mi-a*
black hole	buco nero	*'bu-ko 'ne-ro*
comet	cometa	*ko-'me-ta*
cosmos	cosmo	*'koz-mo*
eclipse	eclissi (f, inv)	*e-'klis-si*
• **lunar eclipse**	eclissi lunare	*e-'klis-si lu-'na-re*
• **solar eclipse**	eclissi solare	*e-'klis-si so-'la-re*
galaxy	galassia	*ga-'las-sya*
• **gravity**	gravità (f, inv)	*gra-vi-'ta*
light	luce (f)	*'lu-če*
• **infrared light**	luce infrarossa	*in-fra-'ros-sa*
• **ultraviolet light**	luce ultravioletta	*ul-tra-vyo-'let-ta*
meteor	meteora	*me-'te-o-ra*
missile	missile (m)	*'mis-si-le*
moon	luna	*'lu-na*
• **full moon**	luna piena	*'lu-na 'pye-na*
• **moonbeam**	raggio lunare	*'raj-jo lu-'na-re*
orbit	orbita	*'or-bi-ta*
• **(to) orbit**	orbitare	*or-bi-'ta-re*
planet	pianeta (m) (pianeti, pl)	*pya-'ne-ta*
• **Earth**	Terra	*'ter-ra*
• **Jupiter**	Giove (m)	*'jo-ve*
• **Mars**	Marte (m)	*'mar-te*
• **Mercury**	Mercurio	*mer-'ku-ryo*
• **Neptune**	Nettuno	*net-'tu-no*
• **Pluto**	Plutone (m)	*plu-'to-ne*
• **Saturn**	Saturno	*sa-'tur-no*
• **Uranus**	Urano	*u-'ra-no*
• **Venus**	Venere (f)	*'ve-ne-re*
satellite	satellite (m)	*sa-'tel-li-te*

Idiomatic Expressions

(to) come to light	=	venire* (ess) alla luce
(to) shed light on	=	gettare luce su
(to) be in a bad mood	=	avere* la luna di traverso

space	spazio	'spa-tsyo
• space shuttle	navetta spaziale	na-'vet-ta spa-'tsya-le
star	stella	'stel-la
sun	sole	'so-le
• solar system	sistema (m) solare	sis-'te-ma so-'la-re
• sun ray	raggio solare	'raj-jo so-'la-re
• sunlight	luce solare	'lu-če so-'la-re
universe	universo	u-ni-'ver-so
world	mondo	'mon-do

B. THE ENVIRONMENT AND PHYSICAL FORMATIONS (COASTS, RIVERS, ETC.)

archipelago	arcipelago	ar-či-'pe-la-go
atmosphere	atmosfera	at-mos-'fe-ra
bay	baia	'ba-ya
beach	spiaggia	'spyaj-ja
boulder	macigno	ma-'či-nyo
cape	capo	'ka-po
cave	grotta	'grot-ta
channel	canale (m)	ka-'na-le
cliff	scogliera	sko-'lye-ra
coast, coastline	costa	'kos-ta
cove	insenatura	in-se-na-'tu-ra
crevasse	crepaccio	kre-'pač-čo
desert	deserto	de-'zer-to
earthquake	terremoto	ter-re-'mo-to
edge, bank	sponda	'spon-da
environment	ambiente (m)	am-'byen-te
estuary	estuario	es-tu-'a-ryo
farmland	terreno agrario	ter-'re-no a-'gra-ryo
field	campo	'kam-po
• field of grass	prato	'pra-to
flood	alluvione (f)	al-lu-'vyo-ne
foam	schiuma	'skyu-ma
forest	foresta	fo-'res-ta
	bosco	'bos-ko
grass	erba	'er-ba
gulf	golfo	'gol-fo
gully	burrone (m)	bur-'ro-ne
hill	collina	kol-'li-na
ice	ghiaccio	'gyač-čo
island	isola	'i-zo-la
lagoon	laguna	la-'gu-na
lake	lago	'la-go
land	terra	'ter-ra
landscape	paesaggio	pa-e-'zaj-jo
layer, stratum	strato	—

maritime	marittimo	*ma-'rit-ti-mo*
mount	monte (m)	*'mon-te*
mountain	montagna	*mon-'ta-nya*
• mountain chain	catena montuosa	*ka-'te-na mon-'two-za*
mud, silt	fango	*'fan-go*
• muddy	fangoso	*fan-'go-zo*
nature	natura	*na-'tu-ra*
• natural	naturale	*na-tu-'ra-le*
ocean	oceano	*o-'če-a-no*
• Antarctic	Antartico	*an-'tar-ti-ko*
• Arctic	Artico	*'ar-ti-ko*
• Atlantic	Atlantico	*at-'lan-ti-ko*
• Pacific	Pacifico	*pa-'ci-fi-ko*
pass	passo	*'pas-so*
peak	vetta	*'vet-ta*
pebble	ciottolo	*'čot-to-lo*
peninsula	penisola	*pe-'ni-zo-la*
plain	pianura	*pya-'nu-ra*
precipice	precipizio	*pre-či-'pi-tsyo*
promontory	promontorio	*pro-mon-'to-ryo*
reef	banco di scogli	*'ban-ko di 'sko-'lyi*
river	fiume (m)	*'fyu-me*
• (to) flow	scorrere*	*'skor-re-re*
• river bank	argine (m)	*'ar-ji-ne*
rock	roccia	*'roč-ča*
salt water	acqua di mare	*'ak-kwa di 'ma-re*
sand	sabbia	*'sab-bya*
sea	mare (m)	*'ma-re*
• seabed	fondo del mare	*'fon-do del 'ma-re*
slab, block	lastra	*'las-tra*
slope	pendio	*pen-'di-o*
steep	ripido	*'ri-pi-do*
stone	pietra	*'pye-tra*
	sasso	*'sas-so*
summit	cima	*'či-ma*
surf	cresta dell'onda	*'kres-ta del-'lon-da*
swamp	palude (f)	*pa-'lu-de*
tide	marea	*ma-'re-a*
tributary	affluente (m)	*af-flu-'en-te*
valley	valle (f)	*'val-le*
vegetation	vegetazione (f)	*ve-je-ta-'tsyo-ne*
volcano	vulcano	*vul-'ka-no*
• eruption	eruzione (f)	*e-ru-'tsyo-ne*
• lava	lava	—
waterfall	cascate (cascata)	*kas-'ka-te*
wave	onda	*'on-da*
whirlpool	gorgo	*'gor-go*
woods	bosco	*'bos-ko*

C. MATTER AND MATERIALS

acid	acido	*'a-či-do*
acrylic	acrilico	*a-'kri-li-ko*
air	aria	*'a-rya*
ammonia	ammoniaca	*am-mo-'ni-a-ka*
asbestos	amianto	*a-'myan-to*
asphalt	asfalto	*as-'fal-to*
atom	atomo	*'a-to-mo*
• electron	elettrone (m)	*e-let-'tro-ne*
• neutron	neutrone (m)	*neu-'tro-ne*
• nucleus	nucleo	*'nu-kle-o*
• proton	protone (m)	*pro-'to-ne*
boiling point	punto di ebollizione	*'pun-to di e-bol-li-'tsyo-ne*
brass	ottone (m)	*ot-'to-ne*
brick	mattone (m)	*mat-'to-ne*
• bricklayer	muratore (m)	*mu-ra-'to-re*
bronze	bronzo	*'bron-dzo*
burlap	tela di sacco	*'te-la di 'sak-ko*
calcium	calcio	*'kal-čo*
carbon (element)	carbonio	*kar-'bo-nyo*
carbon (solid), coal	carbone (m)	*kar-'bo-ne*
cardboard	cartone (m)	*kar-'to-ne*
cast iron	ghisa	*'gi-za*
chalk	gesso	*'jes-so*
chemical	chimico	*'ki-mi-ko*
• chemistry	chimica	*'ki-mi-ka*
chlorine	cloro	*'klo-ro*
clay	argilla	*ar-'jil-la*
cloth	stoffa	*'stof-fa*
compound	composto	*kom-'posto*
concrete. cement	cemento	*ce-'men-to*
copper	rame (m)	*'ra-me*
corduroy	fustagno	*fus-'ta-nyo*
cork	sughero	*'su-ge-ro*
cotton	cotone (m)	*ko-'to-ne*
ebony	ebano	*'e-ba-no*
elastic	elastico	*e-'las-ti-ko*
electrical	elettrico	*e-'let-tri-ko*
• electricity	elettricità (f, inv)	*e-let-tri-či-'ta*
enamel	smalto	*'zmal-to*
energy	energia	*e-ner-'ji-a*
ether	etere (m)	*'e-te-re*
felt	feltro	*'fel-tro*
fiber	fibra	*'fi-bra*
fiberglass	lana di vetro	*'la-na di 've-tro*
filter	filtro	—

fire	fuoco	*'fwo-ko*
flannel	flanella	*fla-'nel-la*
flint	selce (f)	*'sel-če*
freezing point	punto di congelamento	*kon-je-la-'men-to*
fuel	carburante (m)	*kar-bu-'ran-te*
gas	benzina	*ben-'dzi-na*
gauze	garza	*'gar-dza*
glass	vetro	*'ve-tro*
gold	oro	*'o-ro*
granite	granito	*gra-'ni-to*
gravel	ghiaia	*'gya-ya*
greenhouse effect	effetto serra	*ef-'fet-to 'ser-ra*
hardwood	legno duro	*'le-nyo 'du-ro*
heat	calore (m)	*ka-'lo-re*
hydrogen	idrogeno	*i-'dro-je-no*
industry	industria	*in-'dus-trya*
• industrial	industriale	*in-dus-'trya-le*
iodine	iodio	*'yo-di-o*
iron	ferro	—
knot	nodo	—
• knotty	nodoso	*no-'do-zo*
lace	pizzo	*'pi-tso*
lead	piombo	*'pyom-bo*
leather	pelle (f)	*'pel-le*
	cuoio	*'kwo-yo*
linen	lino	—
liquid	liquido	*'li-kwi-do*
magnesium	magnesio	*ma-'nye-zi-o*
mahogany	mogano	*'mo-ga-no*
marble	marmo	—
matter	materia	*ma-'te-rya*
mercury	mercurio	*mer-'ku-ryo*
metal	metallo	*me-'tal-lo*
microscope	microscopio	*mi-kro-'sko-pyo*
microwave	microonda	*mi-kro-'on-da*
mineral	minerale (m)	*mi-ne-'ra-le*
net	rete (f)	*'re-te*
nickel	nichelio	*ni-'ke-lyo*
nitrogen	nitrogeno	*ni-tro-je-no*
organic	organico	*or-'ga-ni-ko*
• inorganic	inorganico	*in-or-'ga-ni-ko*
oxygen	ossigeno	*os-'si-je-no*
particle	particella	*par-ti-'čel-la*
petroleum	petrolio	*pe-'tro-lyo*
phosphate	fosfato	*fos-'fa-to*
physical	fisico	*'fi-zi-ko*
• physics	fisica	*'fi-zi-ka*
plaster	intonaco	*in-'to-na-ko*

plastic	plastica	*'plas-ti-ka*
platinum	platino	*'pla-ti-no*
pollution	inquinamento	*in-kwi-na-'men-to*
• (to) pollute	inquinare	*in-kwi-'na-re*
porcelain	porcellana	*por-čel-'la-na*
potassium	potassio	*po-'tas-syo*
pressure	pressione (f)	*pres-'syo-ne*
radiation	radiazione (f)	*ra-dya-'tsyo-ne*
• radioactive	radioattivo	*ra-dyo-at-'ti-vo*
resin	resina	*'re-zi-na*
resistant	resistente	*re-zis-'ten-te*
rope	corda	*'kor-da*
rubber	gomma	*'gom-ma*
salt	sale	*'sa-le*
scale	bilancia	*bi-'lan-ča*
scrap iron	rottame (m)	*rot-'ta-me*
sheet metal	laminato	*la-mi-'na-to*
silk	seta	*'se-ta*
silver	argento	*ar-jen-to*
smoke	fumo	—
sodium	sodio	*'so-dyo*
solid	solido	*'so-li-do*
stainless steel	acciaio inossidabile	*ač-'ča-yo in-os-si-'da-bi-le*
steel	acciaio	*ač-'ča-yo*
straw	paglia	*'pa-lya*
string	spago	*'spa-go*
stuff	roba	*'ro-ba*
substance	sostanza	*sos-'tan-tsa*
sulfur	zolfo	*'dzol-fo*
synthetic	sintetico	*sin-'te-ti-ko*
tape	nastro	*'nas-tro*
tar	pece (f)	*'pe-če*
test tube	provetta	*pro-'vet-ta*
texture, textile	tessuto	*tes-'su-to*
thermometer	termometro	*ter-'mo-me-tro*
tin	latta	*'la-ta*
	stagno	*'sta-nyo*
vapor	vapore (m)	*va-'po-re*
velvet	velluto	*vel-'lu-to*
virgin wool	lana vergine	*'la-na 'ver-ji-ne*
water	acqua	*'ak-kwa*
wood	legno	*'le-nyo*
wool	lana	—
wrought iron	ferro battuto	*'fer-ro bat-'tu-to*

D. GEOGRAPHY

> For names of countries, cities, etc. see §30a-c

Antarctic Circle	Circolo Polare Antartico	*'čir-ko-lo po-'la-re an-tar-ti-ko*
Arctic Circle	Circolo Polare Artico	*'čir-ko-lo po-'la-re 'ar-ti-ko*
area	area	*'a-re-a*
atlas	atlante (m)	*at-'lan-te*
border (political)	frontiera (m)	*fron-'tye-ra*
climate	clima (m)	*'kli-ma*
compass	bussola	*'bus-so-la*
continent	continente (m)	*kon-ti-'nen-te*
• continental	continentale	*kon-ti-nen-ta-le*
country	paese (m)	*pa-'e-ze*
demographic	demografico	*de-mo-'gra-fi-ko*
east	est	—
• eastern	orientale	*o-ryen-'ta-le*
equator	equatore (m)	*e-kwa-'to-re*
geographical	geografico	*je-o-'gra-fi-ko*
• geography	geografia	*je-o-gra-'fi-a*
globe (planetary)	globo	—
globe (object)	mappamondo	*map-pa-'mon-do*
gulf	golfo	—
hemisphere	emisfero	*e-mis-'fe-ro*
latitude	latitudine (f)	*la-ti-'tu-di-ne*
longitude	longitudine (f)	*lon-ji-'tu-di-ne*
map	mappa	—
meridian	meridiano	*me-ri-'dya-no*
nation	nazione (f)	*na-'tsyo-ne*
• national	nazionale	*na-tsyo-'na-le*
north	nord	—
• northeast	nord-est	—
• northern	settentrionale	*set-ten-tryo-'na-le*
• northwest	nord-ovest	—
pole	polo	—
• North Pole	Polo Nord	—
• South Pole	Polo Sud	—
province	provincia	*pro-'vin-ča*
region	regione (f)	*re-'jo-ne*
south	sud	—
• southeast	sud-est	—
• southern	meridionale	*me-ri-dyo-'na-le*
• southwest	sud-ovest	—

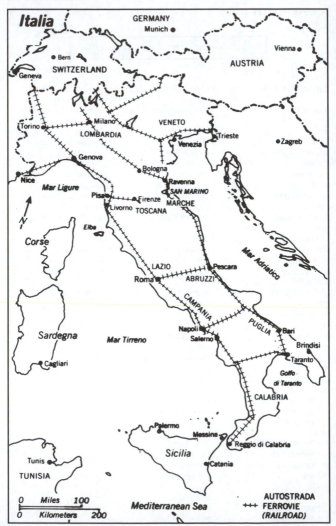

state	stato	—
territory	territorio	ter-ri-'to-ryo
tropic	tropico	'tro-pi-ko
• Tropic of Cancer	Tropico del Cancro	'tro-pi-ko del 'kan-kro
• Tropic of Capricorn	Tropico del Capricorno	'tro-pi-ko del ka-pri-'kor-no
• tropical	tropicale	tro-pi-'ka-le
west	ovest	—
• western	occidentale	oč-či-den-ta-le
zone	zona	'dzo-na

Idiomatic Expressions

It's a small world	=	Tutto il mondo è paese

14. PLANTS

A. GENERAL VOCABULARY

agriculture	agricoltura	a-gri-kol-'tu-ra
bark	corteccia	kor-'teč-ča
barley	orzo	'or-dzo
(to) bloom	sbocciare	zboč-'ča-re
botanical	botanico	bo-'ta-ni-ko
• botany	botanica	bo-'ta-ni-ka
branch	ramo	—
bulb	bulbo	—
clay	argilla	ar-'jil-la
compost	miscela fertilizzante	mi-'še-la fer-ti-li-'dzan-te
corn	granturco	gran-'tur-ko
	mais (m, inv)	—
cultivation	coltivazione (f)	kol-ti-va-'tsyo-ne
• (to) cultivate	coltivare	kol-ti-'va-re
(to) dig	scavare	ska-'va-re
ditch	fossato	fos-'sa-to
dung	letame (m)	le-'ta-me
ear (of corn)	spiga	'spi-ga
fallow, uncultivated	incolto	in-kol-to
farmland	terreno agricolo	ter-'re-no a-'gri-ko-lo
fermentation	fermentazione (f)	fer-men-ta-'tsyo-ne
fertilizer	fertilizzante (m)	fer-ti-li-'dzan-te
flower	fiore (m)	'fyo-re
• (to) flower	fiorire (isc)	fyo-'ri-re

flower garden, flower bed	aiuola	*a-'yuo-la*
fodder	foraggio	*fo-'raj-jo*
foliage	fogliame (m)	*fo-'lya-me*
garden	giardino	*jar-'di-no*
garden seat	panchina	*pan-'ki-na*
gardener	giardiniere (-a)	*jar-di-'nye-re*
grain	grano	—
• **granary**	granaio	*gra-'na-yo*
greenhouse	serra	—
harvest	raccolta	*rak-kol-ta*
• **(to) harvest**	raccogliere*	*rak-'ko-'lye-re*
hay	fieno	*'fye-no*
hedge	siepe (f)	*'sye-pe*
hoe	zappa	*'dzap-pa*
• **(to) hoe**	zappare	*dzap-'pa-re*
hose	tubo	—
• **(to) hose**	innaffiare	*in-naf-'fya-re*
irrigation	irrigazione (f)	*ir-ri-ga-'tsyo-ne*
lawn	prato (erboso)	*'pra-to (er-'bo-zo)*
• **lawn mower**	falciatrice (f)	*fal-ča-'tri-če*
leaf	foglia	*'fo-lya*
manure	concime (m)	*kon-'či-me*
meadow	prato	—
(to) mow, reap	falciare	*fal-'ča-re*
nursery	vivaio	*vi-'va-yo*
oats	avena	*a-'ve-na*
path	sentiero	*sen-'tye-ro*
petal	petalo	*'pe-ta-lo*
pest	parassita (m)	*pa-ras-'si-ta*
• **pesticide**	insetticida (m)	*in-set-ti-'či-da*
pitchfork	forcone (m)	*for-'ko-ne*
plant	pianta	*'pyan-ta*
• **(to) plant**	piantare	*pyan-'ta-re*
plow	aratro	*a-'ra-tro*
• **(to) plow**	arare	*a-'ra-re*
pollen	polline (m)	*'pol-li-ne*
(to) prune	potare	*po-'ta-re*
rake	rastrello	*ras-'trel-lo*
• **(to) rake**	rastrellare	*ras-trel-'la-re*
• **(to) reap**	mietere	*'mye-te-re*
ripe	maturo	*ma-'tu-ro*
root	radice (f)	*ra-'di-če*
rotten	marcio	*'mar-čo*
seed	seme (m)	*'se-me*
• **(to) seed, sow**	seminare	*se-mi-'na-re*
shovel, spade	vanga	*'van-ga*
sickle	falce (f)	*'fal-če*
slab	piastra	*'pyas-tra*

small garden	giardinetto	*jar-di-'net-to*
spade	vanga	—
species	specie (f)	*'spe-če*
spraying	polverizzazione (f)	*pol-ve-ri-dza-'tyo-ne*
sprinkler	spruzzatore (m)	*spru-tsa-'to-re*
stem	stelo	—
storage room, shed	ripostiglio	*ri-pos-'ti-lyo*
straw	paglia	*'pa-lya*
sundial	meridiana	*me-ri-'dya-na*
thorn	spina	—
(to) thresh	trebbiare	*treb-'bya-re*
(to) till	vangare	*van-'ga-re*
tree	albero	*'al-be-ro*
trimmer	potatore (delle piante)	*po-ta-'to-re*
trowel	cazzuola	*ka-'tswo-la*
trunk	tronco	*'tron-ko*
vegetable garden	orto	—
vine	vite (f)	*'vi-te*
vineyard	vigna	*'vi-nya*
weed	erbaccia	*er-'bač-ča*
(to) wilt	appassire (isc)	*ap-pas-'si-re*

B. FLOWERS

buttercup	ranuncolo	*ra-'nun-ko-lo*
camelia	camelia	*ka-'me-lya*
carnation	garofano	*ga-'ro-fa-no*
clematis	clematide (f)	*kle-'ma-ti-de*
cornflower	fiordaliso	*fyor-da-'li-zo*
cyclamen	ciclamino	*či-kla-'mi-no*
daffodil	trombone (m)	*trom-'bo-ne*
dahlia	dalia	*'da-lya*
daisy	margherita	*mar-ge-'ri-ta*
forget-me-not	miosotide (f)	*mi-o-'zo-ti-de*
geranium	geranio	*je-'ra-nyo*
gladiolus	gladiolo	*gla-'di-o-lo*
hyacinth	giacinto	*ja-'čin-to*
hydrangea	ortensia	*or-'ten-sya*
ivy	edera	*'e-de-ra*
lily	giglio	*'ji-lyo*
lily of the valley	mughetto	*mu-'get-to*
magnolia	magnolia	*ma-'nyo-lya*
marigold	calendola	*ka-'len-do-la*
mistletoe	vischio	*'vis-kyo*
nasturtium	nasturzio	*nas-'tur-tsyo*
nettle	ortica	*or-'ti-ka*
orchid	orchidea	*or-ki-'de-a*
pansy	viola del pensiero	*'vyo-la del pen-'sye-ro*

peony	peonia	*pe-'o-nya*
petunia	petunia	*pe-'tu-nya*
poppy	papavero	*pa-'pa-ve-ro*
primrose	primula	*'pri-mu-la*
rose	rosa	*'ro-za*
snowdrop	bucaneve (m, inv)	*bu-ka-'ne-ve*
sunflower	girasole (m)	*ji-ra-'so-le*
tulip	tulipano	*tu-li-'pa-no*
twig	ramoscello	*ra-mo-'šel-lo*
violet	viola	*'vyo-la*
wild rose	rosa selvatica	*'ro-za sel-'va-ti-ka*
wisteria	glicine (m)	*'gli-či-ne*

C. TREES

acorn	ghianda	*'gyan-da*
apple	melo	—
ash	frassino	*'fras-si-no*
beech	faggio	*'faj-jo*
birch	betulla	*be-'tul-la*
cherry	ciliegio	*či-'lye-jo*
chestnut	castagno	*kas-'ta-nyo*
cypress	cipresso	*ci-pres-so*
ebony	ebano	*'e-ba-no*
elm	olmo	—
evergreen	sempreverde (m)	*sem-pre-'ver-de*
fig	fico	*'fi-ko*
fir	abete (m)	*a-'be-te*
hazelnut	nocciolo	*noč-'čo-lo*
lemon	limone (m)	*li-'mo-ne*
maple	acero	*'a-če-ro*
oak	quercia	*'kwer-ča*
olive	olivo (ulivo)	*o-'li-vo*
orange	arancio	*a-'ran-čo*
palm	palma	—
peach	pesco	*'pes-ko*
pear	pero	—
pine	pino	—
poplar	pioppo	*'pyop-po*
sap	linfa	*'lin-fa*
sapling	alberello	*al-be-'rel-lo*
walnut	noce (m)	*'no-če*
willow, weeping willow	salice (m)	*'sa-li-če*
	salice piangente	*pyan-'jen-te*

D. FRUITS AND NUTS

| apple | mela | — |
| **apricot** | albicocca | *al-bi-'kok-ka* |

banana	banana	—
blueberry	mirtillo	*mir-'til-lo*
cherry	ciliegia	*či-'lye-ja*
chestnut	castagna	*kas-'ta-nya*
date	dattero	*'dat-te-ro*
fig	fico	*'fi-co*
fruit	frutta	*'frut-ta*
grapefruit	pompelmo	*pom-'pel-mo*
grapes	uva	*'u-va*
lemon	limone (m)	*li-'mo-ne*
mandarin orange	mandarino	*man-da-'ri-no*
melon	melone (m)	*me-'lo-ne*
olive	oliva	*o-'li-va*
orange	arancia	*a-'ran-ča*
peach	pesca	*'pes-ka*
peanut (as sold in the USA)	nocciolina americana	*noč-čo-'li-na a-me-re-'ka-na*
peanut (in general)	arachide (f)	*a-'ra-ki-de*
pear	pera	—
pineapple	ananas (m, inv)	—
pistachio	pistacchio	*pis-'tak-kyo*
plum	susina	*su-'zi-na*
prune	prugna	*'pru-nya*
raspberry	lampone (m)	*lam-'po-ne*
strawberry	fragola	*'fra-go-la*
walnut	noce (f)	*'no-če*
watermelon	anguria	*an-'gu-rya*

E. VEGETABLES AND GREENS

artichoke	carciofo	*kar-'čo-fo*
asparagus	asparagi (m, pl)	*as-'pa-ra-ji*
basil	basilico	*ba-'zi-li-ko*
bean	fagiolo	*fa-'jo-lo*
beet	barbabietola	*bar-ba-'bye-to-la*
broccoli	broccoli (m, pl)	*'brok-ko-li*
cabbage	cavolo	*'ka-vo-lo*
carrot	carota	*ka-'ro-ta*
cauliflower	cavolfiore (m)	*ka-vol-'fyo-re*
celery	sedano	*'se-da-no*
chick peas	ceci (m, pl)	*'če-či*
cucumber	cetriolo	*če-tri-'o-lo*
eggplant	melanzana	*me-lan-'dza-na*
fennel	finocchio	*fi-'nok-kyo*
garlic	aglio	*'a-lyo*
lentil	lenticchia	*len-'tik-kya*
lettuce	lattuga	*lat-'tu-ga*
lima bean	fava	—
mint	menta	—

mushroom	fungo	—
onion	cipolla	*či-'pol-la*
parsley	prezzemolo	*pre-'tse-mo-lo*
pea	pisello	*pi-'zel-lo*
pepper	peperone (m)	*pe-pe-'ro-ne*
potato	patata	*pa-'ta-ta*
pumpkin	zucca	*'dzuk-ka*
rosemary	rosmarino	*roz-ma-'ri-no*
rhubarb	rabarbaro	*ra-'bar-ba-ro*
salad	insalata	*in-sa-'la-ta*
spinach	spinaci (m, pl)	*spi-'na-či*
string bean	fagiolino	*fa-jo-'li-no*
tomato	pomodoro	*po-mo-'do-ro*
vegetables, greens	verdura	*ver-'du-ra*
zucchini	zucchine (f, pl)	*dzuk-'ki-ne*

15. THE ANIMAL WORLD

A. MAMMALS AND ANIMALS IN GENERAL

animal	animale (m)	*a-ni-'ma-le*
antelope	antilope (f)	*an-'ti-lo-pe*
antler, horn	corno (corna, pl)	*'kor-no*
ape, monkey	scimmia	*'šim-mya*
baboon	babbuino	*bab-'bwi-no*
badger	tasso	*'tas-so*
bat	pipistrello	*pi-pis-'trel-lo*
bear	orso	*'or-so*
beaver	castoro	*kas-'to-ro*
breeding	allevamento	*al-le-va-'men-to*
buffalo	bufalo	*'bu-fa-lo*
burrow, den	tana	—
bull	toro	—
camel	cammello	*kam-'mel-lo*
cat	gatto	*'gat-to*
• (to) hiss	sibilare	*si-bi-'la-re*
• kitten	gattino	*gat-'ti-no*
• (to) meow	miagolare	*mya-go-'la-re*
cow	mucca	*'muk-ka*
• calf	vitello	*vi-'tel-lo*
• (to) moo	muggire (isc)	*muj-'ji-re*
deer	cervo	*'čer-vo*
dog	cane (m)	*'ka-ne*
• (to) bark	abbaiare	*ab-ba-'ya-re*
• bulldog	mastino	*mas-'ti-no*
• female dog	cagna	*'ka-nya*
• German shepherd	cane lupo	*'ka-ne 'lu-po*
• guard dog	cane da guardia	*'ka-ne da 'gwar-dya*

• hound	cane da caccia	'ka-ne da 'kač-ča
• (to) howl	ululare	u-lu-'la-re
• kennel	canile (m)	ka-'ni-le
• poodle	barboncino	bar-bon-'či-no
• puppy	cucciolo	'kuč-čo-lo
donkey	asino	'a-zi-no
elephant	elefante (m)	e-le-'fan-te
• tusk	zanna	'dzan-na
farm	fattoria	fat-to-'ri-a
• barn	granaio	gra-'na-yo
• farmer	contadino (-a)	kon-ta-'di-no
• fence	recinto	re-'čin-to
giraffe	giraffa	ji-'raf-fa
goat	capra	'ka-pra
gorilla	gorilla (m, inv)	go-'ril-la
(to) graze	pascolare	pas-ko-'la-re
hamster	criceto	kri-'če-to
hare	lepre (f)	'la-pre
hedgehog	riccio	'rič-čo
hippopotamus	ippopotamo	ip-po-'po-ta-mo
horse	cavallo	ka-'val-lo
• hoof	zoccolo	'dzok-ko-lo
• (to) neigh	nitrire (isc)	ni-'tri-re
• mane	criniera	kri-'nye-ra
• mare	cavalla	ka-'val-la
hunter	cacciatore (-trice)	kač-ča-'to-re
• hunt	caccia	'kač-ča
hyena	iena	'ye-na
jackal	sciacallo	ša-'kal-lo
kangaroo	canguro	kan-'gu-ro
lamb	agnello	a-'nyel-lo
leopard	leopardo	le-o-'par-do
lion, lioness	leone (-essa)	le-'o-ne
• (to) roar	ruggire (isc)	ruj-'ji-re
livestock	bestiame (m)	bes-'tya-me
mammal	mammifero	mam-'mi-fe-ro
marmot`	marmotta	mar-'mot-ta
mink	visone (m)	vi-'zo-ne
mole	talpa	'tal-pa
monkey	scimmia	'šim-mya
mouse	topo	—
mule	mulo	—
otter	lontra	—
ox	bue (buoi, pl)	'bu-e
panda	panda (m, inv)	—
panther	pantera	pan-'te-ra
pet	animale domestico	a-ni-'ma-le do-'mes-ti-ko

Some Common Animals

il gatto   la mucca   il cavallo   il cane

la tigre   il leone   il cervo

il lupo   il maiale   l'elefante   l'orso

pig	maiale (m)	*ma-'ya-le*
• **sow**	scrofa	*'skro-fa*
polar bear	orso bianco	*'or-so 'byan-ko*
porcupine	porcospino	*por-ko-'spi-no*
rabbit	coniglio	*ko-'ni-lyo*
raccoon	procione (m)	*pro-'čo-ne*
ram	montone (m)	*mon-'to-ne*
rat	ratto	*'rat-to*
reindeer	renna	*'ren-na*
rhinoceros	rinoceronte (m)	*ri-no-če-'ron te*
rodent	roditore (m)	*ro-di-'to-re*
seal	foca	*'fo-ka*
sea lion	leone marino	*le-'o-ne ma-'ri-no*
sheep	pecora	*'pe-ko-ra*
• **shepherd**	pastore (-a)	*pas-'to-re*
skunk	puzzola	*'pu-tso-la*
squirrel	scoiattolo	*sko-'yat-to-lo*

tail	coda	—
(to) tame	addomesticare	*ad-do-mes-ti-'ka-re*
tiger	tigre (f)	*'ti-gre*
trap	trappola	*'trap-po-la*
walrus	tricheco	*tri-'ke-ko*
whale	balena	*ba-'le-na*
wild boar	cinghiale (m)	*čin-'gya-le*
wolf	lupo	—
zebra	zebra	*'dze-bra*
zoo	zoo	*'dzo*
• zoological	zoologico	*dzo-o-'lo-ji-ko*
• zoology	zoologia	*dzo-o-lo-'ji-a*

B. BIRDS AND FOWL

beak	becco	*'bek-ko*
bird	uccello	*uč-'čel-lo*
• bird of prey	uccello rapace	*uč-'čel-lo ra-'pa-če*
birdcage	gabbia	*'gab-bya*
blackbird	merlo	—
brood	covata	*ko-'va-ta*
canary	canarino	*ka-na-'ri-no*
chaffinch	fringuello	*frin-'gwel-lo*
chick	pulcino	*pul-'či-no*
chicken, hen	gallina	*gal-'li-na*
crest	cresta	*'kres-ta*
crow	corvo	*'kor-vo*
cuckoo	cuculo	*ku-'ku-lo*
dove	colomba	*ko-'lom-ba*
duck	anatra (anitra)	*'a-na-tra*
eagle	aquila	*'a-kwi-la*
falcon	falcone (m)	*fal-'ko-ne*
feather	penna	—
flamingo	fenicottero	*fe-ni-'kot-te-ro*
goose	oca	*'o-ka*
hawk	falco	*'fal-ko*
homing pigeon	piccione (m)	*pič-'čo-ne*
kingfisher	martin pescatore	*mar-'tin pes-ka-'to-re*
lark	allodola	*al-'lo-do-la*
magpie	gazza	*'ga-dza*
migratory bird	uccello migratore	*uč-'čel-lo*
nest	nido	—
nightingale	usignolo	*u-zi-'nyo-lo*
ostrich	struzzo	*'stru-tso*
owl	gufo	—
parrot, budgie	pappagallo	*pap-pa-'gal-lo*
partridge	pernice (f)	*per-'ni-če*
peacock	pavone (m)	*pa-'vo-ne*

pelican	pellicano	*pel-li-'ka-no*
penguin	pinguino	*pin-'gwi-no*
pheasant	fagiano	*fa-'ja-no*
robin	pettirosso	*pet-ti-'ros-so*
rooster	gallo	*'gal-lo*
seagull	gabbiano	*gab-'bya-no*
sparrow	passero	*'pas-se-ro*
stork	cicogna	*či-'ko-nya*
swallow	rondine (f)	*'ron-di-ne*
swan	cigno	*'či-nyo*
turkey	tacchino	*tak-'ki-no*
turtle dove	tortora	*'tor-to-ra*
vulture	avvoltoio	*av-vol-'to-yo*
wing	ala (ali, pl)	—
woodpecker	picchio	*'pik-kyo*

Idiomatic Expressions

(to) line up	=	fare la coda
(to) kill two birds with one stone	=	pigliare due piccioni con una fava
(to) be very cold	=	fare un freddo da cani

C. FISH, REPTILES, AMPHIBIANS, AND MARINE MAMMALS

alligator	alligatore (m)	*al-li-ga-'to-re*
boa	serpente boa	*ser-'pen-te 'bo-a*
clam	vongola	*'von-go-la*
cobra	cobra (m, inv)	—
codfish	merluzzo	*mer-'lu-tso*
crab	granchio	*'gran-kyo*
crocodile	coccodrillo	*kok-ko-'dril-lo*
eel	anguilla	*an-'gwil-la*
fish	pesce (m)	*'pe-še*
• fin, flipper	pinna	*'pin-na*
• (to) fish	pescare	*pes-'ka-re*
• fishing	pesca	*'pes-ka*
• fishing rod	canna	*'kan-na*
• gill	branchia	*'bran-kya*
• hook	amo	—
• scale	scaglia	*'ska-lya*
frog	rana	—
• (to) croak	gracidare	*gra-či-'da-re*
goldfish	pesce rosso	*'pe-še ros-so*

herring	aringa	a'-rin-ga
jellyfish	medusa	me-'du-za
lizard	lucertola	lu-'čer-to-la
lobster	aragosta	a-ra-'gos-ta
mackerel	sgombro	'sgom-bro
mollusk, shellfish	mollusco	mol-'lus-ko
mullet	triglia	'tri-lya
mussel	cozza	'ko-tsa
octopus	polipo	'po-li-po
oyster	ostrica	'os-tri-ka
prawn, shrimp	gambero	'gam-be-ro
rattlesnake	serpente a sonagli	ser-'pen-te a so-'na-lyi
reptile	rettile (m)	'ret-ti-le
salmon	salmone (m)	sal-'mo-ne
sardine	sardina	sar-'di-na
scallop, shell	conchiglia	kon-'ki-lya
seahorse	cavalluccio marino	ka-val-'luč-čo ma-'ri-no
shark	squalo	'skwa-lo
shell	conchiglia	kon-'ki-lya
snake	serpente (m)	ser-'pen-te
sole	sogliola	'so-lyo-la
squid	calamaro	ka-la-'ma-ro
swordfish	pesce spada	'pe-še
tadpole	girino	ji-'ri-no
toad	rospo	'ros-po
trout	trota	'tro-ta
tuna	tonno	'ton-no
turtle, tortoise	tartaruga	tar-ta-'ru-ga
viper	vipera	'vi-pe-ra

D. INSECTS AND OTHER INVERTEBRATES

ant	formica	for-'mi-ka
• ant hill	formicaio	for-mi-'ka-yo
bedbug	cimice (f)	'či-mi-če
bee	ape (f)	'a-pe
• (to) buzz	ronzare	ron-'dza-re
• hive	alveare (m)	al-ve-'a-re
• (to) sting	pungere*	'pun-je-re
• swarm	sciame (m)	'ša-me
beetle	maggiolino	maj-jo-'li-no
butterfly	farfalla	far-'fal-la
caterpillar	bruco	'bru-ko
chrysalis	crisalide (f)	kri-'sa-lide
cockroach	scarafaggio	ska-ra-'faj-jo
cocoon	bozzolo	'bo-tso-lo
cricket	grillo	'gril-lo
dragonfly	libellula	li-'bel-lu-la

flatworm	verme (m)	*'ver-me*
flea	pulce (f)	*'pul-če*
glowworm	lucciola	*'luč-čo-la*
grasshopper	cavalletta	*ka-val-'let-ta*
hornet	calabrone (m)	*ka-la-'bro-ne*
housefly	mosca	*'mos-ka*
insect, bug	insetto	*in-'set-to*
ladybug	coccinella	*koč-či-'nel-la*
louse	pidocchio	*pi-'dok-kyo*
midge	moscerino	*mo-še-'ri-no*
mosquito	zanzara	*dzan-'dza-ra*
scorpion	scorpione (m)	*skor-'pyo-ne*
silk worm	baco da seta	*'ba-ko da 'se-ta*
spider	ragno	*'ra-nyo*
• spiderweb	ragnatela	*ra-nya-'te-la*
termite	termite (f)	*'ter-mi-te*
tick	zecca	*'dzek-ka*
wasp	vespa	*'ves-pa*
worm	verme (m)	*'ver-me*

COMMUNICATING, FEELING, AND THINKING

16. BASIC SOCIAL EXPRESSIONS

A. GREETINGS AND FAREWELLS

Adieu!	Addio!	*ad-'di-o*
Good afternoon, Hello!	Buon pomeriggio!	*bwon po-me-'rij-jo*
	Buona sera!	*'bwo-na 'se-ra*
	(later afternoon)	
Good evening, Hello!	Buona sera!	*'bwo-na 'se-ra*
Good luck, Best wishes!	Auguri!	*au-'gu-ri*
Good morning, Good day!	Buongiorno!	*bwon-'jor-no*
Good night!	Buona notte!	*'bwo-na 'not-te*
Good-bye!	Arrivederci! (fam)	*ar-ri-ve-'der-či*
	ArrivederLa! (pol)	*ar-ri-ve-'der-la*
greeting	saluto	*sa-'lu-to*
• (to) greet	salutare	*sa-lu-'ta-re*
Greetings, Hello!	Salve!	*'sal-ve*
Hi, Bye!	Ciao! (fam)	*ča-o*
How are you?	Come stai? (fam)	*'ko-me 'stai*
	Come sta? (pol)	*'ko-me sta*
How's it going?	Come va?	*'ko-me va*
• Bad(ly)!	Male!	*'ma-le*
• Fine, Well!	Bene!	*'be-ne*
• Not bad!	Non c'`e male!	*non če 'ma-le*
• Quite well!	Abbastanza bene!	*ab-bas-'tan-dza 'be-ne*
• So, so!	Così, così!	*ko-'zi ko-'zi*
• Very well!	Molto bene!	*'mol-to 'be-ne*
	Benissimo!	*be-'nis-si-mo*
Please give my regards, greetings to…	Ti prego di salutarmi… (fam)	*'pre-go sa-lu-'tar-mi*
	La prego di salutarmi… (pol)	—
See you!	Ci vediamo!	*či ve-'dya-mo*
See you later!	A più tardi!	*a pyu 'tar-di*
See you soon!	A presto!	*a 'pres-to*
See you Sunday!	A domenica!	*a do-'me-ni-ka*
(to) shake hands	dare* la mano	*'da-re la 'ma-no*
	stringere* la mano	*'strin-je-re*
• handshake	stretta di mano	*'stret-ta*

Alternative Spellings

Buon giorno	*or*	**Buongiorno**
Buona sera	*or*	**Buonasera**
Buona notte	*or*	**Buonanotte**

B. FORMS OF ADDRESS AND INTRODUCTIONS

A pleasure!	Piacere!	*pya-'če-re*
• **The pleasure is mine!**	Il piacere è mio!	—
(to) be on a first-name basis	darsi* del tu	—
(to) be on a formal basis	darsi* del Lei	—
(to) be seated	accomodarsi	*ak-ko-mo-'dar-si*
	sedersi*	*se-'der-si*
Be seated!	Accomodati! (fam)	*ak-'ko-ma-da-ti*
	Siediti! (fam)	*'sye-di-ti*
	Si accomodi! (pol)	*si ak-'ko-mo-di*
	Si sieda! (pol)	*si 'sye-da*
calling (business) card	biglietto da visita	*bi-'lyet-to da 'vi-zi-ta*
Come in!	Avanti!	*a-'van-ti*
	Prego!	*'pre-go*
Delighted!	Molto lieto! (m)	*'mol-to 'lye-to*
	Molto lieta! (f)	—
Happy to make your acquaintance	Felice di fare* la tua conoscenza (fam)	
	Felice di fare* la Sua conoscenza (pol)	*fe'li-če ko-no-'šen-tsa*
introduction	presentazione (f)	*pre-zen-ta-'tsyo-ne*
• **(to) introduce**	presentare	*pre-zen-'ta-re*
• **(to) know someone**	conoscere*	*ko-'no-še-re*
• **Let me introduce you to…**	Ti presento… (fam)	—
	Le presento… (pol)	
• **May I introduce you to…?**	Posso presentarti…? (fam)	—
	Ti posso presentare…? (fam)	
	Posso presentarLe…? (pol)	
	Le posso presentare…? (pol)	
Make yourself comfortable!	Si accomodi!	*si ak-'ko-mo-di*
(to) meet	conoscere*	*ko-'no-še-re*
• **(to) run into**	incontrare	*in-kon-'tra-re*
title	titolo	*'ti-to-lo*

• **Accountant**	Ragioniere (-a)	*ra-jo-'nye-re*
• **Doctor**	Dottore (-essa)	*dot-'to-re*
• **Draftsperson**	Geometra (m/f)	*je-'o-me-tra*
• **Engineer**	Ingegnere (m/f)	*in-je-'nye-re*
• **Lawyer**	Avvocato (m/f)	*av-vo-'ka-to*
• **Miss, Ms.**	Signorina	*si-nyo-'ri-na*
• **Mr.**	Signore	*si-'nyo-re*
• **Mrs., Ms.**	Signora	*si-'nyo-ra*
• **Professor**	Professore (-essa)	*pro-fes-'so-re*
• **Reverend**	Reverendo	*re-ve-'ren-do*
What's your name?	Come ti chiami? (fam)	*'ko-me ti 'kya-mi*
	Come si chiama? (pol)	—
• **My name is…**	Mi chiamo…	*mi 'kya-mo*
• **I'm…**	Sono…	—

C. EXCLAMATIONS AND VARIOUS PROTOCOLS (COMMANDING, BEING COURTEOUS, ETC.)

Are you crazy?	Ma sei pazzo (-a)? (fam)	*'pa-tso*
Attention!	Attenzione!	*at-ten-'tsyo-ne*
Be quiet!	Sta' zitto (-a)! (fam)	*'dzit-to*
	Stia zitto (-a)! (pol)	*'sti-a 'dzit-to*
Best wishes!	Auguri!	*au-'gu-ri*
Bless you!	Salute!	*sa-'lu-te*
Cheers!	Salute!	*sa-'lu-te*
	Cin cin!	*čin čin*
Congratulations!	Congratulazioni!	*kon-gra-tu-la-'tsyo-ni*
	Complimenti!	*kom-pli-'men-ti*
Curses! Damn (it)!	Maledizione!	*ma-le-di-'tsyo-ne*
Don't be stupid (silly)!	Non fare* lo stupido (-a)! (fam)	*'stu-pido*
	Non faccia lo stupido (-a)! (pol)	
Don't mention it!	Figurati! (fam)	*fi-'gu-ra-ti*
	Si figuri! (form)	*si fi-'gu-ri*
Don't talk nonsense!	Non dire* schiocchezze! (fam)	*šok-'ke-tse*
	Non dica schiocchezze! (pol)	
Excuse me!	Scusa! (fam)	*'sku-za*
	Scusi! (pol)	*'sku-zi*
	Mi scusi! (pol)	*mi 'sku-zi*
Excuse me (I need to get through)	Permesso!	*per-'mes-so*
Fantastic!	Fantastico!	*fan-'tas-ti-ko*
Good!	Bene!	*'be-ne*
Good luck!	Buona fortuna!	*'bwo-na for-tu-na*
	In bocca al lupo!	*in 'bok-ka al 'lu-po*

Happy birthday!	Buon compleanno!	bwon kom-ple-'an-no
Happy Easter!	Buona Pasqua!	'bwo-na 'pas-kwa
Happy New Year!	Buon Anno!	bwon 'an-no
	Felice Anno Nuovo!	fe-'li-če an-no 'nwo-vo
Have a good holiday!	Buona vacanza!	'bwo-na va-'kan-dza
Have a good time!	Buon divertimento!	bwon di-ver-ti-'men-to
How lucky!	Che fortuna!	ke for-'tu-na
I wish!	Magari!	ma-'ga-ri
I'll be glad, happy to do it!	Lo farò con piacere!	pya-'če-re
I'm sorry!	Mi dispiace!	mi dis-'pya-če
If you don't mind,	Se non ti dispiace (fam)	dis-'pya-če
If you please…	Se non Le dispiace (pol)	
Incredible!	Incredibile!	in-kre-'di-bi-le
Interesting!	Interessante!	in-te-res-'san-te
It can't be!	Non è possibile!	pos-'si-bi-le
It doesn't matter!	Non importa!	im-'por-ta
Magnificent!	Magnifico!	ma-'nyi-fi-ko
Many thanks!	Grazie mille!	'gra-tsye 'mil-le
Marvelous!	Meraviglioso!	me-ra-vi-'lyo-zo
May I?	È permesso?	per-'mes-so
	Posso?	'pos-so
	Si può?	si 'pwo
May I help you?	Desideri? (fam)	de-'zi-de-ri
	Desidera? (pol)	—
Merry Christmas!	Buon Natale!	bwon na-'ta-le
No way!	Per carità!	per ka-ri-'ta
Please!	Per favore!	per fa-'vo-re
Ouch!	Ahi!	—
Quiet!	Silenzio!	si-'len-tsyo
Really?	Davvero?	dav-'ve-ro
Stay still!	Sta' fermo (-a)! (fam)	—
	Stia fermo (-a)! (pol)	—
Stop it! That's enough!	Basta!	—
Stupendous!	Stupendo!	stu-'pen-do
Thank God!	Grazie a Dio!	'gra-tsye
Thank you!	Grazie!	'gra-tsye
Thank you. It's very kind of you!	Grazie, molto gentile!	'gra-tsye 'mol-to jen-'ti-le
Too bad! Pity! A shame!	Peccato!	pek-'ka-to
Well done!	Bravo (-a)!	'bra-vo
What a bore!	Che noia!	ke 'no-ya
What a drag!	Che barba!	ke 'bar-ba
What a fool!	Che sciocco!	ke šok-ko
What a jam!	Che guaio!	ke 'gwa-yo
What a mess!	Che pasticcio!	ke pas-'tič-čo
	Che casino! (fam)	ke ka-'zi-no

What a nuisance!	Che seccatura!	*ke sek-ka-'tu-ra*
What a nice surprise!	Che bella sorpresa!	*ke 'bel-la sor-'pre-za*
Yah! Sure! There!	Ecco!	*'ek-ko*
You're welcome, Please, go ahead	Prego!	*'pre-go*

17. SPEAKING AND TALKING

A. SPEECH STYLES AND FUNCTIONS

advice	consiglio	*kon-'si-lyo*
• (to) advise	consigliare	*kon-si-'lya-re*
(to) affirm, remark	affermare	*af-fer-'ma-re*
(to) agree	essere* d'accordo	*'es-se-re dak-'kor-do*
(to) allude	alludere*	*al-'lu-de-re*
(to) announce	annunciare	*an-nun-'ča-re*
• announcement	annuncio	*an-'nun-čo*
answer	risposta	*ris-'pos-ta*
• (to) answer	rispondere*	*ris-'pon-de-re*
(to) argue, quarrel	litigare	*li-ti-'ga-re*
• argument	lite (f)	*'li-te*
(to) ask for	chiedere*	*'kye-de-re*
(to) beg to do something	pregare	*pre-'ga-re*
(to) call	chiamare	*kya-'ma-re*
(to) change the subject	cambiare soggetto	*kam-'bya-re soj-'jet-to*
(to) chat	chiacchierare	*kyak-kye-'ra-re*
(to) cheer, acclaim	acclamare	*ak-kla-'ma-re*
(to) communicate	comunicare	*ko-mu-ni-'ka-re*
• communication	comunicazione (f)	*ko-mu-ni-ka-'tsyo-ne*
(to) compare	paragonare	*pa-ra-go-'na-re*
• comparison	paragone (m)	*pa-ra-'go-ne*
(to) complain	lamentarsi	*la-men-'tar-si*
• complaint	lamentela	*la-men-'te-la*
(to) conclude	concludere*	*kon-'klu-de-re*
• conclusion	conclusione (f)	*kon-klu-'zyo-ne*
(to) confirm	confermare	*kon-fer-'ma-re*
(to) congratulate	congratulare	*kon-gra-tu-'la-re*
• congratulations	congratulazioni (f, pl)	*kon-gra-tu-la-'tsyo-ni*
(to) consult, look up	consultare	*kon-sul-'ta-re*
(to) contest, dispute	contestare	*kon-tes-'ta-re*
(to) contradict	contraddire*	*kon-trad-'di-re*
conversation	conversazione (f)	*kon-ver-sa-'tsyo-ne*
• (to) converse	conversare	*kon-ver-'sa-re*
(to) curse	maledire*	*ma-le-'di-re*
debate	dibattito	*di-'bat-ti-to*
• (to) debate	dibattere	*di-'bat-te-re*
(to) decipher	decifrare	*de-či-'fra-re*
(to) declare	dichiarare	*di-'kya-'ra-re*

(to) define	definire (isc)	de-fi-'ni-re
(to) deny	negare	ne-'ga-re
(to) describe	descrivere*	des-'kri-ve-re
• description	descrizione (f)	des-kri-'tsyo-ne
dialogue	dialogo	di-'a-lo-go
(to) disagree	non essere* d'accordo	non 'es-se-re
		dak-'kor-do
• disagreement	malinteso	ma-lin-'te-zo
(to) discuss, argue	discutere*	dis-'ku-te-re
• discussion, argument	discussione (f)	dis-kus-'syo-ne
eloquent	eloquente	e-lo-'kwen-te
(to) emphasize	sottolineare	sot-to-li-ne-'a-re
(to) ensure	assicurare	as-si-ku-'ra-re
excuse	scusa	'sku-za
• (to) excuse oneself	scusarsi	sku-'zar-si
(to) explain	spiegare	spye-'ga-re
• explanation	spiegazione (f)	spye-ga-'tsyo-ne
(to) express	esprimere*	es-'pri-me-re
• (to) express oneself	esprimersi*	es-'pri-mer-si
• expression	espressione (f)	es-pres-'syo-ne
gossip	pettegolezzo	pet-te-go-'le-tso
• (to) gossip	spettegolare	spet-'te-go-la-re
(to) guarantee	garantire (isc)	ga-ran-'ti-re
(to) hesitate	esitare	e-zi-'ta-re
• hesitation	esitazione (f)	e-zi-ta-'tsyo-ne
(to) identify	identificare	i-den-ti-fi-'ka-re
(to) imply	implicare	im-pli-'ka-re
(to) indicate	indicare	in-di-'ka-re
• indication	indicazione (f)	in-di-ka-'tsyo-ne
(to) inform	informare	in-for-'ma-re
• information	informazione (f)	in-for-ma-'tsyo-ne
(to) insinuate	insinuare	in-si-nu-'a-re
(to) interpret	interpretare	in-ter-pre-'ta-re
(to) interrogate	interrogare	in-ter-ro-'ga-re
(to) interrupt	interrompere*	in-ter-'rom-pe-re
• interruption	interruzione (f)	in-ter-ru-'tsyo-ne
(to) invite	invitare	in-vi-'ta-re
(to) jeer	fischiare	fis-'kya-re
(to) jest	scherzare	sker-'tsa-re
• jest, prank	scherzo	'sker-tso
joke (oral)	barzelletta	bar-dzel-'let-ta
• (to) tell a joke	raccontare una	rak-kon-'ta-re u-na
	barzelletta	bar-dzel-'let-ta
(to) keep quiet	stare* zitto	'sta-re 'dzit-to
lecture	conferenza	kon-fe-'ren-dza
lie	bugia	bu-'ji-a
• (to) lie	dire* una bugia	'di-re u-na bu-'ji-a
loquacious	loquace	lo-'kwa-če

malicious gossip	maldicenza	*mal-di-'čen-dza*
(to) malign, speak badly of	malignare	*ma-li-'nya-re*
(to) mean	significare	*si-nyi-fi-'ka-re*
• meaning	significato	*si-nyi-fi-'ka-to*
(to) mention	menzionare	*men-tsyo-'na-re*
misunderstanding	fraintendimento	*fra-in-ten-di-'men-to*
(to) murmur	mormorare	*mor-mo-'ra-re*
(to) note	notare	*no-'ta-re*
(to) object	obiettare	*o-byet-'ta-re*
(to) offend	offendere*	*of-'fen-de-re*
oral	orale	*o-'ra-le*
order	ordine (m)	*'or-di-ne*
• (to) order	ordinare	*or-di-'na-re*
outspoken	schietto	*'skyet-to*
(to) praise	lodare	*lo-'da-re*
(to) pray	pregare	*pre-'ga-re*
• prayer	preghiera	*pre-'gye-ra*
(to) preach	predicare	*pre-di-'ka-re*
promise	promessa	*pro-'mes-sa*
• (to) promise	promettere*	*pro-'met-te-re*
(to) pronounce	pronunciare	*pro-nun-'ča-re*
• pronunciation	pronuncia	*pro-'nun-ča*
(to) propose, suggest	proporre*	*pro-'por-re*
(to) put forward	avanzare	*a-van-'tsa-re*
(to) raise one's voice	alzare la voce	*al-'tsa-re la 'vo-če*
(to) read between the lines	leggere* tra le righe	*'lej-je-re tra le 'ri-ge*
(to) recommend	raccomandare	*rak-ko-man-'da-re*
(to) refer	riferire (isc)	*ri-fe-'ri-re*
(to) repeat	ripetere	*ri-'pe-te-re*
• repetition	ripetizione (f)	*ri-pe-ti-'tsyo-ne*
(to) reply	rispondere*	*ris-'pon-de-re*
report	relazione (f)	*re-la-'tsyo-ne*
• (to) report	riferire (isc)	*ri-fe-'ri-re*
(to) reproach	rimproverare	*rim-pro-ve-'ra-re*
(to) request	richiedere*	*ri-'kye-de-re*
• request	richiesta	*ri-'kyes-ta*
rumor	diceria	*di-če-'ria*
• Rumor has it that…	Corre voce che…	*'kor-re 'vo-če ke*
(to) say, tell	dire*	*'di-re*
shout	grido	—
• (to) shout	gridare	*gir-'da-re*
silence	silenzio	*si-'len-tsyo*
• silent	silenzioso	*si-len-'tsyo-zo*
(to) speak, talk	parlare	*par-'la-re*
• speech, talk	discorso	*dis-'kor-so*
(to) spread gossip	seminare zizzania	*se-mi-'na-re*
		dzi-'dza-nya
(to) state, affirm, maintain	asserire (isc)	*as-se-'ri-re*

• **statement**	affermazione (f)	*af-fer-ma-'tsyo-ne*
story	storia	*'sto-rya*
• **(to) tell a story**	raccontare	*rak-kon-'ta-re*
(to) suggest	suggerire (isc)	*suj-je-'ri-re*
(to) summarize	riassumere*	*ri-as-'su-me-re*
• **summary**	riassunto	*ri-as-'sun-to*
(to) swear, curse	bestemmiare	*bes-tem-'mya-re*
(to) swear, avow	giurare	*ju-'ra-re*
talk, speech	discorso	*dis-'kor-so*
(to) tell (a story), recount	raccontare	*rak-kon-'ta-re*
(to) tell a joke	raccontare una barzelletta	*rak-kon-'ta-re u-na bar-dzel-'let-ta*
(to) testify, vouch	testimoniare	*tes-ti-mo-'nya-re*
(to) thank	ringraziare	*rin-gra-'tsya-re*
threat	minaccia	*mi-'nač-ča*
• **(to) threaten**	minacciare	*mi-nač-'ča-re*
(to) toast	brindare	*brin-'da-re*
• **toast**	brindisi (m, inv)	*'brin-di-zi*
(to) translate	tradurre*	*tra-'dur-re*
• **translation**	traduzione (f)	*tra-du-'tsyo-ne*
(to) uphold, maintain	sostenere*	*sos-te-'ne-re*
vocabulary	vocabolario	*vo-ka-bo-'la-ryo*
(to) warn	avvertire	*av-ver-'ti-re*
• **warning**	avvertimento	*av-ver-ti-'men-to*
(to) whine	piagnucolare	*pya-nyu-ko-'la-re*
(to) whisper	sussurrare	*sus-sur-'ra-re*
witty	spiritoso	*spi-ri-'to-zo*
word	parola	*pa-'ro-la*
(to) yawn	sbadigliare	*zba-di-'lya-re*
(to) yell, scream	urlare	*ur-'la-re*

B. USEFUL EXPRESSIONS IN CONVERSATIONS

(to) be right	avere* ragione	*a-'ve-re ra-'jo-ne*
(to) be wrong	avere* torto	*a-'ve-re 'tor-to*
briefly	in breve	*in 'bre-ve*
by the way	a proposito	*a pro-'po-zi-to*
Go ahead, speak!	Di' pure! (fam)	*'pu-re*
	Dica pure! (pol)	—
How do you say...?	Come si dice...?	*'ko-me si 'di-če*
however	tuttavia	*tut-ta-'vi-a*
	comunque	*ko-'mun-kwe*
I didn't understand!	Non ho capito!	*ka-'pi-to*
I'm sure that...	Sono sicuro (-a) che...	*si-'ku-ro*
in my opinion	a mio parere	*pa-'re-re*
in my own opinion	secondo me	*se-'kon-do*
It seems that...	Sembra che...	*'sem-bra ke*
	Pare che...	*'pa-re ke*

Common Gestures Used in Conversation

	Are you crazy?	Sei pazzo? (fam) È pazzo? (pol)	
	Come here!	Vieni qui (fam) Venga qui! (pol)	*'vye-ni kwi*
	Hello! (pol)	Buon giorno! etc.	
	Hi (fam)	Ciao!	
	Let me introduce you to . . .	Ti presento . . . (fam) Le presento . . . (pol)	
	No way!	Impossibile!!	*im-pos-'si-bi-le*

It's necessary that...	È necessario che...	*ne-čes-'sa-ryo ke*
It's obvious that...	È ovvio che...	*'ov-vyo ke*
It's true!	È vero!	*'ve-ro*
• **It's not true!**	Non è vero!	—
Listen!	Senti! (fam)	*'sen-ti*
	Ascolta! (fam)	*as-'kol-ta*
	Senta! (pol)	—
	Ascolti! (pol)	—
now	ora	*'o-ra*

that is to say	cioè	čo-'e
	vale a dire	va-le a -'di-re
therefore	dunque	'dun-kwe
	quindi	'kwin-di
	allora	al-'lo-ra
to sum up	insomma	in-'som-ma
Who knows?	Chissà?	kis-'sa

18. THE TELEPHONE

A. TELEPHONES AND ACCESSORIES

amplifier	altoparlante (m)	al-to-par-'lan-te
answering machine	segreteria telefonica	se-gre-te-'ri-a te-le-'fo-ni-ka
cable	cavo	—
cell phone	cellulare (m)	cel-lu-'la-re
	telefonino	te-le-fo-'ni-no
digital	digitale	di-ji-'ta-le
carphone	auricolare (m)	au-ri-ko-'la-re
fax machine	fax (m)	—
intercom	citofono	ci-'to-fo-no
modem	modem (m)	—
operator	centralino	cen-tra-'li-no
outlet	presa	'pre-za
phone bill	bolletta del telefono	bol-'let-ta del te-'le-fo-no
phone book	elenco telefonico	e-'len-ko te-le-'fo-ni-ko
phone booth	cabina telefonica	ka-'bi-na te-le-'fo-ni-ka
phone card	scheda telefonica	'ske-da te-le-'fo-ni-ka
phone keyboard	tastiera del telefono	tas-'tye-ra del te-'le-fo-no
portable phone	telefono portatile	te-'le-fo-no por-'ta-ti-le
public phone	telefono pubblico	te-'le-fo-no 'pub-bli-ko
speaker	microfono	mi-'kro-fo-no
telecommunications	telecomunicazioni (f, pl)	te-le-ko-mu-ni-ka-'tsyo-ni
yellow pages	pagine gialle	'pa-ji-ne 'jal-le

B. USING THE TELEPHONE

1-800 number	numero verde	'nu-me-ro 'ver-de
(to) answer	rispondere*	ris-pon-de-re
area code	prefisso	pre-'fis-so
busy, occupied signal	occupato	ok-ku-'pa-to
collect call	telefonata a carico del destinatario	te-le-fo-'na-ta 'ka-ri-ko del des-ti-na-'ta-ryo

(to) dial the number	comporre* il numero	kom-'por-re il 'nu-mero
	fare* il numero	—
direct call	telefonata in teleselezione	te-le-fo-na-ta in te-le-se-le-'tsyo-ne
distress phone line	telefono amico	te-'le-fo-no a-'mi-ko
free signal	libero	
(to) hang up	riattaccare il telefono	ri-at-tak-'ka-re il te-'le-fo-no
information	informazioni (f, pl)	in-for-ma-'tsyo-ni
international call	telefonata internazionale	te-le-fo-'na-ta in-ter-na-tsyo-'na-le
local call	telefonata urbana	te-le-fo-'na-ta ur-'ba-na
long-distance call	telefonata interurbana	te-le-fo-'na-ta in-ter-ur-'ba-na
phone call	telefonata	te-le-fo-'na-ta
• Hello!	Pronto!	—
• I'm sorry, I've dialed the wrong number.	Scusi, ho sbagliato numero.	'sku-zi o zba-'lya-to 'nu-me-ro
• Is Mario in?	C'è Mario?	če 'ma-ryo
• Is Ms. Morelli in?	C'è la signora Morelli?	
• (to) make a call	fare* una telefonata	'fa-re u-na te-le-fo-'na-ta
• May I speak with…?	Posso parlare con…?	—
• I would like to speak with…	Desidererei parlare con…	de-zi-de-re-'rei
• The line is busy.	La linea è occupata.	'li-ne-a ok-ku-'pa-ta
• The line is free.	La linea è libera.	'li-ne-a 'li-be-ra
• This is…	Sono…	—
• Who is it?	Chi è?	ki 'e
• Who's speaking?	Chi parla?	ki 'par-la
phone line for reporting the abuse of children	telefono azzurro	te-'le-fo-no a-'dzur-ro
phone number	numero di telefono	'nu-me-ro di te-'le-fo-no
(to) ring	suonare	swo-'na-re
wrong number	numero sbagliato	'nu-me-ro zba-'lya-to

19. LETTER WRITING

A. FORMAL SALUTATIONS/CLOSINGS

Dear Madam or Sir…	Spettabile (Spett.le) Ditta…	spet-'ta-bi-le
Dear Sir…	Egregio Signore…	egre-jo si-'nyo-re
Dear Madam…	Gentile Signora…	—
Greetings, regards…	Saluti…	sa-'lu-ti
To Whom It May Concern…	A Chi di Competenza…	kom-pe-'ten-dza

With cordial greetings...	Con i più cordiali saluti...	*pyu kor-'dya-li sa-'lu-ti*
With kind wishes...	Un caro saluto...	—
Yours cordially...	Cordiali saluti...	*kor-'dya-li sa-'lu-ti*
Yours truly, sincerely...	Suo (Sua)...	—
	Distinti saluti...	—

Writing to a Company, Corporation, etc.

Dear Madam or Sir	Spettabile Ditta
To Whom It May Concern	A Chi di Competenza
Please accept...	La prego di accettare...

B. FAMILIAR SALUTATIONS/CLOSINGS

A hug...	Un abbraccio...	*un ab-'brač-čo*
Affectionately...	Afettuosamente...	
Dear John...	Caro Giovanni...	—
Dear Mary...	Cara Maria...	—
Dearest John...	Carissimo Giovanni...	—
Dearest Mary...	Carissima Maria...	—
Give my regards to...	Tanti saluti a ...	*'tan-ti sa-'lu-ti a*
	Salutami...	*sa-'lu-ta-mi*
Greetings...	Saluti...	*sa-'lu-ti*
My dear John...	Mio caro Giovanni...	—
My dear Mary...	Mia cara Maria...	—
Yours...	Tuo (Tua)...	

C. PARTS OF A LETTER/PUNCTUATION

body	contenuto	*kon-te-'nu-to*
boldface	grassetto	*gras-'set-to*
(to) center	centrare	*čen-'tra-re*
(to) clear, delete	annullare	*an-nul-'la-re*
closing	chiusa	*'kyu-za*
(to) copy	copiare	*ko-'pya-re*
date	data	—
(to) delete	cancellare	*kan-čel-'la-re*
draft	bozza	*'bo-tsa*
(to) duplicate	duplicare	*du-pli-'ka-re*
(to) enclose, attach	accludere*	*ak-'klu-de-re*
	allegare	*al-le-'ga-re*
• enclosed, attached	accluso	*ak-'klu-zo*
	allegato	*al-le-'ga-to*

Formal Letter

Luogo e data	*Roma, 15 settembre 2005*
Intestazione	*Spettabile Ditta*
Contenuto	*scrivo per informarvi che …*
Chiusa	*Con i più cordiali saluti*
Firma	*Alessandro De Grandi*

Informal Letter

Luogo e data	*Roma, 21 settembre 2005*
Intestazione	*Caro Marco*
Contenuto	*scrivo per dirti che …*
Chiusa	*Un abbraccio*
Firma	*Sara*

English	Italian	Pronunciation
(to) erase, delete	cancellare	*kan-'čel-'la-re*
footnote	nota a piè di pagina	*'no-ta a pye di 'pa-ji-na*
heading	intestazione (f)	*in-tes-ta-'tsyo-ne*
italics	corsivo	*kor-'si-vo*
place	luogo	*'lwo-go*
page	pagina	*'pa-ji-na*
• **page set-up**	impaginazione (f)	*im-pa-ji-na-'tsyo-ne*
punctuation	punteggiatura	*pun-tej-ja-'tu-ra*
• **accent**	accento	*ač-'čen-to*
• **apostrophe**	apostrofo	*a-'pos-tro-fo*
• **asterisk**	asterisco	*as-te-'ris-ko*
• **colon**	due punti	—
• **comma**	virgola	*'vir-go-la*
• **dash**	trattino	*trat-'ti-no*
• **exclamation mark**	punto esclamativo	*es-kla-ma-'ti-vo*
• **lower-case character**	carattere minuscolo	*ka-'rat-te-re*
		mi-'nus-ko-lo
• **parenthesis, bracket**	parentesi (f, inv)	*pa-'ren-te-zi*
• **period**	punto	—

• **question mark**	punto interrogativo	*in-ter-ro-ga-'ti-vo*
• **quotation marks**	virgolette (f, pl)	*vir-go-'let-te*
• **semicolon**	punto e virgola	*'pun-to e 'vir-go-la*
• **slash**	sbarra obliqua	*'zbar-ra o-'bli-kwa*
• **upper-case character**	carattere maiuscolo	*ka-'rat-te-re mi-'yus-ko-lo*
salutation	saluto epistolare	*sa-'lu-to e-pis-to-'la-re*
signature	firma	—
• **(to) sign**	firmare	*fir-'ma-re*
style	stile (m)	*'sti-le*
text	testo	*'tes-to*
• **character**	carattere (m)	*ka-'rat-te-re*
• **line**	riga	—
• **margin**	margine (m)	*'mar-ji-ne*
• **paragraph**	capoverso	*ka-po-'ver-so*
• **phrase**	frase (f)	*'fra-ze*
• **spelling**	ortografia	*or-to-gra-'fi-a*
underline	sottolineatura	*sot-to-li-ne-a-'tu-ra*

D. WRITING MATERIALS AND ACCESSORIES

adhesive tape	nastro adesivo	*'nas-tro a-de-'zi-vo*
ballpoint pen	biro (f, inv)	—
business card	biglietto da visita	*bi-'lyet-to da 'vi-zi-ta*
card, record, file	scheda	*'ske-da*
cartridge	cartuccia	*kar-'tuč-ča*
clip	grappetta	—
computer	computer	—
copy	copia	*'ko-pya*
draft	bozza	*'bo-tsa*
envelope	busta	—
eraser	gomma	—
glue	colla	—
highlighter	evidenziatore (m)	*e-vi-den-tsya-'to-re*
ink	inchiostro	*in-'kyos-tro*
invitation (to a wedding, baptism, and so on)	partecipazione (f)	*par-te-ci-pa-'tsyo-ne*
label	etichetta	*e-ti-'ket-ta*
letter	lettera	*'let-te-ra*
• **letter opener**	tagliacarte (m, inv)	*ta-lya-'kar-te*
• **letterhead**	carta intestata	*'kar-ta in-tes-'ta-ta*
Liquid Paper, White-out	bianchetto	*byan-'ket-to*
marker	pennarello	*pen-na-'rel-lo*
pad	taccuino	*tak-'kwi-no*
paper	carta	*'kar-ta*
• **official paper**	carta protocollo	*pro-to-'kol-lo*
pen	penna	—
photocopy shop	copisteria	*ko-pis-te-'ri-a*

photocopying machine, photocopier	fotocopiatrice (f)	*fo-to-ko-pya-'tri-če*
printer	stampante (f)	*stam-'pan-te*
punch	perforatrice (f)	*per-fo-ra-'tri-če*
ream of paper	risma di carta	*'riz-ma*
ring-binder	quaderno ad anelli	*kwa-'der-no ad a-'nel-li*
rubber band	elastico	*e-'las-ti-ko*
ruler	riga	—
scanner	scanner (m, inv)	—
scissors	forbici (f, pl)	*'for-bi-či*
sheet (of paper)	foglio	*'fo-lyo*
(to) shred	stracciare	*strač-'ča-re*
staple	graffa	*'graf-fa*
• stapler	cucitrice (f)	*ku-či-'tri-če*
string	spago	*'spa-go*
tack	puntina	*pun-'ti-na*
two copies	doppia copia	*'dop-pya 'ko-pya*
wastebasket	cestino	*čes-'ti-no*

For computer terminology, see section (f) below and §42b

E. MAILING

abroad	all'estero	*al-'les-te-ro*
address	indirizzo	*in-di-'ri-tso*
• return address	indirizzo del mittente	*mit-'ten-te*
airmail	posta aerea	*'pos-ta a-'e-re-a*
(to) attach, enclose	allegare	*al-le-'ga-re*
• attached, enclosed	allegato	*al-le-'ga-to*
business letter	lettera commerciale	*'let-te-ra kom-mer-'ča-le*
clerk (postal)	impiegato (-a)	*im-pye-'ga-to*
• clerk's window	sportello	*spor-'tel-lo*
confidential	confidenziale	*kon-fi-den-'tsya-le*
correspondence	corrispondenza	*kor-ris-pon-'den-tsa*
• correspondent	corrispondente (m/f)	*kor-ris-pon-'den-te*
(to) countersign	controfirmare	*kon-tro-fir-'ma-re*
• countersignature	controfirma	*kon-tro-'fir-ma*
courier	corriere (m)	*kor-'rye-re*
envelope	busta	—
express mail	posta celere	*'pos-ta 'če-le-re*
letter carrier	postino (-a)	*pos-'ti-no*
mail	posta	—
• (to) mail	spedire (isc)	*spe-'di-re*

mail delivery	distribuzione (f) della posta	*dis-tri-bu-'tsyo-ne*
mail truck	furgone (m) postale	*fur-'go-ne pos-'ta-le*
mail withheld for pick-up	fermo posta	
mailbox	cassetta postale	*kas-'set-ta pos-'ta-le*
package	pacco	*'pak-ko*
packet	plico	*'pli-ko*
post office	ufficio postale	*uf-'fi-čo pos-'ta-le*
postage	affrancatura	*af-fran-ka-'tu-ra*
postal box	casella postale	*ka-'zel-la pos-'ta-le*
postal card	cartolina postale	*kar-to-'li-na pos-'ta-le*
postal check	assegno postale	*as-'se-nyo pos-'ta-le*
postal code	codice postale	*'ko-di-'če pos-'ta-le*
postal money order	vaglia (m) postale	*'va-lya pos-'ta-le*
postal package	pacco postale	*'pak-ko pos-'ta-le*
postal rate	tariffa postale	*ta-'rif-fa pos-'ta-le*
printed matter	stampe (f, pl)	*'stam-pe*
(to) put into a mailbox	imbucare	*im-bu-'ka-re*
(to) receive	ricevere	*ri-'če-ve-re*
receiver	destinatario	*des-ti-na-'ta-ryo*
registered mail	posta raccomandata	*'pos-ta rak-ko-man-'da-ta*
regular surface mail	posta ordinaria	*'pos-ta or-di-'na-rya*
reply	risposta	*ris-'pos-ta*
• (to) reply	rispondere*	*ris-'pon-de-re*
(to) send	spedire (isc)	*spe-'di-re*
sender	mittente (m/f)	*mit-'ten-te*
stamp	francobollo	*fran-ko-'bol-lo*
telegram	telegramma (m) (telegrammi, pl)	*te-le-'gram-ma*
time between the mailing and reception of mail	giro di posta	*'ji-ro*
(to) wait for	aspettare	*as-pet-'ta-re*
(to) write	scrivere*	*'skri-ve-re*

Envelope Address

Signor(a) G. Ascoli
Via Nazionale, 15
00135 Roma

F. E-MAIL AND THE INTERNET

(to) click	cliccare	*klik-'ka-re*
comma	virgola	*'vir-go-la*
cursor	cursore (m)	*kur-'so-re*
diskette	dischetto	*dis-'ket-to*
e-mail	posta elettronica	*'pos-ta e-let-'tro-ni-ka*
	e-mail (m, inv)	—
e-mail address	indirizzo e-mail	*in-di-'ri-tso*
• at (@)	chiocciola	*'kyoč-čo-la*
• dot	punto	—
hard drive	hard drive (inv)	—
hypertext	ipertesto	*i-per-'tes-to*
inputting on the screen	videoscrittura	*vi-de-o-skrit-'tu-ra*
interactive	interattivo	*in-ter-at-'ti-vo*
internet	internet (m, inv)	—
internet provider	provider (inv)	—
keyboard	tastiera	*tas-'tye-ra*
laptop computer	laptop (m, inv)	—
mouse	mouse (m, inv)	—
(to) navigate	navigare	*na-vi-'ga-re*
peripherals	periferiche (f, pl)	*pe-ri-'fe-ri-ke*
(to) print	stampare	*stam-'pa-re*
• ink-jet printer	stampante a getto d'inchiostro	*stam-'pan-te a 'jet-to din-'kyos-tro*
• laser printer	stampante laser	—
• printer	stampante (f)	—
(to) save	salvare	*sal-'va-re*
search	ricerca	*ri-'čer-ka*
server	server (m, inv)	—
space bar	barra spaziatrice	*'bar-ra spa-tsya-'tri-če*
tab	tabulatore (m)	*ta-bu-la-'to-re*
user	utente (m/f)	*u-ten-te*
• user-friendly	di facile uso	*di 'fa-či-le 'u-zo*
website	sito (web)	—
word processing	trattamento di testi	*trat-ta-'men-to*

20. THE MEDIA

A. PRINT MEDIA

author	autore (-trice)	*au-'to-re*
book	libro	—
(to) cancel a subscription	annullare l'abbonamento	*an-nul-'la-re lab-bo-na-'men-to*
(to) censor	censurare	*čen-su-'ra-re*
• censorship	censura	*čen-'su-ra*
column	rubrica	*ru-'bri-ka*

• columnist, reporter	cronista (m/f)	kro-'nis-ta
comic book	rivista a fumetti	ri-'vis-ta a fu-'met-ti
communiqué	comunicato stampa	ko-mu-ni-'ka-to 'stam-pa
contributor	collaboratore (-trice)	kol-la-bo-ra-'to-re
cover, dust jacket	copertina	ko-per-'ti-na
crime report	cronaca nera	'kro-na-ka 'ne-ra
critic	critico (-a)	'kri-ti-ko
crosswords	parole crociate	pa-'ro-le kro-'ča-te
daily newspaper	quotidiano	kwo-ti-'dya-no
(to) defame, libel	diffamare	dif-fa-'ma-re
(to) edit	redigere*	re-'di-je-re
• editor	redattore (-trice)	re-dat-'to-re
• editorial	articolo di fondo	ar-'ti-ko-lo
• editorial offices, editing, editorial staff	redazione (f)	re-da-'tsyo-ne
• editor-in-chief	caporedattore (-trice)	ka-po-re-dat-'to-re
fashion magazine	rivista di moda	ri-'vis-ta di 'mo-da
fiction, narrative	narrativa	nar-ra-'ti-va
film critic	critico del cinema	'kri-ti-ko del 'či-ne-ma
headline	titolo	'ti-to-lo
illustrated magazine	rivista illustrata	ri-'vis-ta il-lus-'tra-ta
index	indice (m)	'in-di-če
interview	intervista	in-ter-'vis-ta
journalist	giornalista (m/f)	jor-na-'lis-ta
kids magazine	giornalino	jor-na-'li-no
local news	cronaca cittadina	'kro-na-ka čit-ta-'di-na
magazine	rivista	ri-'vis-ta
main story	titolo principale	'ti-to-lo prin-či-'pa-le
national press	stampa nazionale	'stam-pa na-tsyo-'na-le
news item, article, report	cronaca	'kro-na-ka
newspaper	giornale (m)	jor-'na-le
newsroom	sala di redazione	re-da-'tsyo-ne
note	nota	—
novel	romanzo	ro-'man-dzo
• adventure	d'avventura	dav-ven-'tu-ra
• character	personaggio	per-so-'naj-jo
• mystery, detective	giallo	'jal-lo
• plot	trama	—
periodical	periodico	pe-ri-'o-di-ko
play	rappresentazione (f)	rap-pre-zen-ta-'syo-ne
	teatrale	te-a-'tra-le
• comedy	commedia	kom-'me-dya
• drama	dramma	—
• tragedy	tragedia	tra-'je-dya
poem, poetry	poesia	poe-'zi-a
pornographic magazine	rivista pornografica	ri-'vis-ta por-no-'gra-fi-ka

press conference	conferenza stampa	kon-fe-'ren-dza 'stam-pa
press room	sala stampa	'sa-la 'stam-pa
press service, press agency	agenzia di stampa	a-jen-'tsi-a di 'stam-pa
(to) print	stampare	stam-'pa-re
• print (medium)	stampa	'stam-pa
• printing	tipografia	ti-po-gra-'fi-a
print run, circulation	tiratura	ti-ra-'tu-ra
proofs	prove (f, pl)	'pro-ve
(to) publish	pubblicare	pub-bli-'ka-re
• publisher	editore (m)	e-di-'to-re
puzzle section	enigmistica	e-nig-'mis-ti-ka
(to) read	leggere*	'lej-je-re
• readers	lettori (m, pl)	let-'to-ri
• definition	definizione (f)	de-fi-ni-'tsyo-ne
• dictionary	dizionario	di-tsyo-'na-ryo
• encyclopedia	enciclopedia	en-či-klo-pe-'di-a
report, news item, feature	cronaca	'kro-na-ka
report, reporting	servizio	ser-'vi-tsyo
review	recensione (f)	re-čen-'syo-ne
science fiction	fantascienza	fan-ta-'šen-tsa
soap-opera magazine	fotoromanzo	fo-to-ro-'man-dzo
special correspondent	inviato speciale	in-'vya-to spe-'ca-le
sports reporter	cronista sportivo	kro-'nis-ta spor-'ti-vo
(to) subscribe	abbonarsi	ab-bo-'nar-si
• subscription	abbonamento	ab-bo-na-'men-to
teen magazine	rivista per adolescenti	ri-'vis-ta per a-do-le-šen-ti
typographical error	errore tipografico	er-'ro-re ti-po-'gra-fi-ko
women's magazine	rivista femminile	ri-'vis-ta fem-mi-'ni-le

B. ELECTRONIC AND DIGITAL MEDIA

(to) air	mandare in onda	man-'da-re in 'on-da
announcer	annunciatore (-trice)	an-nun-ča-'to-re
antenna	antenna	an-'ten-na
audio receiver, tuner	sintonizzatore (m)	sin-to-ni-dza-'to-re
(to) be on the air	essere* in onda	'es-se-re in 'on-da
broadcast	trasmissione (f)	traz-mis-'syo-ne
• (to) broadcast	trasmettere*	traz-'met-te-re
• cable television	televisione via cavo	te-le-vi-'zyo-ne
cameraman	cameraman (m, inv)	—
cassette tape	audiocassetta	au-dyo-kas-'set-ta
channel	canale (m)	ka-'na-le
children's program	programma per bambini	pro-'gram-ma per bam-'bi-ni
closed-circuit television	televisione a circuito chiuso	te-le-vi-'zyo-ne a čir-'kwi-to 'kyu-zo

commercial	spot	—
commercial channel	canale commerciale	*ka-na-le kom-mer-ča-le*
compact disc, CD	compact disc	
	CD	—
disc	disco	—
disc jockey	disc jockey	—
DVD	DVD (m, inv)	—
(to) go on the air	andare* in onda	*an-'da-re in 'on-da*
headphones	cuffie (f, pl)	*'kuf-fye*
	auricolari (m, pl)	*au-ri-ko-'la-ri*
high-definition television	televisione ad alta	*te•le-vi-'zyo-ne ad*
	definizione	*'al-ta de-fi-ni-'tsyo-ne*
live broadcast	trasmissione (f) in diretta	*traz-mis-'syo-ne*
live program	programma (m) dal vivo	*pro-'gram-ma dal 'vi-vo*
(to) make a connection	collegare	*kol-le-'ga-re*
microphone	microfono	*mi-'kro-fo-no*
news flash	notizia flash	*no-'ti-tsya*
on the air	in onda	—
optic cable	cavo ottico	*'ka-vo 'ot-ti-ko*
optic fiber	fibra ottica	*'fi-bra 'ot-ti-ka*
poll, rating	sondaggio	*son-'daj-jo*
portable radio	radio portatile	*'ra-dyo por-'ta-ti-le*
private channel	canale privato	*ka-'na-le pri-'va-to*
private television	televisione privata	*te-le-vi-'zyo-ne pri-'va-ta*
program	programma (m) (programmi, pl)	*pro-'gram-ma*
projector	proiettore (m)	*pro-yet-'to-re*
public channel	canale pubblico	*ka-'na-le 'pub-bli-ko*
public television	televisione pubblica	*te-le-vi-'zyo-ne 'pub-bli-ka*
radio	radio (m, inv)	*'ra-dyo*
• radio broadcasting	radiodiffusione (f)	*ra-dyo-dif-fu-'zyo-ne*
• radio frequency	banda a modulazione di frequenza	*'ban-da a mo-du-la-'tsyo-ne di fre-'kwen-tsa*
• radio network	rete radiofonica	*'re-te ra-dyo-'fo-ni-ka*
• radio news	giornale (m) radio	*jor-'na-le 'ra-dyo*
• radio station	stazione (f) radio	*sta-'tsyo-ne 'ra-dyo*
• radio wave	onda radiofonica	*'on-da ra-dyo-'fo-ni-ka*
recorder	registratore (m)	*re-jis-tra-'to-re*
remote control	telecomando	*te-le-ko-'man-do*
satellite dish	antenna parabolica	*an-'ten-na pa-ra-'bo-li-ka*
satellite television	televisione (f) via satellite	*te-le-vi-'zyo-ne vi-a sa-'tel-li-te*
serial, series	programma (m) a puntate	*pro-'gram-ma a pun-'ta-te*
short-wave	onde corte	*'on-de -'kor-te*

show	spettacolo	spet-'ta-ko-lo
speaker	cassa acustica	'kas-sa a-'kus-ti-ka
sports program	programma (m) di sport	pro-'gram-ma
talk show	talk show (m, inv)	—
tape	nastro	—
television	televisione (f)	te-le-vi-'zyo-ne
• television broadcasting	telediffusione (f)	te-le-dif-fu-'zyo-ne
• television camera	telecamera	te-le-'ka-me-ra
• television direction booth	cabina di regia	ka-'bi-na di re-'ji-a
• television game show	telequiz (m, inv)	te-le-'kwidz
• television movie	telefilm (m, inv)	te-le-'film
• television network	rete televisiva	're-te te-le-vi-'zi-va
• television news	telegiornale (m)	te-le-jor-'na-le
• television report	telecronaca	te-le-'kro-na-ka
• television reporter	telecronista (m/f)	te-le-kro-'nis-ta
• television studio	studio televisivo	'stu-dyo te-le-vi-'zi-vo
(to) turn off	spegnere*	'spe-nye-re
(to) turn on	accendere*	ač-'čen-de-re
variety program	programma (m) di varietà	pro-'gram-ma di va-rye-'ta
via satellite	via satellite	'vi-a sa-'tel-li-te
video cassette	videocassetta	vi-de-o-kas-'set-ta
videodisc	videodisco	vi-de-o-'dis-ko
viewer	telespettatore (-trice)	te-le-spet-ta-'to-re
weather report	bollettino metereologico	bol-let-'ti-no me-te-o-ro-'lo-ji-ko

C. ADVERTISING

advertisement	messaggio pubblicitario	mes-'saj-jo pub-bli-či-'ta-ryo
	réclame (f, inv)	
advertising	pubblicità (f, inv)	pub-bli-či-'ta
advertising agency	agenzia di pubblicità	a-jen-'tsi-a di pub-'bli-či-'ta
advertising break	spot pubblicitario	pub-bli-či-'ta-ryo
advertising campaign	campagna pubblicitaria	kam-'pa-nya pub-bli-či-'ta-rya
advertising sign	insegna pubblicitaria	in-'se-nya pub-bli-či-'ta-rya
brand, logo	marca	'mar-ka
	marchio	'mar-kyo
brochure	opuscolo	o-'pus-ko-lo
caption	leggenda	lej-'jen-da
coupon, voucher	buono	'bwo-no
cut-out coupon	tagliando	ta-'lyan-do

flier	dépliant (m, inv)	—
free	gratis	—
• **free sample**	campione (m) omaggio	*kam-'pyo-ne*
jingle	jingle (m, inv)	—
logo	logo	—
poster	cartellone pubblicitario	*kar-tel-'lo-ne*
		pub-bli-či-'ta-ryo
radio advertising	pubblicità radiofonica	*pub-bli-či-'ta*
		ra-dyo-'fo-ni-ka
sample	campione (m)	*kam-'pyo-ne*
slogan	slogan (m, inv)	—
sponsor	sponsor (m, inv)	—
• **sponsoring**	sponsorizzazione (f)	*spon-so-ri-dza-'tsyo-ne*
television advertising	pubblicità televisiva	*pub-bli-či-'ta*
		te-le-vi-'zi-va

21. FEELINGS

A. MOODS, ATTITUDES, EMOTIONS

affection	affetto	*af-'fet-to*
(to) agree	essere* d'accordo	*'es-se-re dak-'kor-do*
anger	rabbia	*'rab-bya*
• **angry**	arrabbiato	*ar-rab-'bya-to*
anxiety	ansia	*'an-sya*
• **anxious**	ansioso	*an-'syo-zo*
(to) argue	litigare	*li-ti-'ga-re*
• **argument**	lite (f)	*'li-te*
(to) assure	assicurare	*as-si-ku-'ra-re*
attitude	atteggiamento	*at-tej-ja-'men-to*
bad mood	cattivo umore	*kat-'ti-vo u-'mo-re*
bad-tempered	irascibile	*i-ra-'ši-bi-le*
bawdy	volgare	*vol-'ga-re*
(to) be ashamed	vergognarsi	*ver-go-'nyar-si*
(to) be down	essere* giù	*'es-se-re ju*
(to) be up	essere* su	—
(to) become bored	annoiarsi	*an-no-'yar-si*
benefactor	benefattore (-trice)	*be-ne-fat-'to-re*
bitter	amaro	*a-'ma-ro*
boastful	vanaglorioso	*va-na-glo-'ryo-zo*
bored	annoiato	*an-no-'ya-to*
• **boredom**	noia	*'no-'ya*
braggart	spaccone (-a)	*spak-'ko-ne*
captivating	accattivante	*ak-kat-ti-'van-te*
cautious	cauto	*'kau-to*
ceremonious	cerimonioso	*če-ri-mo-'nyo-zo*
charity	carità (f, inv)	*ka-ri-'ta*
cheeky, cocky	sfacciato	*sfač-'ča-to*

(to) complain	lamentarsi	*la-men-'tar-si*
• **complaint**	lamentela	*la-men-'te-la*
conceited	pieno di sé	*'pye-no*
contact	contatto	*kon-'tat-to*
cordial	cordiale	*kor-'dya-le*
cordiality	cordialità (f, inv)	*kor-dya-li-'ta*
correct, proper	corretto	*kor-'ret-to*
(to) cry	piangere*	*'pyan-je-re*
• **crying**	pianto	*'pyan-to*
(to) dare	osare	*o-'za-re*
decency	decenza	*de-'čen-tsa*
• **decent**	decente	*de-'čen-te*
decorum	decoro	*de-'ko-ro*
deferent	deferente	*de-fe-'ren-te*
degenerate	degenerato	*de-je-ne-'ra-to*
depraved	depravato	*de-pra-'va-to*
depressed	depresso	*de-'pres-so*
• **depression**	depressione (f)	*de-pres-'syo-ne*
desperate	disperato	*dis-pe-'ra-to*
• **desperation**	disperazione (f)	*dis-pe-ra-'tsyo-ne*
devout	devoto	*de-'vo-to*
direct	diretto	*di-'ret-to*
(to) disappoint	deludere*	*de-'lu-de-re*
• **disappointed**	deluso	*de-'lu-zo*
(to) disagree	non essere* d'accordo	*non 'es-se-re dak-'kor-do*
• **disagreement**	disaccordo	*diz-ak-'kor-do*
• **(to) be against**	essere* contrario	*'es-se-re kon-'tra-ryo*
(to) disgust	disgustare	*diz-gus-'ta-re*
• **disgust**	disgusto	*diz-'gus-to*
dishonorable	disonorevole	*diz-o-no-'re-vo-le*
dissatisfaction	insoddisfazione (f)	*in-sod-dis-fa-'tsyo-ne*
• **dissatisfied**	insoddisfatto	*in-sod-dis-'fat-to*
dissolute	dissoluto	*dis-so-'lu-to*
docile	docile	*'do-či-le*
eager	desideroso	*de-zi-de-'ro-zo*
effective	efficace	*ef-fi-'ka-če*
efficient	efficiente	*ef-fi-'čen-te*
egoism	egoismo	*e-go-'iz-mo*
enchanting	incantevole	*in-kan-'te-vo-le*
(to) encourage	incoraggiare	*in-ko-raj-'ja-re*
• **encouraged**	incoraggiato	*in-ko-raj-'ja-to*
(to) enjoy oneself, have fun	divertirsi	*di-ver-'tir-si*
erotic	erotico	*e-'ro-ti-ko*
estimable	stimabile	*sti-'ma-bi-le*
evasive	evasivo	*e-va-'zi-vo*
fanatic	fanatico	*fa-'na-ti-ko*

fear	paura	*pa-'u-ra*
• (to) fear, be afraid	avere* paura (di)	—
• fearful	pauroso	*pau-'ro-zo*
(to) feel like	avere* voglia di	*a-'ve-re 'vo-lya*
feeling	sensibilità (f, inv)	*sen-si-bi-li-'ta*
fierce	violento	*vyo-'len-to*
	feroce	*fe-'ro-če*
(to) flatter	lusingare	*lu-zin-'ga-re*
• flattery	lusinga	*lu-'zin-ga*
frenetic	frenetico	*fre-'ne-ti-ko*
friendship	amicizia	*a-mi-'či-tsya*
fun, enjoyment	divertimento	*di-ver-ti-'men-to*
funny	curioso	*ku-'ryo-zo*
furious	furioso	*fu-'ryo-zo*
generosity	generosità (f, inv)	*je-ne-ro-zi-'ta*
gentility, politeness	gentilezza	*jen-ti-'le-tsa*
good mood	buon umore	*bwon u-'mo-re*
grateful	grato	—
gullible	semplice	*'sem-pli-če*
happiness	felicità (f, inv)	*fe-li-či-'ta*
• happy	felice	*fe-'li-če*
	allegro	*al-'le-gro*
hard-headed	cocciuto	*koč-'ču-to*
haughty	altezzoso	*al-te-'tso-zo*
(to) have patience, be patient	avere* pazienza	*a-'ve-re pa-'tsyen-tsa*
hesitant	restio	*res-'ti-o*
honorable	onorevole	*o-no-'re-vo-le*
hope	speranza	*spe-'ran-dza*
• (to) hope	sperare	*spe-'ra-re*
humor	umorismo	*u-mo-'riz-mo*
hypocrite	ipocrita (m/f)	*i-'po-kri-ta*
• hypocritical	ipocrita	—
idle	ozioso	*o-'tsyo-zo*
immoral	immorale	*im-mo-'ra-le*
indecent	indecente	*in-de-'čen-te*
indifference	indifferenza	*in-dif-fe-'ren-dza*
• indifferent	indifferente	*in-dif-fe-'ren-te*
indolent	indolente	*in-do-'len-te*
inferiority	inferiorità (f, inv)	*in-fe-ryo-ri-'ta*
intrepid	intrepido	*in-'tre-pi-do*
ironic	ironico	*i-'ro-ni-ko*
joy	gioia	*'jo-ya*
lascivious	lascivo	*la-'ši-vo*
laudable	lodevole	*lo-'de-vo-le*
(to) laugh	ridere*	*'ri-de-re*
• laughter	risata	*ri-'za-ta*
(to) let off steam	sfogarsi	*sfo-'gar-si*

lethargic	letargico	le-'tar-ji-ko
level-headed	equilibrato	e-kwi-li-'bra-to
lewd	indecente	in-de-'čen-te
libidinous	libidinoso	li-bi-di-'no-zo
light-hearted	allegro	al-'le-gro
litigious	litigioso	li-ti-'jo-zo
lusty	lussurioso	lus-su-'ryo-zo
magnanimity	magnanimità (f, inv)	ma-nya-ni-'mi-ta
• magnanimous	magnanimo	ma-'nya-ni-mo
malleable	malleabile	mal-le-'a-bi-le
maniacal	maniaco	ma-'ni-a-ko
mean-minded	meschino	mes-'ki-no
mediocre	mediocre	me-'dyo-kre
• mediocrity	mediocrità (f, inv)	me-dyo-kri-'ta
merciful	pietoso	pye-'to-zo
merciless	spietato	spye-'ta-to
mischievous	malizioso	ma-li-'tsyo-zo
mocking, derisive	beffardo	bef-'far-do
modest	modesto	mo-'des-to
mood	umore (m)	u-'mo-re
• moody	lunatico	lu-'na-ti-ko
moralistic	moralistico	mo-ra-'lis-ti-ko
naughty, saucy	spinto	—
noisy	chiassoso	kyas-'so-zo
nosy	ficcanaso	fik-ka-'na-zo
obedient	ubbidiente	ub-bi-'dyen-te
obsequious	ossequioso	os-se-kwi-'o-zo
oddball	bizzarro	bi-'dzar-ro
passion	passione (f)	pas-'syo-ne
patience	pazienza	pa-'tsyen-tsa
• (to) have patience	avere* pazienza	—
perfidious	perfido	'per-fi-do
perverted	pervertito	per-ver-'ti-to
philanthropic	filantropico	fi-lan-'tro-pi-ko
• philanthropy	filantropia	fi-lan-tro-'pi-a
playful	giocoso	jo-'ko-zo
pleased, happy, content	contento	kon-'ten-to
pompous	pomposo	pom-'po-zo
(to) praise	elogiare	e-lo-'ja-re
presentable	presentabile	pre-zen-'ta-bi-le
presumptuous	presuntuoso	pre-zun-'two-zo
provocative	provocante	pro-vo-'kan-te
quality	qualità (f, inv)	kwa-li-'ta
relief	sollievo	so-'lye-vo
respectful	rispettoso	ris-pet-'to-zo
restless	irrequieto	ir-re-'kwye-to
roughness, rudeness	rudezza	ru-'de-tsa
sarcastic	sarcastico	sar-'kas-ti-ko

sardonic	sardonico	sar-'do-ni-ko
satisfaction	soddisfazione (f)	sod-dis-fa-'tsyo-ne
• satisfied	soddisfatto	sod-dis-'fat-to
scheming	intrigante	in-tri-'gan-te
scoundrel	scellerato	šel-le-'ra-to
scrupulous	scrupoloso	skru-po-'lo-zo
sensitive	sensibile	sen-'si-bi-le
• sensitivity	sensibilità (f, inv)	sen-si-bi-li-'ta
sensuous, sensual	sensuale	sen-'swa-le
servile	servizievole	ser-vi-'tsye-vo-le
sexy	sexy	—
shame	vergogna	ver-'go-nya
• shameful	vergognoso	ver-go-'nyo-zo
• shameless	svergognato	zver-go-'nya-to
silly	sciocco	'šok-ko
sincere	sincero	sin-'če-ro
slouch	fannullone (-a)	fan-nul-'lo-ne
(to) smile	sorridere*	sor-'ri-de-re
• smile	sorriso	sor-'ri-zo
smug	compiaciuto	kom-pya-'cu-to
sober	sobrio	'so-bryo
sociable	socievole	so-'če-vo-le
sorrow	dolore (m)	do-'lo-re
spendthrift	spilorcio	spi-'lor-čo
spontaneity	spontaneità (f, inv)	spon-ta-nei-'ta
• spontaneous	spontaneo	spon-'ta-ne-o
steadfast	costante	kos-'tan-te
strict	severo	se-'ve-ro
strong desire	voglia	'vo-lya
sulky	scontroso	skon-'tro-zo
sullen	tetro	te-'tro
sure, certain	sicuro	si-'ku-ro
(to) surprise	sorprendere*	sor-'pren-de-re
• surprise	sorpresa	sor-'pre-za
• surprised	sorpreso	sor-'pre-zo
sympathetic	comprensivo	kom-pren-'si-vo
• sympathy	comprensione (f)	kom-pren-'syo-ne
tenacious	tenace	te-'na-če
tenderness	tenerezza	te-ne-'re-tsa
thankfulness	gratitudine (f)	gra-ti-'tu-di-ne
tolerance	tolleranza	tol-le-'ran-tsa
• tolerant	tollerante	tol-le-'ran-te
touchy, over-sensitive	permaloso	per-ma-'lo-zo
troublemaker	attaccabrighe (m/f, inv)	at-tak-ka-'bri-ge
(to) trust	fidarsi (di)	fi-'dar-si
• trust, faith	fiducia	fi-du-'ča
unbearable	insopportabile	in-sop-por-'ta-bi-le
unfaithful	infedele	in-fe'-de-le

unflustered	pacato	*pa-'ka-to*
ungrateful	ingrato	*in-'gra-to*
unscrupulous	senza scrupoli	*'sen-tsa 'skru-po-li*
upset, angry	adirato	*a-di-'ra-to*
vagabond	vagabondo	*va-ga-'bon-do*
vileness, baseness	viltà (f, inv)	*vil-'ta*
volatile	mutevole	*mu-'te-vo-le*
voracious	vorace	*vo-'ra-če*
vulgar	volgare	*vol-'ga-re*
• **vulgarity**	volgarità (f, inv)	*vol-ga-ri-'ta*
well-disciplined	disciplinato	*di-ši-pli-'na-to*
whimsical	estroso	*es-'tro-zo*
worried	preoccupato	*pre-ok-ku-'pa-to*
worthy	meritorio	*me-ri-'to-ryo*

Colloquial Expressions (Familiar)

Come off it!	Ma va!
Come on!	Su! Dai!
Cut it out!	Piantala!
Damn it!	Accidenti!
Get lost!	Vattene!
Go to the Devil!	Va' al diavolo!
No way!	Macché!
Yuch!	Che schifo!

B. LIKES AND DISLIKES

(to) accept	accettare	*ač-čet-'ta-re*
• **acceptable**	accettabile	*ač-čet-'ta-bi-le*
• **unacceptable**	inaccettabile	*in-ač-čet-'ta-bi-le*
approval	approvazione (f)	*ap-pro-va-'tsyo-ne*
• **(to) approve**	approvare	*ap-pro-'va-re*
(to) be fond of (something)	essere* appassionato di	*'es-se-re ap-pas-syo-'na-to*
(to) detest	detestare	*de-tes-'ta-re*
disgust	disgusto	*diz-'gus-to*
• **disgusted**	disgustato	*diz-gus-'ta-to*
dislike	antipatia	*an-ti-pa-'ti-a*
• **(to) dislike**	non piacere* (ess)	*non pya-'ce-re*
hatred	odio	*'o-dyo*
• **(to) hate**	odiare	*o-'dya-re*
I can't stand…	Non sopporto…	—
kiss	bacio	*'ba-čo*
• **(to) kiss**	baciare	*ba-'ča-re*

(to) like	piacere* (ess) a	*pya-'če-re*
• liking	simpatia	*sim-pa-'ti-a*
love	amore (m)	*a-'mo-re*
• (to) love	amare	*a-'ma-re*
mediocre	mediocre	*me-'dyo-kre*
pleasant	piacevole	*pya-'če-vo-le*
• unpleasant	spiacevole	*spya-'če-vo-le*
(to) prefer	preferire (isc)	*pre-fe-'ri-re*

Tip on Using the Verb Piacere

When saying that you like something, translate the English expression into your mind as "to be pleasing to" and then follow the word order in the formula below.

EXPRESSION	TRANSLATE MENTALLY TO . . .	ITALIAN EXPRESSION
I like that book	"To me is pleasing that book"	*Mi piace quel libro*
We like those books	"To us are pleasing those books"	*Ci piacciono quei libri*

C. EXPRESSIONS

Are you joking?	Scherzi? (fam)	*'sker-tsi*
	Scherza? (pol)	—
Be careful!	Attento (-a)!	*at-'ten-to*
Enough!	Basta!	—
Fortunately!	Per fortuna!	—
I don't believe it!	Non ci credo!	*či 'kre-do*
I don't feel like...	Non mi va di...	—
	Non ho voglia di...	*'vo-lya*
	Non mi sento di...	—
I wish!	Magari!	*ma-'ga-ri*
I'm serious!	Dico sul serio!	*'di-ko sul 'se-ryo*
I'm sorry!	Mi dispiace!	*mi dis-'pya-če*
Impossible!	Impossibile!	*im-pos-'si-bi-le*
It doesn't matter!	Non importa!	*im-'por-ta*
Oh my!	Mamma mia!	—
Poor man!	Poveretto!	*po-ve-'ret-to*
Poor woman!	Poveretta!	*po-ve-'ret-ta*

Quiet!	Silenzio!	*si-'len-tsyo*
Really?	Davvero?	*dav-'ve-ro*
Shut up!	Zitto (-a)!	*'dzit-to*
Thank goodness!	Meno male!	*'me-no 'ma-le*
Too bad!	Peccato!	*pek-'ka-to*
Ugh!	Uffa!	—
Unbelievable!	Incredibile!	*in-kre-'di-bi-le*
Unfortunately!	Purtroppo!	*pur-'trop-po*
What a bore!	Che barba!	*ke 'bar-ba*
	Che noia!	*ke 'no-ya*

22. THOUGHT

A. THE MIND

belief	credenza	*kre-'den-tsa*
complicated	complicato	*kom-pli-'ka-to*
concept	concetto	*kon-'čet-to*
concrete	concreto	*kon-'kre-to*
conscience	coscienza	*ko-šen-dza*
• **conscientious**	coscienzioso	*ko-šen-'tsyo-zo*
creative	creativo	*kre-a-'ti-vo*
• **creativity**	creatività (f, inv)	*kre-a-ti-vi-'ta*
difficult	difficile	*di-'fi-či-le*
doubt	dubbio	*'dub-byo*
• **doubtful**	dubbioso	*dub-'byo-zo*
dream	sogno	*'so-nyo*
easy	facile	*'fa-či-le*
existence	esistenza	*ez-is-'ten-dza*
forgetful	smemorato	*zme-mo-'ra-to*
hypothesis	ipotesi (f, inv)	*i-'po-te-zi*
idea	idea	*i-'de-a*
ignorance	ignoranza	*i-nyo-'ran-tsa*
• **ignorant**	ignorante	*i-nyo-'ran-te*
imagination, fantasy	immaginazione (f)	*im-ma-ji-na-'tsyo-ne*
	fantasia	*fan-ta-'zi-a*
ingenious	ingegnoso	*in-je-'nyo-zo*
• **ingenuity**	ingegno	*in-'je-nyo*
intelligence	intelligenza	*in-tel-li-'jen-tsa*
• **intelligent**	intelligente	*in-tel-li-'jen-te*
interest	interesse (m)	*in-te-'res-se*
• **interesting**	interessante	*in-te-res-'san-te*
judgment, wisdom	giudizio	*ju-'di-tsyo*
knowledge	conoscenza	*ko-no-šen-tsa*
• **knowledgeable**	ben informato	*ben in-for-'ma-to*
logic	logica	*'lo-ji-ka*
memory	memoria	*me-'mo-rya*
mind	mente (f)	*'men-te*

opinion	opinione (f)	*o-pi-'nyo-ne*
problem	problema (m)	*pro-'ble-ma*
	(problemi, pl)	
reason	ragione (f)	*ra-'jo-ne*
reflection	riflessione (f)	*ri-fles-'syo-ne*
sensible	sensato	*sen-'sa-to*
simple	semplice	*'sem-pli-če*
thought	pensiero	*pen-'sye-ro*
wisdom	sapienza	*sa-'pyen-dza*
wrongfulness	torto	—

B. THINKING

(to) be interested in	interessarsi di	*in-te-res-'sar-si*
(to) be right	avere* ragione	*a-'ve-re ra-'jo-ne*
(to) be wrong	avere* torto	*'tor-to*
(to) believe	credere	*'kre-de-re*
(to) conceive	concepire (isc)	*kon-če-'pi-re*
(to) convince	convincere*	*kon-'vin-če-re*
(to) demonstrate	dimostrare	*di-mos-'tra-re*
(to) dissuade	dissuadere*	*dis-swa-'de-re*
(to) doubt	dubitare	*du-bi-'ta-re*
(to) dream	sognare	*so-'nya-re*
(to) exist	esistere (ess)	*e-'zis-te-re*
(to) forget	dimenticare	*di-men-ti-'ka-re*
(to) imagine	immaginare	*im-ma-ji-'na-re*
(to) judge	giudicare	*ju-di-'ka-re*
(to) know	sapere*	*sa-'pe-re*
	conoscere*	*ko-'no-še-re*
(to) learn	imparare	*im-pa-'ra-re*
(to) memorize	memorizzare	*me-mo-ri-'dza-re*
(to) persuade	persuadere*	*per-swa-'de-re*
(to) reason	ragionare	*ra-jo-'na-re*
(to) reflect	riflettere	*ri-'flet-te-re*
(to) remember	ricordare	*ri-kor-'da-re*
(to) solve a problem	risolvere* un problema	*ri-'zol-ve-re un* *pro-'ble-ma*
(to) study	studiare	*stu-'dya-re*
(to) think	pensare	*pen-'sa-re*
(to) understand	capire (isc)	*ka-'pi-re*

DAILY LIFE

23. AT HOME

A. ROOMS, PARTS OF THE HOUSE, AND TYPES OF HOUSES

arch, archway	arco	'ar-ko
	arcata	ar-'ka-ta
attic	attico	'at-ti-ko
balcony	balcone (m)	bal-'ko-ne
banister	balaustra	ba-la-'us-tra
basement	scantinato	skan-ti-'na-to
bathroom	bagno	'ba-nyo
bathtub	vasca	'vas-ka
bedroom	camera (da letto)	'ka-me-ra
blind	avvolgibile (m)	av-vol-'ji-bi-le
burglar alarm	allarme (m) antifurto	al-'lar-me an-ti-'fur-to
ceiling	soffitto	sof-'fit-to
chimney	camino	ka-'mi-no
clothes closet	guardaroba (m, inv)	gwar-da-'ro-ba
clothes rack	attaccapanni (m, inv)	at-tak-ka-'pan-ni
corridor	corridoio	kor-ri-'do-yo
dining room	sala da pranzo	'pran-dzo
door	porta	'por-ta
• **doorbell**	campanello	kam-pa-'nel-lo
• **door knob**	maniglia	ma-'ni-lya
• **hinge**	cardine (m)	'kar-di-ne
• **jamb**	stipite (m)	'sti-pi-te
estate, villa, large home	villa	—
façade	facciata	fač-'ča-ta
fan	ventilatore (m)	ven-ti-la-'to-re
faucet	rubinetto	ru-bi-'net-to
fixture, installation	impianto	im-'pyan-to
floor	pavimento	pa-vi-'men-to
• **floor tile**	piastrella	pyas-'trel-la
forecourt	cortile (m)	kor-'ti-le
foundations	fondamenta (f, pl)	fon-da-'men-ta
garage	garage (m, inv)	—
garden	giardino	jar-'di-no
gutter	grondaia	gron-'da-ya
handle	manico	'ma-ni-ko
handrail	ringhiera	rin-'gye-ra
house	casa	'ka-za

• dwelling	abitazione (f)	a-bi-ta-'tsyo-ne
hut, beach house	capanno	ka-'pan-no
kitchen	cucina	ku-'či-na
landing	pianerottolo	pya-ne-'rot-to-lo
living room	salotto	sa-'lot-to
	soggiorno	soj-'jor-no
loft	soffitta	sof-'fit-ta
mailbox	cassetta delle lettere	kas-'set-ta del-le 'let-te-re
medicine chest	armadietto dei medicinali	ar-'ma-dyet-to dei me-di-či-na-li
mirror	specchio	'spek-kyo
paneling	pannello	pan-'nel-lo
pantry	dispensa	dis-'pen-sa
partition, wall	parete (f)	pa-'re-te
patio	terrazza	ter-'ra-tsa
porch	veranda	ve-'ran-da
prefab	casa prefabbricata	'ka-za pre-fab-bri-'ka-ta
property	proprietà (f, inv)	pro-prye-'ta
roof	tetto	—
room	stanza	'stan-dza
shingle	tegola	'te-go-la
shower	doccia	'doč-ča
shutter, blind	persiana	per-'sya-na
• shutter, leaf	battente (m)	bat-'ten-te
sink	lavandino	la-van-'di-no
sliding door	porta scorrevole	'por-ta skor-'re-vo-le
small villa, cottage home	villino	vil-'li-no
spy-hole	spioncino	spi-on-'či-no
stained-glass window	vetrata dipinta	ve-'tra-ta di-'pin-ta
stairs	scala	'ska-la
• step	gradino	gra-'di-no
storage space	deposito	de-'po-zi-to
switch (light)	interruttore (m)	in-ter-rut-'to-re
terrace	terrazza	ter-'ra-tsa
toilet	bagno	'ba-nyo
• toilet (bowl)	gabinetto	ga-bi-'net-to
towel rack	portasciugamani (m, inv)	por-ta-šu-ga-'ma-ni
veranda	veranda	ve-'ran-da
wall	muro (mura, f, pl)	—
washbasin	lavabo	la-'va-bo
window	finestra	fi-'nes-tra
• window ledge, sill	davanzale (m)	da-van-'tsa-le
• window frame	telaio	te-'la-yo
wine cellar	cantina	kan-'ti-na

B. FURNITURE, DECORATION, APPLIANCES, AND COMMON HOUSEHOLD ITEMS

armchair	poltrona	*pol-'tro-na*
bag	sacco	*'sak-ko*
basket	cesta	*'čes-ta*
bathroom scale	pesapersone (m, inv)	*pe-za-per-'so-ne*
bed	letto	*'let-to*
• bedsheet (sheets)	lenzuolo (lenzuola, f, pl)	*len-'tswo-lo*
• bedding	biancheria da letto	*byan-ke-'ri-a da 'let-to*
• bedside table	comodino	*ko-mo-'di-no*
• bedspread	copriletto	*ko-pri-'let-to*
• blanket	coperta	*ko-'per-ta*
bookcase	libreria	*li-bre-'ri-a*
• bookshelf	scaffale (m)	*skaf-'fa-le*
box, tin	scatola	*'ska-to-la*
broom	scopa	*'sko-pa*
brush	spazzola	*'spa-tso-la*
cabinet	armadietto	*ar-ma-'dyet-to*
cart, movable tray	carrello	*kar-'rel-lo*
chair	sedia	*'se-dya*
cleaning cloth	straccio	*'strač-čo*
clothes dryer	asciugatrice (f)	*a-šu-ga-'tri-če*
clothes hanger	attaccapanni (m, inv)	*at-tak-ka-'pan-ni*
cooker, stove	cucina	*ku-'či-na*
cover, covering	fodera	*'fo-de-ra*
cupboard	armadio	*ar-'ma-dyo*
curtain	tenda	—
cushion	cuscino	*ku-'ši-no*
decor, decoration	arredamento	*ar-re-da-'men-to*
dish cloth	strofinaccio per i piatti	*stro-fi-'nač-čo*
dishwasher	lavastoviglie (m/f, inv)	*la-va-sto-'vi-lye*
doormat	stuoia d'entrata	*'stwo-ya den-'tra-ta*
drawer	cassetto	*kas-'set-to*
dresser, sideboard	credenza	*kre-'den-dza*
dressing table	toilette (f, inv)	—
dust pan	paletta per la spazzatura	*pa-'let-ta per la spa-tsa-'tu-ra*
dustbin	pattumiera	*pat-tu-'mye-ra*
duster	piumino	*pyu-'mi-no*
extension cord	filo di prolungamento	*'fi-lo di pro-lun-ga-'men-to*
fitted carpet	moquette (f, inv)	—
folding chair	sedia pieghevole	*'se-dya pye-'ge-vo-le*
freezer	congelatore (m)	*kon-je-la-'to-re*
funnel	imbuto	*im-'bu-to*
furniture	mobili (m, pl)	*'mo-bi-li*
garbage bin	cestino dei rifiuti	*čes-'ti-no dei ri-'fyu-ti*

glass cabinet	vetrina	ve-'tri-na
heater	termosifone (m)	ter-mo-si-'fo-ne
high chair	seggiolone (m)	sej-jo-'lo-ne
hook	gancio	'gan-čo
household soap	sapone (m) di Marsiglia	sa-'po-ne di mar-'si-lya
ironing board	tavola da stiro	'ta-vo-la da 'sti-ro
kitchen scales	bilancia	bi-'lan-ča
kitchen shelf	mensola	'men-so-la
lamp	lampada	'lam-pa-da
large garbage can	bidone (m)	bi-'do-ne
laundry	biancheria	byan-ke-'ri-a
• laundry basket	cesta del bucato	čes-ta del bu-'ka-to
mattress	materasso	ma-te-'ras-so
microwave oven	forno a microonde	'for-no a mi-kro-'on-de
mop	scopa a stracci	'sko-pa a 'strač-či
oven	forno	—
piece of furniture	mobile (m)	'mo-bi-le
pillow	cuscino	ku-'ši-no
• pillowcase	federa	'fe-de-ra
quilt	trapunta	tra-'pun-ta
recliner	sedia a sdraio	'se-dya a 'zdra-yo
refrigerator	frigorifero	fri-go-'ri-fe-ro
rocking chair	sedia a dondolo	'se-dya a 'don-do-lo
rug	tappeto	tap-'pe-to
sewing machine	macchina per cucire	'mak-ki-na per ku-'či-re
shelf	ripiano	ri-'pya-no
shopping bag	sacchetto della spesa	sak-'ket-to del-la 'spe-za
soap-dish	portasapone (m, inv)	por-ta-sa-'po-ne
sofa, divan	divano	di-'va-no
steam iron	ferro da stiro	'fer-ro da 'sti-ro
stool	sgabello	zga-'bel-lo
stove (kitchen)	cucina	ku-'či-na
• stove element	fornello	for-'nel-lo
stove (heating)	stufa	'stu-fa
table lamp	lampada da tavolo	'lam-pa-da da 'ta-vo-lo
toilet paper	carta igienica	'kar-ta i-'je-ni-ka
towel	asciugamano	a-šu-ga-'ma-no
upholstery	tappezzeria	tap-pe-tse-'ri-a
vacuum cleaner	aspirapolvere (m, inv)	us-pi-ra-'pol-ve-re
wall painting	quadro	'kwa-dro
washing machine	lavatrice (f)	la-va-'tri-če
water-heater	riscaldatore (m) dell'acqua	ris-kal-da-'to-re del-'lak-kwa
wax	cera	'če-ra
writing desk	scrivania	skri-va-'ni-a

C. KITCHENWARE AND MEALTIME OBJECTS

baby bottle	biberon (m, inv)	bi-be-'ron
beaker, tumbler	coppa	'kop-pa
blade	lama	—
blender	frullatore	frul-la-'to-re
bottle	bottiglia	bot-'ti-lya
• **bottled**	imbottigliato	im-bot-ti-'lya-to
• **bottle opener**	cavatappi (m, inv)	ka-va-'tap-pi
bowl	scodella	sko-'del-la
bread basket	cesta del pane	'čes-ta del 'pa-ne
bread knife	coltello da pane	kol-'tel-lo da 'pa-ne
carafe, decanter	caraffa	ka-'raf-fa
casserole	casseruola	kas-se-'rwo-la
chopping (butcher's) knife	coltello da macellaio	kol-'tel-lo da ma-čel-'la-yo
chopping board	tagliere (m)	ta-'lye-re
coffee pot	bricco del caffè	'brik-ko del kaf-'fe
colander	colino	ko-'li-no
cooking pot	pentola	'pen-to-la
cork cap	tappo di sughero	'tap-po di 'su-ge-ro
cup	tazza	'ta-tsa
cutlery	posate (f, pl)	po-'za-te
dessert dish	coppa da dessert	'kop-pa
dessert fork	forchettina	for-ket-'ti-na
dish	piatto	'pyat-to
drinking can	lattina	lat-'ti-na
drinking glass	bicchiere (m)	bik-'kye-re
egg-beater	frullino	frul-'li-no
fork	forchetta	for-'ket-ta
fruit bowl	fruttiera	frut-'tye-ra
frying pan	padella	pa-'del-la
grater	grattugia	grat-'tu-ja
jug	brocca	'brok-ka
kettle	pentolino	pen-to-'li-no
knife	coltello	kol-'tel-lo
ladle	mestolo	'mes-to-lo
masher	pestello	pes-'tel-lo
milk jug	brocca del latte	'brok-ka del 'lat-te
mincer	tritacarne (m)	tri-ta-'kar-ne
mortar	mortaio	mor-'ta-yo
mug	boccale (m)	bok-'ka-le
napkin	tovagliolo	to-va-'lyo-lo
nutcracker	schiaccianoci (m, inv)	skyač-ča-'no-či
pan	padella	pa-'del-la
pepper container	pepiera	pe-'pye-ra
plate-rack	scolapiatti (m, inv)	sko-la-'pyat-ti

pot	pentola	'pen-to-la
	casseruola	kas-se-'rwo-la
	tegame (m)	te-'ga-me
potato masher	schiacciapatate (m, inv)	skyač-ča-pa-'ta-te
potato peeler	pelapatate (m, inv)	pe-la-pa-'ta-te
pressure cooker, steamer	pentola a pressione	'pen-to-la a pres-'syo-ne
salad bowl	insalatiera	in-sa-la-'tye-ra
salt container	saliera	sa-'lye-ra
saucepan	casseruola	kas-se-'rwo-la
saucer	piattino	pyat-'ti-no
spoon	cucchiaio	kuk-'kya-yo
sugar bowl	zuccheriera	dzuk-ke-'rye-ra
tablecloth	tovaglia	to-'va-lya
teacup	tazzina	tat-'tsi-na
teapot	teiera	te-'ye-ra
teaspoon	cucchiaino	kuk-kya-'yi-no
tinfoil	stagnola	sta-'nyo-la
tray, trolley	vassoio	vas-'so-yo
utensil	utensile (m)	u-ten-'si-le
vase	vaso	'va-zo
water glass	bicchiere da acqua	bik-'kye-re da 'ak-kwa
wine glass	bicchiere da vino	bik-'kye-re da 'vi-no
wooden spoon	cucchiaio di legno	kuk-'kya-yo di 'le-nyo

D. SERVICES, TOOLS, AND MAINTENANCE

air conditioning	aria condizionata	'a-rya kon-di-tsyo-'na-ta
adapter	adattatore (m)	a-dat-ta-'to-re
(to) blow a fuse	fare* saltare una valvola	'val-vo-la
bolt	bullone (m)	bul-'lo-ne
• (to) bolt down	bullonare	bul-lo-'na-re
chisel	cesello	če-'zel-lo
clamp	morsetto	mor-'set-to
drill	trapano	'tra-pa-no
electric outlet	presa (elettrica)	'pre-za
electricity	elettricità (f, inv)	e-let-tri-či-'ta
file	lima	'li-ma
flashlight, battery	pila	'pi-la
(to) furnish one's home	ammobiliare la casa	am-mo-bi-'lya-re la 'ka-za
fuse	valvola	'val-vo-la
gas	gas (m, inv)	—
gloss paint, varnish	lacca	'lak-ka
hammer	martello	mar-'tel-lo
hardware	ferramenta (f, pl)	fer-ra-'men-ta
heating	riscaldamento	ris-kal-da-'men-to

insulation	isolante (m)	*i-zo-'lan-te*
light bulb	lampadina	*lam-pa-'di-na*
light, power	luce (f)	*'lu-če*
mallet	mazza	*'ma-tsa*
masking tape	nastro isolante	*'nas-tro i-zo-'lan-te*
nail	chiodo	*'kyo-do*
• (to) nail	inchiodare	*in-kyo-'da-re*
paint	vernice (f)	*ver-'ni-če*
• (to) paint	imbiancare	*im-byan-'ka-re*
• paint brush	pennello	*pen-'nel-lo*
• wet paint	vernice fresca	*ver-'ni-če 'fres-ka*
plane	pialla	*'pyal-la*
pliers, tongs, tweezers	pinze (f, pl)	*'pin-tse*
plug	spina	*'spi-na*
plumbing	sistema idraulico	*sis-'te-ma i-'drau-li-ko*
roller	rullo	*'rul-lo*
sandpaper	carta vetrata	*'kar-ta ve-'tra-ta*
saw	sega	*'se-ga*
screw	vite (f)	*'vi-te*
• (to) screw	avvitare	*av-vi-'ta-re*
• screwdriver	cacciavite (m, inv)	*kač-ča-'vi-te*
• (to) unscrew	svitare	*zvi-'ta-re*
stove air vent	cappa	*'kap-pa*
tool	attrezzo	*at-'tre-tso*
wallpaper	carta da parati	*'kar-ta da pa-'ra-ti*
wire	filo	*'fi-lo*
• wiring	impianto elettrico	*im-'pyan-to e-'let-tri-ko*
wrench	chiave (f) inglese	*'kya-ve in-'gle-ze*

E. APARTMENTS

apartment	appartamento	*ap-par-ta-'men-to*
• apartment building	palazzo (di appartamenti)	*pa-'lat-tso*
building	edificio	*e-di-'fi-čo*
condominium	condominio	*kon-do-'mi-nyo*
elevator	ascensore (m)	*a-šen-'so-re*
entrance	ingresso	*in-'gres-so*
eviction	sfratto	*'sfrat-to*
exit	uscita	*u-'ši-ta*
• emergency exit	uscita di sicurezza	*si-ku-'re-tsa*
flight of stairs	rampa	*'ram-pa*
floor level	piano	*'pya-no*
ground floor	pianterreno	*pyan-ter-'re-no*
intercom	citofono	*či-'to-fo-no*
lease	contratto d'affitto	*kon-'trat-to daf-'fit-to*
lodger, renter, tenant	affittuario (-a)	*af-fit-'twa-ryo*
main door of a building	portone (m)	*por-'to-ne*
remodeling, renovation	rimodernamento	*ri-mo-der-na-'men-to*

rent	affitto	*af-'fit-to*
• overdue rental	morosità (f, inv)	*mo-ro-zi-'ta*
• (to) rent	affittare	*af-fit-'ta-re*
repair	riparazione	*ri-pa-ra'-zyo-ne*
staircase, stairwell	scale (f, pl)	*'ska-le*
tenant	inquilino (-a)	*in-kwi-'li-no*
waste-disposal	eliminazione (f) dei rifiuti	*e-li-mi-na-'tsyo-ne*

F. MISCELLANEOUS VOCABULARY

at home	a casa	*a 'ka-za*
(to) build	costruire (isc)	*kos-tru-'i-re*
(to) buy	comprare	*kom-'pra-re*
(to) clean	pulire (isc)	*pu-'li-re*
(to) clear the table	sparecchiare	*spa-rek-'kya-re*
(to) flush	tirare lo sciacquone	*švak'-kwo-ne*
(to) house	alloggiare	*al-loj-'ja-re*
(to) live in	abitare	*a-bi-'ta-re*
householder, house owner	proprietario (-a)	*pro-prye-'ta-ryo*
(to) iron	stirare	*sti-'ra-re*
key	chiave (f)	*'kya-ve*
(to) move	traslocare	*traz-lo-'ka-re*
• moving (residence)	trasloco	*traz-'lo-ko*
nanny, housekeeper	governante (f)	*go-ver-'nan-te*
occupant, householder	residente (m/f)	*re-zi-'den-te*
(to) sell	vendere	*'ven-de-re*
(to) set the table	apparecchiare	*ap-pa-rek-'kya-re*
(to) wash	lavare	*la-'va-re*
• (to) wash dishes	lavare i piatti	*'pyat-ti*

24. EATING AND DRINKING

A. MEALS, EATING, PREPARATIONS, AND MENUS

appetizer	antipasto	*an-ti-'pas-to*
baked	al forno	*al 'for-no*
banquet	banchetto	*ban-'ket-to*
bitter, sour	amaro	*a-'ma-ro*
(to) boil	bollire	*bol-'li-re*
breakfast	prima colazione	*ko-la-'tsyo-ne*
• (to) have breakfast	fare* colazione	—
breast (chicken, turkey, etc.)	petto	—
broiled	arrostito	*ar-ros-'ti-to*
chop, cutlet	cotoletta	*ko-to-'let-ta*
(to) cook	cucinare	*ku-či-'na-re*

course, dish	piatto	'pyat-to
• first course	primo piatto	—
• second course	secondo piatto	—
cuisine	cucina	ku-'či-na
(to) cut	tagliare	ta-'lya-re
dinner	cena	'če-na
• (to) have dinner	cenare	če-'na-re
filet	filetto	fi-'let-to
food	cibo	'či-bo
French fries	patatine fritte	pa-ta-'ti-ne 'frit-te
fried	fritto	'frit-to
• (to) fry	friggere*	'frij-je-re
grilled	alla griglia	al-la 'gri-lya
juicy	succoso	suk-'ko-zo
leg (chicken, turkey, etc.)	coscia	'ko-ša
lunch	pranzo	'pran-dzo
• (to) have lunch	pranzare	pran-'dza-re
meal	pasto	'pas-to
menu	menù (m, inv)	me-'nu
mild	tiepido	'tye-pi-do
mixed salad	insalata mista	in-sa-'la-ta 'mis-ta
(to) peel	sbucciare	sbuč-'ča-re
platter	piatto misto	'pyat-to 'mis-to
• portion, helping	porzione (f)	por-'tsyo-ne
(to) pour	versare	ver-'sa-re
rare (meat)	al sangue	al 'san-gwe
ripe	maturo	ma-'tu-ro
roast	arrosto	ar-'ros-to
rotten	marcio	'mar-čo
salad	insalata	in-sa-'la-ta
salty	salato	sa-'la-to
side dish	contorno	kon-'tor-no
skin	pelle (f)	'pel-le
(to) slice	affettare	af-fet-'ta-re
snack	spuntino	spun-'ti-no
• (to) have a snack	fare* uno spuntino	—
sour	amaro	a-'ma-ro
spicy, hot	piccante	pik-'kan-te
steak	bistecca	bis-'tek-ka
(to) stir, mix	girare	ji-'ra-re
(to) stuff	farcire (isc)	far-'či-re
sweet	dolce	'dol-če
tasty	gustoso	gus-'to-zo
well-done	ben cotto	ben 'kot-to
with sauce	al sugo	al 'su-go

B. PASTAS, SOUPS, AND RICE

broth	brodo	'bro-do
cannelloni	cannelloni (m, pl)	kan-nel-'lo-ni
dumplings	gnocchi (m, pl)	'nyok-ki
fettuccine	fettuccine (f, pl)	fet-tuč-'či-ne
lasagna	lasagne (f, pl)	la-'za-nye
macaroni	maccheroni (m, pl)	mak-ke-'ro-ni
minestrone soup	minestrone (m)	mi-nes-'tro-ne
pasta	pasta	—
ravioli	ravioli (m, pl)	—
rice	riso	'ri-zo
rice with vegetables	risotto	ri-'zot-to
sauce	sugo	'su-go
	salsa	'sal-sa
soup	minestra	mi-'nes-tra
soup (thick)	zuppa	'dzup-pa
spaghetti	spaghetti (m, pl)	—

C. BREAD, GRAINS, PASTRIES, AND SWEETS

barley	orzo	'or-dzo
biscuit, cookie	biscotto	bis-'kot-to
bread	pane (m)	'pa-ne
breadstick	grissino	gris-'si-no
cake, pie	torta	'tor-ta
candy	caramella	ka-ra-'mel-la
chocolate candy	cioccolatino	čok-ko-la-'ti-no
corn	granturco	gran-'tur-ko
	mais (m, inv)	—
cracker	cracker (m, inv)	—
dessert	dessert (m, inv)	—
	dolce	'dol-če
flour	farina	fa-'ri-na
grain	grano	'gra-no
honey	miele (m)	'mye-le
marmalade, jam	marmellata	mar-mel-'la-ta
oat	avena	a-'ve-na
pudding	budino	bu-'di-no
sandwich (bun)	panino	pa-'ni-no
sandwich (flat)	tramezzino	tra-me-'dzi-no
whole-wheat bread	pane integrale	'pa-ne in-te-'gra-le

D. MEAT AND POULTRY

bacon	pancetta	pan-'čet-ta
beef	manzo	'man-dzo
chicken	pollo	'pol-lo

cold cuts	affettati (m, pl)	*af-fet-'ta-ti*
duck	anatra	*'a-na-tra*
ham	prosciutto	*pro-šut-to*
lamb	agnello	*a-'nyel-lo*
liver	fegato	*'fe-ga-to*
meat	carne (f)	*'kar-ne*
pork	maiale (m)	*ma-'ya-le*
salami sausage	salame (m)	*sa-'la-me*
sausage	salsiccia	*sal-'sič-ča*
turkey	tacchino	*tak-'ki-no*
veal	vitello	*vi-'tel-lo*

E. FISH, SEAFOOD, AND SHELLFISH

anchovy	acciuga	*ač-'ču-ga*
clam	vongola	*'von-gola*
cod	merluzzo	*mer-'lu-tso*
• dried cod	baccalà (m, inv)	*bak-ka-'la*
eel	anguilla	*an-'gwil-la*
fish	pesce (m)	*'pe-še*
herring	aringa	*a-'rin-ga*
lobster	aragosta	*a-ra-'gos-ta*
mussels	cozze (f, pl)	*'ko-tse*
oyster	ostrica	*'os-tri-ka*
prawn	scampo	*'skam-po*
salmon	salmone (m)	*sal-'mo-ne*
sardine	sardina	*sar-'di-na*
seafood	frutti di mare	*'frut-ti di 'ma-re*
shellfish	crostacei (m, pl)	*kros-'ta-če-i*
shrimp	gambero	*'gam-be-ro*
sole	sogliola	*so-'lyo-la*
squid	calamaro (m, pl)	*ka-la-'ma-ro*
trout	trota	*'tro-ta*
tuna	tonno	*'ton-no*

F. VEGETABLES AND GREENS

artichoke	carciofo	*kar-'čo-fo*
asparagus	asparagi (m, pl)	*as-'pa-ra-ji*
bean	fagiolo	*fa-'jo-lo*
beet	barbabietola	*bar-ba-'bye-to-la*
broccoli	broccoli (m, pl)	*'brok-ko-li*
cabbage	cavolo	*'ka-vo-lo*
carrot	carota	*ka-'ro-ta*
cauliflower	cavolfiore (m)	*ka-vol-'fyo-re*
celery	sedano	*'se-da-no*
chick peas	ceci (m, pl)	*'če-ci*
cucumber	cetriolo	*če-tri-'o-lo*

eggplant	melanzana	*me-lan-'dza-na*
fennel	finocchio	*fi-'nok-kyo*
lentil	lenticchia	*len-'tik-kya*
lettuce	lattuga	*lat-'tu-ga*
lima bean	fava	*'fa-va*
mushroom	fungo	*'fun-go*
olive	oliva	*o-'li-va*
onion	cipolla	*či-'pol-la*
pea	pisello	*pi-'zel-lo*
pepper	peperone (m)	*pe-pe-'ro-ne*
potato	patata	*pa-'ta-ta*
pumpkin	zucca	*'dzuk-ka*
radish	ravanello	*ra-va-'nel-lo*
rhubarb	rabarbaro	*ra-'bar-ba-ro*
spinach	spinaci	*spi-'na-či*
string bean	fagiolino	*fa-jo-'li-no*
tomato	pomodoro	*po-mo-'do-ro*
vegetables, greens	verdura	*ver-'du-ra*
zucchini	zucchine (f, pl)	*dzuk-'ki-ne*

G. FRUITS AND NUTS

apple	mela	*'me-la*
apricot	albicocca	*al-bi-'kok-ka*
banana	banana	*ba-'na-na*
blueberry	mirtillo	*mir-'til-lo*
cherry	ciliegia	*či-'lye-ja*
chestnut	castagna	*kas-'ta-nya*
citrus	cedro	*'če-dro*
date	dattero	*'dat-te-ro*
fig	fico	*'fi-ko*
fruit	frutta	*'frut-ta*
fruit salad	macedonia di frutta	*ma-če-'do-nya*
grapefruit	pompelmo	*pom-'pel-mo*
grapes	uva	*'u-va*
lemon	limone (m)	*li-'mo-ne*
mandarin orange	mandarino	*man-da-'ri-no*
melon	melone (m)	*me-'lo-ne*
orange	arancia	*a-'ran-ča*
peach	pesca	*'pes-ka*
peanut (salted)	nocciolina americana	*noč-čo-'li-na a-me-ri-'ka-na*
peanut (in general)	arachide (f)	*a-'ra-ki-de*
pear	pera	*'pe-ra*
pineapple	ananas (m, inv)	*a-na-'nas*
pistachio	pistacchio	*pis-'tak-kyo*
plum	susina	*su-'zi-na*
prune	prugna	*'pru-nya*

raspberry	lampone (m)	*lam-'po-ne*
strawberry	fragola	*'fra-go-la*
walnut	noce (f)	*'no-če*
watermelon	anguria	*an-'gu-rya*

H. DAIRY PRODUCTS, EGGS, AND RELATED FOODS

butter	burro	*'bur-ro*
cheese	formaggio	*for-'maj-jo*
cream	crema	*'kre-ma*
dairy product	latticino	*lat-ti-'či-no*
egg	uovo (uova, f, pl)	*'wo-vo*
ice cream	gelato	*je-'la-to*
milk	latte (m)	*'lat-te*
omelet	frittata	*frit-'ta-ta*
whipping cream	panna montata	*'pan-na mon-'ta-ta*
yogurt	yogurt	—

I. SPICES AND CONDIMENTS

anise	anice (m)	*'a-ni-če*
basil	basilico	*ba-'zi-li-ko*
cinnamon	cannella	*kan-'nel-la*
garlic	aglio	*'a-lyo*
ginger	zenzero	*'dzen-dzero*
herb	erba	*'er-ba*
mint	menta	*'men-ta*
oil	olio	*'o-lyo*
oregano	origano	*o-'ri-ga-no*
parsley	prezzemolo	*pre-'tse-mo-lo*
pepper	pepe (m)	*'pe-pe*
rosemary	rosmarino	*roz-ma-'ri-no*
saffron	zafferano	*dzaf-fe-'ra-no*
salt	sale (m)	*'sa-le*
spice	spezia	*'spe-tsya*
sugar	zucchero	*'dzuk-'ke-ro*
vanilla	vaniglia	*va-'ni-lya*
vinegar	aceto	*a-'če-to*

J. DRINKS AND BEVERAGES

alcoholic beverage	bevanda alcolica	*be-'van-da al-'ko-lika*
beer	birra	*'bir-ra*
• draft beer	birra alla spina	*'bir-ra al-la 'spi-na*
beverage, soft drink	bibita	*'bi-bi-ta*
cappuccino	cappuccino	*kap-puč-'či-no*
chamomile tea	camomilla	*ka-mo-'mil-la*
coffee	caffè (m, inv)	*'kaf-'fe*

• **with a drop of milk**	caffè macchiato	*mak-'kya-to*
• **with a drop of alcohol**	caffè corretto	*kor-'ret-to*
• **with espresso coffee**	caffè espresso	*es-'pres-so*
• **long**	caffè lungo	*'lun-go*
• **short coffee** (concentrated)	caffè ristretto	*ris-'tret-to*
drink, beverage	bevanda	*be-'van-da*
juice	succo	*'suk-ko*
lemonade	limonata	*li-mo-'na-ta*
liqueur	liquore (m)	*li-'kwo-re*
mineral water	acqua minerale	*'ak-kwa mi-ne-'ra-le*
• **carbonated**	gassata	*gas-'sa-ta*
	frizzante	*fri-'dzan-te*
• **non-carbonated**	liscia	*'li-ša*
orangeade	aranciata	*a-ran-'ča-ta*
tea	tè	—
whiskey	whiskey (m, inv)	—
• **with ice, on the rocks**	col ghiaccio	*'gyač-čo*
wine	vino	—

Italian Coffee

cappuccino	cappuccino
coffee with milk	caffellatte
expresso	espresso
long	lungo
regular	normale
short, concentrated	ristretto
with a drop of alcohol	corretto
with a drop of milk	macchiato

K. AT THE TABLE

bottle	bottiglia	*bot-'ti-lya*
cup	tazza	*'tat-tsa*
drinking glass	bicchiere (m)	*bik-'kye-re*
fork	forchetta	*for-'ket-ta*
knife	coltello	*kol-'tel-lo*
napkin	tovagliolo	*to-va-'lyo-lo*
paper cup	bicchiere di carta	*bik-'kye-re di 'kar-ta*
plate	piatto	*'pyat-to*
saucer	piattino	*pyat-'ti-no*
spoon	cucchiaio	*kuk-'kya-yo*
table	tavolo	*'ta-vo-lo*
tablecloth	tovaglia	*to-'va-lya*

tableware	posate (f, pl)	*po-'za-te*
teaspoon	cucchiaino	*kuk-kya-'yi-no*
toothpick	stuzzicadenti (m, inv)	*stu-tsi-ka-'den-ti*
tray	vassoio	*vas-'so-yo*
water bottle	bottiglia da acqua	*bot-'ti-lya da 'ak-kwa*

Table Manners

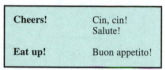

Cheers!	Cin, cin!
	Salute!
Eat up!	Buon appetito!

L. DINING OUT

For menu items see above §24a, and for various food choices, see $24b-j

bartender	barista (m/f)	*ba-'ris-ta*
bill, check	conto	*'kon-to*
cafeteria	mensa	*'men-za*
cover charge	coperto	*ko-'per-to*
pizza parlor	pizzeria	*pi-tse-'ri-a*
price	prezzo	*'pret-tso*
• fixed price	prezzo fisso	*'pret-tso 'fis-so*
reservation	prenotazione (f)	*pre-no-ta-'tsyo-ne*
• reserved	riservato	*ri-zer-'va-to*
restaurant (formal)	ristorante (m)	*ris-to-'ran-te*
restaurant (informal)	trattoria	*trat-to-'ri-a*
service	servizio	*ser-'vi-tsyo*
snack bar	snack bar	—
tip	mancia	*'man-ča*
• (to) tip	dare* la mancia	—
waiter, waitress	cameriere (-a)	*ka-me-'rye-re*
wine list	lista dei vini	—

M. BUYING FOOD AND DRINK

bread store, bakery	panificio	*pa-ni-'fi-čo*
butcher shop	macelleria	*ma-čel-le-'ri-a*
creamery	cremeria	*kre-me-'ri-a*
dairy shop, milk store	latteria	*lat-te-'ri-a*

delicatessen	salumeria	*sa-lu-me-'ri-a*
fish shop	pescheria	*pes-ke-'ri-a*
food store	negozio di alimentari	*ne-'go-tsyo di a-li-men-'ta-ri*
health food store	negozio dietetico	*ne-'go-tsyo di-e-'te-ti-ko*
hypermarket	ipermercato	*i-per-mer-'ka-to*
ice cream parlor	gelateria	*je-la-te-'ri-a*
pastry shop	pasticceria	*pas-tič-če-'ri-a*
produce, fruit vendor	fruttivendolo	*frut-ti-'ven-do-lo*
store	negozio	*ne-'go-tsyo*
supermarket	supermercato	*su-per-mer-'ka-to*
wine shop	enoteca	*e-no-'te-ka*

N. RELATED VOCABULARY

appetizing	appetitoso	*ap-pe-ti-'to-zo*
(to) be hungry	avere* fame	*a-'ve-re 'fa-me*
(to) be thirsty	avere* sete	*a-'ve-re 'se-te*
cheap	a buon mercato	*a bwon mer-'ka-to*
	economico	*e-ko-'no-mi-ko*
(to) cost	costare (ess)	*kos-'ta-re*
(to) drink	bere*	*'be-re*
(to) eat	mangiare	*man-'ja-re*
expensive	caro	—
(to) order	ordinare	*or-di-'na-re*
recipe	ricetta	*ri-'čet-ta*
(to) serve	servire	*ser-'vi-re*
(to) shop for food	fare* la spesa	*'fa-re la 'spe-za*
slice	fetta	*'fet-ta*
• **(to) slice**	affettare	*af-fet-'ta-re*
(to) take out	portare via	*por-ta-re 'vi-a*
(to) toast	brindare	*brin-'da-re*

25. *SHOPPING*

A. GENERAL VOCABULARY

antique shop	negozio dell'antiquariato	*ne-'go-tsyo del'lan-ti-kwa-'rya-to*
bag	sacco	*'sak-ko*
	sacchetto	*sak-'ket-to*
bar code	codice (m) a barre	*'ko-di-če a 'bar-re*
bar-code reader	lettore elettronico	*let-'to-re e-let-'tro-ni-ko*
bill	fattura	*fat-'tu-ra*
brand	marca	*'mar-ka*
	marchio	*'mar-kyo*
(to) bring	portare	*por-'ta-re*
(to) buy	comprare	*kom-'pra-re*

cash register	cassa	'kas-sa
• cashier	cassiere (-a)	kas-'sye-re
change (money)	resto	—
closing (time)	chiusura	kyu-'zu-ra
competition	concorrenza	kon-kor-'ren-tsa
(to) cost	costare (ess)	kos-'ta-re
• costly, expensive	costoso	kos-'to-zo
• How much does it cost?	Quanto costa?	'kwan-to 'kos-ta
• How much does it come to?	Quanto viene?	'kwan-to 'vye-ne
• How much is it?	Quanto è?	—
counter	banco	'ban-ko
customer	cliente (m/f)	kli-'en-te
• clientele	clientela	kli-en-'te-la
delivery	consegna	kon-'se-nya
• home delivery	consegna a domicilio	kon-'se-nya a do-mi-'či-lyo
department	reparto	re-'par-to
department store	grande magazzino	ma-ga-'dzi-no
display, exhibition	mostra	—
entrance	entrata	en-'tra-ta
(to) exchange	cambiare	kam-'bya-re
exit	uscita	u-'ši-ta
flea market	mercato delle pulci	mer-'ka-to
gift	regalo	re-'ga-lo
kiosk, booth	chiosco	'kyos-ko
label, price tag	etichetta	e-ti-'ket-ta
(to) lack	mancare (ess)	man-'ka-re
merchandise	merce (f)	'mer-če
newsstand	edicola	e-'di-ko-la
opening (times)	apertura	a-per-'tu-ra
(to) pack	imballare	im-bal-'la-re
package	pacco	'pak-ko
• small package	pacchetto	pak-'ket-to
(to) pay	pagare	pa-'ga-re
	carta bancaria	'kar-ta ban-'ka-rya
• cash	in contanti	kon-'tan-ti
• check	assegno	as-'se-nyo
• credit card	carta di credito	'kre-di-to
price	prezzo	'pre-tso
• discount	sconto	'skon-to
• expensive	caro	—
• fixed price	prezzo fisso	'pre-tso 'fis-so
• inexpensive	a buon mercato	a bwon mer-'ka-to
	economico	e-ko-'no-mi-ko
• price list	tariffa dei prezzi	ta-rif-fa dei 'pre-tsi
• price tag	etichetta	e-ti-'ket-ta

• **reduced price**	prezzo ridotto	*'pre-tso ri-dot-to*
product	prodotto	*pro-'dot-to*
• **range of products**	gamma di prodotti	*'gam-ma di pro-'dot-ti*
purchase	acquisto	*ak-'kwis-to*
queue, lineup	fila	—
	coda	—
receipt	scontrino	*skon-'tri-no*
refund	rimborso	*rim-'bor-so*
retail	al dettaglio	*al det-'ta-lyo*
• **retail price**	prezzo al dettaglio	*'pre-tso al det-'ta-lyo*
(to) return, bring back	restituire (isc)	*res-ti-tu-'i-re*
sale	saldo	—
• **for sale**	in vendita	*in 'ven-di-ta*
• **on (liquidation) sale**	in svendita	*in 'zven-di-ta*
• **on sale**	in saldo	*in 'sal-do*
• **(to) sell**	vendere	*'ven-de-re*
sample	campione (m)	*kam-'pyo-ne*
shop	negozio	*ne'-go-tsyo*
• **(to) shop**	fare* delle compere	*'fa-re del-le 'kom-pe-re*
• **shop window**	vetrina	*ve-'tri-na*
• **shopkeeper**	negoziante (m/f)	*ne-go-'tsyan-te*
store	negozio	*ne'-go-tsyo*
• **closed**	chiuso	*'kyu-zo*
• **closing time**	chiusura	*kyu-'zu-ra*
• **open**	aperto	*a-'per-to*
• **opening time**	apertura	*a-per-'tu-ra*
• **store chain**	catena di negozi	*ka-'te-na di ne-'go-tsyi*
• **store clerk**	commesso (-a)	*kom-'mes-so*
• **store window**	vetrina	*ve-'tri-na*
• **times (a store is open)**	orario	*o-'ra-ryo*
(to) take	prendere*	*'pren-de-re*
warehouse	magazzino	*ma-ga-'dzi-no*
wholesale	all'ingrosso	*al-lin-'gros-so*
• **wholesale price**	prezzo all'ingrosso	*'pre-tso*
(to) wrap	incartare	*in-kar-'ta-re*

Idiomatic Expression

It costs an arm and a leg! = Costa un occhio della testa!

B. HARDWARE

battery	pila	—
	batteria	bat-te-'ri-a
bolt	bullone (m)	bul-'lo-ne
chisel	cesello	če-'zel-lo
clamp	morsetto	mor-'set-to
drill	trapano	'tra-pa-no
electric outlet	presa (elettrica)	'pre-za
file	lima	—
flashlight	pila	—
fuse	valvola	'val-vo-la
hammer	martello	mar-'tel-lo
hardware	ferramenta (f, pl)	fer-ra-'men-ta
hardware store	negozio di ferramenta	ne-'go-tsyo fer-ra-'men-ta
insulation	isolante (m)	i-zo-'lan-te
light bulb	lampadina	lam-pa-'di-na
• fluorescent	fluorescente	flwuor-eš-'en-te
• neon	al neon	—
mallet	mazza	'ma-tsa
masking tape	nastro isolante	'nas-tro i-zo-'lan-te
nail	chiodo	'kyo-do
paint	vernice (f)	ver-'ni-če
plane	pialla	'pyal-la
pliers, tongs, tweezers	pinze (f, pl)	'pin-tse
	tenaglie (f, pl)	te-'na-lye
plug	spina	—
punch	punzone (m)	pun-'tso-ne
roller	rullo	—
sandpaper	carta vetrata	'kar-ta ve-'tra-ta
saw	sega	'se-ga
screw	vite (f)	'vi-te
screwdriver	cacciavite (m, inv)	kač-ča-'vi-te
shovel	pala	—
tool	attrezzo	at-'tre-tso
transformer	trasformatore (m)	tras-for-ma-'to-re
wallpaper	carta da parati	'kar-ta da pa-'ra-ti
wire	filo	—
wrench	chiave (f) inglese	'kya-ve in-'gle-ze

C. STATIONERY, COMPUTER, AND OFFICE SUPPLIES

adhesive tape	nastro adesivo	'nas-tro a-de-'zi-vo
ballpoint pen	penna a sfera, biro (f, inv)	—
briefcase	cartella	kar-'tel-la
business card	biglietto da visita	bi-'lyet-to da 'vi-zi-ta
calculator	calcolatrice (f)	kal-ko-la-'tri-če

calendar	calendario	*ka-len-'da-ryo*
cartridge	cartuccia	*kar-'tuč-ča*
CD-ROM	CD-ROM (m, inv)	—
color monitor	monitor, schermo a colori	*'sker-mo*
compatible software	software compatibile	*kom-pa-'ti-bi-le*
computer	computer (m, inv)	—
copy shop	copisteria	*ko-pis-te-'ri-a*
diskette	dischetto	*dis-'ket-to*
envelope	busta	—
eraser	gomma	—
file folder	cartella	*kar-'tel-la*
filing card, filing folder	scheda	*'ske-da*
glue	colla	*'kol-la*
highlighter	evidenziatore (m)	*e-vi-den-tsya-'to-re*
ink	inchiostro	*in-'kyos-tro*
ink-jet printer	stampante a getto d'inchiostro	*stam-'pan-te a 'jet-to din-'kyos-tro*
keyboard	tastiera	*tas-'tye-ra*
label	etichetta	*e-ti-'ket-ta*
laptop computer	computer portatile laptop (m, inv)	*por-'ta-ti-le* —
laser printer	stampante laser	*stam-'pan-te*
letterhead	carta intestata	*'karta in-tes-'ta-ta*
Liquid Paper, White-out	bianchetto	*byan-'ket-to*
marker	penrarello	*pen-na-'rel-lo*
modem	modem (m, inv)	—
mouse	mouse (m, inv)	—
notice board	tabella	*ta-'bel-la*
office supplies	forniture (f, inv) per ufficio	*for-ni-'tu-re per uf-'fi-čo*
pad	taccuino	*tak-'kwi-no*
paper	carta	—
pen	penna	—
pencil, crayon	matita	*ma-'ti-ta*
photocopying machine,	fotocopiatrice (f)	*fo-to-ko-pya-'tri-če*
planner	agenda	*a-'jen-da*
printer	stampante (f)	*stam-'pan-te*
punch	perforatrice (f)	*per-fo-ra-'tri-če*
ream of paper	risma di carta	*'riz-ma*
ring-binder	quaderno ad anelli	*kwa-'der-no ad a-'nel-li*
rubber band	elastico	*e-'las-ti-ko*
ruler	riga	—
scanner	scanner (m, inv)	—
scissors	forbici	*'for-bi-či*
sheet (of paper)	foglio	*'fo-lyo*
staple	punto metallico	*'pun-to me-'tal-li-ko*
stapler	cucitrice (f)	*ku-či-'tri-če*

stationery store	cartoleria	*kar-to-le-'ri-a*
string	spago	*'spa-go*
tack	puntina	*pun-'ti-na*
toner	toner (m, inv)	—
wrapping paper	carta da pacchi	*'pak-ki*
writing pad	blocco	*'blok-'ko*
• small writing pad	blocchetto	*blok-'ket-to*

D. PHOTOGRAPHY/CAMERAS

camera	macchina fotografica	*'mak-ki-na fo-to-'gra-fi-ka*
• video, movie camera	cinepresa	*či-ne-'pre-za*
• digital camera	macchina fotografica digitale	*di-ji-'ta-le*
dark room	camera oscura	*'ka-me-ra os-'ku-ra*
digital photography, digital photograph	fotografia digitale	*fo-to-gra-'fi-a di-ji-'ta-le*
film	pellicola	*pel-'li-ko-la*
focus	fuoco	*'fwo-ko*
• (to) focus	mettere* a fuoco	*'met-te-re a 'fwo-ko*
image	immagine (f)	*im-'ma-ji-ne*
lens	lente (f)	*'len-te*
negative	negativo	*ne-ga-'ti-vo*
objective lens	obiettivo	*o'byet-'ti-vo*
photograph	foto (m, inv)	—
	fotografia	*fo-to-gra-'fi-a*
photographer	fotografo (-a)	*fo-'to-gra-fo*
photographic shot	ripresa fotografica	*ri-'pre-za fo-to-'gra-fi-ka*
photo-sensitive	fotosensibile	*fo-to-sen-'si-bi-le*
push button (on a camera)	scatto	*'skat-to*
roll of film	rullino	*rul-'li-no*
slide	diapositiva	*di-a-po-zi-'ti-va*
tripod	treppiede (m, inv)	*trep-'pye-de*
unfocussed	sfocato	*sfo-'ka-to*
video disc	videodisco	*vi-de-o-'dis-ko*
viewer (of a camera), scope	mirino	*mi-'ri-no*
zoom	zoom (m, inv)	—

E. TOBACCO

cigar	sigaro	*'si-ga-ro*
cigarette	sigaretta	*si-ga-'ret-ta*
lighter	accendino	*ač-čen-'di-no*
match	fiammifero	*fyam-'mi-fe-ro*
pipe	pipa	—
(to) smoke	fumare	*fu-'ma-re*

tobacco	tabacco	ta-'bak-ko
tobacconist	tabaccaio	ta-bak-'ka-yo

F. COSMETICS/TOILETRIES

anti-wrinkle cream	crema antirughe	'kre-ma an-ti-'ru-ge
bath oil	olio da bagno	'o-lyo da 'ba-nyo
bath salts	sali da bagno	'sa-li da 'ba-nyo
blade	lametta da barba	la-'met-ta da 'bar-ba
brush	spazzola	'spa-tso-la
cologne	acqua di Colonia	'ak-kwa di ko-'lo-nya
comb	pettine (m)	'pet-ti-ne
cosmetic	cosmetico	koz-'me-ti-ko
cosmetic, perfume shop	profumeria	pro-fu-me-'ri-a
cream, lotion	crema	'kre-ma
curler	bigodino	bi-go-'di-no
deodorant	deodorante (m)	de-o-do-'ran-te
electric razor	rasoio elettrico	ra-'zo-yo e-'let-tri-ko
eyeliner	matita per gli occhi	ma-'ti-ta per lyi 'ok-ki
eye shadow	mascara (m, inv)	mas-'ka-ra
face powder	cipria	'či-prya
facial cream	crema per il viso	'kre-ma per il 'vi-zo
hair cream	brillantina	bril-lan-'ti-na
hairdryer	asciugacapelli (m, inv)	a-šu-ga-ka-'pel-li
hairnet	retina	re-'ti-na
hair remover	crema depilatoria	'kre-ma de-pi-la-'to-ria
hair-dye	tinta	'tin-ta
hairpin	fermaglio	fer-'ma-lyo
hairspray	lacca (per capelli)	'lak-ka
hand cream	crema per le mani	'kre-ma per le 'ma-ni
lipstick	rossetto	ros-'set-to
lotion	lozione (f)	lo-'tsyo-ne
makeup	trucco	'truk-ko
manicure	manicure (f)	ma-ni-'ku-re
mascara	mascara (m, inv)	mas-'ka-ra
moisturizer	crema idratante	'kre-ma i-dra-'tan-te
nail file	lima per unghie	'li-ma per 'un-gye
nail polish	smalto	'zmal-to
perfume	profumo	pro-'fu-mo
razor	rasoio	ra-'zo-yo
shampoo	shampoo (m, inv)	—
shaving cream	crema da barba	'kre-ma da 'bar-ba
soap	sapone (m)	sa-'po-ne
talc, talcum powder	talco	'tal-ko
toiletries	articoli da toilette	ar-'ti-ko-li
tweezers	pinzette (f, pl)	pin-'tset-te
wig, hair piece	parrucca	par-'ruk-ka

G. LAUNDRY

buckle	fibbia	*'fib-bya*
button	bottone (m)	*bot-'to-ne*
clean	pulito	*pu-'li-to*
clothes	abiti (m, pl)	*'a-bi-ti*
clothes basket	cestino del bucato	*čes-'ti-no del bu-'ka-to*
clothespin	molletta	*mol-'let-ta*
collar	colletto	*kol-'let-to*
delicate, soft	delicato	*de-li-'ka-to*
detergent	detergente	*de-ter-'jen-te*
dirty	sporco	*'spor-ko*
dry cleaner	lavanderia a secco	*la-van-de-'ri-a a 'sek-ko*
fabric	tessuto	*tes-'su-to*
fiber	fibra	*'fi-bra*
flannel	flanella	*fla-'nel-la*
fly, zipper	cerniera	*čer-'nye-ra*
heavy	pesante	*pe-'zan-te*
hole	buco	*'bu-ko*
iron	ferro da stiro	*'fer-ro da 'sti-ro*
• (to) iron	stirare	*sti-'ra-re*
• ironed	stirato	*sti-'ra-to*
lace	pizzo	*'pit-tso*
laundry	lavanderia	*la-van-de-'ri-a*
• launderette	lavanderia automatica	*la-van-de-'ri-a au-to-'ma-ti-ka*
light	leggero	*lej-'je-ro*
linen	lino	—
long	lungo	—
loose-fitting	largo	—
material	stoffa	—
(to) mend	rammendare	*ram-men-'da-re*
nylon	nailon (m, inv)	—
pair	paio (paia, f, pl))	*'pa-yo*
pocket	tasca	*'tas-ka*
polyester	poliestere (m)	*po-li-'es-te-re*
rag	cencio	*'čen-čo*
rough	rozzo	*'rot-tso*
(to) sew	cucire	*ku-'či-re*
short	corto	*'kor-to*
size (of clothes)	taglia	*'ta-lya*
sleeve	manica	*'ma-ni-ka*
small	piccolo	*'pik-ko-lo*
smooth	liscio	*'li-šo*
soap powder	sapone (m) in polvere	*sa-'po-ne*
sporty	sportivo	*spor-'ti-vo*
spot, stain	macchia	*'mak-kya*
starch	amido	*'a-mi-do*

stitch	punto	—
striped	a righe	*a 'ri-ge*
tight	stretto	*'stret-to*
tight-fitting	aderente	*a-de-'ren-te*
transparent	trasparente	*tras-pa-'ren-te*
(to) wash	lavare	*la-'va-re*
• washable	lavabile	*la-'va-bi-le*
woolen	lana	—

H. PHARMACY/DRUGSTORE

adhesive bandage	cerotto	*če-'rot-to*
antibiotic	antibiotico	*an-ti-bi-'o-ti-ko*
aspirin	aspirina	*as-pi-'ri-na*
barbiturate	barbiturico	*bar-bi-'tu-ri-ko*
condom	preservativo	*pre-ser-va-'ti-vo*
contraceptive	contracettivo	*kon-trač-čet-'ti-vo*
• contraceptive pill	pillola anticoncezionale	*'pil-lo-la an-ti-kon-če-tsyo-'na-le*
cortisone	cortisone (m)	*kor-ti-'zo-ne*
cough syrup	sciroppo contro la tosse	*ši-'rop-po 'kon-tro la 'tos-se*
covering, bandage	benda	*'ben-da*
cream	crema	*'kre-ma*
crutch	stampella	*stam-'pel-la*
dosage	posologia	*po-zo-lo-'ji-a*
dressing	fascia	*'fa-ša*
drop	goccia	*'goč-ča*
expectorant	espettorante (m)	*es-pet-to-'ran-te*
eyedrop	collirio	*kol-'li-ryo*
first aid	pronto soccorso	*'pron-to sok-'kor-so*
injection, needle	iniezione (f)	*i-nye-'tsyo-ne*
	puntura	*pun-'tu-ra*
insulin	insulina	*in-su-'li-na*
laxative	purga	*'pur-ga*
magnesium citrate	citrato di magnesio	*či-'tra-to*
medicine	medicina	*me-di-'či-na*
ointment	pomata	*po-'ma-ta*
painkiller	analgesico	*a-nal-'je-zi-ko*
palliative	palliativo	*pal-lya-'ti-vo*
pastille	pasticca	*pas-'tik-ka*
penicillin	penicillina	*pe-ni-čil-'li-na*
pharmaceutical	farmaco	*'far-ma-ko*
pharmacist	farmacista (m/f)	*far-ma-'čis-ta*
• pharmacy, drugstore	farmacia	*far-ma-'či-a*
phial	fiala	*'fya-la*
pill	pillola	*'pil-lo-la*
prescription	ricetta medica	*ri-čet-ta 'me-di-ka*

rubber gloves	guanti di gomma	'gwan-ti di 'gom-ma
sedative	sedativo	se-da-'ti-vo
sleeping pill	sonnifero	son-'ni-fe-ro
sling	bendaggio	ben-'daj-jo
sodium bicarbonate	bicarbonato di sodio	bi-kar-bo-'na-to di 'so-dyo
sodium citrate	citrato di sodio	či-'tra-to
suppository	supposta	sup-'pos-ta
tablet	compressa	kom-'pres-sa
thermometer	termometro	ter-'mo-me-tro
tincture of iodine	tintura di iodio	tin-'tu-ra di 'yo-dyo
tonic	tonico	'to-ni-ko
tranquilizer	calmante (m)	kal-'man-te
vitamin	vitamina	vi-ta-'mi-na

I. JEWELRY

alarm clock	sveglia	'zve-lya
artificial	artificiale	ar-ti-fi-'ča-le
bracelet	braccialetto	brač-ča-'let-to
brooch	spilla	'spil-la
carat	carato	ka-'ra-to
chain	catena	ka-'te-na
coral	corallo	ko-'ral-lo
diamond	diamante (m)	dya-'man-te
earring	orecchino	o-rek-'ki-no
emerald	smeraldo	zme-'ral-do
engagement ring	anello di fidanzamento	a-'nel-lo di fi-dan-dza-'men-to
false	falso	—
(to) fix, repair	riparare	ri-pa-'ra-re
gemstone	brillante (m)	bril-'lan-te
gold	oro	—
gold ring	anello d'oro	—
jewel	gioiello	jo-'yel-lo
jewelry store, jeweler	gioielleria	jo-yel-le-'ri-a
locket, medal	medaglia	me-'da-lya
necklace	collana	kol-'la-na
nuptial, wedding ring	fede (f)	'fe-de
opal	opale (m)	o-'pa-le
pearl	perla	—
pendant	pendente	pen-'den-te
precious	prezioso	pre-'tsyo-zo
ring	anello	a-'nel-lo
ruby	rubino	ru-'bi-no
sapphire	zaffiro	dzaf-'fi-ro
silver	argento	ar-'jen-to
silver ring	anello d'argento	a-'nel-lo dar-'jen-to

topaz	topazio	*to-'pa-tsyo*
watch	orologio	*o-ro-'lo-jo*
• band	cinghietta	*čin-'gyet-ta*
• dial	quadrante (m)	*kwa-'dran-te*
• hand	lancetta	*lan-'čet-ta*
• men's watch	orologio da uomo	*'wo-mo*
• quartz watch	orologio al quarzo	*'kwar-tso*
• spring	molla	*'mol-la*
• watchmaker	orologiaio	*o-ro-lo-'ja-yo*
• wind	caricare	*ka-ri-'ka-re*
• women's watch	orologio da donna	*'don-na*
• wristwatch	orologio da polso	*'pol-so*
wedding-ring	fede (f)	*'fe-de*

J. MUSIC AND VIDEO

band	gruppo	*'grup-po*
	complesso	*kom-'ples-so*
blues	blues (m, inv)	—
chamber music	musica da camera	*'mu-zi-ka da 'ka-me-ra*
classical music	musica classica	*'mu-zi-ka 'klas-si-ka*
compact disc	compact disc (m, inv)	—
composer	compositore (-trice)	*kom-po-zi-'to-re*
• composition	composizione (f)	*kom-po-zi-'tsyo-ne*
concert, concerto	concerto	*kon-'čer-to*
conservatory	conservatorio	*kon-ser-va-'to-ryo*
dance music	musica da ballo	*'mu-zi-ka da 'bal-lo*
DVD	DVD (m, inv)	—
folk music	musica folk	*'mu-zi-ka*
folklorist music	musica folcloristica	*'mu-zi-ka fol-klo-'ris-ti-ka*
instrument	strumento	*stru-'men-to*
jazz	jazz (m, inv)	—
light music	musica leggera	*'mu-zi-ka lej-'je-ra*
melody	melodia	*me-lo-'di-a*
music	musica	*'mu-zi-ka*
music stand	portamusica (m, inv)	*por-ta-'mu-zi-ka*
musician	musicista (m/f)	*mu-zi-'čis-ta*
note	nota	—
opera	opera	—
orchestra	orchestra	*or-'kes-tra*
orchestra conductor	direttore (-trice) (d'orchestra)	*di-ret-'to-re*
performer	interprete (m/f)	*in-'ter-pre-te*
player, musician	suonatore (-trice)	*swo-na-'to-re*
rap	rap (m, inv)	—
rhythm	ritmo	—
rock music	musica rock	*'mu-zi-ka*
score	spartito	*spar-'ti-to*

singer	cantante (m/f)	*kan-'tan-te*
song	canzone (f)	*kan-'tso-ne*
symphony	sinfonia	*sin-fo-'ni-a*
tape (cassette)	(audio)cassetta	*kas-'set-ta*
tone	tono	—
tune, aria	aria	—
video camera	videocamera	*vi-de-o-'ka-me-ra*
video recorder	videoregistratore (m)	*vi-de-o-re-jis-tra-'to-re*
videocassette	videocassetta	*vi-de-o-kas-'set-ta*

K. CLOTHING AND APPAREL

apron	grembiule (m)	*grem-'byu-le*
bathrobe	accappatoio	*ak-kap-pa-'to-yo*
blouse	camicetta	*ka-mi-'čet-ta*
bra	reggiseno	*rej-ji-'se-no*
cap	berretto	*ber-'ret-to*
clothes (in general)	abbigliamento	*ab-bi-'lya-'men-to*
• clothing store	negozio di abbigliamento	*ne-'go-tsyo*
• men's clothing store	abbigliamento maschile	*mas-'ki-le*
• women's clothing store	abbigliamento femminile	*fem-mi-'ni-le*
coat	cappotto	*kap-'pot-to*
• fur coat	pelliccia	*pel-'lič-ča*
dress, clothing, suit	vestito	*ves-'ti-to*
	abito	*'a-bi-to*
dressing room	cabina	*ka-'bi-na*
evening attire	abito, vestito da sera	*'a-bi-to ves-'ti-to*
fashion	moda	—
garment	indumento	*in-du-'men-to*
glove	guanto	*'gwan-to*
handkerchief	fazzoletto	*fat-tso-'let-to*
hat	cappello	*kap-'pel-lo*
• felt hat	cappello di feltro	*'fel-tro*
• hood	cappuccio	*kap-'puč-čo*
• straw hat	cappello di paglia	*'pa-lya*
jacket	giacca	*'jak-ka*
• dinner jacket	smoking (m, inv)	—
• double-breasted jacket	giacca a doppio petto	*'jak-ka a 'dop-pyo 'pet-to*
• single-breasted jacket	giacca a un petto	—
• sports jacket	giacca sportiva	*spor-'ti-va*
knickers	calzoni (m, pl)	*kal-'tso-ni*
lingerie, underclothing	biancheria (intima)	*byan-ke-'ri-a*
nightdress	camicia da notte	*ka-'mi-ča da -'not-te*
overcoat	soprabito	*so-'pra-bi-to*
pajamas	pigiama (m)	*pi-'ja-ma*
pants	pantaloni (m, pl)	*pan-to-'lo-ni*

• ski pants	pantaloni da sci	ši
pantyhose, tights	collant (m, inv)	kol-'lant
raincoat	impermeabile (m)	im-per-me-'a-bi-le
shawl	mantello	man-'tel-lo
shirt	camicia	ka-'mi-ča
shorts	pantaloncini (m, pl)	pan-ta-lon-'či-ni
skirt	gonna	—
• pleated skirt	gonna a pieghe	'pye-ge
suit	vestito	ves-'ti-to
	abito	'a-bi-to
• men's suit	abito, vestito da uomo	'wo·mo
• suit (complete), set	completo	kom'-ple-to
• women's suit	abito, vestito da donna	—
sweater	maglia	'ma-lya
	maglione (m)	ma-lyo-ne
swimming cap	cuffia da bagno	'kuf-fya
swimming suit	costume (m) da bagno	kos-'tu-me da 'ba-nyo
• two-piece suit	costume (m) a due pezzi	'pe-tsi
• swimming trunks	pantaloncini (m, pl) da bagno	pan-ta-lon-'či-ni da 'ba-nyo
tailor	sarto (-a)	—
T-shirt	T-shirt (f)	
tie	cravatta	kra-'vat-ta
• bow tie	farfalla	far-'fal-la
underpants, underwear	mutande (f, pl)	mu-'tan-de
undershirt	canottiera	ka-not-'tye-ra
underskirt	sottoveste (f)	sot-to-'ves-te
vest	gilè (m, inv)	ji-'le
wedding dress	abito, vestito da sposa	'a-bi-to ves-'ti-to da 'spo-za
wedding suit (men)	abito, vestito da sposo	'a-bi-to ves-'ti-to da 'spo-zo
wind-breaker	giacca a vento	'jak-ka a 'ven-to
women's suit	tailleur (m, inv)	—

L. DESCRIBING CLOTHING AND RELATED VOCABULARY

beautiful	bello	'bel-lo
big	grande	'gran-de
buckle	fibbia	'fib-bya
button	bottone (m)	bot-'to-ne
checkered	a scacchi	'skak-ki
collar	colletto	kol-'let-to
cotton	cotone	ko-'to-ne
cuff-links	gemelli (m, pl)	je-'mel-li
delicate, soft	delicato	de-li-'ka-to
dirty	sporco	'spor-ko
(to) dress, get dressed	vestirsi	ves-'tir-si

elegant	elegante	*e-le-'gan-te*
(to) enlarge	allargare	*al-lar-'ga-re*
evening	da sera	—
fabric	tessuto	*tes-'su-to*
fiber	fibra	*'fi-bra*
heavy	pesante	*pe-'zan-te*
hole	buco	*'bu-ko*
in style	di moda	—
It looks bad on you.	Ti sta male.	—
It looks good on you.	Ti sta bene.	—
lace	pizzo	*'pi-tso*
(to) lengthen	allungare	*al-lun-'ga-re*
light	leggero	*lej-'je-ro*
linen	lino	—
long	lungo	—
loose-fitting	largo	*'lar-go*
made-to-measure suit	abito, vestito su misura	*'a-bi-to ves-'ti-to su mi-'zu-ra*
material	stoffa	—
nylon	nailon	—
(to) put on (clothes)	mettersi*	*'met-ter-si*
rag	cencio	*'čen-čo*
(to) sew	cucire	*ku-'či-re*
short	corto	*'kor-to*
(to) shorten	accorciare	*ak-kor-'ča-re*
sleeve	manica	*'ma-ni-ka*
small	piccolo	*'pik-ko-lo*
smooth	liscio	*'li-šo*
sporty	sportivo	*spor-'ti-vo*
spot	macchia	*'mak-kya*
stitch	punto	—
string	filo	—
striped	a righe	*'ri-ge*
(to) take off (clothes)	spogliarsi	*spo-'lyar-si*
tight	stretto	*'stret-to*
(to) tighten	stringere*	*'strin-je-re*
tight-fitting	aderente	*a-de-'ren-te*
(to) try on	provarsi	*pro-'var-si*
	provare	*pro-'va-re*
ugly	brutto	*'brut-to*
(to) undress	spogliarsi	*spo-'lyar-si*
(to) wear	indossare	*in-dos-'sa-re*
woolen	di lana	—

M. FOOTWEAR

boot	stivale (m)	*sti-'va-le*
footwear	calzatura	*kal-tsa-'tu-ra*

gym shoes	scarpe (f, pl) da ginnastica	*'skar-pe da jin-'nas-ti-ka*
heel	tacco	*'tak-ko*
• flat-heeled	con tacco piatto	*'pyat-to*
• high-heeled	con tacco alto	—
• low-heeled	con tacco basso	—
leather shoes	scarpe (f, pl) di cuoio	*'kwo-yo*
men's shoes	scarpe (f, pl) da uomo	*'wo-mo*
(to) put on (shoes)	mettersi* (le scarpe)	*'met-ter-si*
sandal	sandalo	*'san-da-lo*
shoe	scarpa	*'skar-pa*
shoe horn	calzascarpe (m, inv)	*kal-tsa-'skar-pe*
shoe repair (shop)	calzolaio	*kal-tso-'la-yo*
shoe size	numero (di scarpa)	*'nu-me-ro*
shoe store	negozio di scarpe	*ne'go-tsyo di 'skar-pe*
shoelace	stringa	*'strin-ga*
slipper	pantofola	*pan-'to-fo-la*
sock	calzino	*kal-'tsi-no*
sole	suola	*'swo-la*
stocking	calza	*'kal-tsa*
suede shoes	scarpe (f, pl) di camoscio	*ka-'mo-šo*
(to) take off (shoes)	togliersi* (le scarpe)	*'to-lyer-si*
tennis shoes	scarpe (f, pl) da tennis	—
women's shoes	scarpe (f, pl) da donna	—

N. BOOKS, MAGAZINES, AND NEWSPAPERS

anthology	antologia	*an-to-lo-'ji-a*
appendix	appendice (f)	*ap-pen-'di-če*
atlas	atlante (m)	*at-'lan-te*
author	autore (-trice)	*au-'to-re*
autobiography	autobiografia	*au-to-bi-o-gra-'fi-a*
biography	biografia	*bi-o-gra-'fi-a*
book	libro	—
bookstore	libreria	*li-bre-'ri-a*
catalogue	catalogo	*ka-'ta-lo-go*
chapter	capitolo	*ka-'pi-to-lo*
character	personaggio	*per-so-'naj-jo*
collection	raccolta	*rak-'kol-ta*
comedy	commedia	*kom-'me-dya*
comic book	rivista a fumetti	*ri-'vis-ta a fu-'met-ti*
cover, dust jacket	copertina	*ko-per-'ti-na*
criticism	critica	*'kri-ti-ka*
crosswords	parole crociate	*pa-'ro-le kro-'ča-te*
daily newspaper	quotidiano	*kwo-ti-'dya-no*
diary	diario	*di-'a-ryo*
dictionary	dizionario	*di-tsyo-'na-ryo*

dissertation	dissertazione (f)	*dis-ser-ta-'tsyo-ne*
drama	dramma (m)	—
	(drammi, pl)	
encyclopedia	enciclopedia	*en-či-klo-pe-'di-a*
episode	episodio	*e-pi-'so-dyo*
essay	saggio	*'saj-jo*
fable	favola	*'fa-vo-la*
fairy tale	fiaba	*'fya-ba*
fashion magazine	rivista di moda	*ri-'vis-ta*
fiction, narrative	narrativa	*nar-ra-'ti-va*
genre	genere (m)	*'je-ne-re*
guidebook	guida	*'gwi-da*
illustrated magazine	rivista illustrata	*ri-'vis-ta il-lus-'tra-ta*
index	indice (m)	*'in-di-če*
interview	intervista	*in-ter-'vis-ta*
kids magazine	giornalino	*jor-na-'li-no*
(to) leaf through	sfogliare	*sfo-'lya-re*
legend	leggenda	*lej-'jen-da*
library	biblioteca	*bib-lyo-'te-ka*
line, verse	verso	—
literacy	alfabetismo	*al-fa-be-'tiz-mo*
• illiteracy	analfabetismo	*an-al-fa-be-'tiz-mo*
• illiterate person	analfabeta (m/f)	*an-al-fa-'be-ta*
literature	letteratura	*let-te-ra-'tu-ra*
magazine	rivista	*ri-'vis-ta*
memoirs	memorie (f, pl)	*me-'mo-rye*
mystery, detective, spy work	giallo	*'jal-lo*
myth	mito	—
• mythology	mitologia	*mi-to-lo-'ji-a*
narrative	narrativa	*nar-ra-'ti-va*
narrator	narratore (-trice)	*nar-ra-'to-re*
newspaper	giornale (m)	*jor-'na-le*
novel	romanzo	*ro-'man-dzo*
• novelist	romanziere (-a)	*ro-man-'dzye-re*
• novelistic	romanzesco	*ro-man-'dzes-ko*
ode	ode (f)	*'o-de*
parody	parodia	*pa-ro-'di-a*
periodical	periodico	*pe-ri-'o-di-ko*
photo-romance	fotoromanzo	*fo-to-ro-'man-dzo*
play	rappresentazione (f)	*rap-pre-zen-ta-'tsyo-ne*
	teatrale	*te-a-'tra-le*
• playwright	commediografo (-a)	*kom-me-'dyo-gra-fo*
plot	trama	*'tra-ma*
poetry	poesia	*po-e-'zi-a*
• poet	poeta (-essa)	*po-'e-ta*
• poetics	poetica	*po-'e-ti-ka*
• poem	poesia	*po-e-'zi-a*

pornographic magazine	rivista pornografica	*ri-'vis-ta por-no-'gra-fi-ka*
preface	prefazione (f)	*pre-fa-'tsyo-ne*
press	stampa	*'stam-pa*
prose	prosa	*'pro-za*
(to) publish	pubblicare	*pub-bli-'ka-re*
publisher	editore (m)	*e-di-'to-re*
puzzle section	enigmistica	*e-nig-'mis-ti-ka*
(to) read	leggere*	*'lej-je-re*
• **reader**	lettore (-trice)	*let-'to-re*
• **reading**	lettura	*let-'tu-ra*
recipe book	libro di ricette	*ri-'čet-te*
reference book	libro di consultazione	*kon-sul-ta-'tsyo-ne*
satire	satira	*'sa-ti-ra*
scene	scena	*'še-na*
science fiction	fantascienza	*fan-ta-'šen-tsa*
short story	novella	*no-'vel-la*
sonnet	sonetto	*so-'net-to*
stanza	strofa	*'stro-fa*
style	stile (m)	*'sti-le*
• **stylistics**	stilistica	*sti-'lis-ti-ka*
table of contents	indice (m) delle materie	*'in-di-če del-le ma-'te-rye*
tale	racconto	*rak-'kon-to*
teen magazine	rivista per adolescenti	*ri-'vis-ta*
text	testo	—
textbook	libro di testo	—
theme	tema (m) (temi, pl)	—
thriller	thriller (m inv)	—
title (of a book)	titolo	*'ti-to-lo*
treatise	trattato	*trat-'ta-to*
volume	volume (m)	*vo-'lu-me*
women's magazine	rivista femminile	*ri-'vis-ta fem-mi-'ni-le*
writer	scrittore (-trice)	*skrit-'to-re*
writing	scrittura	*skrit-'tu-ra*

26. BANKING AND COMMERCE

A. BANKING, FINANCES, AND INSURANCE

account	conto bancario	*'kon-to ban-'ka-ryo*
• **(to) close an account**	chiudere* un conto	*'kyu-de-re*
• **current account**	conto corrente	*kor-'ren-te*
• **(to) open an account**	aprire* un conto	*a-'pri-re*
annuity	rendita	*'ren-di-ta*
automated banking machine	bancomat (m, inv)	—
bank	banca	*'ban-ka*

• branch	filiale (f) di una banca	fi-'lya-le di u-na 'ban-ka
• head office	sede (f) centrale	'se-de čen-'tra-le
• (to) work in a bank	lavorare in banca	la-vo-'ra-re in 'ban-ka
bank book	libretto bancario	li-'bret-to ban-'ka-ryo
bank clerk	impiegato (-a) di banca	im-pye-'ga-to 'ban-ka
bank code	codice (m) bancario	'ko-di-če ban-'ka-ryo
bank money order	vaglia (m, inv) bancario	'va-lya ban-'ka-ryo
bank receipt	ricevuta	ri-če-'vu-ta
bank worker	bancario (-a)	ban-'ka-ryo
banking executive	banchiere (-a)	ban-'kye-re
bill, banknote	banconota	ban-ko-'no-ta
	biglietto di banca	bi-'lyet-to
• large bill	banconota di grosso taglio	ban-ko-'no-ta di 'gros-so 'ta-lyo
• small bill	banconota di piccolo taglio	ban-ko-'no-ta di 'pik-ko-lo 'ta-lyo
blank endorsement	girata in bianco	ji-'ra-ta in 'byan-ko
bond	obbligazione (f)	ob-bli-ga-'tsyo-ne
budget, balance	bilancio	bi-'lan-čo
capital	capitale (m)	ka-pi-'ta-le
cash	contanti (m, pl)	kon-'tan-ti
• cashier, teller	cassiere (-a)	kas-'sye-re
check	assegno	as-'se-nyo
• (to) cash a check	incassare un assegno	in-kas-'sa-re un as-'se-nyo
• check book	libretto degli assegni	li-'bret-to de-lyi as-'se-nyi
• check clearing	compensazione (f) degli assegni	kom-pen-sa-'styo-ne de-'lyi as-'se-nyi
• (to) clear	compensare	kom-pen-'sa-re
• non-transferrable check	assegno barrato	as-'se-nyo bar-'ra-to
counterfeit money	moneta falsa	mo-'ne-ta 'fal-sa
credit	credito	'kre-di-to
• credit card	carta di credito	'kar-ta di 'kre-di-to
• credit institute, trust	istituto di credito	is-ti-'tu-to di 'kre-di-to
• credit limit	fido	'fi-do
• credit transfer	bonifico	bo-'ni-fi-ko
currency value	valuta	va-'lu-ta
debit, bill, debt	debito	'de-bi-to
deficit	deficit (m, inv)	de-fi-'čit
deposit	versamento	ver-sa-'men-to
• (to) deposit	versare	ver-'sa-re
• deposit slip	modulo di versamento	'mo-du-lo di ver-sa-'men-to
devaluation	svaluta	zva-'lu-ta
• (to) devalue	svalutare	zva-lu-'ta-re
discount	sconto	'skon-to

• **discount rate**	tasso di sconto	'tas-so
draft, promissory note	cambiale (f)	kam-'bya-le
endorsement	girata	ji-'ra-ta
• **(to) endorse**	avallare	a-val-'la-re
euro	euro (m, inv)	'eu-ro
exchange	cambio	'kam-byo
• **(to) exchange**	cambiare	kam-'bya-re
financier	finanziere (m)	fi-nan-'tsye-re
form (to fill out)	modulo	'mo-du-lo
funding	finanziamento	fi-nan-tsya-'mento
income	reddito	'red-di-to
inflation	inflazione (f)	in-fla-'tsyo-ne
• **deflation**	deflazione (f)	de-fla-'tsyo-ne
• **inflation rate**	tasso d'inflazione	'tas-so din-fla-'tsyo-ne
• **recession**	recessione (f)	re-ces-'syo-ne
insurance	assicurazione (f)	as-si-ku-ra-'tsyo-ne
• **accident insurance**	assicurazione contro	as-si-ku-ra-'tsyo-ne
	gli infortuni	'kon-tro lyi in-for-'tu-ni
• **anti-theft insurance**	assicurazione contro	
	il furto	'fur-to
• **fire insurance**	assicurazione contro	
	l'incendio	in-'čen-dyo
• **insurable**	assicurabile	as-si-ku-'ra-bi-le
• **insurance company**	società d'assicurazione	so-če-'ta
• **insurance policy**	polizza d'assicurazione	'po-li-tsa
• **(to) insure**	assicurare	as-si-ku-'ra-re
• **insured person**	assicurato (-a)	as-si-ku-'ra-to
• **life insurance**	assicurazione sulla vita	—
interest	interesse (m)	in-te-'res-se
• **compound interest**	interesse composto	kom-'pos-to
• **interest rate**	tasso d'interesse	'tas-so
• **simple interest**	interesse semplice	'sem-pli-če
(to) invest	investire	in-ves-'ti-re
• **investment**	investimento	in-ves-ti-'men-to
liability, loan	ipoteca	i-po-'te-ka
loan	prestito	'pres-ti-to
loose change	spiccioli (m, pl)	'spič-čo-li
manager	direttore (-trice)	di-ret-'to-re
money	denaro	de-'na-ro
	soldi (m, pl)	'sol-di
mortgage	mutuo	'mu-two
• **house mortgage**	mutuo fondiario	fon-'dya-ryo
• **(to) open up a**	accendere* un mutuo	ač-'čen-de-re
mortgage		
• **(to) pay off a**	estinguere* un mutuo	es-'tin-gwe-re
mortgage		
(to) pay	pagare	pa-'ga-re
• **(to) pay off**	saldare	sal-'da-re

• payment	pagamento	pa-ga-'men-to
• payment on delivery	pagamento a pronta cassa	pa-ga-'men-to a 'pron-ta 'kas-sa
portfolio	portafoglio	por-ta-'fo-lyo
rate	tasso	'tas-so
safe	cassaforte (f)	kas-sa-'for-te
safety deposit box	cassetta di sicurezza	kas-'set-ta di si-ku-'re-tsa
(to) save	risparmiare	ris-par-'mya-re
• savings	risparmi	ris-'par-mi
• savings book	libretto di risparmio	li-'bret-to
signature	firma	—
• (to) sign	firmare	fir-'ma-re
• signatory, signer	firmatario (-a)	fir-ma-'ta-ryo
stock, share	azione (f)	a-'tsyo-ne
• stock market	borsa valori	'bor-sa va-'lo-ri
surplus	eccedente (m)	eč-če-'den-te
tax	tassa	—
• taxable income	imponibile (m)	im-po-'ni-bi-le
• tax collector	esattore (-trice)	e-zat-'to-re
teller	cassiere (-a)	kas-'sye-re
• teller's window	sportello	spor-'tel-lo
traveler's check	traveler's check	—
withdrawal	prelevamento	pre-le-va-'men-to
• (to) withdraw	prelevare	pre-le-'va-re
• authorized withdrawal	prelevamento autorizzato	pre-le-va-'men-to auto-ri-'dza-to
• automatic withdrawal	prelevamento automatico	au-to-'ma-ti-ko

B. COMMERCE

amount	ammontare (m)	ammon-'ta-re
balancing the books	compensazione (f)	kom-pen-sa-'tsyo-ne
bankruptcy	bancarotta	ban-ka-'rot-ta
claim	rivendicazione (f)	ri-ven-di-ka-'tsyo-ne
(to) compensate	indennizzare	in-den-ni-'dza-re
competition	concorrenza	kon-kor-'ren-dza
credit letter	lettera di credito	'let-te-ra di 'kre-di-to
damages	danni (m, pl)	'dan-ni
deal	affare (m)	af-'fa-re
deduction	detrazione (f)	de-tra-'tsyo-ne
expenses	spese (f, pl)	'spe-ze
• expenses (business)	uscite (f, pl)	u-'ši-te
(to) export	esportare	es-por-'ta-re
fall in prices	ribasso dei prezzi	ri-'bas-so dei 'pre-tsi
(to) finance	finanziare	fi-nan-'tsya-re
gain	guadagno	gwa-'da-nyo
• gains, profits	entrate (f, pl)	en-'tra-te

import	importare	im-por-'ta-re
interest loan	prestito a interesse	'pres-ti-to a in-te-'res-se
large loan	prestito ingente	'pres-ti-to in-'jen-te
laws of the marketplace	leggi del mercato	'lej-ji del mer-'ka-to
legal tender	corso	
liability	responsabilità (f, inv)	res-pon-sa-bi-li-'ta
liquidation	liquidazione (f)	li-kwi-da-'tsyo-ne
• (to) liquidate	liquidare	li-kwi-'da-re
loaner, creditor	creditore (m)	kre-di-'to-re
loss	perdita	'per-di-ta
lump sum	somma forfettaria	'som-ma for-fet-'ta-rya
market price	prezzo di mercato	'pre-tso di mer-'ka-to
personal income tax	imposta sul reddito delle persone fisiche	im-'pos-ta sul 'red-di-to del-le per'so-ne 'fi-zi-ke
public debt	debito pubblico	'de-bi-to 'pub-bli-ko
quotation	quotazione (f)	kwo-ta-'tsyo-ne
• (to) quote (stock price)	quotare	kwo-'ta-re
realty tax	imposta sugli immobili	im-pos-ta su-lyi im-'mo-bi-li
rise in prices	rialzo dei prezzi	ri-'al-tso dei 'pre-tsi
sales tax	IVA (f. inv)	—
tax payment	prelievo d'imposta	pre-'lye-vo
• taxation office	ufficio delle imposte	uf-'fi-čo de-le im-'pos-te
treasurer	tesoriere (-a)	te-zo-'rye-re
yield	rendimento	ren-di-'men-to

27. GAMES AND SPORTS

A. GAMES, HOBBIES, AND PHYSICAL FITNESS

acrobat	acrobata (m/f)	a-'kro-ba-ta
bet	scommessa	skom-'mes-sa
• (to) bet	scommettere*	skom-'met-te-re
billiards	biliardo	bi-'lyar-do
• billiard ball	palla da biliardo	'pal-la
• billiard cue	stecca da biliardo	'stek-ka
• billiard table	tavolo da biliardo	'ta-vo-lo
bingo	tombola	'tom-bo-la
• bingo card	cartella della tombola	kar-'tel-la
charade	sciarada	ša-'ra-da
(to) cheat	imbrogliare	im-bro-'lya-re
• cheater	imbroglione (-a)	im-bro-'lyo-ne
• cheating	imbroglio	im-'bro-lyo
	truffa	'truf-fa
checkers	dama	—
• checker piece	pedina	pe-'di-na
chess	gioco degli scacchi	'jo-ko de-lyi 'skak-ki
circus	circo	'čir-ko

Cards and Chess

ace	asso
clubs	bastoni (m, pl)
goblets	coppe (f, pl)
hearts	cuori (m, pl)
money	denari (m, pl)
queen of spades	donna di picche
clubs	fiori (m, pl)
hand	mano
spades	picche (f, pl)
diamonds	quadri (m, pl)
swords	spade (f, pl)
bishop	alfiere (m)
knight	cavallo
pawn	pedone (m)
king	re (m, inv)
queen	regina
chess board	scacchiera
chess piece, check	scacco
checkmate	scacco matto
rook	torre (f)

• clown	pagliaccio	*pa-'lyač-čo*
coin	moneta	*mo-'ne-ta*
• coin collecting	numismatica	*nu-miz-'ma-ti-ka*
collecting	collezionismo	*kol-le-tsyo-'niz-mo*
• collector	collezionista (m/f)	*kol-le-tsyo-'nis-ta*
concert	concerto	*kon-čer-to*
crosswords	parole crociate	*pa-'ro-le kro-'ča-te*
dice	dadi	*'da-di*
• die	dado	—
doll	bambola	*'bam-bo-la*
electric toy train	trenino elettrico	*tre-'ni-no e-'let-tri-ko*
embroidery	ricamo	*ri-'ka-mo*
• (to) embroider	ricamare	*ri-ka-'ma-re*
fishing	pesca	*'pes-ka*
• bait	esca	*'es-ka*
• (to) fish	pescare	*pes-'ka-re*
• hook	amo	—
• line	lenza	*'len-tsa*
• reel	mulinello	*mu-li-'nel-lo*
• rod	canna da pesca	*'kan-na da 'pes-ka*
game	gioco	*'jo-ko*
game of chance, gambling	gioco d'azzardo	*'jo-ko dad-'dzar-do*
gardening	giardinaggio	*jar-di-'naj-jo*

hide-and-seek	rimpiattino	*rim-pyat-'ti-no*
hobby	hobby (m, inv)	—
hoop	cerchio	*'čer-kyo*
horse-racing	ippica	*'ip-pi-ka*
hunting	caccia	*'kač-ča*
• **(to) hunt, go hunting**	cacciare	*kač-'ča-re*
instrument	strumento	*stru-'men-to*
• **(to) play**	suonare	*swo-'na-re*
jogging	jogging (m, inv)	—
kite	aquilone (m)	*a-kwi-'lo-ne*
(to) knit	lavorare a maglia	*la-vo 'ra-re u 'ma-'lya*
lawn bowling	bocce (f, pl)	*'boč-če*
(to) lose	perdere*	*'per-de-re*
magic tricks	giochi di prestigio	*'jo-ki di pres-'ti-jo*
• **magician**	prestigiatore (-trice)	*pres-ti-ja-'to-re*
marble	bilia	*'bi-lya*
parade	parata	*pa-'ra-ta*
pinball machine	flipper (m, inv)	—
(to) play (a game)	giocare	*jo-'ka-re*
• **(to) play ball (soccer)**	giocare al pallone	*pal-'lo-ne*
• **(to) play skipping rope**	saltare con la corda	*sal-'ta-re kon la 'kor-da*
playing card	carta da gioco	*'kar-ta da 'jo-ko*
pottery	arte della ceramica	*'ar-te del-la ce-'ra-mi-ka*
puppet theater	teatro dei burrattini	*te-a-tro dei bur-rat-'ti-ni*
• **marionette**	marionetta	*ma-ryo-'net-ta*
puzzle	enigma (m) (enigmi, pl)	*e-'nig-ma*
rebus	rebus (m, inv)	—
recreational activities	attività ricreative	*at-ti-vi-'ta ri-kre-a-'ti-ve*
relaxation	riposo	*ri-'po-zo*
• **(to) relax**	riposarsi	*ri-po-'zar-si*
riddle	indovinello	*in-do-vi-'nel-lo*
(to) sew	cucire	*ku-'či-re*
skateboard	skateboard (m, inv)	—
stamp collecting	filatelia	*fi-la-te-'li-a*
swings	altalena	*al-ta-'le-na*
toboggan, slide	slitta	*'zlit-ta*
toy	giocattolo	*jo-'kat-to-lo*
• **toy car**	macchinina	*mak-ki-'ni-na*
• **toy soldier**	soldatino	*sol-da-'ti-no*
(to) unwind	distendersi	*dis-'ten-der-si*
video game	videogioco	*vi-de-o-'jo-ko*
(to) walk	camminare	*kam-mi-'na-re*
(to) win	vincere*	*'vin-če-re*

B. SPORTS

aerobics	aerobica	*ae-'ro-bi-ka*
amateur	dilettante (m/f)	*di-let-'tan-te*

American football	football americano	a-me-ri-'ka-no
archery	tiro con l'arco	'ti-ro kon 'lar-ko
athlete	atleta (m/f)	at-'le-ta
ball	palla	'pal-la
• (to) catch (the ball)	prendere*	'pren-de-re
• (to) hit	battere	'bat-te-re
• (to) kick	calciare	kal-'ča-re
• (to) pass	passare	pas-'sa-re
• (to) pitch	lanciare	lan-'ča-re
• (to) throw	tirare	ti-'ra-re
baseball	baseball	—
• baseball diamond	diamante (m)	dya-'man-te
• bat	mazza	'ma-tsa
• catcher's mask	maschera	'mas-ke-ra
• chest protector	corazza	ko-'rat-tsa
• helmet	casco	'kas-ko
• mound	pedana di lancio	pe-'da-na di 'lan-čo
• pitcher	lanciatore (m)	lan-ča-'to-re
• runner	corridore (m)	kor-ri-'do-re
basketball	pallacanestro (f, inv)	pal-la-ka-'nes-tro
	basket (m, inv)	—
• ball	pallone (m)	pal-'lo-ne
• basket	canestro	ka-'nes-tro
bicycle racing	corsa ciclistica	'kor-sa či-'klis-ti-ka
boat	barca	'bar-ka
body-building	culturismo	kul-tu-'riz-mo
• (to) lift weights	sollevare pesi	sol-le-'va-re 'pe-zi
• weight lifting	sollevamento pesi	sol-le-va-'men-to 'pe-zi
bowling	bowling (m, inv)	—
• lawn bowling	bocce (f, pl)	'boč-če
• bowling ball	boccia	'boč-ča
• bowling alley	pista	'pis-ta
• bowling pin	birillo	bi-'ril-lo
boxing	pugilato	pu-ji-'la-to
• boxer	pugile (m/f)	'pu-ji-le
• featherweight	peso piuma	'pe-zo 'pyu-ma
• heavyweight	peso massimo	'pe-zo 'mas-si-mo
• middleweight	peso medio	'pe-zo 'me-dyo
(to) break a record	battere un record	'bat-te-re
canoe	canoa	ka-'no-a
car race	corsa automobilistica	'kor-sa au-to-mo-bi-'lis-ti-ka
• car racing	automobilismo	au-to-mo-bi-'liz-mo
champion	campione (m)	kam-'pyo-ne
change room	spogliatoio	spo-lya-'to-yo
coach	allenatore (-trice)	al-le-na-'to-re
competition	agonismo	a-go-'niz-mo
• (to) compete	concorrere*	kom-'kor-re-re

cup	coppa	'kop-pa
cycling	ciclismo	či-'kliz-mo
defeat	sconfitta	skon-'fit-ta
• (to) defeat	sconfiggere*	skon-'fij-je-re
disc, puck	disco	—
diving	(gare di) tuffi	'tuf-fi
• (to) dive	tuffarsi	tuf-'far-si
• diver	tuffatore (-trice)	tuf-fa-'to-re
driver	automobilista (m/f)	au-to-mo-bi-'lis-ta
(to) eliminate	eliminare	e-li-mi-'na-re
elimination round	girone eliminatorio	ji-'ro-ne e-li-mi-na-'to-ryo
fencing	scherma	'sker-ma
• fencing suit	divisa	di-'vi-za
• mask	maschera	'mas-ke-ra
• sword	spada	—
	sciabola	'ša-bo-la
field	campo	—
finalist	finalista (m/f)	fi-na-'lis-ta
foot racing	corsa podistica	'kor-sa po-'dis-ti-ka
game, match	partita	par-'ti-ta
goal, score	gol (m, inv)	—
	rete (f)	're-te
golf	golf (m, inv)	—
gymnastics	ginnastica	jin-'nas-ti-ka
• gymnasium	palestra	pa-'les-tra
• gymnast	ginnasta (m/f)	jin-'nas-ta
• (to) work out	fare* ginnastica	—
high jumping	salto in alto	'sal-to in 'al-to
hockey	hockey (m, inv)	—
• hockey rink	campo di ghiaccio	'kam-po di 'gyač-čo
• hockey stick	bastone (m)	bas-'to-ne
• puck	disco	—
• skate	pattino	'pat-ti-no
horse race	corsa ippica	'kor-sa 'ip-pi-ka
• horse racing	equitazione (f)	e-kwi-ta-'tsyo-ne
ice skating	pattinaggio su ghiaccio	pat-ti-'naj-jo su 'gyač-čo
in record time	a tempo di record	—
javelin throwing	lancio del giavellotto	'lan-čo del ja-vel-'lot-to
• javelin	giavellotto	ja-vel-'lot-to
judo	judo (m, inv)	—
(to) jump	saltare	sal-'ta-re
• jumper	saltatore (-trice)	sal-ta-'to-re
• long jumping	salto in lungo	—
karate	karatè (m, inv)	—
knapsack	zaino	'dzai-no
lap, stage	tappa	—
motorcycling	motociclismo	mo-to-ci-'kliz-mo

mountain climbing	alpinismo	*al-pi-'niz-mo*
• **climber**	alpinista (m/f)	*al-pi-'nis-ta*
oar	remo	—
Olympic games	giochi Olimpici	*'jo-ki o-'lim-pi-či*
opponent	avversario (-a)	*av-ver-'sa-ryo*
parachuting	paracadutismo	*pa-ra-ka-du-'tiz-mo*
player	giocatore (-trice)	*jo-ka-'to-re*
playoffs, championship	campionato	*kam-pyo-'na-to*
point	punto	—
pole vaulting	salto con l'asta	—
(to) practice a sport	praticare uno sport	*pra-ti-'ka-re*
race, racing	corsa	—
• **(to) run**	correre*	*'kor-re-re*
• **runner**	corridore (-trice)	*kor-ri-'do-re*
record	record (m, inv)	—
referee	arbitro (-a)	*'ar-bi-tro*
rival	rivale (m/f)	*ri-'va-le*
roller skating	pattinaggio a rotelle	*pat-ti-'naj-jo a ro-'tel-le*
rope	corda	—
rowing, canoeing	canottaggio	*ka-not-'taj-jo*
sailing	vela	—
score	punteggio	*pun-'tej-jo*
• **draw, tie**	pareggio	*pa-'rej-jo*
• **(to) draw**	pareggiare	*pa-rej-'ja-re*
• **final score**	risultato finale	*ri-zul-'ta-to*
• **(to) lose**	perdere*	*'per-de-re*
• **loser**	perdente	*per-'den-te*
• **loss**	perdita	*'per-di-ta*
• **outcome**	esito	*'e-zi-to*
• **win**	vincita	*'vin-či-ta*
• **(to) win**	vincere*	*'vin-če-re*
• **winner**	vincitore (-trice)	*vin-či-'to-re*
(to) set a record	stabilire (isc) un record	*sta-bi-'li-re*
skating	pattinaggio	*pat-ti-'naj-jo*
• **skate**	pattino	*'pat-ti-no*
• **(to) skate**	pattinare	*pat-ti-'na-re*
• **skater**	pattinatore (-trice)	*pat-ti-na-'to-re*
skiing, ski	sci (m, inv)	*ši*
• **crosscountry skiing**	sci da fondo	—
• **downhill skiing**	discesa	*di-'še-za*
• **(to) ski**	sciare	*ši-'a-re*
• **ski jumping**	salto	*'sal-to*
• **skier**	sciatore (-trice)	*ši-a-'to-re*
• **water skiing**	sci nautico	*'nau-ti-ko*
soccer	calcio	*'kal-čo*
• **goaltender**	portiere (m)	*por-'tye-re*
• **(to) kick**	calciare	*kal-'ča-re*
• **net**	porta	—

• **(to) pass**	passare	*pas-'sa-re*
• **penalty**	rigore (m)	*ri-'go-re*
• **play (action)**	gioco	*'jo-ko*
	azione (f)	*a-'tsyo-ne*
• **(to) save**	parata	*pa-'ra-ta*
• **(to) score**	segnare	*se-'nya-re*
• **(to) shoot, kick**	tirare	*ti-'ra-re*
• **shot, kick**	tiro	*'ti-ro*
• **soccer ball**	pallone (m)	*pal-'lo-ne*
• **soccer player**	calciatore (-trice)	*kal-ča-'to-re*
• **(to) tackle**	contrastare	*kon-tras-'ta-re*
• **sports event**	gara	—
• **sports fan**	tifoso (-a)	*ti-'fo-zo*
• **sporty, of sports**	sportivo	*spor-'ti-vo*
squash	squash (m, inv)	—
stadium	stadio	*'sta-dyo*
standings	classifica	*klas-'si-fi-ka*
surfing	surfing (m, inv)	—
swimming	nuoto	*'nwo-to*
• **(to) swim**	nuotare	*nwo-'ta-re*
• **swimmer**	nuotatore (-trice)	*nwo-ta-'to-re*
• **swimming pool**	piscina	*pi-'ši-na*
target	bersaglio	*ber-'sa-lyo*
team	squadra	*'skwa-dra*
tennis	tennis (m, inv)	—
• **tennis court**	campo da tennis	—
• **tennis player**	tennista (m/f)	*ten-'nis-ta*
• **tennis racket**	racchetta	*rak-'ket-ta*
ticket	biglietto	*bi-'lyet-to*
tournament	tournée (f, inv)	—
track and field	atletica leggera	*at-'le-ti-ka lej-'je-ra*
• **track**	pista	—
training	allenamento	*al-le-na-'men-to*
• **(to) train**	allenarsi	*al-le-'nar-si*
• **trainer, coach**	allenatore (-trice)	*al-le-na-'to-re*
volleyball	pallavolo (f, inv)	*pal-la-'vo-lo*
water polo	pallanuoto (f, inv)	*pal-la-'nwo-to*
World Cup	Coppa del Mondo	—
wrestling	lotta	—
• **(to) wrestle**	lottare	*lot-'ta-re*
• **wrestler**	lottatore (-trice)	*lot-ta-'to-re*

28. THE ARTS

A. CINEMA

actor, actress	attore (-trice)	*at-'to-re*
adventure film	film d'avventura	*dav-ven-'tu-ra*

aisle	corridoio	*kor-ri-'do-yo*
animation	animazione (f)	*a-ni-ma-'tsyo-ne*
balcony (of a movie theater)	galleria	*gal-le-'ri-a*
box office	botteghino	*bot-te-'gi-no*
cartoon	cartone animato	*kar-'to-ne a-ni-'ma-to*
cinema	cinema (m, inv)	*'či-ne-ma*
cowboy movie	film western	—
detective movie	film poliziesco	*po-li-'tsyes-ko*
director	regista (m/f)	*re-'jis-ta*
documentary	documentario	*do-ku-men-'ta-ryo*
dubbed	doppiato	*dop-'pya-to*
• dubbing	doppiaggio	*dop-'pyaj-jo*
editing	montaggio	*mon-'taj-jo*
feature (film)	lungometraggio	*'lun-go-me-'traj-jo*
film, movie	film (m, inv)	—
footage	metraggio	*me-'traj-jo*
ground floor	platea	*pla-'te-a*
horror film	film dell'orrore	*or-'ro-re*
in slow motion	al rallentatore	*ral-len-ta-'to-re*
lobby	ridotto	*ri-'dot-to*
movie camera	cinepresa	*ci-ne-'pre-za*
movie star	stella del cinema	*'stel-la del 'či-ne-ma*
movie theater	cinema (m, inv)	*'či-ne-ma*
musical film	film musicale	*mu-zi-'ka-le*
mystery movie	film giallo	*'jal-lo*
performer	interprete (m/f)	*in-'ter-pre-te*
pornographic movie	film pornografico	*por-no-'gra-fi-ko*
premiere showing	prima visione	*'pri-ma vi-'zyo-ne*
producer	produttore (-trice)	*pro-dut-'to-re*
• production	produzione (m)	*pro-du-'tsyo-ne*
restricted	vietato ai minori	*vye-'ta-to ai mi-'no-ri*
row	fila	—
scenery	sceneggiatura	*še-nej-ja-'tu-ra*
science fiction movie	film di fantascienza	*fan-ta-'šen-tsa*
screen	schermo	*'sker-mo*
(to) shoot a movie	girare un film	*ji-'ra-re*
• shooting on location	riprese (f, pl) in esterni	*ri-'pre-ze*
short (film)	cortometraggio	*kor-to-me-'traj-jo*
shot	ripresa (cinematografica)	*ri-'pre-za*
sound technician	tecnico del suono	*'tek-ni-ko del 'swo-no*
sound track	colonna sonora	*ko-'lon-na so-'no-ra*
spy movie	film di spionaggio	*spyo-'naj-jo*
subtitle	sottotitolo	*sot-to-'ti-to-lo*
thriller	thriller (m, inv)	—
video cassette	videocassetta	*vi-de-o-kas-'set-ta*

B. VISUAL ARTS, SCULPTURE, ARCHITECTURE, AND PHOTOGRAPHY

abstract	astratto	as-'trat-to
(to) aim the lens	puntare l'obiettivo	pun-'ta-re lo-byet-'ti-vo
architecture	architettura	ar-ki-tet-'tu-ra
art	arte (f)	'ar-te
• art exhibition	mostra d'arte	'mos-tra 'dar-te
• art gallery	galleria d'arte	gal-le-'ri-a
• art museum	museo d'arte	mu-'ze-o
• artist	artista (m/f)	ar-'tis-ta
background	sfondo	'sfon-do
Baroque	Barocco	ba-'rok-ko
blueprint	copia cianografica	'ko-'pya ča-no-'gra-fi-ka
bronze sculpture	scultura in bronzo	skul-'tu-ra in 'bron-dzo
brush	pennello	pen-nel-lo
canvas	tela	'te-la
chiaroscuro	chiaroscuro	kya-ro-'sku-ro
chisel	cesello	če-'zel-lo
• (to) chisel	cesellare	če-zel-'la-re
Classicism	Classicismo	klas-si-'čiz-mo
dark room	camera oscura	'ka-me-ra os-'ku-ra
digital photography	fotografia digitale	fo-to-gra-'fi-a di-ji-'ta-le
drawing	disegno	di-'ze-nyo
easel	cavalletto (da pittore)	ka-val-'let-to (da pit-'to-re)
etching	disegno a matita	di-'ze-nyo a ma-'ti-ta
exhibition	mostra	—
fine arts	belle arti	'be-le 'ar-ti
(to) focus	mettere* a fuoco	'met-te-re a 'fwo-ko
foreground	primo piano	'pri-mo -'pya-no
(to) frame	inquadrare	in-kwa-'dra-re
freehand drawing	disegno a mano libera	di-'ze-nyo a 'ma-no 'li-be-ra
fresco painting	affresco	af-'fres-ko
geometric design	disegno geometrico	di-'ze-nyo je-o-'me-tri-ko
image	immagine (f)	im-'ma-ji-ne
Impressionism	Impressionismo	im-pres-syo-'niz-mo
landscape	paesaggio	pa-e-'zaj-jo
marble sculpture	scultura in marmo	skul-'tu ra in 'mar-mo
masterpiece	capolavoro	ka-po-la-'vo-ro
model	modello	mo-'del-lo
movie camera	cinepresa	ci-ne-'pre-za
mural painting	pittura murale	pit-'tu-ra mu-'ra-le
negative	negativo	ne-ga-'ti-vo
nude	nudo	—
oil painting	pittura a olio	pit-'tu-ra a 'o-lyo

(to) paint	dipingere*	di-'pin-je-re
• painter	pittore (-trice)	pit-'to-re
• painting	dipinto	di-'pin-to
	quadro	'kwa-dro
palette	tavolozza	ta-vo-'lo-tsa
pastel	pastello	pas-'tel-lo
pedestal	piedistallo	pye-di-'stal-lo
photograph	fotografia	fo-to-gra-'fi-a
• photographer	fotografo (-a)	fo-'to-gra-fo
• photographic shot	ripresa fotografica	ri-'pre-za fo-to-'gra-fi-ka
portrait	ritratto	ri-'trat-to
pose	posa	'po-za
print, mold	stampa	—
Realism	Realismo	re-a-'liz-mo
relief	rilievo	ri-'lye-vo
Rococo	Rococò	—
Romanticism	Romanticismo	ro-man-ti-'čiz-mo
(to) sculpt	scolpire (isc)	skol-'pi-re
• sculptor, sculptress	scultore (-trice)	skul-'to-re
• sculpture	scultura	skul-'tu-ra
shade, nuance	sfumatura	sfu-ma-'tu-ra
sketch	schizzo	'ski-tso
slide	diapositiva	di-a-po-zi-'ti-va
statue	statua	'sta-tu-a
(to) trace	calcare	kal-'ka-re
tripod	treppiede (m, inv)	trep-'pye-de
visual arts	arti figurative	'ar-ti fi-gu-ra-'ti-ve
water color	acquerello	ak-kwe-'rel-lo
• water colorist	aquerellista (m/f)	ak-kwe-rel-'lis-ta
wax museum	museo delle cere	mu-ze-o del-le 'če-re
work of art	opera d'arte	'o-pe-ra 'dar-te

C. MUSIC/DANCE

accordion	fisarmonica	fi-zar-'mo-ni-ka
• accordionist	fisarmonicista (m/f)	fi-zar-mo-ni-'čis-ta
ballad	ballata	bal-'la-ta
ballet	balletto	bal-'let-to
ballroom	sala da ballo	'sa-la da 'bal-lo
band	gruppo	'grup-po
	complesso	kom-'ples-so
baritone	baritono	ba-'ri-to-no
base	basso	'bas-so
baton	bacchetta	bak-'ket-ta
(to) beat time	battere il tempo	'bat-te-re
brass instruments	ottoni	ot-'to-ni
• horn	corno	'kor-no
• horn player	cornista (m/f)	kor-'nis-ta

• **trombone**	trombone	*trom-'bo-ne*
• **trumpet**	tromba	—
• **trumpeter**	trombettista (m/f)	*trom-bet-'tis-ta*
• **tuba**	tuba	*'tu-ba*
chamber music	musica da camera	*'mu-zi-ka da 'ka-me-ra*
chant	canto	—
choir	coro	—
chord	accordo	*ak-'kor-do*
classical music	musica classica	*'mu-zi-ka*
composer	compositore (-trice)	*kom-po-zi-'to-re*
• **composition**	composizione (f)	*kom-po-zi-'tsyo-ne*
concert, concerto	concerto	*kon-'cer-to*
conservatory	conservatorio	*kon-ser-va-'to-ryo*
contralto	contralto	*kon-'tral-to*
dance	ballo	—
• **(to) dance**	ballare	*bal-'la-re*
• **dance music**	musica da ballo	*'mu-zi-ka da 'bal-lo*
• **dancer**	ballerino (-a)	*bal-le-'ri-no*
disco	discoteca	*dis-ko-'te-ka*
duet	duetto	*du-'et-to*
fandango	fandango	*fan-'dan-go*
folk music	musica folk	*'mu-zi-ka*
	musica folcloristica	*'mu-zi-ka fol-klo-'ris-ti-ka*
harmony	armonia	*ar-mo-'ni-a*
hymn	inno	—
instrument	strumento	*stru-'men-to*
key	chiave (f)	*'kya-ve*
lullaby	ninna nanna	—
madrigal	madrigale (m)	*ma-dri-'ga-le*
masked ball	ballo in maschera	*'bal-lo in 'mas-ke-ra*
melody	melodia	*me-lo-'di-a*
music	musica	*'mu-zi-ka*
• **music stand**	portamusica (m, inv)	*por-ta-'mu-zi-ka*
• **musician**	musicista (m/f)	*mu-zi-'čis-ta*
• **musicologist**	musicologo (-a)	*mu-zi-'ko-lo-go*
note	nota	—
opera	opera	*'o-pe-ra*
orchestra	orchestra	*or-'kes-tra*
orchestra conductor	direttore (-trice)	*di-ret-'to-re*
organ	organo	*'or-ga-no*
• **organist**	organista (m/f)	*or-ga-'nis-ta*
percussion instruments	strumenti a percussione	*stru-'men-ti a per-kus-'syo-ne*
• **bass drum**	grancassa	*gran-'kas-sa*
• **cymbal**	piatto	*'pyat-to*
• **drum, tambourine**	tamburo	*tam-'bu-ro*
• **drummer**	batterista (m/f)	*bat-te-'ris-ta*

• set of drums	batteria	*bat-te-'ri-a*
• timpani	timpano	*'tim-pa-no*
piano	pianoforte (m), piano	*pya-no-'for-te*
• grand piano	piano a coda	
• pianist	pianista (m/f)	*pya-'nis-ta*
• upright piano	piano verticale	*ver-ti-'ka-le*
(to) play	suonare	*swo-'na-re*
• play out of tune	stonare	*sto-'na-re*
• player	suonatore (-trice)	*swo-na-'to-re*
polka	polca	*'pol-ka*
pop music	musica popolare	*'mu-zi-ka po-po-'la-re*
(to) practice	esercitarsi	*e-zer-či-'tar-si*
quadrille, square dance	quadriglia	*kwa-'dri-lya*
quartet	quartetto	*kwar-'tet-to*
quintet	quintetto	*kwin-'tet-to*
rap	rap (m, inv)	—
rehearsal	prova	*'pro-va*
rhythm	ritmo	—
rock music	musica rock	*'mu-zi-ka*
rumba	rumba	—
scale	scala	—
score	spartito	*spar-'ti-to*
sextet	sestetto	*ses-'tet-to*
singer	cantante (m/f)	*kan-'tan-te*
solo	assolo	*as-'so-lo*
• soloist	solista (m/f)	*so-'lis-ta*
song	canzone (f)	*kan-'tso-ne*
soprano	soprano	*so-'pra-no*
string instruments	strumenti a corda	*stru-'men-ti a 'kor-da*
• bow	arco	—
• double bass	contrabbasso	*kon-trab-'bas-so*
• double bass player	contrabbassista (m/f)	*kon-trab-bas-'sis-ta*
• cello	violoncello	*vyo-lon-'čel-lo*
• cellist	violoncellista (m/f)	*vyo-lon-čel-'lis-ta*
• guitar	chitarra	*ki-'tar-ra*
• guitarist	chitarrista (m/f)	*ki-tar-'ris-ta*
• harp	arpa	—
• harpist	arpista (m/f)	—
• harpsichord	clavicembalo	*kla-vi-'čem-ba-lo*
• mandolin	mandolino	*man-do-'li-no*
• mandolin player	mandolinista (m/f)	*man-do-li-'nis-ta*
• string	corda	—
• viola	viola	*'vyo-la*
• viola player	violista (m/f)	*vyo-'lis-ta*
• violin	violino	*vyo-'li-no*
• violinist	violinista (m/f)	*vyo-li-'nis-ta*
symphony	sinfonia	*sin-fo-'ni-a*
tango	tango	—

tap dancing	tip tap (m, inv)	—
tarantella	tarantella	*ta-ran-'tel-la*
tenor	tenore (m)	*te-'no-re*
tone	tono	—
trio	trio	—
(to) tune	accordare	*ak-kor-'da-re*
tune, aria	aria	—
waltz	valzer (m, inv)	—
wind instruments	strumenti a fiato	*stru-'men-ti a 'fya-to*
• bagpipes	zampogne (f, pl)	*dzam-'po-nye*
• bassoon	fagotto	*fa-'got-to*
• bassoonist	fagottista (m/f)	*fa-got-'tis-ta*
• clarinet	clarinetto	*kla-ri-'net-to*
• clarinettist	clarinettista (m/f)	*kla-ri-net-'ti-sta*
• flute	flauto	*'flau-to*
• flautist	flautista (m/f)	*flau-'tis-ta*
• oboe	oboe (m)	*'o-bo-e*
• oboist	oboista (m/f)	*o-bo-'is-ta*
• saxophone	sassofono	*sas-'so-fo-no*
• saxophonist	sassofonista (m/f)	*sas-so-fo-'nis-ta*

D. LITERATURE

adventure	avventura	*av-ven-'tu-ra*
allegory	allegoria	*al-le-go-'ri-a*
anecdote	aneddoto	*a-'ned-do-to*
anthology	antologia	*an-to-lo-'ji-a*
appendix	appendice (f)	*ap-pen-'di-če*
author	autore (-trice)	*au-'to-re*
autobiography	autobiografia	*au-to-bi-o-gra-'fi-a*
ballad	ballata	*bal-'la-ta*
biography	biografia	*bi-o-gra-'fi-a*
catalogue	catalogo	*ka-'ta-lo-go*
chapter	capitolo	*ka-'pi-to-lo*
character	personaggio	*per-son-'aj-jo*
collection	raccolta	*rak-'kol-ta*
colorful, vivacious	vivace	*vi-'va-če*
comedy, play	commedia	*kom-'me-dya*
comics	fumetti (m, pl)	*fu-'met-ti*
compiler, editor of a volume	curatore (-trice)	*ku-ra-'to-re*
concise	conciso	*kon-'či-zo*
confusing	confusionario	*kon-fu-zyo-'na-ryo*
contrast	contrasto	*kon-'tras-to*
controversial, polemical	polemico	*po-'le-mi-ko*
criticism	critica	*'kri-ti-ka*
• (to) criticize	criticare	*kri-ti-'ka-re*

(to) deal with	trattare	*trat-'ta-re*
(to) develop	sviluppare	*zvi-lup-'pa-re*
diary	diario	*di-'a-ryo*
dictionary, lexicon	dizionario	*di-tsyo-'na-ryo*
doodle	scarabocchio	*ska-ra-'bok-kyo*
draft	bozza	*'bot-tsa*
drama	dramma (m) (drammi, pl)	—
elaborate	elaborato	*e-la-bo-'ra-to*
elegy	elegia	*e-le-'ji-a*
(to) emphasize	accentuare	*ač-čen-tu-'a-re*
encyclopedia	enciclopedia	*en-či-'klo-pe-'di-a*
epigram	epigramma (m) (epigrammi, pl)	*e-pi-'gram-ma*
episode	episodio	*e-pi-'zo-dyo*
essay	saggio	*'saj-jo*
• essay-writing	saggistica	*saj-'jis-ti-ka*
(to) explain	spiegare	*spye-'ga-re*
fable	favola	*'fa-vo-la*
fairy tale	fiaba	*'fya-ba*
far-fetched, unusual	inconsueto	*in-kon-'swe-to*
(to) frame	inquadrare	*in-kwa-'dra-re*
genre	genere (m)	*'je-ne-re*
heavy	pesante	*pe-'zan-te*
hero, heroine	eroe (-ina)	*e-'ro-e*
(to) highlight	sottolineare	*sot-to-li-ne-'a-re*
image	immagine (f)	*im-'ma-ji-ne*
index	indice (m)	*'in-di-če*
irony	ironia	*i-ro-'ni-a*
laconic	laconico	*la-'ko-ni-ko*
legend	leggenda	*lej-'jen-da*
light	leggero	*lej-'je-ro*
line, verse	verso	—
literal	letterale	*let-te-'ra-le*
literature	letteratura	*let-te-ra-'tu-ra*
lively	animato	*a-ni-'ma-to*
manuscript	manoscritto	*ma-no-'skrit-to*
memoirs	memorie (f, pl)	*me-'mo-rye*
metaphor	metafora	*me-'ta-fo-ra*
motif	motivo	*mo-'ti-vo*
mystery, detective novel	giallo	*'jal-lo*
myth	mito	—
• mythology	mitologia	*mi-to-lo-'ji-a*
narration	narrazione (f)	*nar-ra-'tsyo-ne*
• narrative, fiction	narrativa	*nar-ra-'ti-va*
• narrator	narratore (-trice)	*nar-ra-'to-re*
novel	romanzo	*ro-'man-dzo*
• novelist	romanziere (-a)	*ro-man-'dzye-re*

ode	ode (f)	'o-de
ornate	adorno	a-'dor-no
(to) outline	tratteggiare	trat-tej-'ja-re
parody	parodia	pa-ro-'di-a
perspective, framework	ottica	'ot-ti-ka
plot	trama	—
poet	poeta (-essa)	po-'e-ta
• poetics	poetica	po-'e-ti-ka
• poetry, poem	poesia	po-e-'zi-a
(to) point out	segnalare	se-nya-'la-re
pompous	pomposo	pom-'po-zo
preface	prefazione (f)	pre-fa-'tsyo-ne
prose	prosa	'pro-za
publisher, publishing house	editore (m)	e-di-'to-re
quotation	citazione (f)	či-ta-'tsyo-ne
• (to) quote	citare	či-'ta-re
(to) read	leggere*	'lej-je-re
• reader	lettore (-trice)	let-'to-re
• reading	lettura	let-'tu-ra
review	recensione (f)	re-čen-'syo-ne
• (to) review	recensire (isc)	re-čen-'si-re
rhetoric	retorica	re-'to-ri-ka
royalty	diritto d'autore	di-'rit-to dau-'to-re
satire	satira	'sa-ti-ra
scene	scena	'še-na
science fiction	fantascienza	fan-ta-'šen-tsa
short story	novella	no-'vel-la
• short-story writer	novellista (m/f)	no-vel-'lis-ta
spicy	piccante	pik-'kan-te
style	stile (m)	'sti-le
• stylistics	stilistica	sti-'lis-ti-ka
symbolic	simbolico	sim-'bo-li-ko
• symbolism	simbolismo	sim-bo-'liz-mo
table of contents	indice (m) delle materie	'in-di-če del-le ma-'te-rye
tale	racconto	rak-'kon-to
terse, succinct	lapidario	la-pi-'da-ryo
text	testo	—
theme	tema (m) (temi, pl)	—
title (of a book)	titolo	'ti-to-lo
tragedy	tragedia	tra-'je-dya
volume	volume (m)	vo-'lu-me
work	opera	'o-pe-ra
(to) write	scrivere*	'skri-ve-re
• writer	scrittore (-trice)	skrit-'to-re
• writing	scrittura	skrit-'tu-ra

E. THEATER

act	atto	*'at-to*
• **(to) act**	recitare	*re-či-'ta-re*
• **actor, actress**	attore (-trice)	*at-'to-re*
applause	applauso	*ap-'plau-zo*
• **(to) applaud**	applaudire (isc)	*ap-plau-'di-re*
aside	a parte	—
audience	pubblico	*'pub-bli-ko*
(to) boo	fischiare	*fis-'kya-re*
character	personaggio	*per-son-'aj-jo*
• **main character, protagonist**	protagonista (m/f)	*pro-ta-go-'nis-ta*
comedy, play	commedia	*kom-'me-dya*
comic, comedian	comico (-a)	*'ko-mi-ko*
costume	costume (m)	*kos-'tu-me*
curtain	tenda	*'ten-da*
• **curtains**	sipario	*si-'pa-ryo*
dialogue	dialogo	*di-'a-lo-go*
director	regista (m/f)	*re-'jis-ta*
drama	dramma (m) (drammi, pl)	—
footlights	luci di ribalta	*'lu-či di ri-'bal-ta*
hero, heroine	eroe (-ina)	*e-'ro-e*
intermission	intervallo	*in-ter-'val-lo*
line (verbal)	battuta	*bat-'tu-ta*
main role	ruolo principale	*'rwo-lo prin-ci-'pa-le*
make-up	trucco	*'truk-ko*
monologue	monologo	*mo-'no-lo-go*
pantomime	pantomima	*pan-to-'mi-ma*
play	recita	*'re-či-ta*
• **performance**	messa in scena	*'še-na*
playwright	commediografo (-a)	*kom-me-'dyo-gra-fo*
plot	trama	—
program	programma (m)	*pro-'gram-ma*

Some Well-Known Italian Playwrights

Carlo Goldoni (1707–93)	*La Locandiera (1753)*
Luigi Pirandello (1867–1936)	*Sei personaggi in cerca d'autore (1921)*
Ugo Betti (1892–1953)	*Corruzione al palazzo di giustizia (1949)*
Dario Fo (1926–)	*Morte accidentale di un anarchico (1971)*

prompter	suggeritore (-trice)	*suj-je-ri-'to-re*
role	ruolo	*'rwo-lo*
scenario, background	scenario	*še-'na-ryo*
scene	scena	*'še-na*
• **scenery**	sceneggiatura	*še-nej-ja-'tu-ra*
script	copione (m)	*ko-'pyo-ne*
show	spettacolo	*spet-'ta-ko-lo*
skit	sketch (inv) comico	*'ko-mi-ko*
spotlights	riflettori (m, pl)	*ri-flet-'to-ri*
stage	palcoscenico	*pal-ko-'še-ni-ko*
star	stella	—
theater	teatro	*te-'a-tro*
tragedy	tragedia	*tra-'je-dya*
usher	maschera	*'mas-ke-ra*
wings (of a stage)	quinte (f, pl)	*'kwin-te*

29. HOLIDAYS/GOING OUT

A. HOLIDAYS/SPECIAL OCCASIONS

anniversary	anniversario	*an-ni-ver-'sa-ryo*
birthday	compleanno	*kom-ple-'an-no*
Christmas	Natale	*na-'ta-le*
Easter	Pasqua	*'pas-kwa*
Feast of the Assumption	Ferragosto	*fer-ra-'gos-to*
holidays	ferie (f, pl)	*'fe-rye*
name day	onomastico	*o-no-'mas-ti-ko*
New Year's Day	Capodanno	*ka-po-'dan-no*
New Year's Eve	Vigilia di Capodanno	*vi-'ji-lya di ka-po-'dan-no*
picnic	picnic (m, inv)	—
vacation	vacanza	*va-'kan-dza*
• **(to) go on vacation**	andare* (ess) in vacanza	—

B. GOING OUT

bar	bar (m, inv)	—
circus	circo	*'čir-ko*
• **clown**	pagliaccio	*pa-'lyač-čo*
concert	concerto	*kon-'čer-to*
dance	ballo	—
date	appuntamento	*ap-pun-ta-'men-to*
disco	discoteca	*dis-ko-'te-ka*
(to) enjoy oneself, have fun	divertirsi	*di-ver-'tir-si*
fortune teller	chiromante (f)	*ki-ro-'man-te*
(to) go out	uscire* (ess)	*u-'ši-re*
good time, enjoyment	divertimento	*di-ver-ti-'men-to*
ice cream	gelato	*je-'la-to*

• ice cream parlor	gelateria	*je-la-te-'ri-a*
invitation	invito	*in-vi-to*
leisure	svago	*'zva-go*
movies	cinema (m, inv)	*'či-ne-ma*
night club	locale notturno	*lo-'ka-le not-'tur-no*
parade	parata	*pa-'ra-ta*
party, feast	festa	—
relaxation	riposo	*ri-'po-zo*
(to) remain	rimanere* (ess)	*ri-ma-'ne-re*
(to) return	ritornare (ess)	*ri-tor-'na-re*
show, performance	spettacolo	*spet-'ta-ko-lo*
(to) stroll	passeggiata	*pas-sej-'ja-ta*
target practice	tiro	—
theater	teatro	*te-'a-tro*
unwind	distendersi	*dis-'ten-der-si*
visit	visita	*'vi-zi-ta*
• (to) visit	visitare	*vi-zi-'ta-re*
walk, stroll	camminata	*kam-mi-'na-ta*
• (to) walk	camminare	*kam-mi-'na-re*

C. SPECIAL GREETINGS

Best wishes!	Auguri!	*au-'gu-ri*
Compliments!	Complimenti!	*kom-pli-'men-ti*
Congratulations!	Congratulazioni!	*kon-gra-tu-la-'tsyo-ni*
Happy Birthday!	Buon compleanno!	*bwon kom-ple-'an-no*
Happy New Year!	Buon anno!	—
Have a good vacation!	Buona vacanza!	*'bwo-na va-'kan-dza*
Have fun!	Buon divertimento!	*bwon di-ver-ti-'men-to*
Merry Christmas!	Buon Natale!	*bwon na-'ta-le*

TRAVEL

30. CHOOSING A DESTINATION

A. AT THE TRAVEL AGENCY

abroad	all'estero	*al-'les-te-ro*
brochure	opuscolo	*o-'pus-ko-lo*
bus tour	viaggio in pullman	*'vyaj-jo in 'pul-man*
charter flight	volo charter	—
class	classe (f)	*'klas-se*
• **economy class**	classe turistica	*tu-'ris-ti-ka*
• **first class**	prima classe	—
continent	continente (m)	*kon-ti-'nen-te*
country, nation	nazione (f)	*na-'tsyo-ne*
down-payment	caparra	*ka-'par-ra*
excursion, tour	gita	*'ji-ta*
guide	guida	*'gwi-da*
high season	alta stagione	*'al-ta sta-'jo-ne*
insurance	assicurazione (f)	*as-si-ku-ra-'styo-ne*
low season	bassa stagione	*'bas-sa sta-'jo-ne*
package tour	viaggio organizzato	*'vyaj-jo*
reservation	prenotazione (f)	*pre-no-ta-'tsyo-ne*
• **on-line reservation**	prenotazione (f) on-line	—
seaside area	zona balneare	*'dzo-na bal-ne-'a-re*
• **seaside vacation**	vacanza al mare	*va-'kan-dza al 'ma-re*
summer vacation	vacanze estive	*va-'kan-dze es-'ti-ve*
ticket	biglietto	*bi-'lyet-to*
• **(to) buy a travel ticket**	fare* il biglietto	—
• **by boat, by ship**	con la nave	*'na-ve*
• **by plane**	in aereo	*a-'e-re-o*
• **by train**	in treno	—
• **one-way ticket**	biglietto di andata	—
• **return ticket**	biglietto di andata e ritorno	—
tour	giro	*'ji-ro*
tourism	turismo	*tu-'riz-mo*
• **tourist**	turista (m/f)	*tu-'ris-ta*
(to) travel	viaggiare	*vyaj-'ja-re*
• **travel agency**	agenzia di viaggi	*a-jen-'tsi-a di 'vyaj-ji*
• **travel agent**	agente (m/f) di viaggio	*a-'jen-te di 'vyaj-jo*
trip, journey	viaggio	*'vyaj-jo*
• **Have a nice trip!**	Buon viaggio!	—

• (to) take a trip	fare* un viaggio	—
vacation	vacanza	va-'kan-dza
• vacation in the mountains	vacanze in montagna	mon-'ta-nya
• winter vacation	vacanze invernali	in-ver-'na-li

B. COUNTRIES AND CONTINENTS

Abyssinia	Abissinia	ab-is-'si-nya
Afghanistan	Afghanistan (m)	—
Africa	Africa	—
Albania	Albania	al-ba-'ni-a
Algeria	Algeria	al-je-'ri-a
America	America	a-'me-ri-ka
• Latin America	America Latina	—
• North America	America del Nord	—
• South America	America del Sud	—
Argentina	Argentina	—
Armenia	Armenia	—
Asia	Asia	'a-zia
Australia	Australia	—
Austria	Austria	—
Bangladesh	Bangladesh (m)	—
Belgium	Belgio	'bel-jo
Bolivia	Bolivia	—
Bosnia	Bosnia	—
Brazil	Brasile (m)	bra-'zi-le
Bulgaria	Bulgaria	bul-ga-'ri-a
Cambodia	Cambogia	kam-'bo-ja
Canada	Canada	—
Caribbean	Caraibi (m, pl)	ka-'ray-bi
Chile	Cile (m)	'či-le
China	Cina	'či-na
Colombia	Colombia	—
Costa Rica	Costa Rica	—
Croatia	Croazia	kro-'a-tsya
Cuba	Cuba	—
Czech Republic	Repubblica Ceca	re-'pub-bli-ka 'če-ka
Denmark	Danimarca	da-ni-'mar-ka
Dominican Republic	Repubblica Dominicana	re-'pub-bli-ka do-mi-ni-'ka-na
Ecuador	Ecuador	—
Egypt	Egitto	e-'jit-to
El Salvador	El Salvador	—
England	Inghilterra	in-gil-'ter-ra
Eritrea	Eritrea	—
Estonia	Estonia	—
Ethiopia	Etiopia	e-'tyo-pya

Europe	Europa	*eu-'ro-pa*
Finland	Finlandia	*fin-'lan-dya*
France	Francia	*'fran-ča*
Georgia	Georgia	—
Germany	Germania	*jer-'ma-nya*
Great Britain	Gran Bretagna	*gran bre-'ta-nya*
Greece	Grecia	*'gre-ča*
Greenland	Groenlandia	*gro-en-'lan-dya*
Guatemala	Guatemala	—
Holland	Olanda	*o-'lan-da*
Honduras	Honduras (f)	—
Hungary	Ungheria	*un-ge-'ri-a*
India	India	—
Indonesia	Indonesia	—
Iran	Iran	—
Iraq	Iraq	—
Ireland	Irlanda	—
Israel	Israele	*iz-ra-'e-le*
Italy	Italia	*i-'ta-li-a*
Jamaica	Giamaica	*ja-'may-ka*
Japan	Giappone (m)	*jap-'po-ne*
Jordan	Giordania	*jor-'da-nya*
Kenya	Kenya	—
Korea	Corea	*ko-'re-a*
Kuwait	Kuwait (m)	—
Laos	Laos (m)	—
Lebanon	Libano	*'li-ba-no*
Liberia	Liberia	—
Libya	Libia	—
Lithuania	Lituania	*li-tu-'a-ni-a*
Luxembourg	Lussemburgo	*lus-sem-'bur-go*
Macedonia	Macedonia	*ma-če-'do-nya*
Malaysia	Malaysia	—
Malta	Malta	—
Melanesia	Melanesia	—
Mexico	Messico	*'mes-si-ko*
Middle East	Medio Oriente	*'me-dyo o-'ryen-te*
Moldavia	Moldavia	—
Monaco	Monaco	—
Mongolia	Mongolia	—
Montenegro	Montenegro	—
Morocco	Marocco	*ma-'rok-ko*
Near East	Vicino Oriente	*vi-'či-no o-'ryen-te*
New Zealand	Nuova Zelanda	*'nwo-va dze-'lan-da*
Nicaragua	Nicaragua	—
Nigeria	Nigeria	—
Norway	Norvegia	*nor-'ve-ja*
Oceania	Oceania	*o-če-'a-nya*

Pakistan	Pakistan (m)	—
Paraguay	Paraguay (m)	—
Peru	Perù (m)	—
Philippines	Filippine (f, pl)	*fi-lip-'pi-ne*
Poland	Polonia	*po-'lo-nya*
Polynesia	Polinesia	—
Portugal	Portogallo	*por-to-'gal-lo*
Puerto Rico	Puerto Rico	—
Rumania	Romania	*ro-ma-'ni-a*
Russia	Russia	*'rus-sya*
San Marino	San Marino	—
Saudi Arabia	Arabia Saudita	*a-'ra-bya sau-'di-ta*
Scandinavia	Scandinavia	—
Scotland	Scozia	*'sko-tsya*
Senegal	Senegal (m)	—
Serbia	Serbia	—
Siberia	Siberia	—
Singapore	Singapore (m)	*sin-ga-'po-re*
Slovakia	Slovacchia	*zlo-'vak-kya*
Slovenia	Slovenia	*zlo-'ve-nya*
Somalia	Somalia	—
South Africa	Sud Africa	—
Spain	Spagna	*'spa-nya*
Sri Lanka	Sri Lanka	—
Sudan	Sudan	—
Sweden	Svezia	*'zve-tsya*
Switzerland	Svizzera	*'zvi-tse-ra*
Syria	Siria	—
Tanzania	Tanzania	—
Thailand	Tailandia	*tai-'lan-dya*
Tunisia	Tunisia	*tu-ni-'zi-a*
Turkey	Turchia	*tur-'ki-a*
Uganda	Uganda	—
United States	Stati Uniti (m, pl)	*'sta-ti u-'ni-ti*
Uruguay	Uruguay	—
Venezuela	Venezuela	—
Vietnam	Vietnam	—
Wales	Galles	*'gal-les*
Zambia	Zambia (m)	—

C. CITIES, PLACES, AND SITES

Adriatic	Adriatico	*a'dri-'a-ti-ko*
Alexandria	Alessandria	*a-les-'san-drya*
Alps	Alpi (f, pl)	*'al-pi*
• **alpine**	alpino	*al-'pi-no*
Amsterdam	Amsterdam	—
Apennines	Appennini (m, pl)	*ap-pen-'ni-ni*

Formulas

to + country	in + *country*
to Italy	in Italia
to + city	a + *city*
to Rome	a Roma

Arno River	Arno	—
Athens	Atene	*a-'te-ne*
• **Athenian**	ateniese	*a-te-'nye-ze*
Atlantic	Atlantico	*at-'lan-ti-ko*
Balkans	Balcani (m, pl)	*bal-'ka-ni*
Barcelona	Barcellona	*bar-čel-'lo-na*
Bari	Bari	—
Beijing	Pechino	*pe-'ki-no*
Belgrade	Belgrado	*bel-'gra-do*
Berlin	Berlino	*ber-'li-no*
Bologna	Bologna	—
Cairo	il Cairo	—
Catanzaro	Catanzaro	—
Caucasian	caucasico	*kau-'ka-zi-ko*
Corsica	Corsica	—
• **Corsican**	corso	—
Dolomites	Dolomiti (f, pl)	*do-lo-'mi-ti*
Edinburgh	Edinburgo	*e-din-'bur-go*
Elba	Elba	—
Etna	Etna	—
Florence	Firenze	*fi-'ren-dze*
French Riviera	Costa Azzurra	*'kos-ta a-'dzur-ra*
Geneva	Ginevra	*ji-'ne-vra*
Genoa	Genova	*'je-no-va*
Ivory Coast	Costa d'Avorio	*'kos-ta da-'vo-ryo*
Lisbon	Lisbona	*liz-'bo-na*
London	Londra	*'lon-dra*
Madrid	Madrid	—
Mediterranean	Mediterraneo	*me-dit-ter-'ra-ne-o*
Milan	Milano	*mi-'la-no*
Moscow	Mosca	*'mos-ka*
Naples	Napoli	*'na-po-li*
New York	New York	—
Pacific	Pacifico	*pa-'či-fi-ko*
Palermo	Palermo	—
Paris	Parigi	*pa-'ri-ji*
Perugia	Perugia	—

Pisa	Pisa	—
Po river	Po	—
Reggio Calabria	Reggio Calabria	'rej-jo ka-'la-brya
Rimini	Rimini	'ri-mi-ni
Rome	Roma	—
Siena	Siena	—
Tiber River	Tevere (m)	'te-ve-re
Turin	Torino	—
Tyrrenean Sea	Tirreno	tir-'re-no
Venice	Venezia	ve-'ne-tsya
Vesuvius	Vesuvio	ve-'zu-vyo
Vienna	Vienna	—

D. ITALIAN REGIONS

Abruzzi	Abruzzo	—
Alto Adige	Alto Adige	'a-di-je
Aosta	Aosta	—
Apulia	Puglia	'pu-lye
Calabria	Calabria	—
Campania	Campania	—
Emilia	Emilia Romagna	ro-'ma-nya
Friuli	Friuli	—
Latium	Lazio	'la-tsyo
Liguria	Liguria	—
Lombardy	Lombardia	lom-bar-'di-a
Lucania	Basilicata	Ba-'zi-li-ka-ta
Molise	Molise (m)	mo-'li-ze
Piedmont	Piemonte (m)	pye-'mon-te
Sardinia	Sardegna	sar-'de-nya
Sicily	Sicilia	si-'či-lya
Trentino Alto-Adige	Trentino Alto-Adige	tren-'ti-no 'al-to 'a-di-je
Tuscany	Toscana	tos-'ka-na
Umbria	Umbria	—
Venetia	Veneto	've-ne-to

E. NATIONALITIES

African	africano	a-fri-'ka-no
Albanian	albanese	al-ba-'ne-ze
Algerian	algerino	al-je-'ri-no
American	americano	a-me-ri-'ka-no
Arabic	arabo	'a-ra-bo
Argentinean	argentino	ar-jen-'ti-no
Armenian	armeno	ar-'me-no
Australian	australiano	aus-tra-'lya-no
Austrian	austriaco	aus-'tri-a-ko
Belgian	belga	'bel-ga

Pattern

All nationalities are given in the masculine form. *In general,* the language
name is the same as the nationality.

tedesco   =   German nationality and language

but

canadese   =   Canadian
inglese/francese   =   Canada's two official languages

Bolivian	boliviano	*bo-li-'vya-no*
Bosnian	bosniaco	*boz-'ni-a-ko*
Brazilian	brasiliano	*bra-zi-'lya-no*
British	britannico	*bri-'tan-ni-ko*
Bulgarian	bulgaro	*'bul-ga-ro*
Cambodian	cambogiano	*kam-bo-'jano*
Canadian	canadese	*ka-na-'de-ze*
Cantonese	cantonese	*kan-to-'ne-ze*
Caribbean	caraibico	*ka-'ray-bi-ko*
Chilean	cileno	*či-'le-no*
Chinese	cinese	*či-'ne-ze*
Colombian	colombiano	*ko-lom-'bya-no*
Congolese	congolese	*kon-go-'le-ze*
Costa Rican	costaricano	*kos-ta-ri-'ka-no*
Croatian	croato	*kro-'a-to*
Cuban	cubano	*ku-'ba-no*
Czech	ceco	*če-ko*
Danish	danese	*da-'ne-ze*
Dominican	dominicano	*do-mi-ni-'ka-no*
Dutch	olandese	*o-lan-'de-ze*
Easterner, Oriental	orientale	*o-ryen-'ta-le*
Ecuadorian	ecuadoriano	*e-kwa-do-'rya-no*
Egyptian	egiziano	*e-ji-'tsya-no*
English	inglese	*in-'gle-ze*
Estonian	estone	*'es-to-ne*
Ethiopian	etiope	*e-'ti-o-pe*
European	europeo	*eu-ro-'pe-o*
Filipino	filippino	*fi-lip-'pi-no*
Finnish	finlandese	*fin-lan-'de-ze*
French	francese	*fran-'če-ze*
German	tedesco	*te-'des-ko*
Greek	greco	*'gre-ko*
Guatemalan	guatemalteco	*gwa-te-mal-'te-ko*

Haitian	haitiano	*ay-'tya-no*
Honduran	honduregno	*on-du-'renyo*
Hungarian	ungherese	*un-ge-'re-ze*
Indian	indiano	*in-'dya-no*
Indonesian	indonesiano	*in-do-ne-'zya-no*
Iranian	iraniano	*i-ra-'nya-no*
Iraqi	iracheno	*i-ra-'ke-no*
Irish	irlandese	*ir-lan-'de-ze*
Israeli	israeliano	*iz-ra-e-'lya-no*
Italian	italiano	*i-ta-'lya-no*
Jamaican	giamaicano	*ja-may-'ka-no*
Japanese	giapponese	*jap-po-'ne-ze*
Jordanian	giordano	*jor-'da-no*
Kenyan	keniano	*ke-'nya-no*
Korean	coreano	*ko-re-'a-no*
Kuwaiti	kuwaitiano	*ku-way-'tya-no*
Laotian	laoziano	*la-o-'tsya-no*
Lebanese	libanese	*li-ba-'ne-ze*
Liberian	liberiano	*li-be-'rya-no*
Libyan	libico	*'li-bi-ko*
Lithuanian	lituano	*li-'twa-no*
Luxembourger	lussemburghese	*lus-sem-bur-'ge-ze*
Macedonian	macedone	*ma-'če-do-ne*
Malaysian	malaysiano	*ma-lay-'sya-no*
Maltese	maltese	*mal-'te-ze*
Mexican	messicano	*mes-si-'ka-no*
Middle Easterner	mediorientale	*me-dyo-ryen-'ta-le*
Moldavian	moldavo	*mol-'da-vo*
Mongolian	mongolo	*'mon-go-lo*
Moroccan	marrocchino	*mar-rok-'ki-no*
New Zealander	neozelandese	*ne-o-dze-lan-'de-ze*
Nicaraguan	nicaraguense	*ni-ka-ra-'gwen-se*
Nigerian	nigeriano	*ni-je-'rya-no*
North American	nordamericano	*nord-a-me-ri-'ka-no*
Norwegian	norvegese	*nor-ve-'je-ze*
Pakistani	pachistano	*pa-kis-'ta-no*
Palestinian	palestinese	*pa-les-ti-'ne-ze*
Paraguayan	paraguaiano	*pa-ra-gwa-'ya-no*
Peruvian	peruviano	*pe-ru-'vya-no*
Polish	polacco	*po-'lak-ko*
Portuguese	portoghese	*por-to-'ge-ze*
Puerto Rican	portoricano	*por-to-ri-'ka-no*
Rumanian	rumeno	*ru-'me-no*
Russian	russo	*'rus-so*
Salvadoran	salvadoregno	*sal-va-do-'re-nyo*
Saudi	saudita	*sau-'di-ta*
Scandinavian	scandinavo	*skan-di-'na-vo*
Scottish	scozzese	*skot-'tse-ze*

Senegalese	senegalese	*se-ne-ga-'le-ze*
Serbian	serbo	*'ser-bo*
Siberian	siberiano	*si-be-'rya-no*
Singaporean	singaporiano	*sin-ga-po-'rya-no*
Slavic	slavo	*'zla-vo*
Slovak	slovacco	*zlo-'vak-ko*
Slovenian	sloveno	*zlo-'ve-no*
Somalian	somalo	*'so-ma-lo*
South African	sudafricano	*sud-a-fri-'ka-no*
South American	sudamericano	*sud-a-me-ri-'ka-no*
Spanish	spagnolo	*spa-'nyo-lo*
Sudanese	sudanese	*su-da-'ne-ze*
Swedish	svedese	*zve-'de-ze*
Swiss	svizzero	*'zvit-tse-ro*
Syrian	siriano	*si-'rya-no*
Thai	tailandese	*tay-lan-'de-ze*
Tunisian	tunisino	*tu-ni-'zi-no*
Turkish	turco	*'tur-ko*
Ugandan	ugandese	*u-gan-'de-ze*
Uruguayan	uruguaiano	*u-ru-gwa-'ya-no*
Venezuelan	venezuelano	*ve-ne-tswe-'la-no*
Vietnamese	vietnamita	*vyet-na-'mi-ta*
Welsh	gallese	*gal-'le-ze*
Westerner	occidentale	*oč-či-den-'ta-le*
Zambian	zambiano	*dzam-'bya-no*

31. PACKING AND GOING THROUGH CUSTOMS

baggage, luggage	bagaglio	*ba-'ga-lyo*
• **hand luggage**	bagaglio a mano	—
border	frontiera	*fron-'tye-ra*
citizenship	cittadinanza	*čit-ta-di-'nan-dza*
customs	dogana	*do-'ga-na*
• **customs officer**	doganiere (-a)	*do-ga-'nye-re*
(to) declare	dichiarare	*di-kya-'ra-re*
• **nothing to declare**	niente da dichiarare	*'nyen-te*
document	documento	*do-ku-'men-to*
duty tax	tassa	—
• **(to) pay duty**	pagare la dogana	*pa-'ga-re la do-'ga-na*
foreign currency	valuta straniera	*va-'lu-ta stra-'nye-ra*
foreigner	straniero (-a)	*stra-'nye-ro*
form (to fill out)	modulo	*'mo-du-lo*
Identification document,	carta d'identità	*'kar-ta di-den-ti-'ta*
proof of identity		
nationality	nazionalità (f, inv)	*na-tsyo-na-li-'ta*
passport	passaporto	*pas-sa-'por-to*
• **passport control**	controllo passaporti	*kon-'trol-lo*
purse	borsa	—

suitcase	valigia	*va-'li-'ja*
tariff	tariffa	*ta-'rif-fa*
visa	visto	—
weight	peso	*'pes-zo*
• heavy	pesante	*pe-'zan-te*
• light	leggero	*lej-'je-ro*

32. TRAVELING BY AIR

A. IN THE TERMINAL

airline	linea aerea	*'li-ne-a a-'e-re-a*
airplane	aereo	*a-'e-re-o*
airport	aeroporto	*a-e-ro-'por-to*
boarding	imbarco	*im-'bar-ko*
• (to) board	salire* (ess) a bordo	*sa-'li-re*
• boarding pass	carta d'imbarco	*dim-'bar-ko*
check-in	accettazione (f)	*ač-čet-ta-'tsyo-ne*
	check-in (m)	—
connection	coincidenza	*ko-in-či-'den-tsa*
economy class	classe turistica	*'klas-se tu-'ris-ti-ka*
first class	prima classe	—
information counter,	banco	*ban-ko*
information desk	informazioni	
lost and found	ufficio oggetti smarriti	*uf-'fi-čo oj-'jet-ti*
		zmar-'ri-ti
no smoking	vietato fumare	*vye-'ta-to fu-'ma-re*
(to) pick up one's baggage	ritirare il bagaglio	*ri-ti-'ra-re il ba-'ga-lyo*
porter	assistente ai bagagli	*ba-'ga-lyi*
reservation	prenotazione (f)	*pre-no-ta-'tsyo-ne*
shuttle vehicle	navetta	*na-'vet-ta*
terminal	terminal (m, inv)	—
ticket	biglietto	*bi-'lyet-to*
• e-ticket	biglietto elettronico	*e-let-'tro-ni-ko*
ticket agent	bigliettaio (-a)	*bi-lyet-'ta-yo*
waiting room	sala d'aspetto	*'sa-la das-pet-to*

B. FLIGHT INFORMATION

arrival	arrivo	*ar-'ri-vo*
canceled	cancellato	*kan-čel-'la-to*
departure	partenza	*par-'ten-dza*
early	in anticipo	*an-'ti-či-po*
flight	volo	—
gate, exit	uscita	*u-'ši-ta*
international flight	volo internazionale	*in-ter-na-tsyo-'na-le*
late, delayed	in ritardo	*ri-'tar-do*
national, domestic flight	volo nazionale	*na-tsyo-'na-le*

on time	in orario	o-'ra-ryo
schedule, times board	orario	o-'ra-ryo
transit	transito	'tran-zi-to
• transit passenger	passeggero (-a) in transito	pas-sej-'je-ro

C. ON THE PLANE

cabin	cabina	ka-'bi-na
captain	comandante (m/f)	ko-man-'dan-te
copilot	copilota (m/f)	ko-pi-'lo-ta
crew	equipaggio	e-kwi-'paj-jo
flight attendant	assistente (m/f) di volo	as-sis-'ten-te
flying time	durata del volo	du-'ra-ta
headphones	auricolari (m, pl,)	au-ri-ko-'la-ri
(to) land	atterrare	at-ter-'ra-re
• landing	atterraggio	at-ter-'raj-jo
• landing gear	carrello	kar-'rel-lo
life jacket	salvagente (m, inv)	sal-va-'jen-te
motor	motore (m)	mo-'to-re
passenger	passeggero (-a)	pas-sej-'je-ro
pilot	pilota (m/f)	pi-'lo-ta
runway	pista	—
seat	posto	—
• aisle	corridoio	kor-ri-'do-yo
• back of the seat	schienale (m)	skye-'na-le
• (to) buckle	allacciare	al-lač-'ča-re
• seat belt	cintura di sicurezza	čin-'tu-ra si-ku-'ret-tsa
• window	finestrino	fi-nes-'tri-no
stopover	scalo	'ska-lo
(to) take off	decollare	de-kol-'la-re
• take-off	decollo	de-'kol-lo
time difference	fuso orario	'fu-zo o-'ra-ryo
toilet	toletta	to-'let-ta
tray	vassoio	vas-'so-yo
turbulence	turbolenza	tur-bo-'lendza
wing	ala	—

33. ON THE ROAD

A. DRIVING

accident	incidente (m)	in-či-'den-te
(to) brake	frenare	fre-'na-re
bridge	ponte (m)	'pon-te
corner (street)	angolo	'an-go-lo
city block	isolato	i-zo-'la-to

curve	curva	*'kur-va*
distance	distanza	*dis-'tan-dza*
(to) drive	guidare	*gwi-'da-re*
• driver	autista (m/f)	*au-'tis-ta*
	conducente (m/f)	*kon-du-'cen-te*
driver's license	patente (di guida)	*pa-'ten-te*
fine, traffic ticket	multa	—
gas station	stazione (f) di servizio	*sta-'tsyo-ne di ser-'vi-tsyo*
• (to) change the oil	cambiare l'olio	*kam-'bya-re 'lo-lyo*
• (to) check the oil	controllare l'olio	*kon-trol-'la-re 'lo-lyo*
• (to) fill up	fare* il pieno	*'fa-re il 'pye-no*
• (to) fix	aggiustare	*aj-jus-'ta-re*
• gas	benzina	*ben-'dzi-na*
• gas attendant	benzinaio (-a)	*ben-dzi-'na-yo*
• mechanic	meccanico (-a)	*mek-'ka-ni-ko*
gears	marcia	*'mar-ča*
• (to) back up	fare* marcia indietro	*in-'dye-tro*
• (to) change gears	cambiare marcia	*kam-'bya-re*
• (to) go forward	fare* marcia avanti	*a-'van-ti*
(to) go through a red light	passare col rosso	*pas-'sa-re*
highway	autostrada	*au-to-'stra-da*
• highway police	polizia stradale	*po-li-'tsi-a stra-'da-le*
insurance card	carta verde	—
intersection	incrocio	*in-'kro-čo*
lane (traffic)	corsia	*kor-'si-a*
ownership papers	libretto di circolazione	*li-'bret-to di čir-ko-la-'styo-ne*
(to) park	parcheggiare	*par-kej-'ja-re*
• parking	parcheggio	*par-'kej-jo*
(to) pass	sorpassare	*sor-pas-'sa-re*
pedestrian	pedone (m)	*pe-'do-ne*
• pedestrian crosswalk	passaggio pedonale	*pas-'saj-jo pe-do-'na-le*
policeman, police woman	carabiniere (-a)	*ka-ra-bi-'nye-re*
	poliziotto (-a)	*po-li-'tsyot-to*
• traffic policeman	vigile (-essa)	*'vi-ji-le*
ramp	rampa	—
road map	mappa stradale	—
road sign	segnale stradale	*se-'nya-le stra-'da-le*
rush hour	ora di punta	—
speed	velocità (f, inv)	*ve-lo-či-'ta*
• (to) slow down	rallentare	*ral-len-'ta-re*
• (to) speed up	accelerare	*ač-če-le-'ra-re*
(to) start the car	mettere* in moto	*'met-te-re*
toll booth	casello (stradale)	*ka-'zel-lo*
(to) tow the car	rimorchiare la macchina	*ri-mor-'kya-re la 'mak-ki-na*
• towing	rimorchio	*ri-'mor-kyo*

Common Road Signs

No U-turn

No passing

Border crossing

Traffic signal ahead

Speed limit

Traffic circle
(roundabout) ahead

Minimum speed limit

All traffic turns left

End of no passing zone

One-way street

Detour

Danger ahead

Entrance to
expressway

Expressway ends

traffic	traffico	'traf-fi-ko
• traffic jam	ingorgo	in-'gor-go
• traffic lights	semaforo	se-'ma-fo-ro
tunnel	galleria	gal-'le-'ri-a
	tunnel (m, inv)	—
turn	svolta	'zvol-ta
• left turn, exit left	svolta a sinistra	si-'nis-tra
• right turn, exit right	svolta a destra	'des-tra
• (to) turn	girare	ji-'ra-re
• (to) turn left	girare a sinistra	—
• (to) turn right	girare a destra	—

B. SIGNS

Bicycle path	Pista ciclabile	či-'kla-bi-le
Closed	Chiuso	'kyu-zo
Closed for holidays	Chiuso per ferie	'fe-rye
Emergency lane	Corsia d'emergenza	kor-'si-a de-mer-'jen-dza
Entrance	Ingresso	in-gres-so
Exit	Uscita	u-'ši-ta
Information	Informazioni	in-for-ma-'tsyo-ni
Lane reserved	Corsia preferenziale	kor-'si-a pre-fe-ren-'tsya-le
Level crossing	Passaggio a livello	pas-'saj-jo a li-'vel-lo
Limited parking	Sosta limitata	li-mi-'ta-ta
Merge	Confluenza	kon-flu-'en-dza
No entrance	Vietato l'ingresso	vye-'ta-to lin-'gres-so
No entry	Divieto di accesso	di-'vye-to dač-'čes-so
No exit	Vietata l'uscita	vye-'ta-ta lu-'ši-ta
No left turn	Divieto di svolta a sinistra	di-'vye-to 'svol-ta a si-'nis-tra
No parking	Sosta vietata	vye-'ta-ta
No passing	Divieto di sorpasso	di-'vye-to di sor-'pas-so
No right turn	Divieto di svolta a destra	di-'vye-to di 'svol-ta
No smoking	Vietato fumare	vye-'ta-to fu-'ma-re
No stopping	Divieto di fermata	di-'vye-to di fer-'ma-ta
No thoroughfare	Divieto di transito	di-'vye-to di 'tran-zi-to
No U-turn	Divieto di inversione a U	di-'vye-to in-ver-'zyo-ne
One way	Senso unico	'sen-so 'u-ni-ko
Open	Aperto	a-'per-to
Out of order	Fuori servizio	'fwo-ri ser-'vi-tsyo
Passing lane	Corsia di sorpasso	kor-'si-a di sor-'pas-so
Slippery when wet	Strada sdrucciolevole	'stra-da zdruč-čo-'le-vo-le
Speed limit	Limite di velocità	'li-mi-te di ve-lo-či-'ta
Stop	Stop	—

Common Road Signs

Guarded railroad crossing

Yield

Stop

Right of way

Dangerous intersection ahead

Gasoline (petrol) ahead

Parking

No vehicles allowed

Dangerous curve

Pedestrian crossing

Oncoming traffic has right of way

No bicycles allowed

No parking allowed

No entry

No left turn

Toll	Pedaggio	*pe-'daj-jo*
Tow-away zone	Zona rimozione	*'dzo-na ri'-mo-zyo-ne*
Underpass	Sottopassaggio	*sot-to-pas-'saj-jo*
Washroom	Toilette	—
	Servizi	*ser-'vi-zi*
Work in progress	Lavori in corso	*la-'vo-ri*
Yield	Precedenza	*pre-če-'den-dza*

C. THE CAR

air conditioning	aria condizionata	*'a-rya kon-di-tsyo-'na-ta*
back seat	sedile (m) posteriore	*se-'di-le pos-te-'ryo-re*
battery	batteria	*bat-te-'ri-a*
brake	freno	—
bumper	paraurti (inv)	*pa-ra-'ur-ti*
car body	carrozzeria	*kar-ro-tse-'ri-a*
car dealer(ship)	concessionario	*kon-čes-syo-'na-ryo*
car door	portiera	*por-'tye-ra*
car roof	tetto	*'tet-to*
car seat	sedile (m)	*se-'di-le*
car window	finestrino	*fi-nes-'tri-no*
carburetor	carburatore (m)	*kar-bu-ra-'to-re*
carpet	tappezzeria	*tap-pe-tse-'ri-a*
choke	valvola dell'aria	*'val-vo-la del-'la-rya*
clutch	frizione (f)	*fri-'tsyo-ne*
dashboard	cruscotto	*krus-'kot-to*
fender	parafango	*pa-ra-'fan-go*
filter	filtro	*'fil-tro*
front seat	sedile (m) anteriore	*se-'di-le an-te-'ryo-re*
gas pedal	acceleratore (m)	*ač-če-le-ra-'to-re*
gas tank	serbatoio	*ser-'ba-'to-yo*
gearshift	leva del cambio	*'le-va del -'kam-byo*
glove compartment	cassetto ripostiglio	*kas-'set-to ri-pos-'ti-lyo*
handle	maniglia	*ma-'ni-lya*
heater	aereatore (m)	*a-e-re-a-'to-re*
hood, bonnet	cofano	*'ko-fa-no*
horn	clacson (m, inv)	—
horse power	cilindrata	*či-lin-'dra-ta*
jack	cric (m, inv)	—
license plate	targa	—
light	faro	—
luggage rack	portabagaglio (inv)	*por-ta-ba-'ga-lyo*
motor	motore (m)	*mo-'to-re*
• fan	ventola	*'ven-to-la*
• gas pump	pompa della benzina	*ben-'dzi-na*
• generator	dinamo (f, inv)	*'di-na-mo*
• piston	pistone (m)	*pis-'to-ne*

• **sparkplug**	candela	*kan-'de-la*
• **valve**	valvola	*'val-vo-la*
muffler	marmitta	*mar-'mit-ta*
oil	olio	*'o-lyo*
power brake	servofreno	*ser-vo-'fre-no*
power steering	servosterzo	*ser-vo-'ster-tso*
pump	pompa	—
radiator	radiatore (m)	*ra-dya-'to-re*
seat belt	cintura di sicurezza	*čin-'tu-ra di si-ku-'re-tsa*
side mirror	specchietto	*spek-'kyet-to*
signal light	luce (f) di posizione	*'lu-če di po-zi-'tsyo-ne*
speedometer	tachimetro	*ta-'ki-me-tro*
steering wheel	volante (m)	*vo-'lan-te*
tire	gomma	—
	pneumatico	*pne-u-'ma-ti-ko*
trunk	baule (m)	*ba-'u-le*
wheel	ruota	*'rwo-ta*
• **spare wheel**	ruota di scorta	*'skor-ta*
windshield	parabrezza (m, inv)	*pa-ra-'bret-tsa*
• **wiper**	tergicristallo	*ter-ji-'kris-'tal-lo*

D. CAR RENTAL

check-out vehicle **conditions**	condizioni del veicolo in uscita	*kon-di-'tsyo-ni del ve-'i-ko-lo in u-'ši-ta*
chip	scheggiatura	*skej-ja-'tu-ra*
dent	ammaccatura	*am-mak-ka-'tu-ra*
rate	tariffa	*ta-'rif-fa*
(to) rent	noleggiare	*no-lej-'ja-re*
• **rental**	noleggio	*no-'lej-jo*
• **rental place**	autonoleggio	*au-to-no-'lej-jo*
return vehicle **conditions**	condizioni del veicolo al rientro	*kon-di-'tsyo-ni del ve-'i-ko-lo al ri-'en-tro*
scratch	graffio	*'graf-fyo*
tear	squarcio	*'skwar-co*

34. TRANSPORTATION

ambulance	ambulanza	*am-bu-'lan-dza*
anchor	ancora	*'an-ko-ra*
automobile	automobile (f)	*au-to-'mo-bi-le*
	auto (f, inv)	—
bicycle	bicicletta	*bi-či-'klet-ta*
• **brake**	freno	*'fre-no*
• **handlebar**	manubrio	*ma-'nu-bryo*
• **pedal**	pedale (m)	*pe-'da-le*
• **seat**	sellino (m)	*sel-'li-no*

• spoke	raggio	*'raj-jo*
• tire	pneumatico	*pne-u-'ma-ti-ko*
bus	autobus (m, inv)	—
• bus driver	autista (m/f)	*au-'tis-ta*
• bus station, depot	capolinea (m)	*ka-po-'li-ne-a*
• courier bus, express	corriera	*kor-'rye-ra*
car	macchina	*'mak-ki-na*
• compact car	utilitaria	*u-ti-li-'ta-rya*
• rented car	macchina, auto noleggiata	*no-lej-'ja-ta*
• sports car	macchina, auto sportiva	*spor-'ti-va*
car-ferry	nave (f) traghetto	*'na-ve tra-'get-to*
commuter	pendolare (m/f)	*pen-do-'la-re*
compass	bussola	*'bus-so-la*
conductor	conduttore (-trice)	*kon-dut-'to-re*
connection	coincidenza	*ko-in-či-'den-dza*
driver (of a public vehicle)	conducente (m/f)	*kon-du-'čen-te*
ferry	traghetto	*tra-'get-to*
(to) hitchhike	fare* l'autostop	—
• hitchhiker	autostoppista (m/f)	*au-to-stop-'pis-ta*
(to) leave, depart	partire (ess)	*par-'ti-re*
• (to) miss (a bus)	perdere*	*'per-de-re*
life-jacket	giubbotto di salvataggio	*jub-'bot-to di sal-va-'taj-jo*
minivan	pulmino	*pul-'mi-no*
motor scooter	motorino	*mo-to-'ri-no*
motorcycle	motocicletta	*mo-to-či-'klet-ta*
newsstand	edicola	*e-'di-ko-la*
oar	remo	—
paddle	pagaia	*pa-'ga-ya*
porthole	oblò (m, inv)	—
propeller	elica	*'e-li-ka*
public transport	trasporto pubblico	*tras-'por-to 'pub-bli-ko*
raft	zattera	*'dzat-te-ra*
railroad	ferrovia	*fer-ro-'vi-a*
• station	stazione (f) ferroviaria	*sta-'tsyo-ne fero-ro-vi-'a-rya*
schedule	orario	*o-'ra-ryo*
• arrival	arrivo	*ar-'ri-vo*
• canceled	cancellato	*kan-čel-'la-to*
• departure	partenza	*par-'ten-dza*
seat	posto	—
stop	fermata	*fer-'ma-ta*
subway	metropolitana	*me-tro-po-li-'ta-na*
• subway entrance	entrata della metropolitana	*en-'tra-ta*
• subway station	stazione (f) della metropolitana	*sta-'tsyo-ne*

ticket	biglietto	*bi-'lyet-to*
• **e-ticket**	biglietto elettronico	*e-let-'tro-ni-ko*
• **ticket agent**	bigliettaio (-a)	*bi-lyet-'ta-yo*
• **ticket office, counter**	biglietteria	*bi-lyet-te-'ri-a*
• **ticket machine**	biglietteria automatica	*au-to-'ma-ti-ka*
transportation	trasporto	*tras-'por-to*
tow truck	autosoccorso	*au-to-sok-'kor-so*
	autorimorchiatore (m)	*au-to-ri-mor-kya-'to-re*
train	treno	—
• **coach**	vagone (m)	*va-'go-ne*
• **compartment**	scompartimento	*skom-par-ti-'men-to*
• **locomotive**	locomotiva	*lo-ko-mo-'ti-va*
• **railway**	ferrovia	*fer-ro-'vi-a*
• **sleeping coach**	vagone (m) letto	—
• **track**	binario	*bi-'na-ryo*
• **train station**	stazione ferroviaria	*sta-tsyo-ne fer-ro-vi-'a-rya*
truck	camion (m, inv)	—
• **fire truck**	autopompa	*au-to-'pom-pa*
• **garbage truck**	autoimmondizie	*au-to-im-mon-'di-tsye*
van	furgone (m)	*fur-'go-ne*
vehicle	veicolo	*ve-'i-ko-lo*
(to) wait for	aspettare	*as-pet-'ta-re*

35. HOTELS

A. LODGING AND HOTELS

all-inclusive price	prezzo forfettario	*'pret-tso for-fet-'ta-ryo*
banquet	banchetto	*ban-'ket-to*
bellhop	fattorino (-a)	*fat-to-'ri-no*
bill	conto	—
bread and breakfast	pensione (f)	*pen-'syo-ne*
breakfast	prima colazione	*'pri-ma ko-la-'tsyo-ne*
• **breakfast included**	colazione compresa	*kom-'pre-za*
camping	campeggio	*kam-'pej-jo*
clerk	impiegato (-a)	*im-pye-'ga-to*
(to) complain	lamentarsi	*la-men-'tar-si*
• **complaint**	lamentela	*la-men-'te-la*
doorman, doorwoman	portiere (-a)	*por-'tye-re*
elevator	ascensore (m)	*a-šen-'so-re*
entrance	ingresso	*in-'gres-so*
exit	uscita	*u-'ši-ta*
floor	piano	—
foyer, lobby	atrio	*'a-tri-o*
ground floor	pianterreno	*pyan-ter-'re-no*
hostel	ostello	*os-'tel-lo*
hotel	albergo	*al-'ber-go*

• five-star hotel	albergo a cinque stelle	*'cin-kwe 'stel-le*
• hotel room	camera	*'ka-me-ra*
• luxury hotel	albergo di lusso	*'lus-so*
• modest hotel	albergo modesto	*mo-'des-to*
identification card	carta d'identità	*i-den-ti-'ta*
key	chiave (f)	*'kya-ve*
lodging, accommodations	alloggio	*al-'loj-jo*
luggage rack	portabagagli (m, inv)	*por-ta-ba-'ga-lyi*
lunch	pranzo	*'pran-dzo*
maid	cameriera	*ka-me-'rye-ra*
main door	portone (m)	*por-'to-ne*
manager	direttore (-trice)	*di-ret-'to-re*
message	messaggio	*mes-'saj-jo*
motel	motel (m, inv)	—
pool	piscina	*pi-'ši-na*
price	prezzo	*'pret-tso*
• high season	alta stagione	*al-ta sta-'jo-ne*
• low season	bassa stagione	*'bas-sa sta-'jo-ne*
• rate	tariffa	*ta-'rif-fa*
receipt	ricevuta	*ri-če-'vu-ta*
reservation	prenotazione (f)	*pre-no-ta-'tsyo-ne*
• (to) reserve	prenotare	*pre-no-'ta-re*
room	camera	*'ka-me-ra*
	stanza	*'stan-dza*
• double room	camera doppia	*'ka-mera 'dop-pya*
• single bed	camera singola	*'sin-go-la*
• with two beds	camera a due letti	—
• with double bed	camera matrimoniale	*ma-tri-mo-'nya-le*
services	servizi (m, pl)	*ser-'vi-tsi*
stairs	scale (f, pl)	*'ska-le*
view	veduta	*ve-'du-ta*
wake-up call	sveglia (telefonica)	*'zve-lya*

B. THE HOTEL ROOM

armchair	poltrona	*pol-'tro-na*
balcony	terrazza	*ter-'ra-tsa*
• sliding door	porta scorrevole	*'por-ta skor-'re-vo-le*
bath tub	vasca	—
bathroom	bagno	*'ba-nyo*
bed	letto	—
• double bed	letto matrimoniale	*ma-tri-mo-'nya-le*
bedside table	comodino	*ko-mo-'di-no*
blanket	coperta	*ko-'per-ta*
chest of drawers	cassettone (m)	*kas-se-'to-ne*
closet	armadio	*ar-'ma-dyo*
clothes hanger	attaccapanni (m, inv)	*at-tak-ka-'pan-ni*

curtain	tenda	'ten-da
dresser	comò (m, inv)	—
faucet	rubinetto	ru-bi-'net-to
lamp	lampada	'lam-pa-da
light	luce (f)	'lu-če
• current	corrente (f)	kor-'ren-te
• switch	interruttore (m)	in-ter-rut-'to-re
• (to) turn off	spegnere*	'spe-nye-re
• (to) turn on	accendere*	ač-'čen-de-re
(to) overlook	guardare su	gwar-'da-re
pillow	cuscino	ku-'ši-no
soap	sapone (m)	sa-'po-ne
shampoo	shampoo (m, inv)	—
sheets	lenzuola (f, pl)	len-'tswo-la
shower	doccia	'doč-ča
soap bar	saponetta	sa-po-'net-ta
sink, wash basin	lavabo	la-'va-bo
• cold water	acqua fredda	'ak-kwa 'fred-da
• hot water	acqua calda	'kal-da
thermostat	termostato	ter-'mos-ta-to
toilet paper	carta igienica	'kar-ta i-'jye-ni-ka
towel	asciugamano	a-šu-ga-'ma-no

36. ON VACATION

A. SIGHTSEEING

alley, lane	vicolo	'vi-ko-lo
amphitheater	anfiteatro	an-fi-te-'a-tro
amusement park	luna park (m, inv)	—
ancient monument	monumento storico	mo-nu-'men-to 'sto-ri-ko
art gallery (museum)	galleria d'arte	gal-le-'ri-a 'dar-te
	museo	mu-'ze-o
avenue, large road	corso	—
barracks	caserma	ka-'zer-ma
basilica	basilica	ba-'zi-li-ka
bell tower	campanile (m)	kam-pa-'ni-le
botanical gardens	giardino botanico	jar-'di-no bo-'ta-ni-ko
bridge	ponte (m)	'pon-te
building	edificio	e-di-'fi-čo
bypass, highway	raccordo stradale	rak-'kor-do stra-'da-le
capital (of the country)	capitale (f)	ka-pi-'ta-le
capital town (of a region)	capoluogo	ka-po-'lwo-go
cathedral	cattedrale (f)	kat-te-'dra-le
chapel	cappella	kap-'pel-la
church	chiesa	'kye-za
city	città (f, inv)	čit-'ta
• city hall	municipio	mu-ni-'či-pyo

• city map	pianta della città	'pyan-ta
• city dweller, citizen	cittadino (-a)	čit-ta-'di-no
commuter	pendolare (m/f)	pen-do-'la-re
condominium	condominio	kon-do-'mi-nyo
courthouse	tribunale (m)	tri-bu-'na-le
district	quartiere (m)	kwar-'tye-re
downtown	centro	'čen-tro
(to) dwell, live in	abitare	a-bi-'ta-re
guide-book	guida	'gwi-da
gutter	fognatura	fo-nya-'tu-ra
intersection	incrocio	in-'kro-čo
kiosk	chiosco	'kyos-ko
law courts	palazzo di giustizia	pa-'lat-tso di jus-'ti-tsya
library	biblioteca	bib-lyo-'te-ka
(to) live (in a place)	vivere*	'vi-ve-re
monument	monumento	mo-nu-'men-to
museum	museo	mu-'ze-o
park	parco	'par-ko
parking meter	parchimetro	par-'ki-me-tro
pavement, sidewalk	marciapiede (m)	mar-ča-'pye-de
pedestrian crossing	passaggio pedonale	pas-'sajjo pe-do-'na-le
police station	questura	kwes-'tu-ra
public notices	affissioni pubbliche	af-fis-'syo-ni 'pub-bli-ke
railway crossing	passaggio a livello	pas-'saj-jo a li-'vel-lo
road, roadway, street	strada	—
souvenir shop	bottega dei souvenir	bot-'te-ga
square	piazza	'pya-tsa
stock exchange	borsa	—
street, road	via	—
tower	torre (f)	—
underpass	passaggio sotterraneo	pas-'saj-jo sot-ter-'ra-ne-o
urban dweller	urbano (-a)	ur-'ba-no
water fountain	fontana	fon-'ta-na
worksite	cantiere (m)	kan-'tye-re

B. GETTING OUT OF THE CITY

beach	spiaggia	'spyaj-ja
boat	barca	—
brook	ruscello	ru-'šel-lo
canoe	canoa	ka-'no-a
chairlift	seggiovia	sej-jo-'vi-a
countryside	campagna	kam-'pa-nya
crafts	artigianato	ar-ti-ja-'na-to
cruise	crociera	kro-'če-ra
deck chair	sedia a sdraio	'se-dya a 'zdra-yo

fishing	pesca	'pes-ka
footpath, trail	sentiero	sen-'tye-ro
(to) go sightseeing	andare* (ess) in giro	an-'da-re in 'ji-ro
highway	autostrada	au-to-'stra-da
in the country	in campagna	kam-'pa-nya
in the mountains	in montagna	mon-'ta-nya
lake	lago	—
motorway restaurant	autogrill (m, inv)	—
mountain boots	scarponi (m, pl)	skar-'po-ni
mountain climbing	alpinismo	al-pi-'niz-mo
on vacation	in vacanza	va-'kan-dza
river	fiume (m)	'fyu-me
scenic route	itinerario panoramico	i-ti-ne-'ra-ryo
sea	mare (m)	'ma-re
ski resort	campo di sci	'kam-po di 'ši
sleeping bag	sacco a pelo	'sak-ko a -'pe-lo
suburb	sobborgo	sob-'bor-go
• suburbs, outskirts	periferia	per-i-fe-'ri-a
suntan	abbronzatura	ab-bron-dza-'tu-ra
	tintarella	tin-ta-'rel-la
• (to) get a suntan	abbronzarsi	ab-bron-'dzar-si
tent	tenda	—
tourist information office	ufficio d'informazioni turistiche	uf-'fi-čo din-for-ma-'tsyo-ni tu-'ris-ti-ke
tourist place, sight-seeing place	posto di villeggiatura	'pos-to di vil-lej-ja-'tu-ra
town (hamlet), village	paese (m)	pa-'e-ze
town (market-town)	borgo	—
town (small city)	cittadina	čit-ta-'di-na
town council	comune (m)	ko-'mu-ne
village	villaggio	vil-'laj-jo

C. ASKING FOR DIRECTIONS

across	attraverso	at-tra-'ver-so
ahead	avanti	a-'van-ti
at the end of	in fondo a	—
at the top of	in cima a	'či-ma
back	indietro	in-'dye-tro
behind	dietro	'dye-tro
(to) cross	attraversare	at-tra-ver-'sa-re
down	giù	ju
east	est	—
• to the east	a est	—
(to) enter	entrare (ess)	en-'tra-re
everywhere	dappertutto	dap-per-'tut-to
(to) exit, go out	uscire* (ess)	u-'ši-re
far	lontano	lon-'ta-no

(to) follow	seguire	se-'gwi-re
(to) go	andare* (ess)	an-'da-re
(to) go down	scendere* (ess)	'šen-de-re
(to) go up	salire* (ess)	sa-'li-re
here	qui	kwi
in front of	di fronte a	—
inside	dentro	—
left	sinistra	si-'nis-tra
• to the left	a sinistra	—
near	vicino	vi-'či-no
north	nord	—
• to the north	a nord	—
outside	fuori	'fwo-ri
right	destra	—
• to the right	a destra	—
south	sud	—
• to the south	a sud	—
straight ahead	diritto (dritto)	di-'rit-to
west	ovest	'o-vest
• to the west	a ovest	—

Basic Formulas

Can you tell me where...?	=	Mi sa dire dove...?
How do you get to...?	=	Come si fa per andare a...?
Where is...?	=	Dov'è...?

SCHOOL AND WORK

37. SCHOOL

A. TYPES OF SCHOOLS AND GENERAL VOCABULARY

coed school	scuola mista	'skwo-la 'mis-ta
commercial school	istituto commerciale	is-ti-'tu-to
compulsory education	istruzione (f)	is-tru-'tsyo-ne
	obbligatoria	ob-bli-ga-'to-rya
conservatory	conservatorio	kon-ser-va-'to-ryo
course	corso	—
• correspondence course	corso per corrispondenza	kor-ris-pon-'den-tsa
daycare	asilo nido	a-'zi-lo 'ni-do
dean, chair of a faculty	preside (m/f) di facoltà	'pre-zi-de di fa-kol-'ta
(to) educate, instruct	istruire (isc)	is-tru-'i-re
• education (as process)	educazione (f)	e-du-ka-'tsyo-ne
• education, instruction	istruzione (f)	is-tru-'tsyo-ne
elementary school	scuola elementare	'skwo-la
evening course	corso serale	'kor-so se-'ra-le
evening school	scuola serale	'skwo-la se-'ra-le
faculty	facoltà (f, inv)	fa-kol-'ta
• architecture	facoltà di architettura	ar-ki-tet-'tu-ra
• arts	facoltà di lettere	'let-te-re
• business and commerce	facoltà di economia e commercio	kom-'mer-čo
• engineering	facoltà di ingegneria	in-je-nye-'ria
• jurisprudence, law	facoltà di giurisprudenza	ju-ris-pru-'den-tsa
• medicine	facoltà di medicina	me-di-'či-na
• sciences	facoltà di scienze	'šen-tse
grade	classe (f)	'klas-se
• grade one	prima	—
high school, lyceum	liceo	li-'če-o
• art lyceum	liceo artistico	ar-'tis-ti-ko
• arts and letters	liceo classico	'klas-si-ko
• languages lyceum	liceo linguistico	lin-'gwis-ti-ko
• scientific lyceum	liceo scientifico	šen-'ti-fi-ko
institute	istituto	is-ti-'tu-to
junior high school, middle school	scuola media	'skwo-la 'me-dya
kindergarten	asilo infantile	a-'zi-lo in-fan-'ti-le

Ministry of Public Education	Ministero della Pubblica Istruzione	—
nursery school	scuola materna	*'skwo-la ma-'ter-na*
primary school	scuola primaria	*'skwo-la pri-'ma-rya*
private school	scuola privata	*'skwo-la pri-'va-ta*
public school	scuola pubblica	*'skwo-la 'pub-bli-ka*
residential school (college)	collegio	*kol-'le-jo*
scholarship, grant	borsa di studio	*'bor-sa di 'stu-dyo*
• scholarship holder	borsista (m/f)	*bor-'sis-ta*
school	scuola	*'skwo-la*
school year	anno scolastico	*'an-no sko-'las-ti-ko*
secondary school	scuola secondaria	*'skwo-la se-kon-'da-rya*
specialization course	corso di specializzazione	*'kor-so di spe-ča-'li-dza-'tsyo-ne*
state school	scuola statale	*'skwo-la sta-'ta-le*
teacher training school	istituto magistrale	*is-ti-'tu-to ma-jis-'tra-le*
technical school, vocational school	istituto tecnico	*is-ti-'tu-to 'tek-ni-ko*
university	università (f, inv)	*u-ni-ver-si-'ta*
• first year	primo anno	—
• second year	secondo anno	—
university chair	cattedra	*'kat-te-dra*
upper school	scuola superiore	*'skwo-la su-pe-'ryo-re*

B. THE CLASSROOM

assignment book	agenda	*a-'jen-da*
ballpoint pen	biro (f, inv)	—
blackboard	lavagna	*la-'va-nya*
blackboard eraser	cancellino	*kan-čel-'li-no*
book	libro	—
calculator	calcolatrice (f)	*kal-ko-la-'tri-če*
• pocket calculator	calcolatrice tascabile	*tas-'ka-bi-le*
chalk	gesso	*'jes-so*
compass	compasso	*kom-'pas-so*
computer	computer (m, inv)	—
desk	banco	—
dictionary	dizionario	*di-tsyo-'na-ryo*
encyclopedia	enciclopedia	*en-či-klo-pe-'di-a*
eraser	gomma	—
glue, paste	colla	—
grammar book	grammatica	*gram-'ma-ti-ka*
highlighter	evidenziatore (m)	*e-vi-den-tsya-'to-re*
ink	inchiostro	*in-'kyos-tro*
knapsack. backpack	zaino	*'dzai-no*
laptop computer	laptop (m, inv)	—
manual	manuale (m)	*ma-'nwa-le*

map	cartina geografica	*kar-'ti-na je-o-'gra-fi-ka*
marker	pennarello	*pen-na-'rel-lo*
notebook, workbook	quaderno	*kwa-'der-no*
• ringed notebook	quaderno a anelli	*a-'nel-li*
• spiral notebook	quaderno a spirale	*spi-'ra-le*
overhead	lucido	*'lu-či-do*
• overhead projector	lavagna luminosa	*la-'va-nya lu-mi-'no-za*
paper	carta	*'kar-ta*
• carton paper	cartoncino	*kar-ton-'či-no*
• drawing paper	carta da disegno	*di-'ze-nyo*
• lined paper	carta a righe	*'ri-ge*
• squared paper	carta a quadretti	*kwa-'dret-ti*
projector	proiettore (m)	*pro-yet-'to-re*
protractor	goniometro	*go-'nyo-me-tro*
reading book	libro di lettura	*let-'tu-ra*
school bag	cartella	*kar-'tel-la*
textbook	libro di testo	—
writing desk	scrivania	*skri-va-'ni-a*

C. AREAS

cafeteria	mensa	—
campus	campus (inv)	—
classroom	aula	*'au-la*
gymnasium	palestra	*pa-'les-tra*
hallway	corridoio	*kor-ri-'do-yo*
laboratory	laboratorio	*la-bo-ra-'to-ryo*
library	biblioteca	*bib-lyo-'te-ka*
main office	segreteria	*se-gre-te-'ri-a*
office (of an instructor)	studio	*'stu-dyo*
school yard	cortile (m)	*kor-'ti-le*

D. PEOPLE

assistant	assistente (m/f)	*as-sis-'ten-te*
class (of students), grade	classe (f)	*'klas-se*
elementary school pupil	scolaro (-a)	*sko-'la-ro*
high school principal	preside (m/f) di liceo	*'pre-zi-de*
janitor	bidello (-a)	*bi-'del-lo*
librarian	bibliotecario (-a)	*bib-lyo-te-'ka-ryo*
non-teaching personnel	personale (m) non docente	*per-so-'na-le non do-'čen-te*
president of a university	rettore	*ret-'to-re*
principal	preside (m/f)	*'pre-zi-de*
pupil	alunno (-a)	*a-'lun-no*
schoolmate	compagno (-a)	*kom-'pa-nyo*
secretary	segretario (-a)	*se-gre-'ta-ryo*
self-learner	privatista	*pri-va-'tis-ta*

special education teacher	insegnante (m/f) di sostegno	*in-se-'nyan-te di sos-'te-nyo*
student	studente (-essa)	*stu-'den-te*
teacher, instructor	insegnante (m/f)	*in-se-'nyan-te*
• **elementary school**	maestro (-a)	*ma-'es-tro*
• **middle, high school**	professore (-essa)	*pro-fes-'so-re*
technician	tecnico (-a)	*'tek-ni-ko*

E. SUBJECTS

anatomy	anatomia	*a-na-to-'mi-a*
anthropology	antropologia	*an-tro-po-lo-'ji-a*
archeology	archeologia	*ar-ke-o-lo-'ji-a*
architecture	architettura	*ar-ki-tet-'tu-ra*
art	arte (f)	—
arts, humanities, letters	lettere (f, pl)	*'let-te-re*
astronomy	astronomia	*as-tro-no-'mi-a*
biology	biologia	*bi-o-lo-'ji-a*
botany	botanica	*bo-'ta-ni-ka*
chemistry	chimica	*'ki-mi-ka*
commerce	commercio	*kom-'mer-čo*
communication sciences	scienze della comunicazione	*'šen-dze del-la ko-mu-ni-ka-'tsyo-ne*
design	disegno	*di-'ze-nyo*
discipline	disciplina	*di-ši-'pli-na*
economics	economia	*e-ko-no-'mi-a*
engineering	ingegneria	*in-je-nye-'ri-a*
geography	geografia	*je-o-gra-'fi-a*
geometry	geometria	*je-o-me-'tri-a*
history	storia	*'sto-rya*
informatics, computer science	informatica	*in-for-'ma-ti-ka*
jurisprudence, law	giurisprudenza	*ju-ris-pru-'den-dza*
	legge (f)	*'lej-je*
languages	lingue (f, pl,)	*'lin-gwe*
linguistics	linguistica	*lin'-gwis-ti-ka*
literature	letteratura	*let-te-ra-'tu-ra*
mathematics	matematica	*ma-te-'ma-ti-ka*
medicine	medicina	*me-di-'či-na*
music	musica	*'mu-zi-ka*
philosophy	filosofia	*fi-lo-so-'fi-a*
physics	fisica	*'fi-zi-ka*
political science	scienze politiche	*'šen-dze po-'li-ti-ke*
psychiatry	psichiatria	*psi-ki-a-'tri-a*
psychology	psicologia	*psi-ko-lo-'ji-a*
science	scienza	*'šen-dza*
sociology	sociologia	*so-čo-lo-'ji-a*
statistics	statistica	*sta-'tis-ti-ka*

subject	materia	ma-'te-rya
trigonometry	trigonometria	tri-go-no-me-'tri-a
zoology	zoologia	dzo-o-lo-'ji-a

F. MISCELLANEOUS

ability	abilità (f, inv)	a-bi-li-'ta
admission test	prova d'ammissione	dam-mis-'syo-ne
answer	risposta	ris-'pos-ta
• (to) answer	rispondere*	ris-'pon-de-re
• brief, short	breve	—
• long	lunga	—
• right	corretta	kor-'ret-ta
• wrong	sbagliata	zba-'lya-ta
aptitude test	test d'attitudine	dat-ti-'tu-di-ne
assignment	compito	'kom-pi-to
(to) attend	frequentare	fre-kwen-'ta-re
• attendance	frequenza	fre-'kwen-dza
average	media	'me-dya
(to) be absent	essere* assente	'es-se-re as-'sen-te
(to) be present	essere* presente	'es-se-re pre'zen-te
(to) be promoted, pass	essere* promosso (-a)	'es-se-re pro-'mos-so
bibliography	bibliografia	bib-li-o-gra-'fi-a
bookmark	segnalibro	se-nya-'li-bro
catalogue	catalogo	ka-'ta-lo-go
class	classe (f)	'klas-se
• class, lesson	lezione (f)	le-'tsyo-ne
• (to) have a class	avere* lezione	—
• (to) skip a class	saltare una lezione	sal-'ta-re
composition	componimento	kom-po-ni-'men-to
computer-assisted learning	apprendimento tramite computer	ap-pren-di-'men-to
conference	convegno	kon-'ve-nyo
copy	copia	'ko-pya
• good, final copy	bella copia	—
• rough copy, draft	brutta copia	—
core subject	materia fondamentale	ma-'te-rya fon-da-men-'ta-le
curriculum	curriculum (m, inv)	—
degree	laurea	'lau-re-a
• (to) get a degree	laurearsi	lau-re 'ar-si
diploma	diploma (m) (diplomi, pl)	di-'plo-ma
• (to) get a diploma	diplomarsi	di-plo-'mar-si
drawing	disegno	di-'ze-nyo
• (to) draw	disegnare	di-ze-'nya-re
(to) drop out	abbandonare gli studi	ab-ban-do-'na-re lyi 'stu-di
educated	istruito	is-tru-'i-to

• education	istruzione (f)	is-tru-'tsyo-ne
(to) erase	cancellare	kan-čel-'la-re
error	errore (m)	er-'ro-re
evaluation, grading	valutazione (f)	va-lu-ta-'tsyo-ne
examination	esame (m)	e-'za-me
• entrance exam	esame d'ammissione	dam-mis-'syo-ne
• oral exam	esame orale	o-'ra-le
• (to) pass an exam	superare un esame	su-pe-'ra-re
• (to) take an exam	sostenere* un esame	sos-te-'ne-re
• written exam	esame scritto	'skrit-to
exercise	esercizio	e-zer-'či-tsyo
(to) fail	essere* bocciato	'es-se-re boč-'ča-to
• (to) fail (someone)	bocciare	boč-'ča-re
field (of study)	campo (di studio)	—
field trip	gita scolastica	'ji-ta sko-'las-ti-ka
grade, mark	voto	—
graph	grafico	'gra-fi-ko
group work	lavoro in gruppo	la-'vo-ro
(to) have a class, a lesson	avere* lezione	a-'ve-re le-'tsyo-ne
high school diploma	diploma (m) di	di-'plo-ma di
	maturità	ma-tu-ri-'ta
(to) learn	imparare	im-pa-'ra-re
• learning	apprendimento	ap-pren-di-'men-to
lesson, class	lezione (f)	le-'tsyo-ne
level of education	titolo di studio	'ti-to-lo di 'stu-dyo
(to) listen to	ascoltare	as-kol-'ta-re
(to) mark, correct	correggere*	kor-'rej-je-re
mistake	sbaglio	'zba-lyo
• (to) make mistakes	sbagliare	zba-'lya-re
note	appunto	ap-'pun-to
optional subject	materia opzionale	ma-'te-rya op-tsyo-'na-le
photocopy	fotocopia	fo-to-'ko-pya
• (to) photocopy	fotocopiare	fo-to-ko-'pya-re
physical education	educazione fisica	e-du-ka-'tsyo-ne 'fi-zi-ka
problem	problema (m) (problemi, pl)	pro-'ble-ma
• (to) solve a problem	risolvere* un problema	'ri-zol-ve-re un pro-'ble-ma
professional development	aggiornamento degli insegnanti	aj-jor-na-'men-to de-lyi in-se-'nyan-ti
professional development course	corso di formazione professionale	'kor-so di for-ma-'tsyo-ne pro-fes-syo-'na-le
quarter term	quadrimestre (m)	kwa-dri-'mes-tre
question	domanda	do-'man-da
• (to) ask a question	fare* una domanda	—
reading, reading passage	lettura	let-'tu-ra

• (to) read	leggere*	*'lej-je-re*
registration	iscrizione (f)	*is-kri-'tsyo-ne*
• registration fee	tassa d'iscrizione	*'tas-sa*
(to) repeat	ripetere	*ri-'pe-te-re*
report card	pagella	*pa-'jel-la*
review	ripasso	*ri-'pas-so*
• (to) review	ripassare	*ri-pas-'sa-re*
round table	tavola rotonda	*'ta-vo-la ro-'ton-da*
school fee, tuition	tassa scolastica	*'tas-sa sko-'las-ti-ka*
school registration	iscrizione (m) a scuola	*is-kri-'tsyo-ne a 'skwo-la*
self-taught	autodidatta (m/f)	*au-to-di-'dat-ta*
semester	semestre (m)	*se-'mes-tre*
seminar, workshop	seminario	*se-mi-'na-ryo*
(to) skip school, play hooky	marinare la scuola	*ma-ri-'na-re la 'skwo-la*
slide	diapositiva	*di-a-po-zi-'ti-va*
study	studio	—
• (to) study	studiare	*stu-'dya-re*
symposium	simposio	*sim-'po-zyo*
(to) take attendance	fare* l'appello	*ap-'pel-lo*
(to) teach	insegnare	*in-se-'nya-re*
teaching aids	materiale didattico	*ma-te-'rya-le di-'dat-ti-ko*
test	prova	—
thesis	tesi (f, inv)	*'te-zi*
• (to) defend one's thesis	discutere* la tesi	*dis-'ku-te-re*
training	formazione (f)	*for-ma-'tsyo-ne*
trimester	trimestre (m)	*tri-'mes-tre*
(to) write	scrivere*	*'skri-ve-re*

38. WORK AND THE BUSINESS WORLD

A. JOBS AND PROFESSIONS

accountant	contabile (m/f)	*kon-'ta-bi-le*
administration	amministrazione (f)	*am-mi-nis-tra-'tsyo-ne*
apprentice	apprendista (m/f)	*ap-pren-'dis-ta*
architect	architetto (-a)	*ar-ki-'tet-to*
auditor	revisore dei conti	*re-vi-'zo-re dei 'kon-ti*
baker	fornaio (-a)	*for-'na-yo*
barber	barbiere (-a)	*bar-'bye-re*
bookseller	libraio (-a)	*li-'bra-yo*
bricklayer	muratore (m)	*mu-ra-'to-re*
business consultant	consulente (m/f) commerciale	*kon-su-'len-te kom-mer-'ča-le*
business person	persona d'affari	*per-'so-na daf-'fa-ri*
butcher	macellaio (-a)	*ma-čel-'la-yo*
carpenter	falegname (m/f)	*fa-le-'nya-me*

cashier	cassiere (-a)	*kas-'sye-re*
chartered accountant	commercialista (m/f)	*kom-mer-ča-'lis-ta*
chief executive	direttore (-trice) generale	*di-ret-'to-re je-ne-'ra-le*
cobbler, shoe-repairer	calzolaio (-a)	*kal-tso-'la-yo*
company lawyer	giurista (m/f) d'impresa	*ju-'ris-ta dim-'pre-za*
computer scientist	informatico (-a)	*in-for-'ma-ti-ko*
consultant	consulente (m/f)	*kon-su-'len-te*
cook	cuoco (-a)	*'kwo-ko*
customs officer	doganiere (-a)	*do-ga-'nye-re*
departmental manager	caporeparto	*ka-po-re-'par-to*
director, CEO	dirigente (m/f)	*di-ri-'jen-te*
doctor	medico	*'me-di-ko*
	dottore (-essa)	*dot-'to-re*
driver	autista (m/f)	*au-'tis-ta*
editor	redattore (-trice)	*re-dat-'to-re*
electrician	elettricista (m/f)	*e-let-tri-'čis-ta*
engineer	ingegnere (m/f)	*in-je-'nye-re*
farmer	contadino (-a)	*kon-ta-'di-no*
firefighter	vigile del fuoco	*'vi-ji-le del 'fwo-ko*
fishmonger	pescivendolo	*pe-ši-'ven-do-lo*
florist	fiorista (m/f)	*fyo-'ris-ta*
fruit vendor	fruttivendolo	*frut-ti-'ven-do-lo*
grocer	droghiere (-a)	*dro-'gye-re*
guard	guardiano (-a)	*gwar-'dya-no*
hairdresser	parrucchiere (-a)	*par-ruk-'kye-re*
house painter	imbianchino (-a)	*im-byan-'ki-no*
industrialist	industriale (m/f)	*in-dus-'trya-le*
jeweler	gioielliere (-a)	*jo-yel-'lye-re*
job	mestiere (m)	*mes-'tye-re*
journalist	giornalista (m/f)	*jor-na-'lis-ta*
lawyer	avvocato (m/f)	*av-vo-'ka-to*
legal consultant	consulente (m/f) legale	*kon-su-'len-te le-'ga-le*
letter carrier	postino (-a)	*pos-'ti-no*
librarian	bibliotecario (-a)	*bib-lyo-te-'ka-ryo*
marriage counselor	consigliere (-a) matrimoniale	*kon-si-'lye-re ma-tri-mo-'nya-le*
mechanic	meccanico (-a)	*mek-'ka-ni-ko*
midwife	levatrice (f)	*le-va-'tri-če*
nurse	infermiere (-a)	*in-fer-'mye-re*
occupation	occupazione (f)	*ok-ku-pa-'tsyo-ne*
oculist	oculista (m/f)	*o-ku-'lis-ta*
office worker	impiegato (-a)	*im-pye-'ga-to*
partner	socio (-a)	*'so-čo*
pharmacist	farmacista (m/f)	*far-ma-'čis-ta*
physical therapist	fisioterapista (m/f)	*fi-zyo-te-ra-'pis-ta*
pilot	pilota (m/f)	*pi-'lo-ta*
plasterer	intonacatore (-trice)	*in-to-na-ka-'to-re*
plumber	idraulico (m/f)	*i-'drau-li-ko*

policeman, policewoman	poliziotto (-a)	*po-li-'tsyot-to*
profession	professione (f)	*pro-fes-'syo-ne*
professional	professionista (m/f)	*pro-fes-syo-'nis-ta*
programmer	programmatore (-trice)	*pro-gram-ma-'to-re*
psychiatrist	psichiatra (m/f)	*psi-ki-'a-tra*
psychologist	psicologo (-a)	*psi-'ko-lo-go*
real-estate agent	agente immobiliare (m/f)	*a-'jen-te im-mo-bi-'lya-re*
sailor	marinaio (-a)	*ma-ri-'na-yo*
sales representative	agente commerciale (m/f)	*a-'jen-te kom-mer-'ča-le*
salesman, saleswoman	venditore (-trice)	*ven-di-'to-re*
scientist	scienziato (-a)	*šen-'tsya-to*
secretary	segretario (-a)	*se-gre-'ta-ryo*
social worker	assistente sociale (m/f)	*as-sis-'ten-te so-'ča-le*
soldier	soldato	*sol-'da-to*
speech therapist	logopedista (m/f)	*lo-go-pe-'dis-ta*
staff, personnel	personale (m)	*per-so-'na-le*
stockbroker	agente di cambio (m/f)	*a-'jen-te di 'kam-byo*
store clerk	commesso (-a)	*kom-'mes-so*
street sweeper	netturbino (-a)	*net-tur-'bi-no*
surgeon	chirurgo (-a)	*ki-'rur-go*
surveyor	geometra (m/f)	*je-'o-me-tra*
tailor	sarto (-a)	*'sar-to*
taxi driver	tassista (m/f)	*tas-'sis-ta*
teacher	insegnante (m/f)	*in-se-'nyan-te*
technical consultant	consulente tecnico (-a)	*kon-su-'len-te 'tek-ni-ko*
theatrical agent	agente teatrale	*a-'jen-te te-a-'tra-le*
upholsterer	tappezziere (-a)	*tap-pe-'tsye-re*
waiter, waitress	cameriere (-a)	*ka-me-'rye-re*
writer	scrittore (-trice)	*skrit-'to-re*

B. INTERVIEWING FOR A JOB

Name	nome (m)	*'no-me*
• surname	cognome (m)	*ko-'nyo-me*
• signature	firma	—
Address	indirizzo	*in-di-'rit-tso*
• street	via	—
• number	numero	*'nu-me-ro*
• city	città (f, inv)	*čit 'ta*
• postal code	codice (m) postale	*'ko-di-če pos-'ta-le*
Telephone Number	numero di telefono	*'nu-me-ro di te-'le-fo-no*
• area code	prefisso	*pre-'fis-so*
• e-mail address	e-mail	—
Date and Place of Birth	Data e luogo di nascita	*'lwo-go di 'na-ši-ta*
• date	data	—
• place	luogo	—

Age	Età	—
Sex	Sesso	—
• male	maschile	'mas-kyle
• female	femminile	'fem-mi-nile
Marital Status	Stato civile	'sta-to či-'vi-le
• divorced	divorziato (-a)	di-vor-'tsya-to
• married	sposato (-a)	spo-'za-to
• single	celibe (m)	'če-li-be
	nubile (f)	'nu-bi-le
• widowed	vedovo (-a)	've-do-vo
Nationality	Nazionalità (f, inv)	na-tsyo-na-li-'ta
Education	Istruzione (f)	is-tru-'tsyo-ne
educational qualifications, credentials	titoli di studio	'ti-to-li
• high school graduate	diplomato (-a)	di-plo-'ma-to
• university graduate	laureato (-a)	lau-re-'a-to
Profession	Professione (f)	pro-fes-'syo-ne
Qualifications	Qualifiche (f, pl)	kwa-'li-fi-ke
References	Referenze (f, pl)	re-fe-'ren-dze
Résumé	Curriculum vitae (m, inv)	—

C. THE OFFICE

adhesive tape	nastro adesivo	'nas-tro a-de-'zi-vo
answering machine	segreteria telefonica	se-gre-te-'ri-a te-le-'fo-ni-ka
at (@)	chiocciola	'kyoč-čo-la
business card	biglietto da visita	bi-'lyet-to da -'vi-zi-ta
calculator	calcolatrice (f)	kal-ko-la-'tri-če
calendar	calendario	ka-len-'da-ryo
carbon paper	carta carbone	'kar-ta kar-'bo-ne
card, record, file	scheda	'ske-da
cartridge	cartuccia	kar-'tuč-ča
CD-ROM	CD-ROM (m, inv)	—
clip	clip	—
compatible software	software (m, inv) compatibile	kom-pa-'ti-bi-le
computer	computer (m, inv)	—
copy	copia	'ko-pya
• (to) copy	copiare	ko-'pya-re
cursor	cursore (m)	kur-'so-re
directory	indirizzario	in-di-ri-'tsya-ryo
diskette	dischetto	dis-'ket-to
document	documento	do-ku-'men-to
• document cover	copertina	ko-per-'ti-na
draft	bozza	'bot-tsa
(to) duplicate	duplicare	du-pli-'ka-re

e-mail	e-mail	—
envelope	busta	—
fax	fax (m, inv)	—
file	archivio	ar-'ki-vyo
	scheda	'ske-da
• **(to) file away**	schedare	ske-'da-re
• **file folder**	cartella	kar-'tel-la
• **file name**	titolo del documento	'ti-to-lo del do-ku-'men-to
• **filing cabinet, box file**	schedario	ske-'da-ryo
(to) fill out	compilare	kom-pi-'la-re
format	format (m, inv)	—
• **(to) format**	formattare	for-mat-'ta-re
• **formatted**	formattato	for-mat-'ta-to
hard drive	hard drive	—
hardware	hardware (m, inv)	—
icon	icona	i-'ko-na
index	indice (m)	'in-di-če
ink	inchiostro	in-'kyos-tro
ink-jet printer	stampante (f) a getto d'inchiostro	stam-'pan-te a 'jet-to din-'kyos-tro
inputting on the screen	videoscrittura	vi-de-o-skrit-'tu-ra
• **(to) input**	digitare	di-ji-'ta-re
installation	installazione (f)	in-stal-la-'tsyo-ne
interactive	interattivo	in-ter-at-'ti-vo
intercom	citofono	či-'to-fo-no
internet	Internet (m, inv)	—
justification	giustificazione (f)	jus-ti-fi-ka-'tsyo-ne
keyboard	tastiera	tas-'tye-ra
label	etichetta	e-ti-'ket-ta
laptop computer	laptop (m, inv)	—
laser printer	stampante (f) laser	stam-'pan-te
letterhead	carta intestata	'kar-ta in-tes-'ta-ta
Liquid Paper, White-out	bianchetto	byan-'ket-to
marker	pennarello	pen-na-'rel-lo
memory	memoria	me-'mo-rya
menu	menu (m, inv)	—
microprocessor	microprocessore (m)	mi-kro-pro-ces-'so-re
modem	modem (m, inv)	—
mouse	mouse (m, inv)	—
(to) navigate	navigare	na-vi-'ga-re
network	network (m, inv)	—
	rete (f)	're-te
notice board	tabella	ta-'bel-la
office hours	orario d'ufficio	o-'ra-ryo duf-'fi-čo
• **office manager, boss**	capoufficio (capo)	ka-po-uf-'fi-čo
• **office personnel**	personale (m) d'ufficio	per-so-'na-le

• office supplies	forniture (f, pl) per ufficio	*for-ni-'tu-re*
on-line (online)	on-line	—
organization chart	organigramma (m)	*or-ga-ni-'gram-ma*
pad	taccuino	*tak-'kwi-no*
paper	carta	—
password	password (m, inv)	—
pen	penna	—
pencil, crayon	matita	*ma-'ti-ta*
permanent memory	memoria fissa	*me-'mo-rya 'fis-sa*
personal organizer	agenda	*a-'jen-da*
photocopier	fotocopiatrice (f)	*fo-to-kopya-'tri-če*
(to) print	stampare	*stam-'pa-re*
• printer	stampante (f)	*stam-'pan-te*
punch	perforatrice (f)	*per-fo-ra-'tri-če*
ruler	riga	—
sheet (of paper)	foglio	*'fo-lyo*
(to) shred	stracciare	*strač-'ča-re*
software	software (m, inv)	—
spreadsheet	foglio elettronico	*'fo-lyo e-let-'tro-ni-ko*
staple	punto metallico	*'pun-to me-'tal-li-ko*
• stapler	cucitrice (f)	*ku-'či-'tri-če*
string	spago	*'spa-go*
supply cupboard	armadietto delle forniture	*ar-ma-'dyet-to del-le for-ni-'tu-re*
systems analyst	analista (m/f) di sistemi	*a-na-'lis-ta dei sis-'te-mi*
tack	puntina	*pun-'ti-na*
teleconference	teleconferenza	*te-le-kon-fe-'ren-tsa*
terminal	terminal (m, inv)	—
toner	toner (m, inv)	—
(to) type in	digitare	*di-ji-'ta-re*
user	utente (m/f)	*u-'ten-te*
user-friendly	di facile uso	*'fa-či-le 'u-zo*
virtual	virtuale	*vir-'twa-le*
virus	virus (m, inv)	—
waiting room	sala d'aspetto	*'sa-la das-'pet-to*
wastebasket	cestino	*čes-'ti-no*
website	sito (web)	—
window	finestra	*fi-'nes-tra*
word-processing	trattamento di testi	*trat-ta-'men-to*
workstation	stazione (f) di lavoro	*sta-'tsyo-ne di la-'vo-ro*
writing desk	scrivania	*skri-va-'ni-a*

D. EMPLOYMENT AND THE BUSINESS WORLD

accounting department	reparto della contabilità	*re-'par-to del-la kon-ta-bi-li-'ta*

advertising	pubblicità (f, inv)	pub-bli-či-'ta
annual leave	congedo annuale	kon-'je-do an-'nwa-le
applicant	candidato	kan-di-'da-to
appointment	appuntamento	ap-pun-ta-'men-to
bargaining, negotiations	trattative (f, pl)	trat-ta-'ti-ve
base salary	paga base	'pa-ga 'ba-ze
(to) be self-employed	lavorare in proprio	la-vo-'ra-re in 'pro-pryo
board of directors	consiglio d'amministrazione	kon-'si-lyo dam-mi-nis-tra-'tsyo-ne
branch	succursale (f)	suk-kur-'sa-le
break	pausa	'pau-za
budget	bilancio	bi-'lan-čo
• **budget prediction**	bilancio preventivo	pre-ven-'ti-vo
career	carriera	kar-'rye-ra
(to) chair a meeting	presiedere una riunione	pre-'sye-de-re
classified ad	piccola pubblicità	'pik-ko-la pub-bli-či-'ta
clientele	clientela	kli-en-'te-la
commerce, trade	commercio	kom-'mer-čo
company	ditta	—
company policy	politica aziendale	po-'li-ti-ka a-dzyen-'da-le
competition	concorrenza	kon-kor-'ren-tsa
• **competitor**	concorrente (m/f)	kon-kor-'ren-te
consumer	consumatore (-trice)	kon-su-ma-'to-re
consumer good	bene (m) di consumo	'be-ne di kon-'su-mo
consumer protection	tutela del consumatore	tu-'te-la del kon-su-ma-'to-re
contract	contratto	kon-'trat-to
corporation	società (f, inv)	so-če-'ta
cost price	prezzo di costo	'pret-tso di 'kos-to
customer	cliente (m/f)	kli-'en-te
delivery	consegna	kon-'se-nya
demonstration	manifestazione (f)	ma-ni-fes-ta-'tsyo-ne
discount	sconto	'skon-to
dividend	dividendo	di-vi-'den-do
(to) earn	guadagnare	gwa-da-'nya-re
employee	dipendente (m/f)	di-pen-'den-te
• **blue-collar worker**	operaio (-a)	o-per-'a-yo
• **employer**	datore di lavoro	da-'to-re di la-'vo-ro
• **employment**	lavoro	la-'vo-ro
• **employment agency**	agenzia di collocamento	a-jen-'tsi-a di kol-lo-ka-'men-to
• **white-collar worker**	impiegato (-a)	im-pye-'ga-to
factory	fabbrica	'fab-bri-ka
(to) fire	licenziare	li-cen-'tsya-re
• **firing**	licenziamento	li-cen-tsya-'men-to
firm, company	azienda	a-'dsyen-da
fixed wage	stipendio fisso	sti-'pen-dyo 'fis-so
franchise	appalto	ap-'pal-to

• franchiser	appaltatore (-trice)	ap-pal-ta-'to-re
general strike	sciopero generale	'šo-pe-ro je-ne-'ra-le
(to) get a job	procurarsi un lavoro	pro-ku-'rar-si un la-'vo-ro
(to) go on strike	scioperare	šo-pe-'ra-re
grievance	lamentela	la-men-'te-la
gross national product	prodotto nazionale lordo	pro-'dot-to na-tsyo-'na-le 'lor-do
gross profit	guadagno lordo	gwa-'da-nyo 'lor-do
head office	sede (f) principale	'se-de prin-ci-'pa-le
(to) hire	assumere*	as-'su-me-re
• hiring	assunzione (f)	as-sun-'tsyo-ne
income	reddito	'red-di-to
labor shortage	scarsezza di manodopera	skar-'set-tsa di ma-no-'do-pe-ra
labor surplus	eccesso di manodopera	eč-'čes-so di ma-no-'do-pe-ra
labor union	sindacato	sin-da-'ka-to
leave-of-absence	congedo	kon-'je-do
(to) lose one's job	perdere* il lavoro	'per-de-re il la-'vo-ro
lunch break	pausa mensa	'pau-za 'men-sa
management	direzione (f)	di-re-'tsyo-ne
	gestione (f)	jes-'tyo-ne
• management board	comitato direttivo	ko-mi-'ta-to di-ret-'ti-vo
• manager	direttore (-trice)	di-ret-'to-re
market	mercato	mer-'ka-to
• market research	ricerche (f, pl) di mercato (di marketing)	ri-čer-'ke di mer-'ka-to
merchandise	merce (f)	'mer-če
(to) merge	fondere*	'fon-de-re
monopoly	monopolio	mo-no-'po-lyo
multinational (company)	multinazionale (f)	mul-ti-na-tsyo-'na-le
net profit	guadagno netto	gwa-'da-nyo 'net-to
night work	lavoro notturno	la-'vo-ro not-'tur-no
occasional job	lavoro saltuario	la-vo-ro sal-'twa-ryo
occupational hazard	rischio del mestiere	'ris-kyo del mes-'tye-re
(to) offer a job	offrire* un lavoro	of-'fri-re un la-'vo-ro
office	ufficio	uf-'fi-čo
overtime work	lavoro straordinario	la-'vo-ro stra-or-di-'na-ryo
partnership	partnership (m, inv)	—
pay	paga	—
pay claim	rivendicazione (f) salariale	ri-ven-di-ka-'tsyo-ne sa-la-'rya-le
pay day	giorno di paga	'jor-no di 'pa-ga
pension, retirement	pensione (f)	pen-'syo-ne
personality test	test psicologico	psi-ko-'lo-ji-ko

piece work	lavoro a cottimo	*la-'vo-ro a 'kot-ti-mo*
plant	stabilimento	*sta-bi-li-'men-to*
(to) privatize	privatizzare	*pri-va-tid-'dza-re*
probation period	tirocinio	*ti-ro-'či-nyo*
producer	produttore (m)	*pro-dut-'to-re*
• product	prodotto	*pro-'dot-to*
profit	profitto	*pro-'fit-to*
	guadagno	*gwa-'da-nyo*
• profit margin	margine (m) di guadagno	*'mar-ji-ne*
promotion	promozione (f)	*pro-mo-'tsyo-ne*
public relations office	ufficio pubbliche relazioni	*uf-'fi-čo 'pub-bli-ke re-la-'tsyo-ni*
(to) register a company	immatricolare un'azienda	*im-ma-tri-ko-'la-re un-a-'dzyen-da*
(to) retire	andare* (ess) in pensione	*an-'da-re in pen-'syo-ne*
second job, moonlighting	secondo lavoro	*se-'kon-do la-'vo-ro*
shift work	turno di lavoro	*'tur-no di la-'vo-ro*
starting wage	stipendio iniziale	*sti-'pen-dyo i-ni-'tsya-le*
stay-at-home job	lavoro a domicilio	*la-'vo-ro a do-mi-'či-lyo*
stock company, corporation	società (f, inv) per azioni	*so-če-'ta per a-'tsyo-ni*
• stockholder	azionista (m/f)	*a-tsyo-'nis-ta*
strike	sciopero	*'šo-pe-ro*
• striker	scioperante (m/f)	*šo-pe-'ran-te*
subsidiary	filiale (f)	*fi-'lya-le*
survey	sondaggio	*son-'daj-jo*
take-home pay	busta paga	—
takeover bid	offerta pubblica d'acquisto	*of-'fer-ta 'pub-bli-ka dak-'kwis-to*
tax on salary	imposta sul reddito	*im-'pos-ta sul 'red-di-to*
temporary work	lavoro temporaneo	*la-'vo-ro tem-po-'ra-ne-o*
unemployed	disoccupato	*diz-ok-ku-'pa-to*
• unemployment	disoccupazione (f)	*diz-ok-ku-pa-'tsyo-ne*
• unemployment benefits	cassa integrazione	*'kas-sa in-te-gra-'tsyo-ne*
union member	sindacalista (m/f)	*sin-da-ka-'lis-ta*
union negotiation	trattativa sindacale	*trat-ta-'ti-va sin-da-'ka-le*
wage, stipend	stipendio	*sti-'pen-dyo*
• wage increase	aumento di stipendio	*au-'men-to di sti-'pen-dyo*
warehouse	magazzino	*ma-gad-'zi-no*
work	lavoro	*la-'vo-ro*
• (to) work	lavorare	*la-vo-'ra-re*
work associate	collega (m/f)	*kol-'le-ga*
work contract	contratto di lavoro	*kon-'trat-to di la-'vo-ro*
working hours	orario di lavoro	*o-'ra-ryo di la-'vo-ro*

EMERGENCIES

39. REPORTING AN EMERGENCY

A. FIRE

alarm	allarme (m)	*al-'lar-me*
arson	incendio doloso	*in-cen-dyo do-'lo-zo*
• arsonist	piromane (m/f)	*pi-'ro-ma-ne*
building	edificio	*e-di-'fi-čo*
burn (on body)	ustione (f)	*us-'tyo-ne*
(to) burn	bruciare	*bru-'ča-re*
(to) call the fire department	chiamare i pompieri	*kya-'ma-re i pom-'pye-ri*
(to) catch fire	incendiarsi	*in-cen-'dyar-si*
danger	pericolo	*pe-'ri-ko-lo*
(to) destroy	distruggere*	*dis-'truj-je-re*
emergency exit	uscita di sicurezza (emergenza)	*u-'ši-ta di si-ku-'ret-tsa*
(to) escape, get out	uscire* (ess) fuori	*u-'ši-re 'fwo-ri*
(to) extinguish, put out	spegnere* il fuoco	*'spe-nye-re il 'fwo-ko*
fire	incendio	*in-'čen-dyo*
	fuoco	*'fwo-ko*
• Fire!	Al fuoco!	—
• fire extinguisher	estintore (m)	*es-tin-'to-re*
• firefighter	vigile del fuoco	*'vi-ji-le*
• fire hose	pompa	—
• fire hydrant	idrante (m)	*i-'dran-te*
• fire truck	autopompa	*au-to-'pom-pa*
fireproof	antincendio	*an-tin-'čen-dyo*
first aid	pronto soccorso	*'pron-to sok-'kor-so*
flame	fiamma	*'fyam-ma*
help	aiuto	*a-'yu-to*
• (to) help	aiutare	*a-yu-'ta-re*
• Help!	Aiuto!	—
• (to) give help	dare* aiuto	—
ladder	scala	*'ska-la*
out	fuori	*'fwo-ri*
• Everybody out!	Tutti fuori!	—
(to) protect	proteggere*	*pro-'tej-je-re*
(to) rescue	soccorrere*	*sok-'kor-re-re*
shout	grido	—
• (to) shout	gridare	*gri-'da-re*
siren	sirena	*si-'re-na*

| smoke | fumo | — |
| victim | vittima | 'vit-ti-ma |

B. ROBBERY, ASSAULT, AND OTHER CRIMES

accomplice	complice (m)	'kom-pliče
(to) argue	litigare	li-ti-'ga-re
arrest	arresto	ar-'res-to
• (to) arrest	arrestare	ar-res-'ta-re
• arrest warrant	mandato di cattura	man-'da-to di kat-'tu-ra
assailant	aggressore (m)	a-gres-'so-re
assassin, murderer	assassino	as-sas-'si-no
assault, attack	aggressione (f)	ag-res-'syo-ne
• armed assault, attack	aggressione a mano armata	ar-'ma-ta
• (to) assault, attack	aggredire (isc)	ag-gre-'di-re
blackmail	ricatto	ri-'kat-to
• (to) blackmail	ricattare	ri-kat-'ta-re
bodyguard	guardia del corpo	'gwar-dya del 'kor-po
break and enter	scasso	'skas-so
bribe	bustarella	bus-ta-'rel-la
• bribery	corruzione (f)	kor-ru-'tsyo-ne
chief of police	commissario di polizia	kom-mis-'sa-ryo di po-li-'tsi-a
clue	indizio	in-'di-tsyo
conspiracy, frame-up	complotto	kom-'plot-to
coroner	magistrato (investigatore)	ma-jis-'tra-to
court-appointed lawyer	difensore d'ufficio	di-fen-'so-re duf-'fi-čo
crime	crimine (m)	'kri-mi-ne
• criminal	criminale (m/f)	kri-mi-'na-le
• criminal act	reato	re-'a-to
• criminal record	passato criminale	pas-'sa-to kri-mi-'na-le
defense lawyer	difensore	di-fen-'so-re
delinquency	delinquenza	de-lin-'kwen-tsa
description	descrizione (f)	des-kri-'tsyo-ne
DNA	DNA (m, inv)	—
drug pusher	spacciatore (m) di droga	spač-ča-'to-re
• drug pushing	spaccio di droga	'spač-čo
• drug traffic	traffico di droga	'traf-fi-ko
• drug trafficker	trafficante di droga	traf-fi-'kan-te
• (to) push drugs	spacciare droga	spač-'ča-re
embezzlement	appropriazione indebita	ap-pro-prya-tsyo-ne in-'de-bi-ta
escape	evasione (f)	e-va-'zyo-ne
(to) fight	picchiarsi	pik-'kyar-si
fingerprint	impronta digitale	im-'pron-ta di-ji-'ta-le
firearm	arma da fuoco	'ar-ma da 'fwo-ko

forensics, forensic science	medicina legale	me-di-'či-na le-'ga-le
forgery	contraffazione (f)	kon-traf-fa-'tsyo-ne
• forger	contraffattore (-trice)	kon-traf-fat-'to-re
fraud	frode (f)	'fro-de
fugitive	evaso (-a)	e-'va-zo
(to) give oneself up	consegnarsi alla polizia	kon-se-'nyar-si al-la po-li-'tsi-a
gun	rivoltella	ri-vol-'tel-la
handcuffs	manette (f, pl)	ma-'net-te
hijacking	dirottamento	di-rot-ta-'men-to
• (to) hijack	dirottare	di-rot-'ta-re
hired killer	sicario	si-'ka-ryo
hostage	ostaggio (-a)	os-'taj-jo
informant	informatore (-trice)	in-for-ma-'to-re
infraction	infrazione (f)	in-fra-'tsyo-ne
injury, wound	ferita	fe-'ri-ta
• (to) injure, wound	ferire (isc)	fe-'ri-re
investigation	investigazione (f)	in-ves-ti-ga-'tsyo-ne
• investigator	investigatore (-trice)	in-ve-ti-ga-'to-re
juvenile delinquency	delinquenza minorile	de-lin-'kwen-tsa mi-no-'ri-le
• juvenile delinquent	delinquente minorile	de-lin-'kwen-te
kidnapping	sequestro	se-kwes-tro
• (to) kidnap	sequestrare	se-kwes-'tra-re
• kidnapper	sequestratore (m)	se-kwes-tra-'to-re
(to) kill	uccidere*	uč-'či-de-re
• killer	assassino	as-sas-'si-no
knife	coltello	kol-'tel-lo
legal assistance	assistenza legale	as-sis-'ten-dza le-'ga-le
loot	bottino	bot-'ti-no
manslaughter	omicidio preterintenzionale	o-mi-'či-dyo pre-ter-in-ten-tsyo-'na-le
murder	assassinio	as-sas-'si-nyo
• (to) murder	uccidere*	uč-'či-de-re
• murderer	omicida (m/f)	o-mi-'či-da
outlaw	fuorilegge (m/f)	fwo-ri-'lej-je
patrol	pattuglia	pat-'tu-lya
• (to) patrol	pattugliare	pat-tu-'lya-re
perjury	falsa testimonianza	'fal-sa tes-ti-mo-'nyan-tsa
pickpocket	scippatore (-trice)	šip-pa-'to-re
• pocket-picking	scippo	'šip-po
pistol	pistola	pis-'to-la
police	polizia	po-li-'tsi-a
• police headquarters	commissariato	kom-mis-sa-'rya-to
• police officer	poliziotto (-a)	po-lit-'tsyot-to
• police station	questura	kwes-'tu-ra

• police van	furgone (m) della polizia	*fur-'go-ne*
premeditated crime	delitto premeditato	*de-'lit-to pre-me-di-'ta-to*
prisoner	detenuto (-a)	*de-te-'nu-to*
private detective	investigatore (-trice) privato (-a)	*in-ves-ti-ga-'to-re pri-'va-to*
questioning	interrogatorio	*in-ter-ro-ga-'to-ryo*
ransom	riscatto	*ris-'kat-to*
rape	violenza carnale	*vyo-'len-tsa kar-'na-le*
• (to) rape	violentare	*vyo-len-'ta-re*
• rapist	violentatore (m)	*vyo-len-ta-'to-re*
rifle	fucile (m)	*fu-'či-le*
robbery, burglary	rapina	*ra-'pi-na*
• armed robbery	rapina a mano armata	—
• (to) rob	rapinare	*ra-pi-'na-re*
• robber, burglar	rapinatore (-trice)	*ra-pi-na-'to-re*
scuffle	baruffa	*ba-'ruf-fa*
search	perquisizione (f)	*per-kwi-zi-'tsyo-ne*
• search warrant	mandato di perquisizione	*man-'da-to*
(to) shoot	sparare	*spa-'ra-re*
smuggling	contrabbando	*kon-trab-'ban-do*
(to) stab	pugnalare	*pu-nya-'la-re*
statement made to authorities	verbale (m)	*ver-'ba-le*
(to) steal	rubare	*ru-'ba-re*
tax evasion	frode (f) fiscale	*'fro-de fis-'ka-le*
thief	ladro (-a)	—
vandal	vandalo (-a)	*'van-da-lo*
• vandalism	vandalismo	*van-da-'liz-mo*
violence	violenza	*vyo-'len-tsa*
warrant	mandato	*man-'da-to*
weapon	arma	—

Useful Expressions

Help!	Aiuto!
Hurry! Come quickly!	Presto!
Fire!	Al fuoco!
Someone assaulted me!	Qualcuno mi ha aggredito (-a)!
Someone stole my…	Qualcuno mi ha rubato…!

C. TRAFFIC ACCIDENTS

accident	incidente (m)	in-či-'den-te
• serious accident	incidente grave	'gra-ve
• traffic accident	incidente stradale	stra-'da-le
ambulance	ambulanza	am-bu-'lan-tsa
	autoambulanza	au-to-am-bu-'lan-tsa
(to) be run over	essere* investito (-a)	'es-se-re in-ves-'ti-to
(to) bleed	sanguinare	san-gwi-'na-re
• blood	sangue (m)	'san-gwe
broken bone	osso rotto	'os-so 'rot-to
(to) bump	sbattere	'zbat-te-re
(to) collide, smash	scontrarsi	skon-'trar-si
• collision, smash	scontro	'skon-tro
crash	schianto	'skyan-to
• (to) crash	schiantarsi	skyan-'tar-si
doctor	medico	'me-di-ko
• (to) get a doctor	chiamare un medico	kya-'ma-re
first aid	pronto soccorso	'pron-to sok-'kor-so
• antiseptic	antisettico	an-ti-'set-ti-ko
• bandage	benda	'ben-da
• gauze	garza	'gar-dza
• splint	stecca	'stek-ka
• tincture of iodine	tintura di iodio	tin-'tu-ra di 'yo-dyo
Help!	Aiuto!	a-'yu-to
hospital	ospedale (m)	os-pe-'da-le
• emergency	pronto soccorso	'pron-to sok-'kor-so
• X-rays	raggi X	'raj-ji
police	polizia	po-li-'tsi-a
• (to) call the police	chiamare la polizia	kya-'ma-re
shock, bang	trauma (m) (traumi, pl)	—
wound, injury	ferita	fe-'ri-ta

40. MEDICAL CARE

A. AT THE DOCTOR'S

abortion	aborto	a-'bor-to
acne	acne (f)	—
acupuncture	agopuntura	a-go-pun-'tu-ra
addiction	dipendenza	di-pen-'den-tsa
adhesive bandage	cerotto	če-'rot-to
AIDS	AIDS (m, inv)	—
ailment	indisposizione (f)	in-dis-po-zi-'tsyo-ne
allergic	allergico	al-'ler-ji-ko
• allergy	allergia	al-ler-'ji-a
anemia	anemia	a-ne-'mi-a
• anemic	anemico	a-'ne-mi-co

anesthesia	anestesia	*a-nes-te-'zi-a*
• anesthetic	anestetico	*a-nes-'te-ti-ko*
ankle sprain	storta alla caviglia	*ka-'vi-lya*
antibiotic	antibiotico	*an-ti-bi-'o-ti-ko*
anxiety	ansietà	*un-sye-'ta*
appendicitis	appendicite (f)	*ap-pen-di-'či-te*
appointment	appuntamento	*ap-pun-ta-'men-to*
arrhythmia	aritmia	*a-rit-'mi-a*
arteriosclerosis	arteriosclerosi (f, inv)	*ar-te-ryo-skle-'ro-zi*
arthritis	artrite (f)	*ar-'tri-te*
aspirin	aspirina	*as-pi-'ri-na*
asthma	asma	*'az-ma*
athlete's foot	micosi (f, inv) dei piedi	*mi-'ko-zi*
autism	autismo	*au-'tiz-mo*
bacillus, bacterium	bacillo	*ba-'čil-lo*
backache	mal di schiena	*'skye-na*
(to) bandage	bendare	*ben-'da-re*
barbiturate	barbiturico	*bar-bi-'tu-ri-ko*
(to) be on call	essere* di turno	*'es-se-re di -'tur-no*
(to) become cured	guarire (isc)	*gwa-'ri-re*
(to) become ill	ammalarsi	*am-ma-'lar-si*
benign	benigno	*be-'ni-nyo*
bile	bile (f)	*'bi-le*
bite	morso	*'mor-so*
blister	vescica	*ve-'ši-ka*
blood	sangue (m)	*'san-gwe*
• blood test	analisi (f, inv) del sangue	*a-'na-'li-zi*
• blood transfusion	trasfusione (f) del sangue	*tras-fu-'zyo-ne*
(to) break a limb	fratturare un arto	*frat-tu-'ra-re*
bronchitis	bronchite (f)	*bron-'ki-te*
bruise	livido	*'li-vi-do*
cancer	cancro	*'kan-kro*
cataract	cateratta	*ka-te-'rat-ta*
catarrh	catarro	*ka-'tar-ro*
(to) catch a chill	prendere* freddo	*'pren-de-re 'fred-do*
cellulite	cellulite (f)	*čel-lu-'li-te*
chest infection	infezione (f) polmonare	*in-fe-'tsyo-ne pol-mo-'na-re*
chicken-pox	varicella	*va-ri-'čel-la*
chill, shiver	brivido	*'bri-vi-do*
cold	raffreddore (m)	*raf-fred-'do-re*
colitis	colite (f)	*ko-'li-te*
concussion	commozione (f) cerebrale	*kom-mo-'tsyo-ne če-re-'bra-le*
condom	preservativo	*pre-zer-va-'ti-vo*

constipation	stitichezza	*sti-ti-'ke-tsa*
contraceptive	contraccettivo	*kon-trač-čet-'ti-vo*
• contraceptive pill	pillola anticoncezionale	*'pil-lo-la an-ti-kon-če-tsyo-'na-le*
convalescence	convalescenza	*kon-va-le-'šen-dza*
corn, callus	callo	—
cortisone	cortisone (m)	*kor-ti-'zo-ne*
cough	tosse (f)	*'tos-se*
• (to) cough	tossire (isc)	*tos-'si-re*
• cough syrup	sciroppo contro la tosse	*ši-rop-po*
• coughing fit	colpo di tosse	*'kol-po di 'tos-se*
cream	crema	—
critical condition	grave stato	—
crutch	stampella	*stam-'pel-la*
cure	cura	—
• (to) cure	curare	*ku-'ra-re*
cyst	cisti (f, inv)	*'čis-ti*
dehydrated	disidratato	*di-si-dra-'ta-to*
• dehydration	disidratazione (f)	*di-si-dra-ta-'tsyo-ne*
depression	depressione (f)	*de-pres-'syo-ne*
dermatitis	dermatite (f)	*der-ma-'ti-te*
diabetes	diabete (m)	*di-a-'be-te*
(to) diagnose	diagnosticare	*di-a-nyos-ti-'ka-re*
• diagnosis	diagnosi (f, inv)	*di-'a-nyo-zi*
diarrhea	diarrea	*di-ar-'re-a*
diet	dieta	*'dye-ta*
discomfort	malessere (m)	*ma-'les-se-re*
disease	malattia	*ma-lat-'ti-a*
dislocated	slogato	*zlo-'ga-to*
• dislocation	slogatura	*zlo-ga-'tu-ra*
diuretic	diuretico	*di-u-'re-ti-ko*
dizziness	giramento di testa	*ji-ra-'men-to*
doctor	medico	*'me-di-co*
	dottore (-essa)	*dot-'to-re*
• doctor's office	gabinetto medico	*ga-bi-'net-to 'me-di-ko*
• family doctor	medico di famiglia	*fa-'mi-lya*
dosage	posologia	*po-zo-lo-'ji-a*
dressing	fascia	*'fa-ša*
drop	goccia	*'goč-ča*
drowsiness	sonnolenza	*son-no-'len-tsa*
drug addiction	tossicodipendenza	*tos-si-ko-di-pen-'den-tsa*
ear infection	otite (f)	*o-'ti-te*
electrocardiogram	elettrocardiogramma (m)	*e-let-tro-kar-dyo-'gram-ma*
embolism	embolia	*em-bo-'li-a*
epidemic	epidemia	*e-pi-de-'mi-a*
epileptic fit	crisi epilettica	*'kri-zi e-pi-'let-ti-ka*

estrogen	estrogeno	es-'tro-je-no
(to) examine	visitare	vi-zi-'ta-re
expectorant	espettorante (m)	es-pet-to-'ran-te
eye-drop	collirio	kol-'li-ryo
(to) faint	svenirsi*	zve-'nir-si
fainting spell	svenimento	zve-ni-'men-to
(to) feel nauseous	avere* la nausea	'nau-ze-a
fever, temperature	febbre (f)	'feb-bre
flu, influenza	influenza	in-flu-'en-dza
food poisoning	intossicazione (f) alimentare	in-tos-si-ka-'tsyo-ne a-li-men-'ta-re
fracture	frattura	frat-'tu-ra
gallstones	calcoli biliari	'kal-ko-li bi-'lya-ri
(to) gargle	fare* gargarismi	gar-ga-'riz-mi
(to) get better	migliorare	mi-lyo-'ra-re
gonorrhea	gonorrea	gon-nor-'re-a
gynecologist	ginecologo (-a)	ji-ne-'ko-lo-go
• gynecology	ginecologia	ji-ne-ko-lo-'ji-a
(to) have...	avere*	a-'ve-re
• a backache	avere* mal di schiena	'skye-na
• a headache	avere* mal di testa	—
• a sore throat	avere* mal di gola	—
• a sore, upset stomach	avere* mal di stomaco	'sto-ma-ko
• a temperature	avere* la febbre	—
(to) heal	guarire	gwa-'ri-re
hearing aid	apparecchio acustico	ap-pa-'rek-kyo a-'kus-ti-ko
heart attack	infarto cardiaco	in-'far-to kar-'di-a-ko
heartburn	bruciore (m) di stomaco	bru-'čo-re di 'sto-ma-ko
hematoma	ematoma (m)	e-ma-'to-ma
hemorrhage, bleeding	emorragia	e-mor-raj-'ji-a
hernia	ernia	'er-nya
herpes	erpete (m)	'er-pe-te
high blood pressure	ipertensione (f)	i-per-ten-'syo-ne
HIV-positive	sieropositivo	sye-ro-po-zi-'ti-vo
homeopathy	omeopatia	o-me-o-pa-'ti-a
hormone	ormone (m)	or-'mo-ne
house call	visita domiciliare	'vi-zi-ta do-mi-či-'lya-re
incontinence	incontinenza	in-kon-ti-'nen-dza
indigestion	indigestione (f)	in-di-jes-'tyo-ne
infection	infezione (f)	in-fe-'tsyo-ne
• inflamed	infiammato	in-fyam-'ma-to
• inflammation	infiammazione (f)	in-fyam-ma-'tsyo-ne
injection, needle	puntura	pun-'tu-ra
injury	infortunio	in-for-'tu-nyo
insomnia	insonnia	in-'son-nya
insulin	insulina	in-su-'li-na

intensive care unit	sala di rianimazione	ri-a-ni-ma-'tsyo-ne
(to) itch	prudere	'pru-de-re
• itchiness	prurito	pru-'ri-to
kidney stone	calcolo renale	'kal-ko-lo re-'na-le
laryngitis	laringite (f)	la-rin-'ji-te
laxative	purga	—
lesion	lesione (f)	le-'zyo-ne
leukemia	leucemia	leu-če-'mi-a
magnesium citrate	citrato di magnesio	či-'tra-to di ma-'nye-zyo
(to) make an appointment	fissare un appuntamento	fis-'sa-re un ap-pun-ta-'men-to
malignant	maligno	ma-'li-nyo
measles, red measles	morbillo	mor-'bil-lo
	roseola	ro-'ze-o-la
medical checkup	visita di controllo	'vi-zi-ta di kon-'trol-lo
• medical examination	esame (m) medico	e-'za-me 'me-di-ko
menopause	menopausa	me-no-'pau-za
menstruation	mestruazione (f)	mes-tru-a-'tsyo-ne
miscarriage	aborto spontaneo	a-'bor-to spon-'ta-ne-o
mumps	orecchioni (m, pl)	o-rek-'kyo-ni
nausea	nausea	'nau-ze-a
nurse	infermiere (-a)	in-fer-'mye-re
obstetrician	ostetrico (-a)	os-'te-tri-ko
oculist, eye specialist	oculista (m/f)	o-ku-'lis-ta
ointment	pomata	po-'ma-ta
(to) operate	operare	o-pe-'ra-re
• operating room	sala operatoria	'sa-la o-pe-ra-'to-rya
• operation	intervento chirurgico	in-ter-'ven-to ki-'rur-ji-ko
optometrist	optometrista (m/f)	op-to-me-'tris-ta
orthopedic surgeon	chirurgo ortopedico	ki-'rur-go or-to-'pe-di-ko
pain	dolore (m)	do-'lo-re
• painful	doloroso	do-lo-'ro-zo
• painkiller	analgesico	a-nal-'je-zi-ko
pale	pallido	'pal-li-do
palliative	palliativo	pal-lya-'ti-vo
paralysis	paralisi (f, inv)	pa-'ra-li-zi
paramedic	paramedico	pa-ra-'me-di-ko
pastille	pasticca	pas-'tik-ka
pathologist	patologo (-a)	pa-'to-lo-go
patient	paziente (m/f)	pa-'tsyen-te
pediatrician	pediatra (m/f)	pe-di-'a-tra
penicillin	penicillina	pe-ni-čil-'li-na
pharmaceutical	farmaco	'far-ma-ko
• pharmacist	farmacista (m/f)	far-ma-'čis-ta
phial	fiala	'fya-la
pill	pillola	'pil-lo-la
plaster	ingessatura	in-jes-sa-'tu-ra
• plaster cast	fascia gessata	'fa-ša jes-'sa-ta

plastic surgeon	chirurgo estetico	*ki-'rur-go es-'te-ti-ko*
pneumonia	polmonite (f)	*pol-mo-'ni-te*
pregnancy	gravidanza	*gra-vi-'dan-dza*
• **pregnant**	incinta	*in-'čin-ta*
(to) prescribe	prescrivere*	*pre-'skri-ve-re*
• **prescription**	ricetta medica	*ri-'čet-ta 'me-di-ka*
(to) probe	sondare	*son-'da-re*
prognosis	prognosi (f, inv)	*'pro-nyo-zi*
psychiatrist	psichiatra (m/f)	*psi-ki-'a-tra*
psychosomatic	psicosomatico	*psi-ko-so-'ma-ti-ko*
psychotherapist	psicoterapista (m/f)	*psi-ko-te-ra-'pis-ta*
pulse	polso	—
pus	pus (m, inv)	—
radiography	radiografia	*ra-dyo-gra-'fi-a*
radiologist	radiologo (-a)	*ra-'dyo-lo-go*
rash	eruzione cutanea	*e-ru-'tsyo-ne ku-'ta-ne-a*
(to) recover	rimettersi*	*ri-met-ter-si*
redness	rossore (m)	*ros-'so-re*
(to) resuscitate	rianimare	*ri-a-ni-'ma-re*
rheumatism	reumatismo	*reu-ma-'tiz-mo*
rubber gloves	guanti di gomma	*'gwan-ti*
scar	cicatrice (f)	*či-ka-'tri-če*
scarlet fever	scarlattina	*skar-lat-'ti-na*
scurvy	scorbuto	*skor-'bu-to*
sedative	sedativo	*se-da-'ti-vo*
self-examination	autopalpazione (f)	*au-to-pal-pa-'tsyo-ne*
shingles	fuoco di Sant'Antonio	*'fwo-ko di sant-an-'to-nyo*
sick person	ammalato (-a)	*am-ma-'la-to*
• **sickly**	malaticcio	*ma-la-'tič čo*
sinusitis	sinusite (f)	*si-nu-'zi-te*
sleeping pill	sonnifero	*son-'ni-fe-ro*
sling	bendaggio	*ben-'daj-jo*
sneeze	starnuto	*star-'nu-to*
• **(to) sneeze**	starnutire (isc)	*star-nu-'ti-re*
sodium bicarbonate	bicarbonato di sodio	*bi-kar-bo-'na-to di 'so-dyo*
spasm	spasimo	*'spa-zi-mo*
speech therapist	logopedista (m/f)	*lo-go-pe-'dis-ta*
sprain	distorsione (f)	*dis-tor-'syo-ne*
	storta	*'stor-ta*
squint	strabismo	*stra-'biz-mo*
stiff neck	torcicollo	*tor-či-'kol-lo*
• **stiffness**	rigidezza	*ri-ji-'det-tsa*
stitch	punto	—
stomachache	mal di stomaco	*'sto-ma-ko*
stone	calcolo	*'kal-ko-lo*
stress	stress (m, inv)	—

stretcher	barella	ba-'rel-la
stroke	ictus cerebrale	če-re-'bra-le
strong	forte	'for-te
sunstroke	colpo di sole	'kol-po di -'so-le
suppository	supposta	sup-'pos-ta
surgeon	chirurgo (-a)	ki-'rur-go
• surgery	chirurgia	ki-rur-'ji-a
• surgical appliance	protesi (f, inv)	'pro-te-zi
swab	tampone (m)	tam-'po-ne
sweat	sudore (m)	su-'do-re
• (to) sweat	sudare	su-'da-re
swelling	gonfiore (m)	gon'fyo-re
• (to) swell	gonfiare	gon'fya-re
• swollen	gonfio	'gon-fyo
symptom	sintomo	'sin-to-mo
syphilis	sifilide (f)	si-'fi-li-de
syringe	siringa	si-'rin-ga
tablet	compressa	kom-'pres-sa
(to) take one's temperature	misurare la febbre	mi-zu-'ra-re la 'feb-bre
tetanus	tetano	'te-ta-no
therapist	terapista (m/f)	te-ra-'pis-ta
• therapy	terapia	te-ra-'pi-a
thermometer	termometro	ter-'mo-me-tro
tincture of iodine	tintura di iodio	tin-'tu-ra di 'yo-dyo
tonic	tonico	'to-ni-ko
tonsillitis	tonsillite (f)	ton-sil-'li-te
tourniquet	laccio emostatico	'lač-čo
tranquilizer	calmante (m)	kal-'man-te
transplant	trapianto	tra-'pyan-to
tumor	tumore (m)	tu-'mo-re
ulcer	ulcera	'ul-če-ra
ultrasound	ecografia	e-ko-gra-'fi-a
unconscious	inconscio	in-'kon-šo
urologist	urologo (-a)	u-ro-lo-go
(to) vaccinate	vaccinare	vač-či-'na-re
• vaccination	vaccino	vač-'či-no
varicose vein	vena varicosa	've-na va-ri-'ko-za
vasectomy	vasectomia	va-zek-to-'mi-a
venereal disease	malattia venerea	ma-lat-'ti-a ve-'ne-re-a
virus	virus (m, inv)	—
• viral infection	infezione virale	in-fe-'tsyo-ne vi-'ra-le
visiting hours	ore di visita	'o-re di -'vi-zi-ta
vitamin	vitamina	vi-ta-'mi-na
vomit	vomito	'vo-mi-to
• (to) vomit	vomitare	vo-mi-'ta-re
waiting room	sala d'aspetto	'sa-la das-'pet-to
wart	verruca	ver-'ru-ka

weak	debole	'de-bo-le
wheelchair	sedia a rotelle	'se-dya a ro-'tel-le
whooping cough	pertosse (f)	per-'tos-se
(to) worsen, deteriorate	aggravarsi	ag-gra-'var-si
wound	ferita	fe-'ri-ta

B. AT THE DENTIST'S

anesthetic	anestetico	a-nes-'te-ti-ko
appointment	appuntamento	ap-pun-ta-'men-to
braces	apparecchio per denti	ap-pa-'rek-kyo per i-'den-ti
cavity, tooth decay	carie (f, inv)	'ka-rye
dental assistant	assistente (m/f)	as-sis-'ten-te
dentist	dentista (m/f)	den-'tis-ta
• at the dentist's	dal dentista	—
• dentist's office	gabinetto dentistico	ga-bi-'net-to den-'tis-ti-ko
drill	trapano	'tra-pa-no
false teeth, denture	dentiera	den-'tye-ra
(to) fill a tooth	impiombare un dente	im-pyom-'ba-re
• filling	piombatura	pyom-ba-'tu-ra
injection, needle	iniezione (f)	in-ye-'tsyo-ne
mouth	bocca	'bok-ka
• gums	gengive (f, pl)	jen-'ji-ve
• jaw	mandibola	man-'di-bo-la
• lip	labbro (labbra, f, pl)	'lab-bro
• Open!	Apra!	—
• palate	palato	pa-'la-to
• tongue	lingua	'lin-gwa
office hours	orario	o-'ra-ryo
orthodontist	ortodontista (m/f)	or-to-don-'tis-ta
plaque	placca dentaria	'plak-ka den-'ta-rya
(to) pull a tooth	estrarre* un dente	es-'trar-re
(to) rinse	sciacquarsi la bocca	šak-'kwar-si la 'bok-ka
tartar	tartaro	'tar-ta-ro
tooth	dente (m)	'den-te
• canine	canino	ka-'ni-no
• molar	molare (m)	mo-'la-re
• root	radice (f)	ra-'di-če
• tooth extraction	estrazione (f)	es-tra-'tsyo-ne
• wisdom tooth	dente del giudizio	ju-'di-tsyo
toothache	mal di denti	—
• (to) have a toothache	avere* mal di denti	—
toothpaste	dentifricio	den-ti-'fri-čo
X-rays	raggi X	'raj-ji iks

41. LEGAL MATTERS

accusation	imputazione (f)	*im-pu-ta-'tsyo-ne*
• **(to) accuse**	accusare	*ak-ku-'za-re*
• **accused**	imputato (-a)	*im-pu-'ta-to*
(to) acquit	assolvere*	*as-'sol-ve-re*
(to) admit	ammettere*	*am-me-te-re*
attorney	avvocato (-essa)	*av-vo-'ka-to*
bail	cauzione (f)	*kau-'tsyo-ne*
(to) be on trial	essere* sotto processo	*'es-se-re 'sot-to pro-'čes-so*
(to) carry out a sentence	eseguire una sentenza	*e-ze-'gwi-re u-na sen-'ten-dza*
(to) charge	incolpare	*in-kol-'pa-re*
civil right	diritto civile	*di-'rit-to či-'vi-le*
closed-door hearing	udienza a porte chiuse	*u-'dyen-sza a 'por-te 'kyu-ze*
controversy	controversia	*kon-tro-'ver-sya*
(to) convince	convincere*	*kon-'vin-če-re*
court	tribunale (m)	*tri-bu-'na-le*
• **court for serious crimes**	corte (m) d'assise	*'kor-te das-'si-ze*
• **court for the administration of public funds**	corte (m) dei conti	—
• **court of appeal**	corte (m) d'appello	*dap-'pel-lo*
courtroom	aula del tribunale	*'au-la del tri-bu-'na-le*
• **courtroom hearing**	udienza in tribunale	*u-'dyen-tsa in tri-bu-'na-le*
criminal hearing	udienza penale	*u-'dyen-tsa pe-'na-le*
debate	dibattito	*di-'bat-ti-to*
• **(to) debate**	dibattere	*di-'bat-te-re*
(to) defend oneself	difendersi*	*di-'fen-der-si*
deferred sentence	sentenza di rinvio a giudizio	*sen-'ten-dza di rin-'vi-o a ju-'di-tsyo*
deposition, testimony	deposizione (f)	*de-po-zi-'tsyo-ne*
(to) detain	detenere*	*de-te-'ne-re*
detention	detenzione (f)	*de-ten-'tsyo-ne*
(to) disagree	non essere* d'accordo	*non-'es-se-re dak-'kor-do*
(to) discuss, argue	discutere*	*dis-'ku-te-re*
evidence	prove (f, pl)	*'pro-ve*
• **(to) examine the witness**	interrogare il testimone	*in-ter-ro-'ga-re il tes-ti-'mo-ne*
extradition	estradizione (f)	*es-tra-di-'tsyo-ne*
fault, guilt	colpa	—
freedom on bail	libertà (f, inv) su cauzione	*li-ber-'ta su kau-'tsyo-ne*

guilt	colpevolezza	*kol-pe-vo-'let-tsa*
• guilty	colpevole	*kol-'pe-vo-le*
hearing	udienza	*u-'dyen-tsa*
hostile party	parte avversa	*'par-te av-'ver-sa*
illegal	illegale	*il-le-'ga-le*
(to) imprison	incarcerare	*in-kar-če-'ra-re*
innocence	innocenza	*in-no-'čen-tsa*
• innocent	innocente	*in-no-'čen-te*
insufficient evidence	insufficienza di prove	*insuf-fi-'čen-'tsa di 'pro-ve*
(to) issue a sentence	pronunciare una sentenza	*pro-nun-'ča-re u-na sen-'ten-tsa*
judge	giudice (m/f)	*'ju-di-če*
• (to) judge	giudicare	*ju-di-'ka-re*
juror	giurato (-a)	*ju-'ra-to*
• jury	giuria	*ju-'ri-a*
justice	giustizia	*jus-'ti-tsya*
justice of the peace	giudice di pace	*'ju-di-če di 'pa-če*
law	legge (f)	*'lej-je*
lawsuit	querela	*kwe-'re-la*
lawyer	avvocato	*av-vo-'ka-to*
legal	legale	*le-'ga-le*
life imprisonment	ergastolo	*er-'gas-to-lo*
litigation, legal case	causa	*'kau-za*
• (to) litigate	fare* causa	—
magistrate	magistrato	*ma-jis-'tra-to*
(to) pay bail	versare la cauzione	*ver-'sa-re la kau-'tsyo-ne*
(to) persuade	persuadere*	*per-swa-'de-re*
plaintiff	querelante (m/f)	*kwe-re-'lan-te*
plea	supplica	*'sup-pli-ka*
• (to) postpone, adjourn	rimandare	*ri-man-'da-re*
power of attorney	procura	*pro-'ku-ra*
prison	prigione (f)	*pri-'jo-ne*
probation	libertà vigilata	*li-ber-'ta vi-ji-'la-ta*
proof	prova	—
public prosecutor	pubblico accusatore	*'pub-bli-ko ak-ku-za-'to-re*
(to) release on bail	rilasciare sotto cauzione	*ri-la-'ša-re sot-to kau-'tsyo-ne*
sentence	sentenza	*sen-'ten-tsa*
(to) sue	querelare	*kwe-re-'la-re*
summons	citazione (f)	*či-ta-'tsyo-ne*
supreme court	corte (f) di cassazione	*'kor-te di kas-sa-'tsyo-ne*
(to) testify	testimoniare	*tes-ti-mo-'nya-re*
testimony	testimonianza	*tes-ti-mo-'nyan-tsa*
trial	processo	*pro-'čes-so*
verdict	verdetto	*ver-det-to*
witness	testimone (m/f)	*tes-ti-'mo-ne*
• eyewitness	testimone oculare	*o-ku-'la-re*

THE CONTEMPORARY WORLD

42. SCIENCE AND TECHNOLOGY

A. TECHNOLOGY AND TELECOMMUNICATIONS

acoustics	acustica	a-'kus-ti-ka
antenna	antenna	an-'ten-na
audio	audio	'au-dyo
by cable	via cavo	—
distortion	distorsione (f)	dis-tor-'syo-ne
emission	emissione (f)	e-mis-'syo-ne
fee	tariffa	ta-'rif-fa
fidelity	fedeltà (f, inv)	fe-del-'ta
frequency	frequenza	fre-'kwen-tsa
interference	interferenza	in-ter-fe-'ren-dza
light signal	segnale luminoso	se-'nya-le lu-mi-'no-zo
message	messaggio	mes-'saj-jo
network	rete (f)	're-te
optical reader	lettore ottico (m)	let-to-re 'ot-ti-ko
optics	ottica	'ot-ti-ka
real time	tempo reale	re-'a-le
reception	ricezione (f)	ri-če-'tsyo-ne
satellite	satellite (m)	sa-'tel-li-te
• satellite dish	antenna parabolica	an-'ten-na pa-ra-'bo-li-ka
sound signal	segnale sonoro	se-'nya-le so-'no-ro
subscription	abbonamento	ab-bo-na-'men-to
• subscription fee	canone (m) d'abbonamento	'ka-no-ne
technology	tecnologia	tek-no-lo-'ji-a
telecommunication	telecomunicazione (f)	te-le-ko-mu-ni-ka-'tsyo-ne
teleconference	teleconferenza	te-le-kon-fe-'ren-dza
transmission	trasmissione (f)	traz-mis-'syo-ne
video conference	videoconferenza	vi-deo-o-kon-fe-'ren-dza
• video game	videogioco	vi-de-o-'jo-ko
• video telephone	videotelefono	vi-de-o-te-'le-fo-no
volume	volume (m)	vo-'lu-me
wavelength	lunghezza d'onda	lun-'ge-tsa 'don-da
wireless	senza fili	'sen-tsa 'fi-li

B. COMPUTERS, COMPUTER SCIENCE, AND THE INTERNET

(to) align	allineare	*al-li-ne-'a-re*
analog	analogico	*a-na-'lo-ji-ko*
animated image	immagine animata	*im-'ma-ji-ne a-ni-'ma-ta*
artificial intelligence	intelligenza artificiale	*in-tel-li-'jen-tsa ar-ti-fi-'ca-le*
automation	automazione (f)	*au-to-ma-'tsyo-ne*
byte	byte (m, inv)	—
cartridge	cartuccia	*kar-'tuč-ča*
CD reader, drive	lettore	*let-'to-re*
CD-ROM	CD-ROM (inv)	—
(to) center	centrare	*čen-'tra-re*
chip	chip (m, inv)	—
(to) clear, delete	annullare	*an-nul-'la-re*
(to) click	cliccare	*klik-'ka-re*
color monitor	schermo a colori	*'sker-mo a ko-'lo-ri*
command	comando	*ko-'man-do*
compatible	compatibile	*kom-pa-'ti-bi-le*
computer	computer (m, inv)	
computer science	informatica	*in-for-'ma-ti-ka*
computerization	computerizzazione (f)	*kom-pu-te-ri-tsa-'tsyo-ne*
(to) copy	copiare	*ko-'pya-re*
cursor	cursore (m)	*kur-'so-re*
datum, data	dato (sing.)	—
	dati (pl.)	—
• data bank	banca dati	—
• data file	file (m, inv) di dati	—
• data processing	elaborazione (f) dati	*e-la-bo-ra-'tsyo-ne*
(to) delete	cancellare	*kan-'čel-'la-re*
digital	digitale	*di-ji-'ta-le*
diskette	dischetto	*dis-ket-to*
document	cartella (documento)	*kar-'tel-la*
(to) duplicate	duplicare	*du-pli-'ka-re*
editing	editing (m, inv)	—
electronic file	archivio elettronico	*ar-'ki-vyo e-let-'tro-ni-ko*
e-mail	e-mail	—
(to) erase, delete	cancellare	*kan-'cel-'la-re*
file	archivio	*ar-'ki-vyo*
	file (m, inv)	—
• file manager	file manager (m, inv)	—
• file name	titolo del documento	*'ti-to-lo del do-ku-men-to*
floppy disc	dischetto	*dis-'ket-to*
format	format (m, inv)	—
• (to) format	formattare	*for-mat-'ta-re*

• formatted	formattato	*for-mat-'ta-to*
grammar check	controllo della	*kon-'trol-lo del-la*
	grammatica	*gram-'ma-ti-ka*
graphic, graph	grafico	*'gra-fi-ko*
• graphic interface	interfaccia grafica	*in-ter-'fač-ča*
hard drive	hard drive	—
hardware	hardware (m, inv)	—
help command	comando help (m, inv)	*ko-'man-do*
	aiuto	*a-'yu-to*
hypertext	ipertesto	*i-per-'tes-to*
icon	icona	*i-'ko-na*
index	indice (m)	*'in-di-če*
information	informazione (f)	*in-for-ma-'tsyo-ne*
inputting on the screen	videoscrittura	*vi-de-o-skrit-'tu-ra*
installation	installazione (f)	*in-stal-la-'tsyo-ne*
integrated circuit	circuito integrato	*čir-ku-'i-to in-te-'gra-to*
interactive	interattivo	*in-ter-at-'ti-vo*
interface	interfaccia	*in-ter-'fač-ča*
internet provider	provider (m, inv)	—
justification	giustificazione (f)	*jus-ti-fi-ka-'tsyo-ne*
keyboard	tastiera	*tas-'tye-ra*
keyword	parola chiave	*pa-'ro-la 'kya-ve*
laser printer	stampante (f) laser	*stam-'pan-te*
lock	bloccaggio	*blok-'kaj-jo*
margin	margine (m)	*'mar-ji-ne*
memory	memoria	*me-'mo-rya*
• memory capacity	capacità (f, inv) di	*ka-pa-či-'ta*
	memoria	
• permanent memory	memoria fissa	*'fis-sa*
• RAM memory	RAM	—
menu	menu (m, inv)	—
microprocessor	microprocessore (m)	*mi-kro-pro-čes-'so-re*
modem	modem (m, inv)	—
mouse	mouse (m, inv)	—
multimedia	multimedialità (f, inv)	*mul-ti-me-dya-li-'ta*
(to) navigate	navigare	*na-vi-'ga-re*
network	network (m, inv)	—
	rete (f)	—
on-line	on-line	—
optical reader	lettore ottico	*let-'to-re 'ot-ti-ko*
page set-up	impaginazione (f)	*im-pa-ji-na-'tsyo-ne*
peripheral	unità (f, inv) periferica	*pe-ri-'fe-ri-ka*
• peripherals	periferiche (f, pl)	*pe-ri-'fe-ri-ke*
personal organizer	agenda elettronica	*a-'jen-da e-let-'tro-ni-ka*
(to) print	stampare	*stam-'pa-re*
printer	stampante (f)	*stam-'pan-te*
program	programma (m)	*pro-'gram-ma*
	(programmi, pl)	

• **program instruction**	istruzione (f)	*is-tru-'tsyo-ne*
• **programmer**	programmatore (-trice)	*program-ma-'to-re*
• **program language**	linguaggio di	*lin-'gwaj-jo di*
	programmazione	*pro-gram-ma-'tsyo-ne*
• **pirate program**	programma (m) pirata	*pro-'gram-ma pi-'ra-ta*
(to) put a space	interlineare	*in-ter-li-ne-'a-re*
(to) save	salvare	*sal-'va-re*
screen	schermo	*'sker-mo*
search	ricerca	*ri-'čer-ka*
server	server (m, inv)	—
(to) set up a page	impaginare	*im-pu-ji-'na-re*
software	software (m, inv)	—
space bar	barra spaziatrice	*'bar-ra spa-tsya-'tri-če*
spell check	controllo dell'ortografia	*kon-'trol-lo del-lor-to-gra-'fi-a*
spreadsheet	foglio elettronico	*'fo-lyo e-let-'tro-ni-ko*
(to) store	immagazzinare	*im-ma-ga-tsi-'na-re*
style	stile (m)	*'sti-le*
symbols table	tavola dei simboli	*'ta-vo-la dei 'sim-bo-li*
tab	tabulatore (m)	*ta-bu-la-'to-re*
• **(to) tab**	tabulare	*ta-bu-'la-re*
terminal	terminal (m, inv)	—
transistor	transistor (m, inv)	—
(to) type in	digitare	*di-ji-'ta-re*
underline	sottolineatura	*sot-to-li-ne-a-'tu-ra*
user	utente (m/f)	*u-'ten-te*
virtual	virtuale	*vir-'twa-le*
virus	virus (m, inv)	—
website	sito web	—
window	finestra	*fi-'nes-tra*
word processing	word processing	
work station	stazione (f) di lavoro	*sta-'tsyo-ne di la-'vo-ro*

C. COMPUTER FUNCTIONS AND COMMANDS

Attachment	Allegato	*al-le-'ga-to*
Back	Indietro	*in-'dye-tro*
Close	Chiudi	*'kyu-di*
Connect	Connetta	*kon-'net-ta*
Control	Controlla	*kon-'trol-la*
Copy	Copia	*'ko-pya*
Customize	Personalizza	*per-so-na-'li-dza*
Cut	Taglia	*'ta-lya*
Delete	Annulla	*an-nul-la*
Dialogue Window	Finestra di Dialogo	*fi-'nes-tra di di-'a-lo-go*
Edit	Modifica	*mo-'di-fi-ka*
Eliminate	Elimina	*e-'li-mi-na*
File	File	—

Find	Trova	*'tro-va*
Format	Formato	*for-'ma-to*
Forward	Avanti	*a-'van-ti*
Forward (e-mail)	Inoltra	*i-'nol-tra*
Go to	Vai a	—
Incoming mail	Posta in arrivo	*'pos-ta in ar-'ri-vo*
Insert	Inserisci	*in-se-'ri-ši*
Layout	Layout	—
Menu	Menu	—
Message	Messaggio	*mes-'saj-jo*
Move	Sposta	—
Nicknames	Rubrica	*ru-'bri-ka*
Open	Apri	—
Options	Opzioni	*op-'tsyo-ni*
Outgoing mail	Posta in uscita	*u-'ši-ta*
Page layout	Impaginazione	*im-pa-ji-na-'tsyo-ne*
Password	Password	—
Paste	Incolla	*in-kol-la*
Preferences	Preferiti	*pre-fe-'ri-ti*
Print	Stampa	—
Remove	Rimuovi	*ri-'mwo-vi*
Reply	Rispondi	*ris-'pon-di*
Return	Invio	*in-'vi-o*
Save	Salva	—
Select	Seleziona	*se-le-'tsyo-na*
Send	Invia	*in-'vi-a*
Sent mail	Posta inviata	*in-'vya-ta*
Spell check	Controllo ortografia	*kon-'trol-lo or-to-gra-'fi-a*
Table	Tabella	*ta-'bel-la*
Tools	Strumenti	*stru-'men-ti*
Trashed mail	Posta eliminata	*e-li-mi-'na-ta*
Update	Aggiorna	*aj-'jor-na*
User name	Nome utente	*'no-me u-'ten-te*
View	Visualizza	*vi-zwa-'li-dza*
Window	Finestra	*fi-'nes-tra*

43. POLITICS AND HISTORY

A. THE POLITICAL WORLD

administration	amministrazione (f)	*am-mi-nis-tra-'tsyo-ne*
agenda (of a meeting)	ordine del giorno	*'or-di-ne del 'jor-no*
assembly	assemblea	*as-sem-'ble-a*
ballot	scheda elettorale	*'ske-da e-let-to-'ra-le*
• ballot box	urna elettorale	*'ur-na*
• balloting	ballottaggio	*bal-lot-'taj-jo*
bicameral	bicamerale	*bi-ka-me-'ra-le*

bill (of the legislature)	disegno di legge	*di-'ze-nyo di 'lej-je*
cabinet	gabinetto	*ga-bi-'net-to*
• **cabinet head**	capo di gabinetto	—
• **cabinet meeting**	consiglio di gabinetto	*kon-'si-lyo*
(to) call (a meeting, etc.)	convocare	*kon-vo-'ka-re*
center (political)	di centro	*čen-tro*
chamber of representatives	camera dei deputati	*'ka-me-ra dei de-pu-'ta-ti*
citizen	cittadino (-a)	*čit-ta-'di-no*
• **citizenship**	cittadinanza	*čit-ta-di-'nan-dza*
civic duty	dovere civico	*do-'ve-re 'či-vi-ko*
civil affairs	affari civili	*af-'fa-ri či-'vi-li*
civil right	diritto civile	*di-'rit-to či-'vi-le*
civil servant	funzionario	*fun-tsyo-'na-ryo*
coalition	coalizione (f)	*ko-a-li-'tsyo-ne*
commission	commissione (f)	*kom-mis-'syo-ne*
commission of inquiry	commissione d'inchiesta	*din-'kyes-ta*
committee	comitato	*ko-mi-'ta-to*
communism	comunismo	*ko-mu-'niz-mo*
confederation	confederazione (f)	*kon-fe-de-ra-'tsyo-ne*
conservative	conservatore (-trice)	*kon-ser-va-'to-re*
constitution	costituzione (f)	*kos-ti-tu-'tsyo-ne*
consulate	consolato	*kon-so-'la-to*
council	consiglio	*kon-'si-lyo*
• **Council of Europe**	Consiglio d'Europa	—
• **council of ministers**	consiglio dei ministri	*mi-'nis-tri*
• **councilor**	consigliere (-a)	*kon-si-'lye-re*
country of origin	paese (m) d'origine	*pa-'e-ze do-'ri-ji-ne*
decentralization	decentramento	*de-čen-tra-'men-to*
decree	decreto	*de-'kre-to*
democracy	democrazia	*de-mo-kra-'tsi-a*
• **democratic party**	partito democratico	*par-'ti-to de-mo-'kra-ti-ko*
• **democratic society**	società democratica	*so-če-'ta*
demonstration	dimostrazione (f)	*di-mos-tra-'tsyo-ne*
economy	economia	*e-ko-no-'mi-a*
(to) elect	eleggere*	*e-'lej-je-re*
• **elected representative**	deputato (-a)	*de-pu-'ta-to*
• **election**	elezione (f)	*e-le-'tsyo-ne*
• **electoral campaign**	campagna elettorale	*kam-'pa-nya e-let-to-'ra-le*
embassy	ambasciata	*am-ba-'ša-ta*
euro	euro (m, inv)	—
executive	esecutivo	*e-ze-ku-'ti-vo*
external affairs	affari esteri	*af-'fa-ri 'es-te-ri*
federation	federazione (f)	*fe-de-ra-'tsyo-ne*
foreign country	paese straniero	*pa-'e-ze stra-'nye-ro*
(to) govern	governare	*go-ver-'na-re*

• **government**	governo	go-'ver-no
• **government bond**	buono del tesoro	'bwo-no del te-'zo-ro
• **governmental**	governativo	go-ver-na-'ti-vo
• **head of government**	capo del governo	'ka-po
• **head of state**	capo dello stato	—
ideology	ideologia	i-de-o-lo-'ji-a
imperialism	imperialismo	im-pe-rya-'liz-mo
inflation	inflazione (f)	in-fla-'tsyo-ne
internal affairs	affari interni	af-'fa-ri in-'ter-ni
judiciary	giudiziario	ju-di-'tsya-ryo
juridical, legal, authorized	giuridico	ju-'ri-di-ko
king	re (m, inv)	—
labor union	sindacato	sin-da-'ka-to
left-wing	di sinistra	si-'nis-tra
legislation	legislazione (f)	le-jis-la-'tsyo-ne
• **legislative**	legislativo	le-jis-la-'ti-vo
• **legislature**	legislatura	le-jis-la-'tu-ra
liberal	liberale	li-be-'ra-le
• **liberal party**	partito liberale	par-'ti-to
local agency	ente locale (m)	'en-te lo-'ka-le
mayor	sindaco	'sin-da-ko
minister	ministro	mi-'nis-tro
• **ministry**	ministero	mi-nis-'te-ro
monarchist party	partito monarchico	par-'ti-to mo-'nar-ki-ko
• **monarchy**	monarchia	mo-nar-'ki-a
motion	mozione (f)	mo'tsyo-ne
• **abstention**	astensione (f)	as-ten-'syo-ne
• **against**	sfavorevole	sfa-vo-'re-vo-le
• **amendment**	emendamento	e-men-da-'men-to
• **in favor**	favorevole	fa-vo-'re-vo-le
• **passing**	approvazione (f)	ap-pro-va-'tsyo-ne
municipal	municipale	mu-ni-či-'pa-le
national	nazionale	na-tsyo-'na-le
parliament	parlamento	par-la-'men-to
party	partito	par-'ti-to
platform	programma (m)	pro-'gram-ma
	elettorale	e-let-to-'ra-le
policy (in general)	politica	po-'li-ti-ka
politician	politico (m/f)	po-li-ti-'ko
poll	sondaggio	son-'daj-jo
power	potere (m)	po-'te-re
president	presidente (m/f)	pre-zi-'den-te
prime minister	primo ministro	'pri-mo mi-'nis-tro
prince	principe (m)	'prin-či-pe
princess	principessa	prin-či-'pes-sa
progressive party	partito progressista	par-'ti-to pro-gres-'sis-ta
protest	protesta	pro-'tes-ta

provincial	provinciale	pro-vin-'ča-le
queen	regina	re-'ji-na
(to) ratify	ratificare	ra-ti-fi-'ka-re
referendum	referendum (m)	—
reform	riforma	ri-'for-ma
regional	regionale	re-jo-'na-le
representation (political)	rappresentanza	rap-pre-zen-'tan-dza
republic	repubblica	re-'pub-bli-ka
republican party	partito repubblicano	par-'ti-to re-pub-bli-'ka-no
revolt, riot	rivolta	ri-'vol-ta
revolution	rivoluzione (f)	ri-vo-lu-'tsyo-ne
right to vote	diritto al voto	di-'rit-to al 'vo-to
right to work	diritto al lavoro	di-'rit-to al la-'vo-ro
right-wing	di destra	—
seat (political)	seggio	'sej-jo
security services	servizi di sicurezza	ser-'vi-tsi
senate	senato	se-'na-to
session	sessione (f)	ses-'syo-ne
sitting (of the house)	seduta	se-'du-ta
socialism	socialismo	so-ča-'liz-mo
• socialist party	partito socialista	par-ti-to so-ča-'lis-ta
speech	discorso	dis-'kor-so
statute	statuto	sta-'tu-to
task, duty	incarico	in-'ka-ri-ko
treasurer	tesoriere (-a)	te-zo-'rye-re
• treasury	tesoreria	te-zo-re-'ri-a
universal suffrage	suffragio universale	suf-'fra-jo u-ni-ver-'sa-le
(to) violate a right	violare un diritto	vyo-'la-re un di-'rit-to
vote	voto	—
• (to) vote	votare	vo-'ta-re
• confidence vote	fiducia	fi-'du-ča
• non-confidence vote	sfiducia	sfi-'du-ča

B. HISTORY

alliance	alleanza	al-le-'an-tsa
• ally	alleato	al-le-'a-to
ancient Greece	Antica Grecia	an-'ti-ka 'gre-ča
ancient Rome	Antica Roma	an-'ti-ka 'ro-ma
antiquity	antichità (f, inv)	an-ti-ki-'ta
archivist	archivista (m/f)	ar-ki-'vis-ta
Baroque	Barocco	ba-'rok-ko
century	secolo	'se-ko-lo
civil war	guerra civile	'gwer-ra či-'vi-le
Classicism	Classicismo	klas-si-'čiz-mo
curfew	coprifuoco	ko-pri-'fwo-ko
decade	decennio	de-'čen-nyo

decline	declino	de-'kli-no
defeat	sconfitta	skon-'fit-ta
defense	difesa	di-'fe-za
document	documento	do-ku-'men-to
Enlightenment	Illuminismo	il-lu-mi-'niz-mo
epoch	epoca	'e-po-ka
era	era	—
faction	fazione (f)	fa-'tsyo-ne
feudal	feudale	fe-u-'da-le
First World War	Prima Guerra Mondiale	'pri-ma 'gwer-ra mon-'dya-le
fossil	fossile (m)	'fos-si-le
Hellenic	ellenico	el-'le-ni-ko
history	storia	'sto-rya
• **historian**	storico (-a)	'sto-ri-ko
Industrial Revolution	Rivoluzione (f) Industriale	ri-vo-lu-'tsyo-ne in-dus-'trya-le
insurrection	insurrezione (f)	in-sur-re-'tsyo-ne
medieval	medioevale	me-dyo-e-'va-le
Middle Ages	Medioevo	me-dyo-'e-vo
paleontology	paleontologia	pa-le-on-to-lo-'ji-a
period	periodo	pe-'ri-o-do
plebeian	plebeo	ple-'be-o
prehistoric	preistorico	pre-is-'to-ri-ko
• **prehistory**	preistoria	pre-is-'to-rya
Renaissance	Rinascimento	ri-na-ši-'men-to
Roman Empire	Impero Romano	im-pe-ro ro-'ma-no
Romanticism	Romanticismo	ro-man-ti-'čiz-mo
ruin	rovina	ro-'vi-na
Second World War	Seconda Guerra Mondiale	se-'kon-da 'gwer-ra mon-'dya-le
World War	Guerra Mondiale	'gwer-ra mon-'dya-le

44. CONTROVERSIAL ISSUES

A. THE ENVIRONMENT

air pollution	inquinamento atmosferico	in-kwi-na-'men-to at-mos-'fe-ri-ko
biosystem	biosistema (m)	bi-o-sis-'te-ma
disposal, waste, discharge	scarico	'ska-ri-ko
energy	energia	e-ner-'ji-a
• **energy conservation**	conservazione (f) dell'energia	kon-ser-va-'tsyo-ne
• **energy crisis**	crisi (f, inv) energetica	'kri-zi e-ner-'je-ti-ka
• **energy waste**	spreco d'energia	'spre-ko
environment	ambiente (f)	am-'byen-te
• **environmentalist**	ambientalista (m/f)	am-byen-ta-'lis-ta

fossil fuel	combustibile (m)	*kom-bus-'ti-bi-le*
natural resources	risorse naturali (f, inv)	*ri-'sor-se na-tu-'ra-li*
petroleum	petrolio	*pe-'tro-lyo*
pollution	inquinamento	*in-kwi-na-'men-to*
• polluted	inquinato	*in-kwi-'na-to*
radiation	radiazione (f)	*ra-dya-'tsyo-ne*
• radioactive waste	rifiuto radioattivo	*ri'fyu-to ra-dyo-at-'ti-vo*
sewage	acque di scarico	*'ak-kwe di 'ska-ri-ko*
• sewage system	fognatura	*fo-nya-'tu-ra*
solar energy	energia solare	*e-ner-'ji-a so-'la-re*
thermal energy	energia termica	*e-ner-'ji-a 'ter-mi-ka*
toxic	tossico	*'tos-si-ko*
waste	rifiuto	*ri-'fyu-to*
waste disposal	scarico delle immondizie	*'ska-ri-ko del-le im-mon-'di-tsye*
water pollution	inquinamento delle acque	*in-kwi-na-'men-to del-le 'ak-kwe*

B. SOCIAL ISSUES

abortion	aborto	*a-'bor-to*
AIDS	AIDS (m, inv)	—
alcohol	alcool (m, inv)	—
• alcoholism	alcolismo	*al-ko-'liz-mo*
(to) beg	mendicare	*men-di-'ka-re*
• beggar	mendicante (m/f)	*men-di-'kan-te*
censorship	censura	*čen-'su-ra*
death penalty	pena di morte	—
depressed area	zona depressa	*'dzo-na de-'pres-sa*
disadvantage	svantaggio	*zvan-'taj-jo*
ghetto	ghetto	—
health assistance	assistenza sanitaria	*sa-ni-'ta-rya*
homeless	senzatetto	*sen-tsa-'tet-to*
homosexuality	omosessualità (f, inv)	*o-mo-ses-swa-li-'ta*
legal assistance	assistenza legale	*as-sis-'ten-tsa le-'ga-le*
lesbian	lesbica	*'lez-bi-ka*
National Welfare Agency	Istituto Nazionale della Previdenza Sociale	*is-ti-'tu-to na-tsyo-'na-le del-la pre-vi-'den-dza so-'ča-le*
overpopulation	sovrappopolazione (f)	*so-vrap-po-po-la-'tsyo-ne*
pornography	pornografia	*por-no-gra-'fi-a*
poverty	povertà (f, inv)	*po-ver-'ta*
prostitution	prostituzione (f)	*pros-ti-tu-'tsyo-ne*
provision of welfare services	previdenza sociale	*pre-vi-'den-tsa so-'ča-le*
racism	razzismo	*rat-'tsiz-mo*

(to) receive benefits	ricevere assistenza sociale	ri-'če-ve-re as-sis-'ten-dza so-'ča-le
shelter	rifugio	ri-'fu-jo
social assistance, welfare	assistenza, previdenza sociale	as-sis-'ten-dza pre-vi-'den-dza so-ča-le

C. DRUGS

amphetamine	amfetamina	am-fe-ta-'mi-na
cocaine	cocaina	ko-ka-'i-na
(to) detoxify oneself, come clean	disintossicarsi	diz-in-tos-si-'kar-si
drug addict	tossicodipendente (m/f)	tos-si-ko-di-pen-'den-te
drug dependency, addiction	tossicodipendenza	tos-si-ko-di-pen-'den-tsa
drug pusher	spacciatore (-trice) di droga	spač-ča-'to-re
drug traffic	traffico degli stupefacenti	'traf-fi-ko de-lyi stu-pe-fa-'čen-ti
drugs	droga	—
(to) get out of drugs	uscire* (ess) dalla droga	u-'ši-re
hallucination, high	allucinazione (f)	al-lu-či-na-'tsyo-ne
hard drug	droga pesante	pe-'zan-te
heroin	eroina	e-ro-'i-na
marijuana	marijuana	—
needle	ago	—
overdose	overdose (m, inv)	—
soft drug	droga leggera	lej-'je-ra
syringe	siringa	si-'rin-ga
trip	trip (m, inv)	—

D. GLOBAL ISSUES

armed conflict	conflitto a fuoco	kon-'flit-to a 'fwo-ko
armistice	armistizio	ar-mi-'sti-tsyo
arms dealer	mercante d'armi	mer-'kan-te 'dar-mi
arms reduction	diminuzione (f) delle armi	di-mi-nu-'tsyo-ne del-le 'ar-mi
arms trade	mercato delle armi	mer-'ka-to del-le 'ar-mi
army	esercito	e-'zer-ci-to
attack	attacco	at-'tak-ko
automatic weapon	arma automatica	'ar-ma au-to-'ma-ti-ka
ballistic missile	missile balistico	'mis-si-le ba-'lis-ti-ko
biological war	guerra batteriologica	'gwer-ra bat-te-ryo-'lo-ji-ka
biological weapon	arma batteriologica	'ar-ma bat-te-ryo-'lo-ji-ka

bomb	bomba	'bom-ba
• atomic bomb	bomba atomica	a-'to-mika
• hand bomb	bomba a mano	—
• molotov cocktail	bomba molotov	—
• smoke bomb	bomba fumogena	fu-'mo-je-na
chemical war	guerra chimica	'gwer-ra 'ki-mi-ka
conflict	conflitto	kon-'flit-to
conventional weapon	arma convenzionale	'ar-ma kon-ven-tsyo-'na-le
disarmament	disarmo	diz-'ar-mo
emigrant	emigrante (m/f)	e-mi-'gran-te
• emigration	emigrazione (f)	e-mi-gra-'tsyo-ne
espionage	spionaggio	spyo-'naj-jo
• spy	spia	'spi-a
fight, struggle	lotta	—
grenade	granata	gra-'na-ta
guerrilla warfare	guerriglia	gwer-'ri-lya
headquarters	quartiere (m) generale	kwar-'tye-re je-ne-'ra-le
holy war	guerra santa	'gwer-ra 'san-ta
hostage	ostaggio	os-'taj-jo
human rights	diritti umani	di-'rit-ti u-'ma-ni
immigrant	immigrante (m/f)	im-mi-'gran-te
• immigration	immigrazione (f)	im-mi-gra-'tsyo-ne
missile	missile (m)	'mis-si-le
multiracial society	società (f, inv)	so-če-'ta mul-ti-ra-'tsya-le
	multirazziale	
nerve gas	gas (m, inv) nervino	ner-'vi-no
peace	pace (f)	'pa-če
poison gas	gas (m, inv) tossico	'tos-si-ko
racism	razzismo	rat-'tsiz-mo
• racist	razzista (m/f)	rat-'tsis-ta
refugee	profugo (-a)	'pro-fu-go
• refugee camp	campo profughi	'kam-po 'pro-fu-gi
state of war	stato di guerra	'sta-to di 'gwer-ra
supplies	viveri (m, pl)	'vi-ve-ri
tank	carro armato	'kar-ro ar-'ma-to
tear gas	gas (m, inv) lacrimogeno	la-kri-'mo-je-no
terrorism	terrorismo	ter-ro-'riz-mo
• terrorist	terrorista (m/f)	ter-ro-'ris-ta
totalitarian	totalitario	to-ta-li-'ta-ryo
• totalitarianism	totalitarismo	to-ta-li-ta-'riz-mo
truce	tregua	'tre-gwa
United Nations	Nazioni Unite (f, pl)	na-'tsyo-ni u-'ni-te
visa	visto	
war	guerra	'gwer-ra
weapon	arma	'ar-ma

E. EXPRESSING YOUR OPINION

according to me	secondo me	se-'kon-do me
as a matter of fact	anzi	'an-tsi
by the way	a proposito	a pro-'po-zi-to
for example	per esempio	per e-'zem-pyo
from my point of view	dal mio punto di vista	—
however	tuttavia	tut-ta-'vi-a
	comunque	ko-'mun-kwe
I believe that...	credo che...	—
I don't know if...	non so se...	—
I doubt that...	dubito che...	'du-bi-to
I think that...	penso che...	'pen-so
I would like to say that...	vorrei dire che...	'vor-'rey 'di-re
I'm not sure that...	non sono sicuro (-a) che...	si-'ku-ro
I'm sure that...	sono sicuro (-a) che...	si-'ku-ro
in conclusion	in conclusione	kon-klu-'zyo-ne
in my opinion	a mio avviso	av-'vi-zo
	a mio parere	pa-'re-re
it seems that...	sembra che...	'sem-bra
	pare che...	'pa-re
it's clear that...	è chiaro che...	'kya-ro
no	no	—
that is to say	cioè	čo-'e
	vale a dire	'va-le a 'di-re
there's no doubt that...	non c'è dubbio che...	non če 'dub-byo ke
therefore	allora	al-'lo-ra
	dunque	'dun-kwe
	quindi	'kwin-di
unless	a meno che	—
yes	sì	—

IRREGULAR VERBS

The following verbs used in this book have some irregularity in their conjugation. Only the irregular feature or tense is given here.

accadere (conjugated like **cadere**)

accendere
Past Participle	acceso
Past Absolute	(io) accesi, (tu) accendesti, (Lei) accese, (lui/lei) accese, (noi) accendemmo, (voi) accendeste, (loro) accesero

accludere (conjugated like **concludere**)

aggiungere (conjugated like **piangere**)

alludere (conjugated like **concludere**)

ammettere (conjugated like **mettere**)

andare
Present Indicative	(io) vado, (tu) vai, (Lei) va, (lui/lei) va, (noi) andiamo, (voi) andate, (loro) vanno
Future	(io) andrò, (tu) andrai, (Lei) andrà, (lui/lei) andrà, (noi) andremo, (voi) andrete, (loro) andranno
Conditional	(io) andrei, (tu) andresti, (Lei) andrebbe, (lui/lei) andrebbe, (noi) andremmo, (voi) andreste, (loro) andrebbero
Present Subjunctive	(io) vada (tu) vada, (Lei) vada, (lui/lei) vada, (noi) andiamo, (voi) andiate, (loro) vadano
Imperative	(tu) va', (Lei) vada, (noi) andiamo, (voi) andate, (Loro) vadano

apprendere (conjugated like **prendere**)

aprire
Past Participle	aperto

assolvere (conjugated like **risolvere**)

assumere
Past Participle	assunto
Past Absolute	(io) assunsi, (tu) assumesti, (Lei) assunse, (lui/lei) assunse, (noi) assumemmo, (voi) assumeste, (loro) assunsero

astrarre
Present Indicative	(io) astraggo, (tu) astrai, (Lei) astrae, (lui/lei) astrae, (noi) astraiamo, (voi) astraete, (loro) astraggono
Past Participle	astratto
Imperfect	(io) astraevo, (tu) astraevi, (Lei) astraeva, (lui/lei) astraeva, (noi) astraevamo, (voi) astraevate, (loro) astraevano
Past Absolute	(io) astrassi, (tu) astraesti, (Lei) astrasse, (lui/lei) astrasse, (noi) astraemmo, (voi) astraeste, (loro) astrassero
Present Subjunctive	(io) astragga, (tu) astragga, (Lei) astragga, (lui/lei) astragga, (noi) astraiamo, (voi) astraiate, (loro) astraggano
Imperfect Subjunctive	(io) astraessi, (tu) astraessi, (Lei) astraesse, (lui/lei) astraesse, (noi) astraessimo, (voi) astraeste, (loro) astraessero
Imperative	(tu) astrai, (Lei) astragga, (noi) astraiamo, (voi) astraete, (Loro) astraggano
Gerund	astraendo

attendere
Past Participle	atteso
Past Absolute	(io) attesi, (tu) attendesti, (Lei) attese, (lui/lei) attese, (noi) attendemmo, (voi) attendeste, (loro) attesero

avere
Present Indicative	(io) ho, (tu) hai, (Lei) ha, (lui/lei) ha, (noi) abbiamo, (voi) avete, (loro) hanno
Past Absolute	(io) ebbi, (tu) avesti, (Lei) ebbe, (lui/lei) ebbe, (noi) avemmo, (voi) aveste, (loro) ebbero
Future	(io) avrò, (tu) avrai, (Lei) avrà, (lui/lei) avrà, (noi) avremo, (voi) avrete, (loro) avranno
Conditional	(io) avrei, (tu) avresti, (Lei) avrebbe, (lui/lei) avrebbe, (noi) avremmo, (voi) avreste, (loro) avrebbero
Present Subjunctive	(io) abbia (tu) abbia, (Lei) abbia, (lui/lei) abbia, (noi) abbiamo, (voi) abbiate, (loro) abbiano
Imperative	(tu) abbi, (Lei) abbia, (noi) abbiamo, (voi) abbiate, (Loro) abbiano

avvenire (conjugated like **venire**)

benedire (conjugated like **dire**)

bere
Present Indicative   (io) bevo, (tu) bevi, (Lei) beve, (lui/lei) beve, (noi)
                        beviamo, (voi) bevete, (loro) bevono
Past Participle   bevuto
Past Absolute   (io) bevvi (bevetti), (tu) bevesti, (Lei) bevve (bevette),
                        (lui/lei) bevve (bevette), (noi) bevemmo, (voi) beveste,
                        (loro) bevvero (bevettero)
Future   (io) berrò, (tu) berrai, (Lei) berrà, (lui/lei) berrà, (noi)
                        berremo, (voi) berrete, (loro) berranno
Conditional   (io) berrei, (tu) berresti, (Lei) berrebbe, (lui/lei)
                        berrebbe, (noi) berremmo, (voi) berreste, (loro) berreb-
                        bero
Present Subjunctive   (io) beva, (tu) beva, (Lei) beva, (lui/lei) beva, (noi)
                        beviamo, (voi) beviate, (loro) bevano
Imperfect   (io) bevevo, (tu) bevevi, (Lei) beveva, (lui/lei) beveva,
                        (noi) bevevamo, (voi) bevevate, (loro) bevevano
Imperative   (tu) bevi, (Lei) beva, (noi) beviamo, (voi) bevete,
                        (Loro) bevano
Gerund   bevendo

cadere
Past Absolute   (io) caddi, (tu) cadesti, (Lei) cadde, (lui/lei) cadde,
                        (noi) cademmo, (voi) cadeste, (loro) caddero
Future   (io) cadrò, (tu) cadrai, (Lei) cadrà, (lui/lei) cadrà, (noi)
                        cadremo, (voi) cadrete, (loro) cadranno
Conditional   (io) cadrei, (tu) cadresti, (Lei) cadrebbe, (lui/lei)
                        cadrebbe, (noi) cadremmo, (voi) cadreste, (loro)
                        cadrebbero
Present Subjunctive   (io) cada, (tu) cada, (Lei) cada, (lui/lei) cada, (noi)
                        cadiamo, (voi) cadiate, (loro) cadano

chiedere
Past Participle   chiesto
Past Absolute   (io) chiesi, (tu) chiedesti, (Lei) chiese, (lui/lei) chiese,
                        (noi) chiedemmo, (voi) chiedeste, (loro) chiesero

chiudere
Past Participle   chiuso
Past Absolute   (io) chiusi, (tu) chiudesti, (Lei) chiuse, (lui/lei) chiuse,
                        (noi) chiudemmo, (voi) chiudeste, (loro) chiuscro

comporre (conjugated like **porre**)

comprendere (conjugated like **prendere**)

concludere
Past Participle concluso
Past Absolute (io) conclusi, (tu) concludesti, (Lei) concluse, (lui/lei) concluse, (noi) concludemmo, (voi) concludeste, (loro) conclusero

concorrere (conjugated like **correre**)

conoscere
Past Absolute (io) conobbi, (tu) conoscesti, (Lei) conobbe, (lui/lei) conobbe, (noi) conoscemmo, (voi) conosceste, (loro) conobbero

contenere (conjugated like **tenere**)

contraddire (conjugated like **dire**)

convincere (conjugated like **vincere**)

convivere (conjugated like **vivere**)

correggere
Past Participle corretto
Past Absolute (io) corressi, (tu) correggesti, (Lei) corresse, (lui/lei) corresse, (noi) correggemmo, (voi) correggeste, (loro) corressero

correre
Past Participle corso
Past Absolute (io) corsi, (tu) corresti, (Lei) corse, (lui/lei) corse, (noi) corremmo, (voi) correste, (loro) corsero

crescere
Past Absolute (io) crebbi, (tu) crescesti, (Lei) crebbe, (lui/lei) crebbe, (noi) crescemmo, (voi) cresceste, (loro) crebbero

cuocere
Past Participle cotto
Past Absolute (io) cossi, (tu) cocesti, (Lei) cosse, (lui/lei) cosse, (noi) cocemmo, (voi) coceste, (loro) cossero

dare
Present Indicative (io) do, (tu) dai, (Lei) dà, (lui/lei) dà, (noi) diamo, (voi) date, (loro) danno
Past Participle dato
Imperfect (io) davo, (tu) davi, (Lei) dava, (lui/lei) dava, (noi) davamo, (voi) davate, (loro) davano
Past Absolute (io) diedi, (tu) desti, (Lei) diede, (lui/lei) diede, (noi) demmo, (voi) deste, (loro) diedero

Future	(io) darò, (tu) darai, (Lei) darà, (lui/lei) darà, (noi) daremo, (voi) darete, (loro) daranno
Conditional	(io) darei, (tu) daresti, (Lei) darebbe, (lui/lei) darebbe, (noi) daremmo, (voi) dareste, (loro) darebbero
Present Subjunctive	(io) dia (tu) dia, (Lei) dia, (lui/lei) dia, (noi) diamo, (voi) diate, (loro) diano
Imperfect Subjunctive	(io) dessi, (tu) dessi, (Lei) desse, (lui/lei) desse, (noi) dessimo, (voi) deste, (loro) dessero
Imperative	(tu) da', (Lei) dia, (noi) diamo, (voi) date, (Loro) diano
Gerund	dando

darsi (conjugated like **dare**)

decidere

Past Participle	deciso
Past Absolute	(io) decisi, (tu) decidesti, (Lei) decise, (lui/lei) decise, (noi) decidemmo, (voi) decideste, (loro) decisero

deludere (conjugated like **concludere**)

deporre (conjugated like **porre**)

descrivere (conjugated like **scrivere**)

detenere (conjugated like **tenere**)

difendere

Past Participle	difeso
Past Absolute	(io) difesi, (tu) difendesti, (Lei) difese, (lui/lei) difese, (noi) difendemmo, (voi) difendeste, (loro) difesero

difendersi (conjugated like **difendere**)

diffondere

Past Participle	diffuso
Past Absolute	(io) diffusi, (tu) diffondesti, (Lei) diffuse, (lui/lei) diffuse, (noi) diffondemmo, (voi) diffondeste, (loro) diffusero

dipingere

Past Participle	dipinto
Past Absolute	(io) dipinsi, (tu) dipingesti, (Lei) dipinse, (lui/lei) dipinse, (noi) dipingemmo, (voi) dipingeste, (loro) dipinsero

dire

Present Indicative	(io) dico, (tu) dici, (Lei) dice, (lui/lei) dice, (noi) dici-amo, (voi) dite, (loro) dicono
Past Participle	detto

Imperfect	(io) dicevo, (tu) dicevi, (Lei) diceva, (lui/lei) diceva, (noi) dicevamo, (voi) dicevate, (loro) dicevano
Past Absolute	(io) dissi, (tu) dicesti, (Lei) disse, (lui/lei) disse, (noi) dicemmo, (voi) diceste, (loro) dissero
Future	(io) dirò, (tu) dirai, (Lei) dirà, (lui/lei) dirà, (noi) diremo, (voi) direte, (loro) diranno
Conditional	(io) direi, (tu) diresti, (Lei) direbbe, (lui/lei) direbbe, (noi) diremmo, (voi) direste, (loro) direbbero
Present Subjunctive	(io) dica, (tu) dica, (Lei) dica, (lui/lei) dica, (noi) diciamo, (voi) diciate, (loro) dicano
Imperfect Subjunctive	(io) dicessi, (tu) dicessi, (Lei) dicesse, (lui/lei) dicesse, (noi) dicessimo, (voi) diceste, (loro) dicessero
Imperative	(tu) di', (Lei) dica, (noi) diciamo, (voi) dite, (Loro) dicano
Gerund	dicendo

discutere
Past Participle	discusso
Past Absolute	(io) discussi, (tu) discutesti, (Lei) discusse, (lui/lei) discusse, (noi) discutemmo, (voi) discuteste, (loro) discussero

dissuadere (conjugated like persuadere)

distruggere
Past Participle	distrutto
Past Absolute	(io) distrussi, (tu) distruggesti, (Lei) distrusse, (lui/lei) distrusse, (noi) distruggemmo, (voi) distruggeste, (loro) distrussero

dividere
Past Participle	diviso
Past Absolute	(io) divisi, (tu) dividesti, (Lei) divise, (lui/lei) divise, (noi) dividemmo, (voi) divideste, (loro) divisero

dovere
Present Indicative	(io) devo, (tu) devi, (Lei) deve, (lui/lei) deve, (noi) dobbiamo, (voi) dovete, (loro) devono
Future	(io) dovrò, (tu) dovrai, (Lei) dovrà, (lui/lei) dovrà, (noi) dovremo, (voi) dovrete, (loro) dovranno
Conditional	(io) dovrei, (tu) dovresti, (Lei) dovrebbe, (lui/lei) dovrebbe, (noi) dovremmo, (voi) dovreste, (loro) dovrebbero
Present Subjunctive	(io) deva (debba), (tu) deva (debba), (Lei) deva (debba), (lui/lei) deve (debba), (noi) dobbiamo, (voi) dobbiate, (loro) devano (debbano)

eleggere (conjugated like leggere)

emettere (conjugated like **mettere**)

espandere
Past Participle   espanso
Past Absolute   (io) espansi, (tu) espandesti, (Lei) espanse, (lui/lei)
                        espanse, (noi) espandemmo, (voi) espandeste, (loro)
                        espansero

esprimere
Past Participle   espresso
Past Absolute   (io) espressi, (tu) esprimesti, (Lei) espresse, (lui/lei)
                        espresse, (noi) esprimemmo, (voi) esprimeste, (loro)
                        espressero

esprimersi (conjugated like **esprimere**)

essere
Present Indicative   (io) sono, (tu) sei, (Lei) è, (lui/lei) è, (noi) siamo, (voi)
                        siete, (loro) sono
Past Participle   stato
Imperfect   (io) ero, (tu) eri, (Lei) era, (lui/lei) era, (noi) eravamo,
                        (voi) eravate, (loro) erano
Past Absolute   (io) fui, (tu) fosti, (Lei) fu, (lui/lei) fu, (noi) fummo,
                        (voi) foste, (loro) furono
Future   (io) sarò, (tu) sarai, (Lei) sarà, (lui/lei) sarà, (noi) sare-
                        mo, (voi) sarete, (loro) saranno
Conditional   (io) sarei, (tu) saresti, (Lei) sarebbe, (lui/lei) sarebbe,
                        (noi) saremmo, (voi) sareste, (loro) sarebbero
Present Subjunctive   (io) sia, (tu) sia, (Lei) sia, (lui/lei) sia, (noi) siamo,
                        (voi) siate, (loro) siano
Imperfect Subjunctive (io) fossi, (tu) fossi, (Lei) fosse, (lui/lei) fosse, (noi)
                        fossimo, (voi) foste, (loro) fossero
Imperative   (tu) sii, (Lei) sia, (noi) siamo, (voi) siate, (Loro) siano

estinguere
Past Participle   estinto
Past Absolute   (io) estinsi, (tu) estinguesti, (Lei) estinse, (lui/lei)
                        estinse, (noi) estinguemmo, (voi) estingueste, (loro)
                        estinsero

estrarre (conjugated like **astrarre**)

fare
Present Indicative   (io) faccio, (tu) fai, (Lei) fa, (lui/lei) fa, (noi) facciamo,
                        (voi) fate, (loro) fanno
Past Participle   fatto
Imperfect   (io) facevo, (tu) facevi, (Lei) faceva, (lui/lei) faceva,
                        (noi) facevamo, (voi) facevate, (loro) facevano

Past Absolute	(io) feci, (tu) facesti, (Lei) fece, (lui/lei) fece, (noi) facemmo, (voi) faceste, (loro) fecero
Future	(io) farò, (tu) farai, (Lei) farà, (lui/lei) farà, (noi) faremo, (voi) farete, (loro) faranno
Conditional	(io) farei, (tu) faresti, (Lei) farebbe, (lui/lei) farebbe, (noi) faremmo, (voi) fareste, (loro) farebbero
Present Subjunctive	(io) faccia, (tu) faccia, (Lei) faccia, (lui/lei) faccia, (noi) facciamo, (voi) facciate, (loro) facciano
Imperfect Subjunctive	(io) facessi, (tu) facessi, (Lei) facesse, (lui/lei) facesse, (noi) facessimo, (voi) faceste, (loro) facessero
Imperative	(tu) fa', (Lei) faccia, (noi) facciamo, (voi) fate, (Loro) facciano
Gerund	facendo

farsi (conjugated like **fare**)

fondere

Past Participle	fuso
Past Absolute	(io) fusi, (tu) fondesti, (Lei) fuse, (lui/lei) fuse, (noi) fondemmo, (voi) fondeste, (loro) fusero

friggere

Past Participle	fritto
Past Absolute	(io) frissi, (tu) friggesti, (Lei) frisse, (lui/lei) frisse, (noi) friggemmo, (voi) friggeste, (loro) frissero

indurre (conjugated like **riprodurre**)

interrompere (conjugated like **rompere**)

leggere

Past Participle	letto
Past Absolute	(io) lessi, (tu) leggesti, (Lei) lesse, (lui/lei) lesse, (noi) leggemmo, (voi) leggeste, (loro) lessero

maledire (conjugated like **dire**)

mettere

Past Participle	messo
Past Absolute	(io) misi, (tu) mettesti, (Lei) mise, (lui/lei) mise, (noi) mettemmo, (voi) metteste, (loro) misero

mettersi (conjugated like **mettere**)

morire

Present Indicative	(io) muoio, (tu) muori, (Lei) muore, (lui/lei) muore, (noi) moriamo, (voi) morite, (loro) muoiono
Past Participle	morto

Present Subjunctive   (io) muoia, (tu) muoia, (Lei) muoia, (lui/lei) muoia,
                          (noi) moriamo, (voi) moriate, (loro) muoiano

muovere
Past Participle   mosso
Past Absolute   (io) mossi, (tu) movesti, (Lei) mosse, (lui/lei) mosse,
                          (noi) movemmo, (voi) moveste, (loro) mossero

muoversi (conjugated like **muovere**)

nascere
Past Participle   nato
Past Absolute   (io) nacqui, (tu) nascesti, (Lei) nacque, (lui/lei) nacque,
                          (noi) nascemmo, (voi) nasceste, (loro) nacquero

offendere
Past Participle   offeso
Past Absolute   (io) offesi, (tu) offendesti, (Lei) offese, (lui/lei) offese,
                          (noi) offendemmo, (voi) offendeste, (loro) offesero

offrire
Past Participle   offerto

ottenere (conjugated like **tenere**)

perdere
Past Participle   perso
Past Absolute   (io) persi, (tu) perdesti, (Lei) perse, (lui/lei) perse, (noi)
                          perdemmo, (voi) perdeste, (loro) persero

persuadere
Past Participle   persuaso
Past Absolute   (io) persuasi, (tu) persuadesti, (Lei) persuase, (lui/lei)
                          persuase, (noi) persuademmo, (voi) persuadeste, (loro)
                          persuasero

piacere
Present Indicative   (io) piaccio, (tu) piaci, (Lei) piace, (lui/lei) piace, (noi)
                          piacciamo, (voi) piacete, (loro) piacciono
Past Absolute   (io) piacqui, (tu) piacesti, (Lei) piacque, (lui/lei) piacque,
                          (noi) piacemmo, (voi) piaceste, (loro) piacquero
Present Subjunctive   (io) piaccia, (tu) piaccia, (Lei) piaccia, (lui/lei) piaccia,
                          (noi) piacciamo, (voi) piacciate, (loro) piacciano

piangere
Past Participle   pianto
Past Absolute   (io) piansi, (tu) piangesti, (Lei) pianse, (lui/lei) pianse,
                          (noi) piangemmo, (voi) piangeste, (loro) piansero

porre

Present Indicative	(io) pongo, (tu) poni, (Lei) pone, (lui/lei) pone, (noi) poniamo, (voi) ponete, (loro) pongono
Past Participle	posto
Imperfect	(io) ponevo, (tu) ponevi, (Lei) poneva, (lui/lei) poneva, (noi) ponevamo, (voi) ponevate, (loro) ponevano
Past Absolute	(io) posi, (tu) ponesti, (Lei) pose, (lui/lei) pose, (noi) ponemmo, (voi) poneste, (loro) posero
Future	(io) porrò, (tu) porrai, (Lei) porrà, (lui/lei) porrà, (noi) porremo, (voi) porrete, (loro) porranno
Conditional	(io) porrei, (tu) porresti, (Lei) porrebbe, (lui/lei) porrebbe, (noi) porremmo, (voi) porreste, (loro) porrebbero
Present Subjunctive	(io) ponga, (tu) ponga, (Lei) ponga, (lui/lei) ponga, (noi) poniamo, (voi) poniate, (loro) pongano
Imperfect Subjunctive	(io) ponessi, (tu) ponessi, (Lei) ponesse, (lui/lei) ponesse, (noi) ponessimo, (voi) poneste, (loro) ponessero
Imperative	(tu) poni, (Lei) ponga, (noi) poniamo, (voi) ponete, (Loro) pongano
Gerund	ponendo

potere

Present Indicative	(io) posso, (tu) puoi, (Lei) può, (lui/lei) può, (noi) possiamo, (voi) potete, (loro) possono
Future	(io) potrò, (tu) potrai, (Lei) potrà, (lui/lei) potrà, (noi) potremo, (voi) potrete, (loro) potranno
Conditional	(io) potrei, (tu) potresti, (Lei) potrebbe, (lui/lei) potrebbe, (noi) potremmo, (voi) potreste, (loro) potrebbero
Present Subjunctive	(io) possa, (tu) possa, (Lei) possa, (lui/lei) possa, (noi) possiamo, (voi) possiate, (loro) possano

prendere

Past Participle	preso
Past Absolute	(io) presi, (tu) prendesti, (Lei) prese, (lui/lei) prese, (noi) prendemmo, (voi) prendeste, (loro) presero

prescrivere (conjugated like **scrivere**)

promettere (conjugated like **mettere**)

proporre (conjugated like **porre**)

proteggere

Past Participle	protetto
Past Absolute	(io) protessi, (tu) proteggesti, (Lei) protesse, (lui/lei) protesse, (noi) proteggemmo, (voi) proteggeste, (loro) protessero

pungere
| *Past Participle* | punto |
| *Past Absolute* | (io) punsi, (tu) pungesti, (Lei) punse, (lui/lei) punse, (noi) pungemmo, (voi) pungeste, (loro) punsero |

raccogliere
Present Indicative	(io) raccolgo, (tu) raccogli, (Lei) raccoglie, (lui/lei) raccoglie, (noi) raccogliamo, (voi) raccogliete, (loro) raccolgono
Past Participle	raccolto
Past Absolute	(io) raccolsi, (tu) raccogliesti, (Lei) raccolse, (lui/lei) raccolse, (noi) raccogliemmo, (voi) raccoglieste, (loro) raccolsero
Present Subjunctive	(io) raccolga, (tu) raccolga, (Lei) raccolga, (lui/lei) raccolga, (noi) raccogliamo, (voi) raccogliete, (loro) raccolgano
Imperative	(tu) raccogli, (Lei) raccolga, (noi) raccogliamo, (voi) raccogliete, (Loro) raccolgano

raggiungere
| *Past Participle* | raggiunto |
| *Past Absolute* | (io) raggiunsi, (tu) raggiungesti, (Lei) raggiunse, (lui/lei) raggiunse, (noi) raggiungemmo, (voi) raggiungeste, (loro) raggiunsero |

redigere
| *Past Participle* | redatto |
| *Past Absolute* | (io) redassi, (tu) redigesti, (Lei) redasse, (lui/lei) redasse, (noi) redigemmo, (voi) redigeste, (loro) redassero |

riassumere (conjugated like **assumere**)

richiedere (conjugated like **chiedere**)

ridere
| *Past Participle* | riso |
| *Past Absolute* | (io) risi, (tu) ridesti, (Lei) rise, (lui/lei) rise, (noi) ridemmo, (voi) rideste, (loro) risero |

ridurre (conjugated like **riprodurre**)

rimanere
| *Present Indicative* | (io) rimango, (tu) rimani, (Lei) rimane, (lui/lei) rimane, (noi) rimaniamo, (voi) rimanete, (loro) rimangono |
| *Past Participle* | rimasto |

Past Absolute	(io) rimasi, (tu) rimanesti, (Lei) rimase, (lui/lei) rimase, (noi) rimanemmo, (voi) rimaneste, (loro) rimasero
Future	(io) rimarrò, (tu) rimarrai, (Lei) rimarrà, (lui/lei) rimarrà, (noi) rimarremo, (voi) rimarrete, (loro) rimarranno
Conditional	(io) rimarrei, (tu) rimarresti, (Lei) rimarrebbe, (lui/lei) rimarrebbe, (noi) rimarremmo, (voi) rimarreste, (loro) rimarrebbero
Present Subjunctive	(io) rimanga, (tu) rimanga, (Lei) rimanga, (lui/lei) rimanga, (noi) rimaniamo, (voi) rimaniate, (loro) rimangano
Imperative	(tu) rimani, (Lei) rimanga, (noi) rimaniamo, (voi) rimanete, (Loro) rimangano

rimettere/rimettersi (conjugated like **mettere**)

riprodurre

Present Indicative	(io) riproduco, (tu) riproduci, (Lei) riproduce, (lui/lei) riproduce, (noi) riproduciamo, (voi) riproducete, (loro) riproducono
Past Participle	riprodotto
Imperfect	(io) riproducevo, (tu) riproducevi, (Lei) riproduceva, (lui/lei) riproduceva, (noi) riproducevamo, (voi) riproducevate, (loro) riproducevano
Past Absolute	(io) riprodussi, (tu) riproducesti, (Lei) riprodusse, (lui/lei) riprodusse, (noi) riproducemmo, (voi) riproduceste, (loro) riprodussero
Future	(io) riprodurrò, (tu) riprodurrai, (Lei) riprodurrà, (lui/lei) riprodurrà, (noi) riprodurremo, (voi) riprodurrete, (loro) riprodurranno
Conditional	(io) riprodurrei, (tu) riprodurresti, (Lei) riprodurrebbe, (lui/lei) riprodurrebbe, (noi) riprodurremmo, (voi) riprodurreste, (loro) riprodurrebbero
Present Subjunctive	(io) riproduca, (tu) riproduca, (Lei) riproduca, (lui/lei) riproduca, (noi) riproduciamo, (voi) riproduciate, (loro) riproducano
Imperfect Subjunctive	(io) riproducessi, (tu) riproducessi, (Lei) riproducesse, (lui/lei) riproducesse, (noi) riproducessimo, (voi) riproduceste, (loro) riproducessero
Imperative	(tu) riproduci, (Lei) riproduca, (noi) riproduciamo, (voi) riproducete, (Loro) riproducano
Gerund	riproducendo

riscuotere

Past Participle	riscosso
Past Absolute	(io) riscossi, (tu) riscotesti, (Lei) riscosse, (lui/lei) riscosse, (noi) riscuotemmo, (voi) riscoteste, (loro) riscossero

risolvere
Past Participle   risolto
Past Absolute   (io) risolsi, (tu) risolvesti, (Lei) risolse, (lui/lei) risolse,
                          (noi) risolvemmo, (voi) risolveste, (loro) risolsero

rispondere
Past Participle   risposto
Past Absolute   (io) risposi, (tu) rispondesti, (Lei) rispose, (lui/lei)
                          rispose, (noi) rispondemmo, (voi) rispondeste, (loro)
                          risposero

rivolgersi
Past Participle   rivolto
Past Absolute   (io) mi rivolsi, (tu) ti rivolgesti, (Lei) si rivolse,
                          (lui/lei) si rivolse, (noi) ci rivolgemmo, (voi) vi riv-
                          olgeste, (loro) si rivolsero

rompere
Past Participle   rotto
Past Absolute   (io) ruppi, (tu) rompesti, (Lei) ruppe, (lui/lei) ruppe,
                          (noi) rompemmo, (voi) rompeste, (loro) ruppero

salire
Present Indicative   (io) salgo, (tu) sali, (Lei) sale, (lui/lei) sale, (noi)
                          saliamo, (voi) salite, (loro) salgono
Present Subjunctive   (io) salga, (tu) salga, (Lei) salga, (lui/lei) salga, (noi)
                          saliamo, (voi) saliate, (loro) salgano
Imperative   (tu) sali, (Lei) salga, (noi) saliamo, (voi) salite, (Loro)
                          salgano

sapere
Present Indicative   (io) so, (tu) sai, (Lei) sa, (lui/lei) sa, (noi) sappiamo,
                          (voi) sapete, (loro) sanno
Past Absolute   (io) seppi, (tu) sapesti, (Lei) seppe, (lui/lei) seppe,
                          (noi) sapemmo, (voi) sapeste, (loro) seppero
Future   (io) saprò, (tu) saprai, (Lei) saprà, (lui/lei) saprà, (noi)
                          sapremo, (voi) saprete, (loro) sapranno
Conditional   (io) saprei, (tu) sapresti, (Lei) saprebbe, (lui/lei)
                          saprebbe, (noi) sapremmo, (voi) sapreste, (loro)
                          saprebbero
Present Subjunctive   (io) sappia, (tu) sappia, (Lei) sappia, (lui/lei) sappia,
                          (noi) sappiamo, (voi) sappiate, (loro) sappiano
Imperative   (tu) sappi, (Lei) sappia, (noi) sappiamo, (voi) sappiate,
                          (Loro) sappiano

scegliere
Present Indicative   (io) scelgo, (tu) scegli, (Lei) sceglie, (lui/lei) sceglie,
                          (noi) scegliamo, (voi) scegliete, (loro) scelgono

Past Participle	scelto
Past Absolute	(io) scelsi, (tu) scegliesti, (Lei) scelse, (lui/lei) scelse, (noi) scegliemmo, (voi) sceglieste, (loro) scelsero
Present Subjunctive	(io) scelga, (tu) scelga, (Lei) scelga, (lui/lei) scelga, (noi) scegliamo, (voi) scegliate, (loro) scelgano
Imperative	(tu) scegli, (Lei) scelga, (noi) scegliamo, (voi) scegliete, (Loro) scelgano

scendere

Past Participle	sceso
Past Absolute	(io) scesi, (tu) scendesti, (Lei) scese, (lui/lei) scese, (noi) scendemmo, (voi) scendeste, (loro) scesero

sciogliere

Past Participle	sciolto
Past Absolute	(io) sciolsi, (tu) sciogliesti, (Lei) sciolse, (lui/lei) sciolse, (noi) sciogliemmo, (voi) scioglieste, (loro) sciolsero

scommettere (conjugated like **mettere**)

sconfiggere

Past Participle	sconfitto
Past Absolute	(io) sconfissi, (tu) sconfiggesti, (Lei) sconfisse, (lui/lei) sconfisse, (noi) sconfiggemmo, (voi) sconfiggeste, (loro) sconfissero

scorrere (conjugated like **correre**)

scrivere

Past Participle	scritto
Past Absolute	(io) scrissi, (tu) scrivesti, (Lei) scrisse, (lui/lei) scrisse, (noi) scrivemmo, (voi) scriveste, (loro) scrissero

scuotere

Past Participle	scosso
Past Absolute	(io) scossi, (tu) scotesti, (Lei) scosse, (lui/lei) scosse, (noi) scotemmo, (voi) scoteste, (loro) scossero

sedersi

Present Indicative	(io) mi siedo, (tu) ti siedi, (Lei) si siede, (lui/lei) si siede, (noi) ci sediamo, (voi) vi sedete, (loro) si siedono
Present Subjunctive	(io) mi sieda, (tu) ti sieda, (Lei) si sieda, (lui/lei) si sieda, (noi) ci sediamo, (voi) vi sediate, (loro) si siedano
Imperative	(tu) siediti, (Lei) si sieda, (noi) sediamoci, (voi) sedetevi, (Loro) si siedano

sedurre (conjugated like **riprodurre**)

soccorrere (conjugated like **correre**)

sorprendere (conjugated like **prendere**)

sorridere (conjugated like **ridere**)

sostenere (conjugated like **tenere**)

sottrarre (conjugated like **estrarre**)

spargere
Past Participle	sparso
Past Absolute	(io) sparsi, (tu) spargesti, (Lei) sparse, (lui/lei) sparse, (noi) spargemmo, (voi) spargeste, (loro) sparsero

spegnere
Present Indicative	(io) spengo, (tu) spegni, (Lei) spegne, (lui/lei) spegne, (noi) spegniamo, (voi) spegnete, (loro) spengono
Past Participle	spento
Past Absolute	(io) spensi, (tu) spegnesti, (Lei) spense, (lui/lei) spense, (noi) spegnemmo, (voi) spegneste, (loro) spensero
Present Subjunctive	(io) spenga, (tu) spenga, (Lei) spenga, (lui/lei) spenga, (noi) spegniamo, (voi) spegniate, (loro) spengano
Imperative	(tu) spegni, (Lei) spenga, (noi) spegniamo, (voi) spegnete, (Loro) spengano

spingere (conjugated like **dipingere**)

stare
Present Indicative	(io) sto, (tu) stai, (Lei) sta, (lui/lei) sta, (noi) stiamo, (voi) state, (loro) stanno
Past Participle	stato
Imperfect	(io) stavo, (tu) stavi, (Lei) stava, (lui/lei) stava, (noi) stavamo, (voi) stavate, (loro) stavano
Past Absolute	(io) stetti, (tu) stesti, (Lei) stette, (lui/lei) stette, (noi) stemmo, (voi) steste, (loro) stettero
Future	(io) starò, (tu) starai, (Lei) starà, (lui/lei) starà, (noi) staremo, (voi) starete, (loro) staranno
Conditional	(io) starei, (tu) staresti, (Lei) starebbe, (lui/lei) starebbe, (noi) staremmo, (voi) stareste, (loro) starebbero
Present Subjunctive	(io) stia, (tu) stia, (Lei) stia, (lui/lei) stia, (noi) stiamo, (voi) stiate, (loro) stiano
Imperfect Subjunctive	(io) stessi, (tu) stessi, (Lei) stesse, (lui/lei) stesse, (noi) stessimo, (voi) steste, (loro) stessero
Imperative	(tu) sta', (Lei) stia, (noi) stiamo, (voi) state, (Loro) stiano
Gerund	stando

stringere
Past Participle   stretto
Past Absolute   (io) strinsi, (tu) stringesti, (Lei) strinse, (lui/lei) strinse, (noi) stringemmo, (voi) stringeste, (loro) strinsero

stringersi (conjugated like **stringere**)

svenirsi (conjugated like **venire**)

svolgere
Past Participle   svolto
Past Absolute   (io) svolsi, (tu) svolgesti, (Lei) svolse, (lui/lei) svolse, (noi) svolgemmo, (voi) svolgeste, (loro) svolsero

svolgersi (conjugated like **svolgere**)

tacere (conjugated like **piacere**)

tenere
Present Indicative   (io) tengo, (tu) tieni, (Lei) tiene, (lui/lei) tiene, (noi) teniamo, (voi) tenete, (loro) tengono
Past Absolute   (io) tenni, (tu) tenesti, (Lei) tenne, (lui/lei) tenne, (noi) tenemmo, (voi) teneste, (loro) tennero
Future   (io) terrò, (tu) terrai, (Lei) terrà, (lui/lei) terrà, (noi) terremo, (voi) terrete, (loro) terranno
Conditional   (io) terrei, (tu) terresti, (Lei) terrebbe, (lui/lei) terrebbe, (noi) terremmo, (voi) terreste, (loro) terrebbero
Present Subjunctive   (io) tenga, (tu) tenga, (Lei) tenga, (lui/lei) tenga, (noi) teniamo, (voi) teniate, (loro) tengano
Imperative   (tu) tieni, (Lei) tenga, (noi) teniamo, (voi) tenete, (Loro) tengano

tenersi (conjugated like **tenere**)

tingere (conjugated like **dipingere**)

tingersi (conjugated like **dipingere**)

togliersi (conjugated like **raccogliere**)

torcere
Past Participle   torto
Past Absolute   (io) torsi, (tu) torcesti, (Lei) torse, (lui/lei) torse, (noi) torcemmo, (voi) torceste, (loro) torsero

tradurre (conjugated like **riprodurre**)

trascorrere (conjugated like **correre**)

trasmettere (conjugated like **mettere**)

uccidere
Past Participle   ucciso
Past Absolute   (io) uccisi, (tu) uccidesti, (Lei) uccise, (lui/lei) uccise,
                        (noi) uccidemmo, (voi) uccideste, (loro) uccisero

udire
Present Indicative   (io) odo, (tu) odi, (Lei) ode, (lui/lei) ode, (noi) udiamo,
                        (voi) udite, (loro) odono
Present Subjunctive   (io) oda, (tu) oda, (Lei) oda, (lui/lei) oda, (noi) udiamo,
                        (voi) udiate, (loro) odano
Imperative   (tu) oda, (Lei) oda, (noi) udiamo, (voi) udite, (Loro)
                        odano

ungere
Past Participle   unto
Past Absolute   (io) unsi, (tu) ungesti, (Lei) unse, (lui/lei) unse, (noi)
                        ungemmo, (voi) ungeste, (loro) unsero

uscire
Present Indicative   (io) esco, (tu) esci, (Lei) esce, (lui/lei) esce, (noi)
                        usciamo, (voi) uscite, (loro) escono
Present Subjunctive   (io) esca, (tu) esca, (Lei) esca, (lui/lei) esca, (noi)
                        usciamo, (voi) usciate, (loro) escano
Imperative   (tu) esci, (Lei) esca, (noi) usciamo, (voi) uscite, (Loro)
                        escano

vedere
Past Participle   visto/veduto
Past Absolute   (io) vidi, (tu) vedesti, (Lei) vide, (lui/lei) vide, (noi)
                        vedemmo, (voi) vedeste, (loro) videro
Future   (io) vedrò, (tu) vedrai, (Lei) vedrà, (lui/lei) vedrà, (noi)
                        vedremo, (voi) vedrete, (loro) vedranno
Conditional   (io) vedrei, (tu) vedresti, (Lei) vedrebbe, (lui/lei)
                        vedrebbe, (noi) vedremmo, (voi) vedreste, (loro)
                        vedrebbero

venire
Present Indicative   (io) vengo, (tu) vieni, (Lei) viene, (lui/lei) viene, (noi)
                        veniamo, (voi) venite, (loro) vengono
Past Participle   venuto
Past Absolute   (io) venni, (tu) venisti, (Lei) venne, (lui/lei) venne,
                        (noi) venimmo, (voi) veniste, (loro) vennero
Future   (io) verrò, (tu) verrai, (Lei) verrà, (lui/lei) verrà, (noi)
                        verremo, (voi) verrete, (loro) verranno

Conditional	(io) verrei, (tu) verresti, (Lei) verrebbe, (lui/lei) verrebbe, (noi) verremmo, (voi) verreste, (loro) verrebbero
Present Subjunctive	(io) venga, (tu) venga, (Lei) venga, (lui/lei) venga, (noi) veniamo, (voi) veniate, (loro) vengano
Imperative	(tu) vieni, (Lei) venga, (noi) veniamo, (voi) venite, (Loro) vengano

vincere
| *Past Participle* | vinto |
| *Past Absolute* | (io) vinsi, (tu) vincesti, (Lei) vinse, (lui/lei) vinse, (noi) vincemmo, (voi) vinceste, (loro) vinsero |

vivere
| *Past Participle* | vissuto |
| *Past Absolute* | (io) vissi, (tu) vivesti, (Lei) visse, (lui/lei) visse, (noi) vivemmo, (voi) viveste, (loro) vissero |

volere
Present Indicative	(io) voglio, (tu) vuoi, (Lei) vuole, (lui/lei) vuole, (noi) vogliamo, (voi) volete, (loro) vogliono
Past Absolute	(io) volli, (tu) volesti, (Lei) volle, (lui/lei) volle, (noi) volemmo, (voi) voleste, (loro) vollero
Future	(io) vorrò, (tu) vorrai, (Lei) vorrà, (lui/lei) vorrà, (noi) vorremo, (voi) vorrete, (loro) vorranno
Conditional	(io) vorrei, (tu) vorresti, (Lei) vorrebbe, (lui/lei) vorrebbe, (noi) vorremmo, (voi) vorreste, (loro) vorrebbero
Present Subjunctive	(io) voglia, (tu) voglia, (Lei) voglia, (lui/lei) voglia, (noi) vogliamo, (voi) vogliate, (loro) vogliano

ENGLISH-ITALIAN WORDFINDER

The following *Wordfinder* contains all the items used in this book. It will enable you to find the information you need quickly and efficiently. It all you want is the Italian equivalent of an entry word, you will find it here. If you also want pronunciation details and other kinds of information, the numbers(s) and letter(s) will tell you where to locate such information.

adenoids adenoidi 12a
adhesive bandage cerotto 25h, 40a
adhesive tape nastro adesivo 19d, 25c, 38c
Adieu! Addio! 16a
adjacent adiacente 2b
adjective aggettivo 8a
administration amministrazione 38a, 43a
admission test prova d'ammissione 37f
admit ammettere 41
adolescence adolescenza 11b
adolescent, teenager adolescente 11b
adopt adottare 11c
adoption adozione 11c
adorable adorabile 11a
adrenaline adrenalina 12a
Adriatic Adriatico 30c
adult adulto 11b
adultery adulterio 11c
adulthood, maturity maturità 11b
adventure avventura 20a, 28d
adventure film film d'avventura 28a
adverb avverbio 8a
advertisement messaggio pubblicitario, réclame 20c
advertising pubblicità 20c, 38d
advertising agency agenzia di pubblicità 20c
advertising break spot pubblicitario 20c
advertising campaign campagna pubblicitaria 20c
advertising sign insegna pubblicitaria 20c
advice consiglio 17a
advise consigliare 17a
aerobics aerobica 27b
affable affabile 11e
affection affetto 21a
affectionate affettuoso 11e
Affectionately affettuosamente… 19b

affirm, remark affermare 17a
affluent benestante 11e
Afghanistan Afghanistan 30b
Africa Africa 30b
African africano 30e
after dopo 4c
afternoon pomeriggio 4b
again ancora (una volta), di nuovo 4c, 8j
against sfavorevole 43a
age età 11b, 38b
agenda (of a meeting) ordine del giorno 43a
aggressive aggressivo 11e
agile agile 11a
agnostic agnostico 11d
ago fa 4c
agree essere d'accordo 21a, 17a
agriculture agricoltura 14a
ahead, forward avanti 3c, 36c
AIDS AIDS 40a, 44b
ailment indisposizione 40a
aim the lens puntare l'obiettivo 28b
air aria, mandare in onda 6a, 13c, 20b
air conditioning aria condizionata 23d, 33c
air pollution inquinamento atmosferico 44a
airline linea aerea 32a
airmail posta aerea 19e
airplane aereo, aereoplano 32a
airport aeroporto 32a
aisle corridoio 28a, 32c
alarm allarme 39a
alarm clock sveglia 4d, 25i
Albania Albania 30b
Albanian albanese 30e
alcohol alcool, bevanda alcolica 44b
alcoholic beverage bevanda alcolica 24j
alcoholism alcolismo 44b
alert sveglio 11a
Alexandria Alessandria 30c

algebra   algebra   1f, 1g

algebraic   algebrico   1f

Algeria   Algeria   30b

Algerian   algerino   30e

algorithm   algoritmo   1f

align   allineare   42b

alimentary canal   tubo digestivo   12a

alimony   alimenti   11c

all day   tutta la giornata   4b

all, everything   tutto   3b

all-inclusive price   prezzo forfettario   35a

allegory   allegoria   28d

allergic   allergico   40a

allergy   allergia   40a

alley, lane   vicolo   36a

alliance   alleanza   43b

alligator   alligatore   15c

allude   alludere   17a

ally   alleato   43b

almost   quasi   8j

almost always   quasi sempre   4c

almost, nearly   circa, quasi   3b

alphabet   alfabeto   8a

alpine   alpino   30c

Alps   Alpi   30c

already   già   4c, 8j

also, too   anche   8i, 8j

altar   altare   11d

altar-boy   chierichetto   11d

although   benché, sebbene   8i

Alto Adige   Alto Adige   30d

altruist   altruista   11e

always   sempre   4c

amateur   dilettante   27b

ambitious   ambizioso   11e

ambulance   ambulanza, autoambulanza   34

amendment   emendamento   43a

America   America   30b

American   americano   30e

American football   football americano   27b

ammonia   ammoniaca   13c

among, between   fra, tra   3c, 8f

amount   ammontare   26b

at (@)   chiocciola   19f, 38c

amphetamine   amfetamina   44c

amphitheater   anfiteatro   36a

amplifier   altoparlante   18a

Amsterdam   Amsterdam   30c

amusement park   luna park   36a

analog   analogico   42b

analytical geometry   geometria analitica   1g

anatomy   anatomia   37e

ancestor   antenato   11c

anchor   ancora   34

anchovy   acciuga   24e

ancient Greece   Antica Grecia   43b

ancient monument   monumento storico   36a

ancient Rome   Antica Roma   43b

and   e   8i

anecdote   aneddoto   28d

anemia   anemia   40a

anemic   anemico   40a

anesthesia   anestesia   40a

anesthetic   anestetico   40a, 40b

angel   angelo   11d

anger   rabbia   21a

angle   angolo   2b

angry   arrabbiato   21a

animal   animale   15a

animated image   immagine animata   42b

animation   animazione   28a

anise   anice   24i

ankle   caviglia   12a

ankle sprain   storta alla caviglia   40a

anniversary   anniversario   11c, 29a

announce   annunciare   17a

announcement   annuncio   17a

announcer   annunciatore (-trice)   20b

annoying, unpleasant   antipatico   11e

annual leave congedo annuale 38d

annuity rendita 26a

anoint ungere 11d

answer risposta, rispondere 9, 17a, 18b, 37f

answering machine segreteria telefonica 18a, 38c

ant formica 15d

ant hill formicaio 15d

Antarctic Antartico 13b

Antarctic Circle Circolo Polare Antartico 13d

antelope antilope 15a

antenna antenna 20b, 42a

anterior, before anteriore 4c

anthology antologia 25n, 28d

anthropology antropologia 37e

anti-theft insurance assicurazione contro il furto 26a

anti-wrinkle cream crema antirughe 25f

antibiotic antibiotico 25h, 40a

antique shop negozio dell'antiquariato 25a

antiquity antichità 43b

antiseptic antisettico 39c

antler, horn corno 15a

anus, bottom ano 12a

anxiety, anxiousness ansia, ansietà 21a, 40a

anxious ansioso 11e, 21a

Aosta Aosta 30d

apartment appartamento 23e

apartment building palazzo (di appartamenti) 23e

ape, monkey scimmia 15a

Apennines Appennini 30c

apostrophe apostrofo 19c

appendicitis appendicite 40a

appendix appendice 24a, 25n, 28d

appetizer antipasto 24a

appetizing appetitoso 24n

applaud applaudire 28e

applause applauso 28e

apple mela 24g, 14d

apple tree melo 14c

applicant candidato 38d

appointment appuntamento 38d, 40a, 40b

apprentice apprendista 38a

approach avvicinarsi a 3f

approval approvazione 21b

approve approvare 21b

approximately approssimativamente 3b

apricot albicocca 14d, 24g

April aprile 5b

apron grembiule 25k

aptitude test test d'attitudine 37f

Apulia Puglia 30d

Aquarius Acquario 5d

Arabic arabo 1d, 30e

arc arco 2a

arch, archway arco, arcata 23a

archbishop arcivescovo 11d

archeology archeologia 37e

archery tiro con l'arco 27b

archipelago arcipelago 13b

architect architetto (-a) 38a

architecture architettura 28b, 37e

architecture faculty facoltà di architettura 37a

archivist archivista 43b

Arctic Artico 13b

Arctic Circle Circolo Polare Artico 13d

Are you crazy? Ma sei pazzo (-a)? 16c

Are you joking? Scherzi? Scherza? 21c

area area, superficie 3a, 13d

area code prefisso 11f, 18b, 38b

Argentina Argentina 30b

Argentinean argentino 30e

argue litigare 17a, 21a, 39b

argument lite 17a, 21a

Aries Ariete 5d

arithmetic aritmetica 1f, 1g

arithmetical aritmetico 1f

arithmetical operations
  operazioni aritmetiche   1e

arm   braccio   12a

armchair   poltrona   23b, 35b

armed assault, attack
  aggressione a mano armata   39b

armed conflict   conflitto a fuoco
44d

armed robbery   rapina a mano
  armata   39b

Armenia   Armenia   30b

Armenian   armeno   30e

armistice   armistizio   44d

armpit   ascella   12a

arms dealer   mercante d'armi
44d

arms reduction   diminuzione
  delle armi   44d

arms trade   mercato delle armi
44d

army   esercito   44d

Arno River   Arno   30c

aroma   aroma   12e

arrest   arresto, arrestare   39b

arrest warrant   mandato di
  cattura   39b

arrhythmia   aritmia   40a

arrival   arrivo   32b, 34

arrive   arrivare   3f

arrogant   arrogante   11e

arson   incendio doloso   39a

arsonist   piromane   39a

art   arte   28b, 37e

art exhibition   mostra d'arte   28b

art gallery   galleria d'arte, museo
  d'arte   28b, 36a

art lyceum   liceo artistico   37a

arteriosclerosis   arteriosclerosi
40a

artery   arteria   12a

arthritis   artrite   40a

artichoke   carciofo   14e, 24f

article   articolo   8a

artificial   artificiale   25i

artificial insemination
  fecondazione artificiale   11c

artificial intelligence   intelligenza
  artificiale   42b

artist   artista   28b

artistic   artistico   11e

arts and letters lyceum   liceo
  classico   37a

arts faculty   facoltà di lettere
37a

arts, humanities, letters   lettere
37e

as   come   8i

as a matter of fact   anzi   8j

as if   come se   8i

as much as   tanto…quanto   3b

as soon as   appena   4c, 8i

asbestos   amianto   13c

ascent   salita, ascesa   3f

ash   frassino   14c

Ash Wednesday   Ceneri   11d

Asia   Asia   30b

aside   a parte   28e

ask a question   fare una domanda
9, 37f

ask for   chiedere   9, 17a

asparagus   asparagi   14e, 24f

asphalt   asfalto   13c

aspirin   aspirina   25h, 40a

assailant   aggressore   39b

assassin, murderer   assassino
39b

assault, attack   aggressione,
  aggredire   39b

assembly   assemblea   43a

assignment   compito   37f

assignment book   agenda   37b

assistant   assistente   37d

assure   assicurare   21a

asterisk   asterisco   19c

asthma   asma   40a

astronomy   astronomia   13a,
37e

astute, bright   astuto   11e

at   a, in   8f

At 1:00.   All'una.   4a

At 2:00.   Alle due.   4a

At 3:00.   Alle tre.   4a

at home   a casa   23f

at midnight   a mezzanotte   4b

at night   di notte, della notte   4b

at noon   a mezzogiorno   4b

at the bottom   in fondo   3c
at the dentist's   dal dentista
40b
at the end of   in fondo a   36c
at the same time   allo stesso
tempo   4c
at the top of   in cima a   36c
At what time?   A che ora?   4a
atheism   ateismo   11d
atheist   ateo   11d
Athenian   ateniese   30c
Athens   Atene   30c
athlete   atleta   27b
athlete's foot   micosi dei piedi
40a
athletic   atletico   11a
Atlantic   Atlantico   13b, 30c
atlas   atlante   13d
atmosphere   atmosfera   6a, 13b
atmospheric conditions
condizioni atmosferiche   6a
atom   atomo   13c
atomic bomb   bomba atomica
44d
atone for one's sins   scontare i
propri peccati   11d
attach, enclose   allegare   19e
attached, enclosed   allegato
19e
Attachment   Allegato   42c
attack   attacco   44d
attend   frequentare   37f
attendance   frequenza   37f
Attention!   Attenzione!   16c
attentive   attento   11e
attic   attico   23a
attitude   atteggiamento   21a
attorney   avvocato (-essa)   41
attractive   attraente   11a
audacious, bold   audace   11e
audience   pubblico   28e
audio   audio   42a
audio receiver, tuner
sintonizzatore   20b
auditor   revisore dei conti   38a
August   agosto   5b
aunt   zia   10a
Australia   Australia   30b

Australian   australiano   30e
Austria   Austria   30b
Austrian   austriaco   30e
author   autore (-trice)   20a,
25n
authorized withdrawal
prelevamento autorizzato   26a
autism   autismo   40a
autobiography   autobiografia
25n, 28d
automated bank machine
bancomat   26a
automatic weapon   arma
automatica   44d
automatic withdrawal
prelevamento automatico   26a
automobile   automobile, auto
34
autumn   autunno   5c
avenue   viale, corso   11f, 36a
average   media   1f, 37f
average height   altezza media
11a
avoid   evitare   3f
away   via   3c
axis   asse   2b

B

baboon   babbuino   15a
baby bottle   biberon   11c, 23c
baby, child   bambino (-a)   11b
bachelor   scapolo (-a)   11c
bacillus, bacterium   bacillo
40a
back (behind)   dietro, indietro
3c, 36c, 42c
back (of the body)   schiena
12a
back and forth   avanti e indietro
3f
back of the seat   schienale   32c
back seat   sedile posteriore   33c
back up   fare marcia indietro
33a
backache   mal di schiena   40a
background   sfondo   28b
backward   indietro   3c
bacon   pancetta   24d

bad male, malamente 8j, 16a

bad mood cattivo umore 21a

bad, mean cattivo 11e

bad-tempered irascibile 21a

badger tasso 15a

bag, sac sacco, sacchetto 3e, 23b, 25a

baggage, luggage bagaglio 31

bagpipes zampogne 28c

bail cauzione 41

bait esca 27a

baked al forno 24a

baker fornaio (-a) 38a

balance scale bilancia 3b

balancing the books compensazione 26b

balcony terrazza, balcone 23a, 35b

balcony (of a theater) galleria 28a

bald calvo 11a

baldness calvizie 11a

Balkans Balcani 30c

ball palla, pallone 27b

ballad ballata 28c, 28d

ballet balletto 28c

ballistic missile missile balistico 44d

ballot scheda elettorale 43a

ballot box urna elettorale 43a

balloting ballottaggio 43a

ballpoint pen biro 19d, 25c, 37b

ballroom sala da ballo 28c

banana banana 14d, 24g

band (watch) cinghietta 25i

band (musical) gruppo, complesso 25j, 28c

bandage benda, bendare 39c, 40a

bang colpo 12c

Bangladesh Bangladesh 30b

banister balaustra 23a

bank banca 26a

bank book libretto bancario 26a

bank card carta bancaria 25a

bank clerk impiegato (-a) di

banca 26a

bank code codice bancario 26a

bank money order vaglia bancario 26a

bank receipt ricevuta 26a

bank worker bancario (-a) 26a

banking executive banchiere (-a) 26a

bankruptcy bancarotta 26b

banquet banchetto 24a, 35a

baptism battesimo 11d

baptismal font fonte battesimale 11d

baptistery battistero 11d

bar bar 29b

bar code codice a barre 25a

bar-code reader lettore elettronico 25a

barber barbiere (-a) 12f, 38a

barbiturate barbiturico 25h, 40a

Barcelona Barcellona 30c

bargaining, negotiations trattative 38d

Bari Bari 30c

baritone baritono 28c

bark (of a tree) corteccia, scorza 14a

bark (dog) abbaiare 15a

barley orzo 14a, 24c

barn granaio 15a

barometer barometro 6c

barometric pressure pressione barometrica 6c

Baroque Barocco 28b, 43b

barracks caserma 36a

barrel botte 3e

bartender barista 24l

base basso 28c

base salary paga base 38d

baseball baseball 27b

baseball diamond diamante 27b

basement scantinato 23a

basil basilico 14e, 24i

basilica basilica 36a

basket cesto, cestino, canestro 3e, 23b, 27b

basketball pallacanestro, basket 27b

bass drum grancassa 28c

bassoon fagotto 28c

bassoonist fagottista 28c

bat (baseball) mazza 27b

bat (mammal) pipistrello 15a

bath oil olio da bagno 25f

bath salts sali da bagno 25f

bathrobe accappatoio 25k

bathroom bagno 23a, 35b

bathroom scale pesapersone 23b

bathtub vasca 23a, 35b

baton bacchetta 28c

battery pila, batteria, 25b, 33c

bawdy volgare 21a

bay baia 13b

be about to stare per 4c

be absent essere assente 37f

be against essere contrario 21a

be ashamed vergognarsi 21a

be bad (awful) weather fare (essere) brutto, cattivo tempo 6a

be born nascere 11c

Be careful! Attento (-a)! 21c

be cold avere freddo, fare freddo 6a, 6b, 12b

be cool fare fresco 6a

be down essere giù 21a

be early essere in anticipo 4c

be enough bastare, essere abbastanza 3b

be equal to essere uguale a 1f

be equivalent to essere equivalente a 1f)

be fond of (something) essere appassionato di 21b

be from essere di 11f

be good weather fare bel tempo, essere bel tempo 6a

be greater than essere maggiore di 1f

be hot avere caldo, fare caldo 6a, 6b, 12b

be hungry avere fame 12b, 24n

be in a bad mood avere la luna di traverso 13a

be in mourning essere in lutto 11c

be interested in interessarsi di 22b

be late essere in ritardo 4c

be less than essere minore di 1f

be mild essere mite 6a

be of...origin essere d'origine... 11f

be on a first-name basis darsi del tu 16b

be on a formal basis darsi del Lei 16b

be on call essere di turno 40a

be on the air essere in onda 20b

be on the point, verge of essere sul punto di 4c

be on time essere in orario 4c

be on trial essere sotto processo 41

be pregnant essere incinta 11c

be present essere presente 37f

be promoted, pass essere promosso 37f

be punctual essere puntuale 4c

Be quiet! Sta' zitto (-a)! Stia zitto (-a)! 16c

be right avere ragione 17b, 22b

be run over essere investito (-a) 39c

be seated accomodarsi, sedersi 16b

be self-employed lavorare in proprio 38d

be similar to essere simile a 1f

be sleepy avere sonno 12b

be slightly built avere un fisico debole 11a

be strongly built avere un fisico forte 11a

be sufficient essere sufficiente 3b

be thirsty avere sete 12b, 24n

be tired essere stanco 12b

be up essere su 21a

be very cold fare un freddo da cani 15b

be windy, blow wind tirare vento 6a

be wrong avere torto 17b, 22b

beach spiaggia 13b, 36b

beak becco 15b

beaker, tumbler coppa 23c

bean fagiolo 14e, 24f

bear (animal) orso 15a

bear, put up with sopportare 6b

beard barba 12a

beat time battere il tempo 28c

beautician estetista 12f

beautiful, handsome bello 11, 25l

beauty bellezza 11a

beaver castoro 15a

because perché 8i

become bored annoiarsi 21a

become cured guarire 40a

become fat ingrassare 11a

become friends diventare amici, fare amicizia 10b

become ill ammalarsi 40a

become old invecchiarsi 11b

become small impiccolire, rimpiccolire 3b

become thin dimagrire 11a

bed letto 23b, 35b

bedbug cimice 15d

bedsheet lenzuolo 23b

bedding biancheria da letto 23b

bedroom camera (da letto) 23a

bedside table comodino 23b, 35b

bedspread copriletto 23b

bee ape 15d

beech faggio 14c

beef manzo 24d

beer birra 24j

beet barbabietola 14e, 24f

beetle maggiolino 15d

before prima 4c

beg (alms) mendicare 44b

beg to do something pregare 17a

beggar mendicante 44b

behind dietro 3c, 36c

Beijing Pechino 30c

Belgian belga 30e

Belgium Belgio 30b

Belgrade Belgrado 30c

belief credenza 11d, 22a

believe credere 11d, 22b

believer credente 11d

bell tower campanile 11d, 36a

bellhop fattorino (-a) 35a

belly pancia 12a

belly button ombelico 12a

below sotto 8f

below zero sotto zero 6c

bend piegare 3f

Benedictine Benedettino 11d

benefactor benefattore (-trice) 21a

benign benigno 40a

Berlin Berlino 30c

beside, next to accanto a 3c

best man testimone (dello sposo) 11c

Best wishes! Auguri! 16c, 29c

bet scommessa, scommettere 27a

Better late than never! Meglio tardi che mai! 4c

between fra, tra 8f

beverage, soft drink bibita 24j

beyond oltre 3c

be...years old avere...anni 11b

Bible Bibbia 11d

bibliography bibliografia 37f

bicameral bicamerale 43a

bicycle bicicletta 34

bicycle lane, path pista ciclabile 33b

bicycle racing corsa ciclistica 27b

big grande, grosso 11a, 11b, 25l

bigoted bigotto 11e

bile   bile   40a

bill (to pay)   conto, fattura   24l, 25a, 35a

bill (of the legislature)   disegno di legge   43a

bill, banknote   banconota, biglietto di banca   26a

billiard ball   palla da biliardo   27a

billiard cue   stecca da biliardo   27a

billiard table   tavolo da biliardo   27a

billiards   biliardo   27a

billionth   miliardesimo   1b

bingo   tombola   27a

bingo card   cartella della tombola   27a

biography   biografia   25n, 28d

biological war   guerra batteriologica   44d

biological weapon   arma batteriologica   44d

biology   biologia   37e

biosystem   biosistema   44a

birch   betulla   14c

bird   uccello   15b

bird of prey   uccello rapace   15b

birdcage   gabbia   15b

birth   nascita   11c, 11f

birth certificate   certificato di nascita   11c

birth pain   doglie   11c

birthday   compleanno   11c, 29a

biscuit, cookie   biscotto   24c

bisector   bisettrice   2b

bishop   vescovo   11d

bite   morso   40a

bitter   aspro, amaro   12e, 21a, 24a

black   nero   7a

black hole   buco nero   13a

blackbird   merlo   15b

blackboard   lavagna   37b

blackboard eraser   cancellino   37b

blackmail   ricatto, ricattare   39b

bladder   vescica   12a

blade (for cutting)   lama   23c

blade (razor)   lametta da barba   25f

blank endorsement   girata in bianco   26a

blanket   coperta   23b, 35b

blasphemy   blasfemia   11d

bleed   sanguinare   39c

blender   frullatore   23c

bless   benedire   11d

Bless you!   Salute!   16c

blessing   benedizione   11d

blind (for a window)   avvolgibile   23a

blind (sightless)   cieco, accecare   12d

blindness   cecità   12d

blink   battere le palpebre   3f, 12d

blister   vescica   40a

blond, blonde   biondo (-a)   11a

blood   sangue   12a, 39c, 40a

blood group   gruppo sanguigno   12a

blood pressure   pressione del sangue   12a

blood test   analisi del sangue   40a

blood transfusion   trasfusione del sangue   40a

blood vessel   vaso sanguigno   12a

bloom   sbocciare   14a

blouse   camicetta, blusa   25k

blow a fuse   fare saltare una valvola   23d

blue   azzurro   7a

blue-collar worker   operaio (-a)   38d

blueberry   mirtillo   14d, 24g

blueprint   copia cianografica   28b

blues   blues   25j, 28d

blush   arrossire   11a

boa   serpente boa   15c

board   salire a bordo   32a

board of directors   consiglio d'amministrazione   38d

boarding   imbarco   32a

boarding pass   carta d'imbarco
32a

boastful   vanaglorioso   21a

boat   barca   27b, 36b

body   corpo   11a, 12a

body (of a letter)   contenuto
19c

body-building   culturismo   27b

bodyguard   guardia del corpo
39b

boil   bollire   24a

boiling point   punto di
ebollizione, dell'acqua bollente
6c, 13c

boldface   grassetto   19c

Bolivia   Bolivia   30b

Bolivian   boliviano   30e

Bologna   Bologna   30c

bolt   bullone   23d, 25b

bolt down   bullonare   23d

bomb   bomba   44d

bond   obbligazione   26a

bone   osso   12a

boo   fischiare   28e

book   libro   20a, 25n, 37b

bookcase   libreria   23b

bookmark   segnalibro   37f

bookseller   libraio (-a)   38a

bookshelf   scaffale   23b

bookstore   libreria   25n

boot   stivale   25m

border (political)   frontiera
13d, 31

bored   annoiato   21a

boredom   noia   21a

Bosnia   Bosnia   30b

Bosnian   bosniaco   30e

botanical   botanico   14a

botanical gardens   giardino
botanico   36a

botany   botanica   14a, 37e

both   ambedue, tutti e due   3b

bothersome, irksome   noioso
11e

bottle   bottiglia   23c, 24k

bottle opener   cavatappi   23c

bottled   imbottigliato   23c

bottom   fondo   3c

boulder   macigno   13b

boundary   confine   3d

bow (archery)   arco   28c

bow   inchino, inchinarsi   3f

bow tie   farfalla   25k

bowl   scodella   23c

bowling   bowling   27b

bowling alley   pista   27b

bowling ball   boccia   27b

bowling pin   birillo   27b

box, tin   scatola   3e, 23b

box office   botteghino   28a

boxer   pugile   27b

boxing   pugilato   27b

boy   ragazzo   11a, 11b

boyfriend   amico, ragazzo   10b

bra   reggiseno   25k

braces   apparecchio per i denti
40b

bracelet   braccialetto   25i

braggart   spaccone (-a)   21a

brain   cervello   12a

brake   freno, frenare   33a, 33c,
34

branch (bank)   filiale di una
banca   26a

branch (company)   succursale
38d

branch (tree)   ramo   14a

brand   marca, marchio   20c,
25a

brash, bold   sfacciato   11e

brass   ottone   13c

brass instruments   ottoni   28c

brawny   poderoso   11a

Brazil   Brasile   30b

Brazilian   brasiliano   30e

bread   pane   24c

bread and breakfast   pensione
35a

bread basket   cesta del pane
23c

bread knife   coltello da pane
23c

bread store, bakery   panificio
24m

breadstick   grissino   24c

break pausa 38d
break a limb fratturare un arto 40a
break a record battere un record 27b
break and enter scasso 39b
break off a friendship rompere un'amicizia 10b
breakfast prima colazione 24a, 35a
breakfast included colazione compresa 35a
breast seno, petto 12a, 24a
breast-feed allattare 11c
breath respiro 12b
breathe respirare 12b
breathing respirazione 12b
breeding allevamento 15a
bribe bustarella 39b
bribery corruzione 39b
brick mattone 13c
bricklayer muratore 13c, 38a
bride sposa 11c
bridesmaid damigella 11c
bridge ponte 33a
brief, short breve 4c, 37f
briefcase cartella 25c
briefly in breve 4c, 17b
bright acceso, brillante 7b, 12d
brilliant brillante 11e
bring portare 25a
British britannico 30e
broad chin mento largo 11a
broad forehead fronte spaziosa 11a
broad-minded di ampie vedute 11e
broad-shouldered con le spalle larghe 11a
broadcast trasmissione, trasmettere 20b
broccoli broccoli 14e, 24f
brochure opuscolo 20c, 30a
broiled arrostito 24a
broke (financially) al verde 7a
broken spezzata 2b
broken bone osso rotto 39c

bronchitis bronchite 40a
bronze bronzo 13c
bronze sculpture scultura in bronzo 28b
brooch spilla 25i
brood covata, nidiata 15b
brook ruscello 36b
broom (sweeper) scopa 23b
broth brodo 24b
brother fratello 10a
brother-in-law cognato 10a
brow, forehead fronte 12a
brown marrone 7a
brown eyes occhi castani 11a
brown skin pelle bruna 11a
bruise livido 40a
brush spazzola, pennello 7b, 12f, 25f, 28b
brush against sfiorare 3f
brush oneself spazzolarsi 12f
brusque brusco 11e
bucket secchio 3e
buckle allacciare, fibbia 25g, 25l, 32c
Buddhism Buddismo 11d
Buddhist Buddista 11d
budget, balance bilancio 26a, 38d
budget prediction bilancio preventivo 38d
buffalo bufalo 15a
build costruire 23f
build (of the body) fisico 11a
building edificio 23e, 36a, 39a
bulb bulbo 14a
Bulgaria Bulgaria 30b
Bulgarian bulgaro 30e
bull toro 15a
bulldog mastino 15a
bump sbattere 39c
bump into imbattersi in 3f
bumper paraurti 33c
burglar alarm allarme antifurto 23a
burial sepultura 11c
burlap tela di sacco 13c
burn bruciatura, bruciare, ustione 39a

Canada Canada 30b
Canadian canadese 30e
canary canarino 15b
cancel a subscription annullare l'abbonamento 20a
canceled cancellato 32b, 34
cancer cancro 40a
Cancer Cancro 5d
candy caramella 24c
canine canino 40b
cannelloni cannelloni 24b
canoe canoa 27b, 36b
Cantonese cantonese 30e
canvas tela 28b
cap berretto 25k
capacity capienza, capacità 3b
cape capo 13b
capital (money) capitale 26a
capital (of the country) capitale 36a
capital town (of a region) capoluogo 36a
cappuccino cappuccino 24j
Capricorn Capricorno 5d
captain comandante 32c
caption leggenda 20c
captivating accattivante 21a
car macchina 34
car body carrozzeria 33c
car dealer(ship) concessionario 33c
car door portiera 33c
car race corsa automobilistica 27b
car racing automobilismo 27b
car roof tetto 33c
car seat sedile 33c
car window finestrino 33c
car-ferry nave traghetto 34
carafe, decanter caraffa 23c
carat carato 25i
carbon (element) carbonio 13c
carbon (solid), coal carbone 13c
carbonated gassata, frizzante 24j
carburetor carburatore 33c

card, record, file scheda 19d, 38c
cardboard cartone 13c
cardboard box scatola di cartone 3e
cardinal cardinale 1d, 11d
cardiovascular system sistema cardiovascolare 12a
career carriera 11f, 38d
carefree spensierato 11e
careful cauto 11e
careless spericolato 11e
Caribbean Caraibi, caraibico 30b, 30e
carnation garofano 14b
carpenter falegname 38a
carpet tappezzeria 33c
carrot carota 14e, 24f
carry out a sentence eseguire una sentenza 41
cart, movable tray carrello 23b
carte blanche carta bianca 7a
cartilage cartilagine 12a
carton paper cartoncino 37b
cartoon cartone animato 28a
cartridge cartuccia 19d, 25c, 38c, 42b
case cassa 3e
cash contanti 25a, 26a
cash a check incassare un assegno 26a
cash register cassa 25a
cashier cassiere (-a) 25a, 26a, 38a
cask barile 3e
casserole casseruola 23c
cassette tape audiocassetta 20b
cast a glance gettare uno sguardo 12d
cast iron ghisa 13c
cat gatto 15a
catalogue catalogo 25n, 28d, 37f
Catanzaro Catanzaro 30c
cataract cateratta 40a
catarrh catarro 40a

catch   afferrare   3f
catch (the ball)   prendere   27b
catch a chill   prendere freddo
40a
catch fire   incendiarsi   39a
catcher's mask   maschera   27b
catechism   catechismo   11d
caterpillar   bruco   15d
cathedral   cattedrale   11d,
36a
Catholic   Cattolico (-a)   11d
Catholicism   Cattolicesimo   11d
Caucasian   caucasico   30c
cauliflower   cavolfiore   14e, 24f
cautious   cauto   21a
cave   grotta   13b
cavity, tooth decay   carie   40b
CD reader, drive   lettore CD
42b
CD-ROM   CD-ROM   25c, 38c,
42b
ceiling   soffitto   23a
celery   sedano   14e, 24f
cell   cellula   12a
cell phone   cellulare, telefonino
18a
cellist   violoncellista   28c
cello   violoncello   28c
cellulite   cellulite   40a
Celsius   Celsius   6c
cement truck   betoniera   34
censor   censurare   20a
censorship   censura   20a,
44b
center   centro, centrare   2a, 19c,
42b
center (political)   di centro   43a
Centigrade   centigrado   6c
centimeter   centimetro   3a
century   secolo   4b, 43b
ceremonious   cerimonioso   21a
chaffinch   fringuello   15b
chain   catena   25i
chair   sedia   23b
chair a meeting   presiedere una
riunione   38d
chairlift   seggiovia   36b
chalice   calice   11d

chalk   gesso   13c, 37b
chamber music   musica da
camera   25j, 28c
chamber (representative)   camera
dei deputati   43a
chamomile tea   camomilla   24j
champion   campione   27b
change (money)   resto   25a
change gears   cambiare marcia
33a
change room   spogliatoio   27b
change the oil   cambiare l'olio
33a
change the subject   cambiare
soggetto   17a
channel   canale   13b, 20b
chant   canto   28c
chapel   cappella   11d, 36a
chapped hands   mani screpolate
11a
chapter   capitolo   25n, 28d
character   carattere, personaggio
19c, 25n, 28d
charade   sciarada   27a
charge (someone)   incolpare
41
charity   carità   21a
charming, fascinating
affascinante   11e
charter flight   volo charter   30a
chartered accountant
commercialista   38a
chase   inseguire   3f
chat   chiacchierare   17a
cheap   a buon mercato, economico
24n
cheat   imbrogliare   27a
cheater   imbroglione (-a)   27a
cheating   imbroglio, truffa   27a
check (money)   assegno   25a, 26a
check (shape, figure)   quadretto
3d
checkbook   libretto degli assegni
26a
check clearing   compensazione
degli assegni   26a
check the oil   controllare l'olio
33a

check-in accettazione, check-in 32a

check-out vehicle condizioni del veicolo in uscita. 33d

checker piece pedina 27a

checkered a scacchi, a quadretti 3d, 25l

checkers dama 27a

cheek guancia 12a

cheekbone zigomo 12a

cheeky, cocky sfacciato 21a

cheer, acclaim acclamare 17a

Cheers! Cin, cin! Salute! 16c, 24k

cheese formaggio 24h

chemical chimico 13c

chemical war guerra chimica 44d

chemistry chimica 13c, 37e

cherry ciliegia 14d, 24g

cherry (tree) ciliegio 14c

chess gioco degli scacchi 27a

chest petto 12a

chest infection infezione polmonare 40a

chest of drawers cassettone 35b

chest protector corazza 27b

chestnut castagna 14d, 24g

chestnut (tree) castagno 14c

chiaroscuro chiaroscuro 28b

chick pulcino 15b

chick peas ceci 14e, 24f

chicken, hen gallina, pollo 15b, 24d

chickenpox varicella 40a

chief executive direttore (-trice) generale 38a

chief of police commissario di polizia 39b

child fanciullo (-a), bambino (-a) 10a

childbirth parto 11c

childhood fanciullezza 11b

children bambini 11b

children's program programma per i bambini 20b

Chile Cile 30b

Chilean cileno 30e

chill, shiver brivido 40a

chimney camino 23a

chin mento 12a

China Cina 30b

Chinese cinese 30e

chip (computer) chip 42b

chip (wood) scheggiatura 33d

chisel cesello, cesellare 23d, 25b, 28b

chlorine cloro 13c

chocolate cioccolato 7b

chocolate candy cioccolatino 24c

choir coro 11d, 28c

choke (of a car) valvola dell'aria 33c

choke strozzarsi 12b

cholesterol colesterolo 12b

chop, cutlet cotoletta 24a

chopping (butcher's) knife coltello da macellaio 23c

chopping board tagliere 23c

chord accordo 28c

Christian Cristiano (-a) 11d

Christianity Cristianesimo 11d

Christmas Natale 5f, 29a

chrysalis crisalide 15d

chubby grassottello 11a

chum compagno (-a) 10b

church chiesa 11d, 36a

church candle cero 11d

cigar sigaro 25e

cigarette sigaretta 25e

cinema cinema 28a

cinnamon cannella 24i

circle cerchio 2a

circuit circuito 3d

circular, round circolare, rotondo 3d

circulate circolare 3f

circulation circolazione 3f

circumference circonferenza 2a

circus circo 27a, 29b

citizen cittadino (-a) 43a

citizenship cittadinanza 11f, 31, 43a

citrus   cedro   24g

city   città   36a, 38b

city block   isolato   33a

city hall   municipio   36a

city map   pianta della città   36a

city dweller, citizen   cittadino (-a)   36a

civic duty   dovere civico   43a

civil affairs   affari civili   43a

civil right   diritto civile   41, 43a

civil servant   funzionario   43a

civil war   guerra civile   43b

claim   rivendicazione   26b

clam   vongola, mollusco bivalve   15c, 24e

clamp   morsetto   23d, 25b

clap   applaudire   3f

clarinet   clarino, clarinetto   28c

clarinetist   clarinettista   28c

clash   cozzare   12c

class   classe, lezione   30a, 37d, 37f

classical music   musica classica   25j, 28c

Classicism   Classicismo   28b, 43b

classified ad   piccola pubblicità   38d

classroom   aula   37c

clause   proposizione   8a

clay   argilla   13c, 14a

clean   pulire, pulito   11a, 23f, 25g

clean oneself   pulirsi   12f

cleaning cloth   straccio   23b

clear (a check)   compensare   26a

clear   sereno   6a, 12d

clear skin   pelle chiara   11a

clear the table   sparecchiare   23f

clear, delete   annullare   19c, 42b

clearness   chiarezza   12d

clematis   clematide   14b

clergy   clero   11d

clerk   impiegato (-a)   19e, 35a

clerk's window   sportello   19e

click   cliccare   19f, 42b

clientele   clientela   25a, 38d

cliff   scogliera   13b

climate   clima   6a, 13d

climb, go up   salire   3f

climber   alpinista   27b

cling on   appiccicarsi, stringersi   3f

clip   grapetta, clip   19d, 38c

clock   orologio   4d

cloister   chiostro   11d

Close   Chiudi   42c

close an account   chiudere un conto   26a

close friend   amico (-a) intimo (-a)   10b

closed   chiuso   25a, 33b

Closed for holidays   Chiuso per ferie   33b

closed-circuit television   televisione a circuito chiuso   20b

closed-door hearing   udienza a porte chiuse   41

closet   armadio   35b

closing   chiusa   19c

closing (time)   chiusura   25a

cloth   stoffa   13c

clothes   abiti, abbigliamento   25g, 25k

clothes basket   cestino del bucato   25g

clothes closet   guardaroba   23a

clothes dryer   asciugatrice   23b

clothes hanger   attaccapanni   23b, 35b

clothes rack   attaccapanni   23a

clothespin   molletta   25g

clothing store   negozio di abbigliamento   25k

cloud   nuvola   6a

cloudburst   nubifragio   6a

cloudy   nuvoloso   6a

clown   pagliaccio   27a, 29b

clue   indizio   39b

clutch   frizione   33c

coach (sports) allenatore (-trice) 27b

coach (train) vagone 34

coalition coalizione 43a

coast, coastline costa 13b

coat cappotto 25k

cobbler, shoe-repairer calzolaio (-a) 38a

cobra cobra 15c

cocaine cocaina 44c

cockroach scarafaggio 15d

cocoon bozzolo 15d

cod merluzzo 24e

codfish merluzzo 15c

coed school scuola mista 37a

coffee caffè 24j

coffee pot bricco del caffè 23c

coffin bara 11c

cohabit, live together coabitare, convivere 11c

cohabitation convivenza 11c

coin moneta 27a

coin collecting numismatica 27a

colander colino 23c

cold (sickness) raffreddore 40a

cold freddo 6a

cold cuts affettati 24d

cold water acqua fredda 35b

colitis colite 40a

collapse crollare 3f

collar colletto 25g, 25l

colleague collega 10b

collect call telefonata a carico del destinatario 18b

collecting collezionismo 27a

collection colletta, raccolta 11d, 25n, 28d

collector collezionista 27a

collide sccontrarsi 39c

collision, smash scontro, scontrarsi, investirsi 39c

cologne acqua di Colonia 25f

Colombia Colombia 30b

Colombian colombiano 30e

colon due punti 19c

color colore, colorare 7b

color monitor schermo a colori 25c

color one's hair tingersi i capelli 11a

colored a colori 7b

colorful, vivacious vivace 28d

column (in a newspaper) rubrica 20a

column colonna 3d

columnist, reporter cronista 20a

comb pettine 12f, 25f

comb oneself pettinarsi 11a, 12f

come venire 3f

Come in! Avanti! Prego! 16b

Come off it! Ma va! 21a

Come on! Su! Dai! 21a

come to light venire alla luce 13a

comedy, play commedia 20a, 28d, 28e

comet cometa 13a

comic book rivista a fumetti 20a, 25n

comic, comedian comico (-a) 28e

comics fumetti 28d

comma virgola 19c, 19f

command comando 42b

Commandment Comandamento 11d

commerce, trade commercio 37e, 38d

commercial spot 20b

commercial channel canale commerciale 20b

commercial school istituto commerciale 37a

commission commissione 43a

commission of inquiry commissione d'inchiesta 43a

committee comitato 43a

communicate comunicare 17a

communication comunicazione 17a

communication sciences scienze della comunicazione 37e

Communion Comunione 11d
communiqué comunicato stampa 20a
communism comunismo 43a
commuter pendolare 34, 36a
compact compatto 3b
compact car utilitaria 34
compact disc compact disc 20b, 28c
company ditta 38d
company lawyer giurista d'impresa 38a
company policy politica aziendale 38d
compare paragonare 17a
comparison paragone 17a
compartment scompartimento 34
compass bussola, compasso 2b, 13d, 34, 37b
compatible compatibile 42b
compatible software software compatibile 25c, 38c
compensate indennizzare 26b
compete concorrere 27b
competent, skilled competente 11e
competition concorrenza, agonismo 25a, 27b, 38d
competitor concorrente 38d
compiler of a volume curatore (-trice) 28d
complain lamentarsi 17a, 21a, 35a
complaint lamentela 17a, 21a, 35a
complementary complementare 2b
complex complesso 1d
complexion carnagione 12a
complicated complicato 22a
Compliments! Complimenti! 29c
composer compositore (-trice) 25j, 28c
composition componimento, tema, composizione 25j, 28c, 37f

compost miscela fertilizzante 14a
compound composto 13c
compound interest interesse composto 26c
compulsory education istruzione obbligatoria 37a
computer computer 19d, 38c, 42b
computer science informatica 42b
computer scientist informatico (-a) 38a
computer-learning apprendimento tramite computer 37f
concave concavo 2b
conceited pieno di sé 21a
conceive concepire 22b
concept concetto 22a
concert concerto 25j, 29b
concise conciso 28d
conclude concludere 17a
conclusion conclusione 17a
concrete concreto 22a
concrete (cement) cemento 13c
concussion commozione cerebrale 40a
conditional condizionale 8a
condom preservativo 25h, 40a
condominium condominio 23e, 36a
conductor conduttore (-trice) 34
cone cono 2a
confederation confederazione 43a
conference convegno 37f
confess confessarsi 11d
Confession Confessione 11d
confessional box confessionale 11d
confidence vote fiducia 43a
confidential confidenziale 19e
confirm confermare 17a
confirmation Cresima 11d
conflict conflitto 44d

conformist conformista 11e

confusing confusionario 28d

Congolese congolese 30e

congratulate congratulare 17a

congratulations congratulazioni 16c, 17a, 29c

congregation congregazione 11d

conical conico 3d

conjugation coniugazione 8a

conjunction congiunzione 8a

Connect Connetta 42c

connection coincidenza 32a, 34

conscience coscienza 22a

conscientious coscienzioso 11e, 22a

consecutive consecutivo 2b

conservative conservatore (-trice) 43a

conservatory conservatorio 25j, 28c, 37a

consonant consonante 8a

conspiracy, frame-up complotto 39b

constant costante 1f

constipation stitichezza 40a

constitution costituzione 43a

consulate consolato 43a

consult, look up consultare 17a

consultant consulente 38a

consumer consumatore (-trice) 38d

consumer good bene di consumo 38d

consumer protection tutela del consumatore 38d

contact contatto 21a

contact lenses lenti a contatto 12d

contain contenere 3e

container contenitore 3e

contents contenuto 3e

contest, dispute contestare 17a

continent continente 13d, 30a

continental continentale 6a, 13d

contraceptive contraccettivo 25h, 40a

contraceptive pill pillola anticoncezionale 25h, 40a

contract contratto 38d

contradict contraddire 17a

contralto contralto 28c

contrast contrasto 28d

contributor collaboratore (-trice) 20a

Control Controlla 42c

controversial, polemical polemico 28d

controversy controversia 41

convalescence convalescenza 40a

convent convento 11d

conventional weapon arma convenzionale 44d

conversation conversazione 17a

converse conversare 17a

convex convesso 2b

convince convincere 22a, 22b, 41

cook cuoco (-a), cucinare 24a, 38a

cooker, stove cucina 23b

cooking pot pentola 23c

cool fresco 6a

coordinate coordinata 2b

copilot copilota 32c

copper rame 13c

copy copia, copiare 19c, 19d, 42b

copy shop copisteria 25c

coral corallo 25i

cordial cordiale 21a

cordiality cordialità 21a

corduroy fustagno 13c

core subject materia fondamentale 37f

cork sughero 13c

cork cap tappo di sughero 23c

corn granturco, mais 14a, 24c

corn, callus callo 40a

cornea cornea 12d

corner angolo 33a

cornflower   fiordaliso   14b

coroner   magistrato (investigatore)
39b

corporation   società   38d

corpulent   corpulento   11a

correct, proper   corretto   21a

correspondence   corrispondenza
19e

correspondence course   corso per
corrispondenza   37a

correspondent   corrispondente
19e

corridor   corridoio   23a

corrupt   vizioso, corrotto   11e

Corsica   Corsica   30c

Corsican   corso   30c

cortisone   cortisone   25h, 40a

cosecant   cosecante   2b

cosine   coseno   2b

cosmetic   cosmetico   12f, 25f

cosmetics, perfume shop
profumeria   25f

cosmos   cosmo   13a

cost   costare   24n, 25a

cost price   prezzo di costo   38d

Costa Rica   Costa Rica   30b

Costa Rican   costaricano   30e

costly, expensive   costoso   25a

costume   costume   28e

cotangent   cotangente   2b

cotton   cotone   13c, 25l

cough   tosse, tossire   40a

cough syrup   sciroppo contro la
tosse   25h, 40a

coughing fit   colpo di tosse   40a

council   consiglio   43a

Council of Europe   Consiglio
d'Europa   43a

council of ministers   consiglio dei
ministri   43a

councilor   consigliere   43a

count   contare   1f

counter   banco   25a

counterfeit money   moneta falsa
26a

countersign   controfirmare   19e

countersignature   controfirma
19e

country   paese   13d

country of origin   paese d'origine
43a

country, nation   nazione   30a

countryside   campagna, paesaggio
36b

coupon, voucher   buono   20c

courageous   coraggioso   11e

courier   corriere   19e

courier bus, express   corriera
34

course   corso   37a

course, dish   piatto   24a

court   tribunale   41

court for public funds   corte dei
conti   41

court for serious crimes   corte
d'assise   41

court of appeal   corte d'appello
41

court-appointed lawyer
difensore d'ufficio   39b

courteous   cortese   11e

courthouse   tribunale   36a

courtroom   aula del tribunale
41

courtroom hearing   udienza in
tribunale   41

cousin   cugino, cugina   10a

cove   insenatura   13b

cover charge   coperto   24l

cover, covering   fodera   23b

cover, dust jacket   copertina
20a, 25n

covering, bandage   benda   25h

cow   mucca   15a

cowardly   codardo   11e

cowboy movie   film western
28a

crab   granchio   15c

cracker   cracker   24c

crackle, squeak   scricchiolare
12c

crafts   artigianato   36b

crawl   strisciare carponi   3f

crazy   pazzo, matto   11e

creak   cigolio, cigolare   12c

cream   crema   25h, 25f, 40a

creamery   cremeria   24m
creative   creativo   11e, 22a
creativity   creatività   22a
credit   credito   26a
credit card   carta di credito   25a, 26a
credit institute, trust   istituto di credito   26a
credit letter   lettera di credito   26b
credit limit   fido   26a
credit transfer   bonifico   26a
cremation   cremazione   11c
crest   cresta   15b
crevasse   crepaccio   13b
crew   equipaggio   32c
cricket   grillo   15d
crime   crimine   39b
crime rate   criminalità   39b
crime report   cronaca nera   20a
criminal   criminale   39b
criminal act   reato   39b
criminal hearing   udienza penale   41
criminal record   passato criminale   39b
critic   critico (-a)   20a
critical   critico   11e
critical condition   grave stato   40a
criticism   critica   25n, 28d
criticize   criticare   28d
croak   gracidare   15c
Croatia   Croazia   30b
Croatian   croato   30e
crocodile   coccodrillo   15c
cross (the road)   attraversare   36c
cross oneself   farsi il segno della croce   11d
cross, crucifix   croce   3d, 11d
cross-country skiing   sci di fondo   27b
crosswords   parole crociate   20a, 25n, 27a
crow   corvo   15b
crucifix   Crocifisso   11d
cruel   crudele   11e

cruise   crociera   36b
crutch   stampella   25h, 40a
cry   piangere   21a
crying   pianto   21a
Cuba   Cuba   30b
Cuban   cubano   30e
cube   cubo   2a
cube root   radice cubica   1e
cubed   al cubo   1e
cubic centimeter   centimetro cubico   3a
cubic kilometer   chilometro cubico   3a
cubic meter   metro cubico   3a
cubic millimeter   millimetro cubico   3a
cuckoo   cuculo   15b
cucumber   cetriolo   14e, 24f
cuff-links   gemelli   25l
cuisine   cucina   24a
cult   culto   11d
cultivate   coltivare   14a
cultivation   coltivazione   14a
cultured   colto   11e
cup   tazza, coppa   23c, 24k, 27b
cupboard   armadio   23b
cure   cura, curare   40a
curfew   coprifuoco   43b
curler   bigodino   25f
curlers   bigodini   12f
curls   ricci   12f
curly   riccio   11a
currency value   valuta   26a
current   corrente   35b
current account   conto corrente   26a
curriculum   curriculum   37f
curse   maledire   17a
Curses! Damn (it)!   Maledizione!   16c
cursor   cursore   19f, 38c, 42b
curtain   tenda   23b, 28e, 35b
curtains   sipario   28e
curve   curva   33a
curved   curva   2b
cushion   cuscino   23b
customer   cliente   25a, 38d
Customize   Personalizza   42c

customs   dogana   31
customs officer   doganiere (-a)   31, 38a
cut   tagliare   24a, 42c
Cut it out!   Piantala!   21a
cut-out coupon   tagliando   20c
cute   simpatico   11a
cutlery   posate   23c
cyclamen   ciclamino   14b
cycling   ciclismo   27b
cylinder   cilindro   2a
cylindrical   cilindrico   3d
cymbal   piatto   28c
cypress   cipresso   14c
cyst   cisti   40a
Czech   ceco   30e
Czech Republic   Repubblica Ceca   30b

D
dad   papà   10a
daffodil   trombone   14b
dahlia   dalia   14b
daily   quotidianamente   4b
daily newspaper   quotidiano   20a, 25n
dairy product   latticino   24h
dairy shop, milk store   latteria   24m
daisy   margherita   14b
damages   danni   26b
Damn it!   Accidenti!   21a
dance   ballo, danza, ballare   28c
dance music   musica da ballo   25j, 28c
dancer   ballerino (-a)   28c
dandruff   forfora   12b
danger   pericolo   39a
Danish   danese   30e
dare   osare   21a
dark   buio, scuro   6a, 7b, 12d
dark blue   blu   7a
dark mood   umore nero   7a
dark room   camera oscura   25d, 28b
dark skin   pelle nera   11a
dark-haired   bruno   11a
darkness   oscurità   12d

dash   trattino   19c
dashboard   cruscotto   33c
data bank   banca dati   42b
data file   file dati   42b
data processing   elaborazione dati   42b
date (calendar)   data   19c, 38b
date (fruit)   dattero   14d, 24g
date (with someone)   appuntamento   29b
date and place of birth   data e luogo di nascita   38b
date of birth   data di nascita   11f
datum, data   dato, dati   42b
daughter   figlia   10a
daughter-in-law   nuora   10a
dawn, sunrise   alba   4b
day   giorno   4b
day after tomorrow   dopodomani   4b
day before yesterday   l'altro ieri   4b
day of the week   giorno della settimana   5a
daycare   asilo nido   37a
deacon, deaconess   diacono (-essa)   11d
deadly sin   peccato mortale   11d
deaf   sordo   12c
deafness   sordità   12c
deal   affare   26b
deal with   trattare   28d
dean, chair of a faculty   preside di facoltà   37a
dear friend   caro (-a) amico (-a)   10b
Dear John   Caro Giovanni   19b
Dear Madam   Gentile Signora   19a
Dear Madam or Sir   Spettabile (Spett.le) Ditta   19a
Dear Mary   Cara Maria   19b
Dear Sir   Egregio Signore   19a
Dearest John   Carissimo Giovanni   19b
Dearest Mary   Carissima Maria   19b

death morte 11c
death certificate certificato di morte 11c
death penalty pena di morte 44b
debate dibattito, dibattere 17a, 41
debit, bill, debt debito 26a
decade decennio 4b, 43b
decagon decagono 2a
deceased, late defunto 11c
December dicembre 5b
decency decenza 21a
decent decente 21a
decentralization decentramento 43a
decimal decimale 1d, 1f
decipher decifrare 17a
deck chair sedia a sdraio 36b
declarative dichiarativa 8a
declare dichiarare 17a, 31
decline declino 43b
decor, decoration arredamento 23b
decorum decoro 21a
decrease, diminish diminuzione, diminuire 3b
decree decreto 43a
deduction detrazione 26b
deep profondo 3c
deer cervo 15a
defame, libel diffamare 20a
defeat sconfitta, sconfiggere 27b, 43b
defecate defecare 12b
defend one's thesis discutere la tesi 37f
defend oneself difendersi 41
defense difesa 43b
defense lawyer difensore (difenditrice) 39b
deferent deferente 21a
deferred sentence sentenza di rinvio a giudizio 41
deficit deficit 26a
define definire 17a
definite (article) determinativo 8a

definition definizione 20a
deflation deflazione 26a
degenerate degenerato 21a
degree (university) laurea 37f
degree grado 2b, 6c
dehydrated disidratato 40a
dehydration disidratazione 40a
delete cancellare 19c, 42b
Delete Annulla 42c
delicate delicato 11a, 25g, 25l
delicatessen salumeria 24m
delicious squisito 12e
Delighted! Molto lieto (-a)! 16b
delinquency delinquenza 39b
delivery consegna 25a, 38d
democracy democrazia 43a
democratic party partito democratico 43a
democratic society società democratica 43a
demographic demografico 13d
demonstrate dimostrare 22b
demonstration dimostrazione, manifestazione 38d, 43a
demonstrative dimostrativo 8a
Denmark Danimarca 30b
denomination confessione 11d
dense denso 3b
density densità 3b
dent ammaccatura 33d
dental assistant assistente 40b
dentist dentista 40b
dentist's office gabinetto dentistico 40b
deny negare 17a
deodorant deodorante 25f
department reparto 25a
department store grande magazzino 25a
departmental manager caporeparto 38a
departure partenza 32b, 34
dependency tossicodipendenza 44c

dependent   persona a carico   11c

deposit   versamento, versare   26a

deposit slip   modulo di versamento   26a

deposition, testimony   deposizione   41

depraved   depravato   21a

depressed   depresso   11e, 21a

depressed area   zona depressa   44b

depression   depressione   21a, 40a

depth   profondità   3c

dermatitis   dermatite   40a

descend   scendere   3f

descent   discesa   3f

describe   descrivere   17a

description   descrizione   17a, 39b

descriptive (adjective)   qualificativo   8a

descriptive geometry   geometria descrittiva   1g

desert   deserto   13b

design   disegno   3d, 37e

desk   banco   37b

desperate   disperato   11e, 21a

desperation   disperazione   21a

despite   malgrado, nonostante   8i

dessert   dessert, dolce   24c

dessert dish   coppa da dessert   23c

dessert fork   forchettina   23c

destroy   distruggere   39a

detain   detenere   41

detective movie   film poliziesco   28a

detention   detenzione   41

detergent   detergente   25g

detest   detestare   21b

detoxify oneself   disintossicarsi   44c

devaluation   svaluta   26a

devalue   svalutare   26a

develop   sviluppare   28d

Devil   Diavolo   11d

devotion   devozione   11d

devout   devoto   11d, 21a

dew   rugiada   6a

diabetes   diabete   40a

diagnose   diagnosticare   40a

diagnosis   diagnosi   40a

diagonal   diagonale   2b

dial   quadrante   4d, 25i

dial the number   comporre il numero, fare il numero   18b

dialogue   dialogo   17a, 28e

Dialogue Window   Finestra di Dialogo   42c

diameter   diametro   2a

diamond   diamante   11c, 25i

diaphragm   diaframma   12a

diary   diario   25n, 28d

dice   dadi   27a

dictionary   vocabolario, dizionario, lessico   20a, 28d

die   morire   11c

die (singular of dice)   dado   27a

diet   dieta   40a

difference   differenza   1f

differential calculus   calcolo differenziale   1g

difficult   difficile   22a

diffusion, spread   diffusione   3c

dig   vangare, scavare   14a

digestion   digestione   12b

digestive system   sistema digerente   12b

digit   cifra   1d

digital   digitale   18a, 42b

digital camera   macchina fotografica digitale   25d

digital photography   fotografia digitale   25d, 28b

digital watch   orologio digitale   4d

diligent   diligente   11e

dimension   dimensione   3b, 3c

dimple   fossetta (del mento)   11a, 12a

dining room   sala da pranzo   23a

dinner cena 24a
dinner jacket smoking 25k
diploma diploma 11f, 37f
diplomatic diplomatico 11e
direct diretto 8a, 21a
direct call telefonata in teleselezione 18b
direction direzione 3c
director regista 28a, 28e
director, CEO dirigente 38a
dirty sporco 11a, 25g, 25l
disadvantage svantaggio 44b
disagree non essere d'accordo 21a
disagreement malinteso, disaccordo 17a, 21a
disappoint deludere 21a
disappointed deluso 21a
disarmament disarmo 44d
disc disco 12a, 20b
disc jockey disc jockey 20b
disc, puck disco 27b
discipline disciplina 37e
disco discoteca 28c, 29b
discomfort malessere 40a
discount sconto 25a, 26a, 38d
discount rate tasso di sconto 26a
discourse discorso 8a
discuss, argue discutere 17a, 41
discussion, argument discussione 17a
disease malattia, morbo 40a
disgust disgusto, disgustare 21a, 21b
disgusted disgustato 11e, 21b
dish piatto 23c
dish cloth strofinaccio per i piatti 23b
dish towel asciugapiatti 23b
dishwasher lavapiatti, lavastoviglie 23b
dishonest disonesto 11e
dishonorable disonorevole 21a
disinterested disinteressato 11e
disk disco 3d

diskette dischetto 19f, 25c, 38c
dislike antipatia, non piacere 21b
dislocated slogato 40a
dislocation slogatura 40a
dispatch dispaccio 20a
display, exhibition mostra 25a
disposal, waste scarico 44a
dissatisfaction insoddisfazione 21a
dissatisfied insoddisfatto 21a
dissertation dissertazione 25n, 28d, 37f
dissolute dissoluto 21a
dissuade dissuadere 22a, 22b
distance distanza 3c, 33a
distortion distorsione 42a
distress phone line telefono amico 18b
district quartiere 36a
ditch fosso, fossato 14a
diuretic diuretico 40a
dive tuffarsi 27b
diver tuffatore (-trice) 27b
divide dividere 1e
divided by diviso (per) 1e
dividend dividendo 38d
diving tuffo 27b
division divisione 1e
divorce divorzio, divorziare 11c
divorced divorziato (-a) 11c, 11f, 38b
dizziness giramento di testa 40a
DNA DNA 39b
docile docile 21a
doctor medico, dottore (-essa) 38a, 39c, 40a
doctor's office gabinetto medico 40a
document cartella, documento 38c, 42b, 43b
document cover copertina 38c
documentary documentario, filmato 28a

dodecahedron   dodecaedro   2a

dodge   schivare   3f

dog   cane   15a

doll   bambola   27a

Dolomites   Dolomiti   30c

Dominican (national)
  dominicano   30e

Dominican (relig.)   Domenicano
  11d

Dominican Republic   Repubblica
  Dominicana   30b

Don't be stupid (silly)!   Non fare
  (faccia) lo stupido (-a)!   16c

Don't mention it!   Figurati! Si
  figuri!   16c

Don't talk nonsense!   Non dire
  (dica) schiocchezze!   16c

donkey   asino   15a

doodle   scarabocchio   28d

door   porta   23a

doorbell   campanello   23a

door-knob   maniglia   23a

doorman, doorwoman   portiere
  (-a)   35a

doormat   stuoia d'entrata   23b

dosage   posologia   25h, 40a

dot   punto   3d, 19f

double   doppio, raddoppiare
  1b, 3b

double bass   contrabbasso   28c

double bass player
  contrabbassista   28c

double bed   letto matrimoniale
  35b

double-breasted jacket   giacca a
  doppio petto   25k

double chin   doppio mento   11a

double citizenship   doppia
  cittadinanza   11f

double room   camera doppia
  35a

double salary   paga doppia   38d

doubt   dubbio, dubitare   22a,
  22b

doubtful   dubbioso   22a

dove   colomba   15b

down   giù   3c, 36c

down-payment   caparra   30a

downhill skiing   sci da discesa
  27b

downpour   pioggia insistente
  6a

downtown   centro   11f, 36a

downtrodden   avvilito   11e

dowry   dote   11c

dozen   dozzina   1b

draft   bozza   19d, 28d, 38c

draft beer   birra alla spina   24j

draft, promissory note   cambiale
  26a

draftsperson   geometra   11f,
  16b

dragonfly   libellula   15d

drama   dramma   25n, 28d, 28e

draw, design   disegnare   2b, 37f

draw, tie   pareggio, pareggiare
  27b

drawer   cassetto   23b

drawing   disegno   28b, 37f

drawing instruments   strumenti
  del disegno   2b

drawing paper   carta da disegno
  37b

dream   sogno, sognare   22a,
  22b

dress, clothing, suit   vestito, abito
  25k

dress, get dressed   vestirsi   25l

dresser   comò   35b

dresser, sideboard   credenza
  23b

dressing   fascia   25h, 40a

dressing room   cabina   25k

dressing-table   toilette   23b

dried cod   baccalà   24e

drill   trapano   23d, 25b, 40b

drink, beverage   bere, bevanda
  12b, 24n, 24j

drinking can   lattina   23c

drinking glass   bicchiere   23c,
  24k

drive   guidare   3f, 33a

driver   autista, conducente,
  guidatore (-trice)   27b, 33a, 38a

driver's license   patente (di guida)
  33a

drizzle pioggerellina 6a
drizzly piovigginoso 6a
drop goccia 6a, 25h, 40a
drop out abbandonare gli studi 37f
drowsiness sonnolenza 40a
drug addict tossicodipendente 44c
drug addiction tossicodipendenza 40a, 44c
drug pusher spacciatore (-trice) di droga 39b, 44c
drug pushing spaccio di droga 39b
drug traffic traffico degli stupefacenti, di droga 39b, 44c
drug trafficker trafficante di droga 39b
drugs droga, stupefacenti 44c
drum, tambourine tamburo 28c
drummer batterista 28c
dry asciutto, secco 6a
dry cleaner lavanderia a secco 25g
dry oneself asciugarsi 12f
dry skin pelle secca 11a
dubbed doppiato 28a
dubbing doppiaggio 28a
duck anatra (anitra) 15b, 24d
duet duetto 28c
dull cupo, spento 7b
dull life una vita grigia 7a
dumplings gnocchi 24b
dung letame 14a
duplicate duplicare 19c, 38c, 42b
duration durata 4c
during durante 4c
dust pan paletta per la spazzatura 23b
dustbin pattumiera 23b
duster piumino 23b
Dutch olandese 30e
duty tax tassa 31
DVD DVD 20b, 25j
dwell, live in abitare 36a
dwelling abitazione 23a
dynamic dinamico 11e

E
e-mail e-mail, posta elettronica 19f, 38c, 42b
e-mail address indirizzo elettronico, e-mail 19f, 38b
e-ticket biglietto elettronico 32a
each, every ogni 3b
eager desideroso 21a
eagle aquila 15b
ear orecchio 12a
ear (of corn) spiga 14a
ear infection otite 40a
eardrum timpano 12a
early presto, in anticipo 4c, 8j, 32b
earn guadagnare 38d
earphone auricolare 18a
earring orecchino 25i
Earth Terra 5c, 13a
earthquake terremoto 13b
easel cavalletto (da pittore) 28b
east est 3c, 13d, 36c
Easter Pasqua 5f, 29a
eastern orientale 3c, 13d
Easterner, Oriental orientale 30e
easy facile 22a
eat mangiare 12b, 24n
Eat up! Buon appetito! 24k
ebony ebano 13c, 14c
ecclesiastic ecclesiastico 11d
echo echeggiare 12c
eclipse eclissi 13a
economics economia 37e
economy economia 43a
economy class classe turistica 30a
Ecuador Ecuador 30b
Ecuadorian ecuadoriano 30e
edge orlo, margine 3c
edge, bank sponda 13b
Edinburgh Edinburgo 30c
edit redigere, editare 20a
Edit Modifica 42c
editing montaggio, editing 28a, 42b
editor redattore (-trice) 20a, 38a

editor-in-chief caporedattore (-trice) 20a
editorial articolo di fondo 20a
editorial offices redazione 20a
educate, instruct istruire 37a
educated istruito 37f
education istruzione 37a, 37f, 38b
education (as process) educazione 37a
education (level) titolo di studio 11f, 38b
eel anguilla 15c, 24e
effective efficace 21a
efficient efficiente 21a
egg uovo 24h
egg-beater frullino 23c
eggplant melanzana 14e, 24f
egoism egoismo 21a
egoist, self-centered egoista 11e
Egypt Egitto 30b
Egyptian egiziano 30e
eight otto 1a
eighteen diciotto 1a
eighth ottavo 1b
eighty ottanta 1a
El Salvador El Salvador 30b
elaborate elaborato 28d
elastic elastico 13c
Elba Elba 30c
elbow gomito 12a
elect eleggere 43a
elected representative deputato (-a) 43a
election elezione 43a
electoral campaign campagna elettorale 43a
electric outlet presa (elettrica) 23d, 25b
electric piano piano elettrico 28c
electric razor rasoio elettrico 12f, 25f
electric toy train trenino elettrico 27a
electrical elettrico 13c

electrician elettricista 38a
electricity elettricità 13c, 23d
electrocardiogram elettrocardiogramma 40a
electron elettrone 13c
electronic file archivio elettronico 42b
elegant elegante 11e, 25l
elegy elegia 28d
elementary school scuola elementare 37a
elementary school pupil scolaro (-a) 37d
elementary teacher maestro (-a) 37d
elephant elefante 15a
elevator ascensore 23e, 35a
eleven undici 1a
eleventh undicesimo 1b
eliminate eliminare 27b, 42c
elimination round girone eliminatorio 27b
elm olmo 14c
eloquent eloquente 11e, 17a
emaciated emaciato 11a
embassy ambasciata 43a
embezzlement appropriazione indebita 39b
emblem emblema 3d
embrace, hug abbracciare 3f
embroider ricamare 27a
embroidery ricamo 27a
emerald smeraldo 25i
emergency pronto soccorso 39c
emergency exit uscita di sicurezza (emergenza) 23e, 39a
Emergency lane Corsia d'emergenza 33b
emetic emetico 40a
emigrant emigrante 44d
emigration emigrazione 44d
Emilia Emilia Romagna 30d
emission emissione 42a
emphasize sottolineare 17a, 28d
employee dipendente 11f, 38d
employer datore di lavoro 11f, 38d

employment lavoro 11f, 38d
employment agency agenzia di collocamento 38d
empty vuoto 3b
enamel smalto 13c
enchanting incantevole 21a
enclose, attach accludere, allegare 19c
enclosed, attached accluso, allegato 19c
enclosed, surrounded circoscritto, racchiuso 3d
enclosure recinto 3d
encourage incoraggiare 21a
encouraged incoraggiato 21a
encyclopedia enciclopedia 20a, 25n, 37b
end, finish fine, finire 4c
endorse avallare 26a
endorsement girata 26a
enemy nemico (-a) 10b
energetic energico 11a
energy energia 13c, 44a
energy conservation conservazione dell'energia 44a
energy crisis crisi energetica 44a
energy waste spreco d'energia 44a
engagement fidanzamento 11c, 29a
engagement ring anello di fidanzamento 25i
engineer ingegnere 11f, 16b, 38a
engineering ingegneria 37e
engineering faculty facoltà di ingegneria 37a
England Inghilterra 30b
English inglese 30e
enjoy oneself, have fun divertirsi 21a, 29b
enlarge allargare 25l
Enlightenment Illuminismo 43b
enough abbastanza 8j, 3b
Enough! Basta! 21c
ensure assicurare 17a

enter entrare 3f, 36c
entire intero 3b
entrance ingresso 23e, 33b, 35a
entrance exam esame d'ammissione 37f
envelope busta 19d, 25c, 38c
envious invidioso 11e
environment ambiente 13b, 44a
environmentalist ambientalista 44a
epidemic epidemia 40a
epigram epigramma 28d
epileptic fit crisi epilettica 40a
episode episodio 25n, 28d
epoch epoca 43b
equality uguaglianza 1f
equation equazione 1f
equation in one unknown equazione a una incognita 1f
equation in two unknowns equazione a due incognite 1f
equator equatore 13d
equilateral equilatero 2a
equinox equinozio 4c
era era 43b
erase, delete cancellare 19c, 37f, 42b
eraser gomma 25c, 37b
erotic erotico 21a
error errore 37f
erudite erudito 11e
eruption eruzione 13b
escape evasione 39b
esophagus esofago 12a
espionage spionaggio 44d
essay saggio 25n, 28d
essay-writing saggistica 28d
estate (succession) successione 11c
estate, villa, large home villa 23a
estimable stimabile 21a
Estonia Estonia 30b
Estonian estone 30e
estrogen estrogeno 40a

estuary   estuario   13b

etching   disegno a matita   28b

ether   etere   13c

Ethiopia   Etiopia   30b

Ethiopian   etiope   30e

Etna   Etna   30c

Eucharist   Eucarestia   11d

Euclidean geometry   geometria euclidea   1g

euro euro   26a, 43a

Europe   Europa   30b

European   europeo   30e

evaluation, grading   valutazione   37f

evangelist   evangelista   11d

evasive   evasivo   21a

even   pari , uguale   1d, 3d

even though   anche se   8i

evening   sera   4b, 25l

evening attire   abito, vestito da sera   25k

evening course   corso serale   37a

evening school   scuola serale   37a

evergreen   sempreverde   14c

every once in a while   di tanto in tanto   4c

Everybody out!   Tutti fuori!   39a

everyone   tutti, ciascuno, ognuno   3b, 8h

everything   tutto   8h

everywhere   dappertutto   36c

eviction   sfratto   23e

evidence   prove   41

examination   esame   37f

examine   visitare   40a

examine the witness   interrogare il testimone   41

exchange   cambio, cambiare   25a, 26a

exclamation mark   punto esclamativo   19c

exclamatory   esclamativa   8a

excursion, tour   gita   30a

excuse   scusa   17a

Excuse me!   Scusa! Scusi! Mi scusi!   16c

excuse oneself   scusarsi   17a

executive   esecutivo   43a

exercise   esercizio   37f

exhale   espirare   12b

exhibition   mostra   28b

exist   esistere   22b

existence   esistenza   22a

exit   uscita   23e, 33b, 35a

exit, go out   uscire   36c

Exodus   Esodo   11d

expand   espandere   3b

expansion   espansione   3b

expectant mother   futura mamma   11c

expectorant   espettorante   25h, 40a

expenses   spese , uscite   26b

expensive   caro   24n, 25a

explain   spiegare   17a, 28d

explanation   spiegazione   17a

explode, blast   scoppiare   12c

exponent   esponente   1f

export   esportare   26b

express   esprimere   17a

express mail   posta celere   19e

express oneself   esprimersi   17a

expression   espressione   11a, 17a

extension   estensione   3b, 3c

extension cord   filo di prolungamento   23b

external affairs   affari esteri   43a

extinguish, put out   spegnere il fuoco   39a

extract the root   estrarre la radice   1e

extradition   estradizione   41

extraordinary   straordinario   11e

extremely angry   giallo dalla rabbia   7a

extroverted   estroverso   11e

eye   occhio   12a

eyewitness   testimone oculare   41

eyedrop   collirio   25h, 40a

eyeliner   matita per gli occhi   25f

eye shadow   mascara   25f

eyebrow sopracciglio 12a
eyeglasses occhiali 12d
eyelash ciglio 12a
eyelid palpebra 12a

F

fable favola 25n, 28d
fabric tessuto 25g, 25l
façade facciata 23a
face faccia 12a
face powder cipria 25f
face, countenance faccia, viso 11a
facial cream crema per il viso 25f
faction fazione 43b
factor fattore, fattorizzare 1f
factorization fattorizzazione 1f
factory fabbrica 38d
faculty facoltà 37a
fade sbiadire 12d
Fahrenheit Fahrenheit 6c
fail essere bocciato 37f
fail (someone) bocciare 37f
fainting spell svenimento 40a
fairy tale fiaba 25n, 28d
faith fede 11d
faithful fedele 11d, 11e
falcon falcone 15b
fall caduta, cadere 3f
fall asleep addoremntarsi 12b
fall down cadere per terra 3f
fall in love innamorarsi 11c
fall in prices ribasso dei prezzi 26b
fallow, uncultivated incolto 14a
false falso 25i
false teeth, denture dentiera 40b
family famiglia 10a
family doctor medico di famiglia 40a
family friend amico (-a) di famiglia 10b
family relation parentela 10a
family tree albero genealogico 11c

fan ventola, ventilatore 23a, 33c
fanatic fanatico 21a
fandango fandango 28c
Fantastic! Fantastico! 16c
far lontano 3c, 8j, 36c
far-fetched, unusual inconsueto 28d
far-sighted ipermetrope 12d
farm fattoria 15a
farmer contadino (-a) 15a, 38a
farmland terreno agrario 13b, 14a
fascinating affascinante 11a
fashion moda 25k
fashion magazine rivista di moda 20a, 25n
fast (from food) digiuno 11d
fast veloce 3f
fat grasso 11a
father padre 10a
father-in-law suocero 10a
faucet rubinetto 23a, 35b
fault, guilt colpa 41
fax fax 18a, 38c
fear, be afraid paura, avere paura (di) 21a
fearful pauroso, timoroso 11e, 21a
Feast of the Assumption Ferragosto 5f, 29a
feather penna 15b
featherweight peso piuma 27b
feature (film) lungometraggio 28a
February febbraio 5b
federation federazione 43a
fee tariffa 42a
feel bad sentirsi male, stare male 12b
feel like avere voglia di 21a
feel nauseous avere la nausea 40a
feel well sentirsi bene, stare bene 12b
feeling sensibilità 21a
felt feltro 13c
felt hat cappello di feltro 25k

felt pen   pennarello   7b
female   femmina, femminile   11a, 38b
female dog   cagna   15a
feminine   femminile   8a, 11a
fence   recinto   15a
fencing   scherma   27b
fencing suit   divisa   27b
fender   parafango   33c
fennel   finocchio   14e, 24f
fermentation   fermentazione   14a
ferry   traghetto   34
fertilizer   fertilizzante   14a
fetid   fetido   12e
fettuccine   fettuccine   24b
feudal   feudale   43b
fever, temperature   febbre   40a
fiancé, fiancée   fidanzato, (-a)   10b
fiber   fibra   13c, 25g, 25l
fiberglass   lana di vetro   13c
fiction, narrative   narrativa   20a, 25n
fidelity   fedeltà   42a
field   campo   13b, 27b
field (of study)   campo (di studio)   37f
field of grass   prato   13b
field trip   gita scolastica   37f
fierce   violento, feroce   21a
fifteen   quindici   1a
fifth   quinto   1b
fifty   cinquanta   1a
fifty-one   cinquantuno   1a
fifty-three   cinquantatré   1a
fifty-two   cinquantadue   1a
fig   fico   14c, 14d, 24g
fight   battersi, picchiarsi, lotta   39b, 44d
figure -   figura   2a
file (office)   archivio, file, scheda   38c, 42b, 42c
file (tool)   lima   23d, 25b
file away   schedare   38c
file folder   cartella, scheda   25c, 38c
file manager   file manager   42b

file name   titolo del documento   38c, 42b
filet   filetto   24a
filing cabinet, box file   schedario   38c
filing card, filing folder   scheda   25c
Filipino   filippino   30e
fill   riempire   3b
fill a tooth   impiombare un dente   40b
fill out   compilare   38c
fill up   fare il pieno   33a
filling   piombatura   40b
film   pellicola   25d
film critic   critico del cinema   20a
film, movie   film   28a
filter   filtro   13c, 33c
fin, flipper   pinna   15c
final score   risultato finale   27b
finalist   finalista   27b
finance   finanziare   26b
financier   finanziere   26a
Find   Trova   42c
fine arts   belle arti   28b
fine, traffic ticket   multa   33a
Fine, Well!   Bene!   16a
finger, toe   dito   12a
fingernail   unghia   12a
fingerprint   impronta digitale   39b
finish school   finire la scuola   11f
Finland   Finlandia   30b
Finnish   finlandese   30e
fir   abete   14c
fire   incendio, fuoco   13c, 39a
Fire!   Al fuoco!   39a, 39b
fire (from work)   licenziare   38d
fire extinguisher   estintore   39a
fire hose   pompa   39a
fire hydrant   idrante   39a
fire insurance   assicurazione contro l'incendio   26a
fire truck   autopompa   39a
firearm   arma da fuoco   39b

firefighter   vigile del fuoco   39a
fireproof   antincendio   39a
firing   licenziamento   38d
firm, company   azienda   38d
first   primo, prima   1b, 8a, 8j
first aid   pronto soccorso   25h, 39a, 39c
first class   prima classe   30a
first course   primo piatto   24a
first name   nome   11f
first year   primo anno   37a
first-born   primogenito   11c
fish   pesce, pescare   15c, 24e, 27a
fish shop   pescheria   24m
fishing   pesca   15c, 27a, 36b
fishing rod   canna   15c
fishmonger   pescivendolo   38a
fist   pugno   12a
fitted carpet   moquette   23b
five   cinque   1a
five thousand   cinquemila   1a
five-star hotel   albergo a cinque stelle   35a
fix, repair   aggiustare, riparare   25l, 33a
fixed price   prezzo fisso   24l, 25a
fixed wage   stipendio fisso   38d
fixture, installation   impianto   23a
flame   fiamma   39a
flamingo   fenicottero   15b
flannel   flanella   13c, 25g
flash   lampeggiare   6a
flash of lightning   fulmine   6a
flashlight, battery   pila   23d, 25b
flat-chested   col seno piatto   11a
flat-heeled   con tacco piatto   25m
flatter   lusingare   21a
flattery   lusinga   21a
flatworm   verme   15d
flautist   flautista   28c
flavor   sapore, gusto   12e
flea   pulce   15d

flea market   mercato delle pulci   25a
flesh   carne   12a
fleshy   carnoso   11a
flexible   flessibile   11e
flier   dépliant   20c
flight   volo   32b
flight attendant   assistente di volo   32c
flight of stairs   rampa   23e
fling   lanciare   3f
flint   selce   13c
flood   alluvione   13b
floor   pavimento   23a
floor level   piano   23e, 35a
floor tile   piastrella   23a
floppy disc   dischetto   42b
Florence   Firenze   30c
florist   fiorista, fioraio (-a)   38a
flour   farina   24c
flow   scorrere   13b
flower   fiore, fiorire   14a
flower basket   canestro di fiori   3e
flower garden, flower bed   aiuola   14a
flu, influenza   influenza   40a
fluorescent   fluorescente   25b
flush   tirare lo sciacquone   23f
flute   flauto   28c
fly, zipper   cerniera   25g, 25l
flying time   durata del volo   32c
foam   schiuma   13b
focus   fuoco, mettere a fuoco   25d
fodder   foraggio   14a
fog   nebbia   6a
foggy   nebbioso   6a
folding chair   sedia pieghevole   23b
foliage   fogliame   14a
folk music   musica folk, musica folcloristica   25j, 28c
follow   seguire   3f, 36c
food   cibo   24a
food poisoning   intossicazione alimentare   40a

food store   negozio di alimentari
24m
foot   piede   3a, 12a
foot racing   corsa podistica   27b
footage   metraggio   28a
footlights   luci di ribalta   28e
footnote   nota a piè di pagina
19c
footpath, trail   sentiero   36b
footwear   calzatura   25m
for   per   8f
for example   per esempio   44e
for sale   in vendita   25a
for three days   da tre giorni   4c
forearm   avambraccio   12a
forecourt   cortile   23a
foreground   primo piano   28b
foreign country   paese straniero
43a
foreign currency   valuta straniera
31
foreigner   stranico (-a)   31
forensic science   medicina legale
39b
forest   foresta, bosco   13b
forger   contraffattore (-trice)
39b
forgery   contraffazione   39b
forget   dimenticare   22a, 22b
forget-me-not   miosotide   14b
forgetful   smemorato   22a
fork   forchetta   23c, 24k
form   forma   3d
form (to fill out)   modulo   26a,
31
format   format, formattare   38c,
42b, 42c
formatted   formattato   38c, 42b
Fortunately!   Per fortuna!   21c
fortune teller   chiromante   29b
forty   quaranta   1a
forty-one   quarantuno   1a
forty-third   quarantatreesimo
1b
forty-three   quarantatré   1a
forty-two   quarantadue   1a
Forward   Avanti   42c
Forward (e-mail)   Inoltra   42c

forwarding address   recapito
11f
fossil   fossile   43b
fossil fuel   combustibile   44a
foul weather   tempaccio   6a
foundations   fondamenta   23a
four   quattro   1a
four thousand   quattromila   1a
four-sided figure   figura a quattro
lati   2a
fourteen   quattordici   1a
fourth   quarto   1b
foyer, lobby   atrio   35a
fraction   frazione   1d
fractional   frazionario   1d
fracture   frattura   40a
fragrance   fragranza   12e
frail, slender   gracile   11a
frame   cornice, inquadrare   3d,
28b, 28d
frame (bodily)   ossatura   12a
France   Francia   30b
franchise   appalto   38d
franchiser   appaltatore (-trice)
38d
Franciscan   Francescano   11d
fraternal   fraterno   10a
fraud   frode   39b
freckles   lentiggini   11a, 12a
freckled   lentigginoso   11a
free   gratis   20c
free sample   campione omaggio,
esemplare omaggio   20c
free signal   libero   18b
freedom on bail   libertà su
cauzione   41
freehand drawing   disegno a
mano libera   28b
freeze   gelare   6a
freezer   congelatore   23b
freezing point   punto di
congelamento   13c
French   francese   30e
French fries   patatine fritte   24a
French Riviera   Costa Azzurra
30c
frenetic   frenetico   21a
frequency   frequenza   42a

frequent frequente 4c
fresco painting affresco 28b
fresh fresco 12e
Friday venerdì 5a
fried fritto 24a
friend amico (-a) 10b
friendly socievole 11e
friendship amicizia 10b, 21a
Friuli Friuli 30d
frivolous frivolo 11e
frizzy, fuzzy hair capelli crespi 11a
frog rana 15c
from da 3c, 8f
from my point of view dal mio punto di vista 44e
from now on d'ora in poi 4c
front fronte, facciata 3c
front seat sedile anteriore 33c
frost gelo 6a
frozen gelato, ghiacciato 6a
fruit frutta 14d, 24g
fruit basket canestro di frutta 3e
fruit bowl fruttiera 23c
fruit salad macedonia di frutta 24g
fruit vendor fruttivendolo 38a
fry friggere 24a
frying pan padella 23c
fuel carburante 13c
fugitive evaso (-a) 39b
full pieno 3b
full moon luna piena 13a
fullness ampiezza 3b
fun, enjoyment divertimento 21a
function funzione 1f
funding finanziamento 26a
funeral funerale 11c
funnel imbuto 23b
funny buffo 21a
fur coat pelliccia 25k
furious furioso 21a
furnish one's home ammobiliare la casa 23d
furniture mobili 23b
furrow solco 3d

fuse valvola 23d, 25b
fussy fastidioso 11e
future futuro 4c, 8a

G

gain guadagno 26b
gains, profits entrate 26b
galaxy galassia 13a
gallbladder cistifellea 12a
gallstones calcoli biliari 40a
game gioco 27a
game of chance gioco d'azzardo 27a
game, match partita 27b
garage garage 23a
garbage bin cestino dei rifiuti 23b
garbage truck autoimmondizie 34
garden giardino 14a, 23a
garden seat panchina 14a
gardener giardiniere (-a) 14a
gardening giardinaggio 27a
garlic aglio 14e, 24i
garment indumento 25k
gas benzina, gas 13c, 23d, 33a
gas attendant benzinaio (-a) 33a
gas pedal acceleratore 33c
gas pump pompa della benzina 33c
gas station stazione di servizio 33a
gas tank serbatoio 33c
gate, exit uscita 32b
gauze garza 13c, 39c
gears marcia 33a
gearshift leva del cambio 33c
Gemini Gemelli 5d
gemstone brillante, cristallo 25i
gender (grammatical) genere 8a
general strike sciopero generale 38d
generator dinamo 33c
generosity generosità 21a

generous   generoso   11e
Geneva   Ginevra   30c
Genoa   Genova   30c
genre   genere   25n, 28d
gentility, politeness   gentilezza   21a
gentle   gentile   11e
gentleman   signore   11a
geographical   geografico   13d
geography   geografia   13d, 37e
geometric design   disegno   geometrico   28b
geometrical   geometrico   2b
geometry   geometria   1g, 2b, 37e
Georgia   Georgia   30b
geranium   geranio   14b
German   tedesco   30e
German shepherd   cane lupo   15a
Germany   Germania   30b
gerund   gerundio   8a
gesture   gesto   3f
get a degree   laurearsi   37f
get a diploma   diplomarsi   37f
get a doctor   chiamare un medico   39c
get a job   procurarsi un lavoro   38d
get a suntan   abbronzarsi   36b
get better   migliorare   40a
get engaged   fidanzarsi   11c
get going   cominciare   3f
Get lost!   Vattene!   21a
get married   sposarsi   11c
get out   uscire fuori   39a
get out of drugs   uscire dalla   droga   44c
get up, rise   alzarsi   3f, 12b
ghetto   ghetto   44b
giant   gigante   11a
gift   regalo   25a
gill   branchia   15c
ginger   zenzero   24i
giraffe   giraffa   15a
girl   ragazza   11b
girlfriend   amica, ragazza   10b
give birth   partorire   11c

give help   dare aiuto   39a
Give my regards to   Tanti saluti   a, Salutami   19b
give oneself up   consegnarsi alla   polizia   39b
gladiolus   gladiolo   14b
glance   sguardo   12d
gland   ghiandola   12a
glare at someone   fissare   qualcuno   12d
glass   vetro   13c
glass cabinet   vetrina   23b
glimpse   occhiata fugace   12d
globe   globo, mappamondo   13d
gloomy   malinconico   11e
gloss paint, varnish   lacca   23d
glove   guanto   25k
glove compartment   cassetto   ripostiglio   33c
glow   risplendere   12d
glowworm   lucciola   15d
glue   colla   19d, 25c, 37b
go   andare   3f, 36c
go across   attraversare   3f
Go ahead, speak!   Di' (Dica)   pure!   17b
go around   andare in giro   3f
go away   andare via, andarsene   3f
go backwards   andare indietro   3f
go down   scendere   36c
go forward   andare avanti, fare   marcia avanti   3f, 33a
go on foot   andare a piedi   3f
go on strike   scioperare   38d
go on the air   andare in onda   20b
go on vacation   andare in vacanza   29a
go out   uscire   3f, 29b
go sightseeing   andare in giro   36b
go through a red light   passare   col rosso   33a
Go to   Vai a   42c
go to school   andare a scuola   11f

Go to the Devil!   Va' al diavolo!
21a
go toward   andare verso   3f
go up   salire   36c
goal   rete, gol   27b
goaltender   portiere   27b
goat   capra   15a
God   Dio, Signore   11d
godchild   figlioccio (-a)   10a
godfather   padrino   10a
godmother   madrina   10a
gold   oro   7a, 13c, 25i
gold ring   anello d'oro   25i
golden   d'oro   11c
goldfish   pesce rosso   15c
golf   golf   27b
Good!   Bene!   16c
good (at heart)   buono   11e
Good afternoon, Hello!   Buon
pomeriggio! Buona sera!   16a
Good-bye!   Arrivederci!
ArrivederLa!   16a
good complexion   carnagione
bella   11a
Good evening, Hello!   Buona
sera!   16a
good figure, shapely   bella figura
11a
good, final copy   bella copia
37f
Good Friday   Venerdì Santo
11d
Good luck! Best wishes!   Buona
fortuna! In bocca al lupo! Auguri!
16a, 16c
good mood   buon umore   21a
Good morning! Good day!   Buon
giorno!   16a
Good night!   Buona notte!   16a
good time, enjoyment
divertimento   29b
goose   oca   15b
gorilla   gorilla   15a
Gospel   Vangelo   11d
gossip   pettegolezzo, spettegolare
17a
govern   governare   43a
government   governo   43a

government bond   buono del
tesoro   43a
governmental   governativo   43a
grab   afferrare   3f
graceful   grazioso   11e
grade   classe   37a
grade one   prima   37a
grade, mark   voto   37f
graduate   laureato (-a), diplomato
(-a)   11f
grain   grano   14a, 24c
gram   grammo   3a
grammar   grammatica   8a
grammar book   grammatica
37b
grammar check   controllo della
grammatica   42c
granary   granaio   14a
grand piano   piano a coda   28c
grandchild   nipote   10a
grandfather   nonno   10a
grandfather clock   orologio a
pendolo   4d
grandmother   nonna   10a
granite   granito   13c
grapefruit   pompelmo   14d, 24g
grapes   uva   14d, 24g
graph   grafico   3d, 37f, 42b
graphic interface   interfaccia
grafica   42b
grass   erba   13b
grasshopper   cavalletta   15d
grate   grattugiare   12c
grateful   grato   21a
grater   grattugia   23c
gravel   ghiaia   13c
gravity   gravità   13a
gray   grigio   7a
gray hair   capelli grigi   11a
graze   pascolare   15a
Great Britain   Gran Bretagna
30b
great grandchild   pronipote
10a
great grandfather   bisnonno
10a
great grandmother   bisnonna
10a

great-aunt   prozia   10a
great-uncle   prozio   10a
Greece   Grecia   30b
greedy   avaro   11e
Greek   greco   30e
green   verde   7a
greenhouse   serra   14a
greenhouse effect   effetto serra
    13c
Greenland   Groenlandia   30b
greet   salutare   3f, 16a
greeting   saluto   16a, 19c
Greetings!   Saluti! Salve!   16a,
    19a, 19b
grenade   granata   44d
grievance   lamentela   38d
grilled   alla griglia   24a
grind   sgretolare   12c
grocer   droghiere (-a)   38a
groom   sposo   11c
gross national product   prodotto
    nazionale lordo   38d
gross profit   guadagno lordo
    38d
ground floor   pianterreno, platea
    23e, 28a, 35a
group work   lavoro in gruppo
    37f
grow   crescere   3b
grow up   crescere   11b
growth   crescita   3b
grumpy   scorbutico   11e
guarantee   garantire   17a
guard   guardiano (-a)   38a
guard dog   cane da guardia   15a
Guatemala   Guatemala   30b
Guatemalan   guatemalteco   30e
guerrilla warfare   guerriglia
    44d
guide   guida   30a
guidebook   guida   25n, 36a
guilt   colpevolezza   41
guilty   colpevole   41
guitar   chitarra   28c
guitarist   chitarrista   28c
gulf   golfo   13b, 13d
gullible   semplice   21a
gully   burrone   13b

gums   gengive   40b
gun   rivoltella   39b
guts   ventre   12a
gutter   fognatura, grondaia   23a,
    36a
gym shoes   scarpe da ginnastica
    25m
gymnasium   palestra   27b, 37c
gymnast   ginnasta   27b
gymnastics   ginnastica   27b
gynecologist   ginecologo (-a)
    40a
gynecology   ginecologia   40a

H
haggard face   viso stravolto
    11a
hail   grandine, grandinare   6a
Hail Mary   Ave Maria   11d
hailstorm   tempesta di grandine
    6a
hair (bodily)   pelo   12a
hair (head)   capelli   12a
hair cream   brillantina   25f
hairnet   retina   25f
hair remover   crema depilatoria
    25f
hair dye   tinta   25f
hairdresser   parrucchiere (-a)
    12f, 38a
hairdryer   asciugacapelli   12f,
    25f
hairpin   fermaglio   25f
hairspray   lacca (per capelli)
    25f
hairstyle   acconciatura (dei
    capelli)   11a
hairy   peloso   11a
Haitian   haitiano   30e
half   metà, mezzo   3b
half-brother   fratellastro   10a
half-sister   sorellastra   10a
hallucination, high   allucinazione
    44c
hallway   corridoio   37c
ham   prosciutto   24d
hammer   martello   23d, 25b
hamster   criceto   15a

hand (of a clock, watch) lancetta
4d, 12a, 25i

hand mano 12a

hand bomb bomba a mano 44d

hand cream crema per le mani
25f

hand luggage bagaglio a mano
31

handbag borsa 3e

handcuffs manette 39b

handful manciata 3b

handkerchief fazzoletto 25k

handle maniglia, manico,
maneggiare 3f, 23a, 33c

handlebar manubrio 34

handrail ringhiera 23a

handshake stretta di mano 16a

hang up riattaccare il telefono
18b

happen, occur accadere, avvenire
4c

happiness felicità 21a

happy felice, allegro 11e, 21a

Happy Birthday! Buon
compleanno! 11c, 16c, 29c

Happy Easter! Buona Pasqua!
5f, 16c

happy face viso allegro 11a

Happy New Year! Buon anno!
5f, 16c, 29c

hard drive hard drive 19f

hard drug droga pesante 44c

hard-headed cocciuto 21a

hard-working laborioso 11e

hardware ferramenta, hardware
23d, 38c, 42b

hardware store negozio di
ferramenta 25b

hardwood legno duro 13c

hare lepre 15a

harmony armonia 28c

harp arpa 28c

harpist arpista 28c

harpsichord clavicembalo 28c

harvest raccolta, raccogliere
14a

hat cappello 25k

hate odiare 21b

hateful odioso 11e

hatred odio 21b

haughty altezzoso 21a

have avere 40a

have a backache avere mal di
schiena 40a

have a class, a lesson avere
lezione 37f

Have a good time! Buon
divertimento! 16c

Have a good vacation! Buona
vacanza! 16c, 29c

have a headache avere mal di
testa 40a

Have a nice trip! Buon viaggio!
30a

have a slim waistline avere una
vita snella 11a

have a snack fare uno spuntino
24a

have a sore throat avere mal di
gola 40a

have a sore stomach avere mal di
stomaco 40a

have a temperature avere la
febbre 40a

have a toothache avere mal di
denti 40b

have breakfast fare colazione
24a

have chills avere i brividi 6b

have dinner cenare 24a

Have fun! Buon divertimento!
29c

have lunch pranzare 24a

have patience, be patient avere
pazienza 21a

hawk falco 15b

hay fieno 14a

hazelnut nocciolo 14c

he lui, egli 8g

head testa 12a

head of government capo del
governo 43a

head of state capo dello stato
43a

head of the family capofamiglia
10a

head office sede principale 26a, 38d

heading intestazione 19c

headline titolo 20a

headphones cuffie, auricolari 20b, 32c

headquarters quartiere generale 44d

heal guarire 40a

health salute 12b

health food store negozio dietetico 24m

healthy sano 12b

hear, feel, sense sentire 12c

hearing (legal) udienza 41

hearing udito 12c

hearing aid apparecchio acustico 40a

heart cuore 12a

heart attack infarto cardiaco 40a

heartbeat battito del cuore 12a

heartburn bruciore di stomaco 40a

heat calore 13c

heater termosifone 23b

heating riscaldamento 23d

heaven, paradise paradiso 11d

heavy pesante 3b, 11a, 25g, 31

heavy-weight peso massimo 27b

hectare ettaro 3a

hectogram ettogrammo, etto 3a

hedge siepe 14a

hedgehog riccio 15a

heel tallone, tacco 12a, 25m

hefty robusto, pesante 11a

height altezza, statura 3a, 11a

hell inferno 11d

Hellenic ellenico 43b

Hello! Pronto! 18b

helmet casco 27b

help aiuto, aiutare 39a

Help! Aiuto! 39a, 39b, 39c

help command comando help, aiuto 42b

help line il telefono azzurro 7a

hematoma ematoma 40a

hemorrhage, bleeding emorragia 40a

heptagon ettagono 2a

her, to her la, lei, le, a lei 8g

herb erba 24i

here qua, qui 3c, 36c

heredity eredità 11c

hernia ernia 40a

hero, heroine eroe (-ina) 28d, 28e

heroin eroina 44c

herpes erpete 40a

herring aringa 15c, 24e

herself si 8g

hesitant restio 21a

hesitate esitare 17a

hesitation esitazione 17a

hexagon esagono 2a

Hi, Bye! Ciao! 16a

hide-and-seek rimpiattino 27a

high altar altare maggiore 11d

high blood pressure ipertensione 40a

high chair seggiolone 23b

high definition television televisione ad alta definizione 20b

high forehead fronte alta 11a

high jumping salto in alto 27b

high school, lyceum liceo 37a

high school diploma diploma (certificato) di maturità 11f, 37f

high school graduate diplomato (-a) 38b

high school principal preside di liceo 37d

high season alta stagione 30a, 35a

high, tall alto 3b

high-heeled con tacco alto 25m

highlight sottolineare 28d

highlighter evidenziatore 25c, 37b

highway autostrada 33a, 36b

highway police polizia stradale 33a
hijack dirottare 39b
hijacking dirottamento 39b
hill colle, collina 13b
himself si 8g
Hindu Indù 11d
Hinduism Induismo 11d
hinge cardine 23a
hip anca 12a
hippopotamus ippopotamo 15a
hire assumere 38d
hired killer sicario 39b
hiring assunzione 38d
hiss sibilare 15a
historian storico (-a) 43b
history storia 37e, 43b
hit battere, colpire 3f, 27b
hitchhike fare l'autostop 34
hitchhiker autostoppista 34
HIV positive sieropositivo 40a
hive alveare 15d
hoarfrost brina 6a
hobby hobby 27a
hockey hockey 27b
hockey rink campo di ghiaccio 27b
hockey stick bastone 27b
hoe zappa, zappare 14a
hold hands tenersi per mano 3f
hole buco 25g, 25l
holiday giorno festivo 29a
Holland Olanda 30b
Holy Ghost Santo Spirito 11d
Holy Trinity Santa Trinità 11d
holy war guerra santa 44d
home delivery consegna a domicilio 25a
homeless senzatetto 44b
homeopathy omeopatia 40a
homily omelia 11d
homing pigeon piccione 15b
homosexuality omosessualità 44b
Honduran honduregno 30e
Honduras Honduras 30b

honest onesto 11e
honesty onestà 11e
honey miele 24c
honeymoon luna di miele 11c
honorable onorevole 21a
hood cappuccio 25k
hood, bonnet cofano 33c
hoof zoccolo 15a
hook gancio, amo 15c, 23b, 27a
hoop cerchio 27a
hope speranza, sperare 21a
horizontal orizzontale 2b, 3c
hormone ormone 40a
horn (car) clacson 33c
horn (animal) corno 28c
horn player cornista 28c
hornet calabrone (m) 15d
horoscope oroscopo 5d
horror film film dell'orrore 28a
horse cavallo 15a
horse power cilindrata 33c
horse race corsa ippica 27b
horse racing ippica, equitazione 27a, 27b
hose tubo, innaffiare 14a
hospital ospedale 39c
host ostia 11d
hostage ostaggio (-a) 39b, 44d
hostel ostello 35a
hostile party parte avversa 41
hot caldo 6a
hot water acqua calda 35b
hotel albergo 35a
hotel room camera 35a
hound cane da caccia 15a
hour ora 4b
house casa, alloggiare 23a, 23f
house call visita domiciliare 40a
house mortgage mutuo fondiario 26a
house number numero di casa 11f
house painter imbianchino (-a) 38a
housefly mosca 15d

household   casa, domicilio, focolare   10a

household soap   sapone di Marsiglia   23b

householder   proprietario (-a)   23f

how   come   9

How are you?   Come sta (stai)?   16a

How come?   Come mai?   9

How do you get to…?   Come si fa per andare a…?   36c

How do you say…?   Come si dice…?   17b

How lucky!   Che fortuna!   16c

how much   quanto   3b

How much does it cost?   Quanto costa?   25a

How much is it?   Quanto è?   25a

How's it going?   Come va?   16a

How's the weather?   Che tempo fa?, Com'è il tempo?   6b

however   tuttavia, comunque   8I, 17b, 44e

howl   ululare   15a

hum   mormorare   12c

human rights   diritti umani   44d

humanity   umanità   11e

humble   umile   11e

humid, damp   umido   6a

humidity   umidità   6a

humor   umorismo   21a

hunched   curvo   11a

hundredth   centesimo   1b

Hungarian   ungherese   30e

Hungary   Ungheria   30b

hunger   fame   12b

hunt   caccia, cacciare   15a, 27a

hunter   cacciatore (-trice)   15a

hunting   caccia   27a

hurricane   uragano   6a

hurry   affrettarsi, sbrigarsi   3f

Hurry! Come quickly!   Presto!   39b

hurt   fare male a   12b

husband   marito   10a, 11c

husky, manly   aitante   11a

hut, beach house   capanno   23a

hyacinth   giacinto   14b

hydrangea   ortensia   14b

hydrogen   idrogeno   13c

hyena   iena   15a

hygiene   igiene   12f

hygienic   igienico   12f

hymn   inno, cantico   11d, 28c

hypermarket   ipermercato   24m

hypertext   ipertesto   19f, 42b

hypocrite   ipocrita   21a

hypocritical   ipocrita   21a

hypotenuse   ipotenusa   2b

hypothesis   ipotesi   22a

I

I   io   8g

I am 55 years old.   Ho cinquantacinque anni.   11b

I believe that…   credo che…   44e

I can't stand the cold.   Non sopporto il freddo.   6b

I can't stand the heat.   Non sopporto il caldo.   6b

I can't stand…   Non sopporto…   21b

I didn't understand!   Non ho capito!   17b

I don't believe it!   Non ci credo!   21c

I don't feel like…   Non mi va (ho voglia) di…   21c

I don't know if…   non so se…   44e

I don't understand.   Non capisco.   9

I doubt that…   dubito che…   44e

I think that…   penso che…   44e

I want some   ne voglio   3b

I was born in 1994.   Sono nato (-a) nel 1994.   5e

I wish!   Magari!   16c, 21c

I would like to say that . . .   vorrei dire che . . .   44e

I would like to speak with   Posso parlare con   18b

I'll be glad, happy to do it!   Lo farò con piacere!   16c

I'm not sure that...   non sono sicuro (-a) che...   44e

I'm serious!   Dico sul serio!   21c

I'm sorry!   Mi dispiace!   16c, 21c

I'm sorry, wrong number.   Scusi, ho sbagliato numero.   18b

I'm sure that...   sono sicuro (-a) che...   17b, 44e

ice   ghiaccio   6a, 13b

ice cream   gelato   24h, 29b

ice cream parlor   gelateria   24m, 29b

ice skating   pattinaggio su ghiaccio   27b

icon   icona   38c, 42b

icosahedron   icosaedro   2a

idea   idea   22a

idealist   idealista   11e

identification   identificazione   11f

identification card   carta d'identità   31, 35a

identify   identificare   17a

identity   identità   11f

ideology   ideologia   43a

idle   ozioso   21a

if   se   8i

If you don't mind...   Se non ti (Le) dispiace...   16c

ignorance   ignoranza   22a

ignorant   ignorante   11e, 22a

ill-mannered   maleducato   11e

illegal   illegale   41

illiteracy   analfabetismo   25n

illiterate person   analfabeta   25n

illumination   illuminazione   12d

illustrated magazine   rivista illustrata   20a, 25n

image   immagine   25d, 28b, 28d

imaginary   immaginario   1d

imagination, fantasy   immaginazione, fantasia   22a

imaginative   immaginativo   11e

imagine   immaginare   22b

immigrant   immigrante   44d

immigration   immigrazione   44d

immoral   immorale   21a

immune system   sistema immunitario   12a

impatient   impaziente   11e

imperative   imperativo   8a

imperfect   imperfetto   8a

imperialism   imperialismo   43a

impetuous   impetuoso   11e

imply   implicare   17a

import   importare   26b

Impossible!   Impossibile!   21c

impressionable   impressionabile   11e

Impressionism   Impressionismo   28b

imprison   imprigionare, incarcerare   41

imprudent   imprudente   11e

impulsive   impulsivo   11e

in   in   3c, 8f

in a hurry   in fretta   8j

in a little while   fra (tra) poco   8j

in an hour's time   tra un'ora   4c

in conclusion   in conclusione   44e

in fact   infatti   8i

in favor   favorevole   43a

in front of   di fronte, davanti   3c, 36c

in love   innamorato   11c

in my opinion   a mio parere   17b, 44e

in my own opinion   secondo me   17b

in record time   a tempo di record   27b

in slow motion   al rallentatore   28a

in style   di moda   25l

in the afternoon   nel pomeriggio,
di pomeriggio   4b

in the city   in città   11f

in the country   in campagna
11f, 36b

in the evening   di sera   4b

in the event that   nel caso che
8i

in the long run   a lungo andare
4c

in the long term   a lungo termine
4c

in the meanwhile   intanto, nel
frattempo   4c, 8j

in the middle   in mezzo (nel
mezzo)   3c

in the morning   di mattina   4b

in the mountains   in montagna
36b

in the short term   a breve
scadenza, a breve termine   4c

in the suburbs   in periferia   11f

in time   in orario   4c

incense   incenso   11d

inch   pollice   3a

income   reddito   26a, 38d

Incoming mail   Posta in arrivo
42c

incompetent   incompetente   11e

inconsiderate   incosciente   11e

incontinence   incontinenza   40a

incorruptible   incorruttibile
11e

increase   aumento, incremento
3b

Incredible!   Incredibile!   16c

indecent   indecente   21a

indecisive   indeciso   11e

indefinite   indeterminativo   8a

independent   indipendente   11e

index   indice   38c, 42b

index finger   indice   12a

India   India   30b

Indian   indiano   30e

indicate   indicare   17a

indication   indicazione   17a

indicative   indicativo   8a

indifference   indifferenza   21a

indifferent   indifferente   11e,
21a

indigent   indigente   11e

indigestion   indigestione   40a

indirect (object)   di termine,
indiretto   8a

individualist   individualista   11e

indolent   indolente   21a

Indonesia   Indonesia   30b

Indonesian   indonesiano   30e

industrial   industriale   13c

Industrial Revolution
rivoluzione industriale   43b

industrialist   industriale   38a

industry   industria   13c

inept, unfortunate   disgraziato
11e

inexpensive   a buon mercato,
economico   25a

infallible   infallibile   11e

infancy   infanzia   11b

infantile   infantile   11b

infection   infezione   40a

inferiority   inferiorità   21a

infinitive   infinito   8a

inflamed   infiammato   40a

inflammation   infiammazione
40a

inflation   inflazione   26a, 43a

inflation rate   tasso d'inflazione
26a

inform   informare   17a

informant   informatore (-trice)
39b

informatics   informatica   37e

information   informazione,
informazioni   17a, 33b, 42b

information counter   banco,
informazioni   11f

information radio   l'onda verde
7a

infraction   infrazione   39b

infrared light   luce infrarossa
13a

ingenious   ingegnoso   11e, 22a

ingenuity   ingegno   22a

ingenuous, naive   ingenuo   11e

inhale inspirare 12b
inherit ereditare 11c
inheritor erede 11c
injection, needle iniezione, puntura 25h, 40a
injure, wound ferire 39b
injury, wound ferita, infortunio 39b, 40a
ink inchiostro 25c, 37b, 38c
ink-jet printer stampante a getto d'inchiostro 38c
innocence innocenza 41
innocent innocente 41
inorganic inorganico 13c
input digitare 38c
inputting on the screen videoscrittura 19f, 38c, 42b
insect insetto 15d
insensitive insensibile 11e
Insert Inserisci 42c
inside dentro 3c, 36c
insinuate insinuare 17a
insipid insipido 12e
insistent, unrelenting insistente 11e
insolent insolente 11e
insomnia insonnia 40a
installation installazione 38c, 42b
instant istante 4b
instead invece 8j
institute istituto 37a
instrument strumento 25j, 27a, 28c
insufficient evidence insufficienza di prove 41
insulation isolante 23d, 25b
insulin insulina 25h, 40a
insurable assicurabile 26a
insurance assicurazione 26a, 30a
insurance card carta verde 33a
insurance company società d'assicurazione 26a
insurance policy polizza d'assicurazione 26a
insure assicurare 26a

insured person assicurato (-a) 26a
insurrection insurrezione 43b
integer intero 1d
integral calculus calcolo integrale 1g
integrated circuit circuito integrato 42b
intellectual intellettuale 11e
intelligence intelligenza 22a
intelligent intelligente 11e, 22a
intensive care unit sala di rianimazione 40a
interactive interattivo 19f, 38c, 42b
intercom citofono 18a, 23e, 38c
interest interesse 22a, 26a
interest loan prestito a interesse 26b
interest rate tasso d'interesse 26a
interesting interessante 16c, 22a
interests, hobbies interessi 11f
interface interfaccia 42b
interference interferenza 42a
intermission intervallo 28e
internal affairs affari interni 43a
international call telefonata internazionale 18b
international flight volo internazionale 32b
internet internet 19f, 38c
internet provider provider 19f, 42b
interpret interpretare 17a
interrogate interrogare 17a
interrogative interrogativa 8a
interrupt interrompere 17a
interruption interruzione 17a
intersection incrocio 33a, 36a
interview intervista 20a, 25n
intestine, bowel intestino 12a
intransitive intransitivo 8a
intrepid intrepido 21a

It's very hot.   Fa molto caldo.
  6b
It's windy.   Tira vento.   6b
Italian   italiano   30e
italics   corsivo   19c
Italy   Italia   30b
itch   prudere   12e, 40a
itchiness (itch)   prurito   40a
itchy   pruriginoso   12e
ivory   avorio   7a
Ivory Coast   Costa d'Avorio
  30c
ivy   edera   14b

J
jack   cric   33c
jackal   sciacallo   15a
jacket   giacca   25k
Jamaica   Giamaica   30b
Jamaican   giamaicano   30e
jamb   stipite   23a
janitor   bidello (-a)   37d
January   gennaio   5b
Japan   Giappone   30b
Japanese   giapponese   30e
jar, tin   barattolo   3e
javelin   giavellotto   27b
javelin throwing   lancio del
  giavellotto   27b
jaw   mandibola   12a, 40b
jawbone   mascella   12a
jazz   jazz   25j
jealous   geloso   11e
jeer   fischiare   17a
jellyfish   medusa   15c
jest   scherzare   17a
jest, prank   scherzo   17a
Jesuit   Gesuita   11d
Jesus Christ   Gesù Cristo   11d
jewel   gioiello   25i
jeweler   gioielliere (-a)   38a
jewelry store, jeweler   gioielleria,
  orefice   25i
jingle, clink, jangle   jingle,
  tintinnare   12c, 20c
job   mestiere   11f, 38a
jogging   jogging   27a
joint   articolazione   12a

joke (oral)   barzelletta   17a
Jordan   Giordania   30b
Jordanian   giordano   30e
journalist   giornalista   20a, 38a
jovial   gioviale   11e
joy   gioia   21a
joyous   gioioso   11e
Judaism   Giudaismo   11d
judge   giudice, giudicare   22b,
  41
judgment, wisdom   giudizio
  22a
judiciary   giudiziario   43a
judo   judo   27b
jug   brocca   23c
juice   succo   24j
juicy   succoso   24a
July   luglio   5b
jump   saltare   3f, 27b
jumper   saltatore (-trice)   27b
June   giugno   5b
June 23   il ventitré giugno   5e
junior high school   scuola media
  37a
Jupiter   Giove   13a
juridical, legal, authorized
  giuridico   43a
jurisprudence, law
  giurisprudenza, legge   37e
juror   giurato (-a)   41
jury   giuria   41
just, as soon as, barely   appena
  4c, 8j
justice   giustizia   41
justice of the peace   giudice di
  pace   41
justification   giustificazione
  38c, 42b
juvenile delinquency   delinquenza
  minorile   39b
juvenile delinquent   delinquente
  minorile   39b

K
kangaroo   canguro   15a
karate   karatè   27b
keep quiet   stare zitto   17a
kennel   canile   15a

Kenya   Kenya   30b
Kenyan   keniano   30e
kettle   pentolino   23c
key   chiave   23f, 28c, 35a
keyboard   tastiera   25c, 38c, 42b
keyword   parola chiave   42b
kick   calciare, dare un calcio, prendere a calci   3f, 27b
kidnap   sequestrare   39b
kidnapper   sequestratore   39b
kidnapping   sequestro   39b
kidney   rene   12a
kidney stone   calcolo renale   40a
kids magazine   giornalino   20a, 25n
kill   uccidere   39b
kill two birds with one stone   pigliare due piccioni con una fava   15b
killer   assassino, sicario   39b
kilogram   chilogrammo, chilo   3a
kilometer   chilometro   3a
kindergarten   asilo infantile   37a
kindness   gentilezza   11e
king   re   43a
kingfisher   martin pescatore   15b
kiosk, booth   chiosco   25a, 36a
kiss   bacio, baciare   11c, 21b
kitchen   cucina   23a
kitchen scales   bilancia   23b
kitchen shelf   mensola   23b
kite   aquilone   27a
kitten   gattino   15a
knapsack   zaino   27b
knee   ginocchio   12a
kneel   inginocchiarsi   3f, 11d
knickers   calzoni   25k
knife   coltello   23c, 24k, 39b
knit   lavorare a maglia   27a
knobby   nodoso   12e
knock   bussare   3f
knot   nodo   13c
knotty   nodoso   13c

know   sapere, conoscere   22b
know someone   conoscere   16b
knowledge   conoscenza   22a
knowledgeable   ben informato   22a
Koran   Corano   11d
Korea   Corea   30b
Korean   coreano   30e
Kuwait   Kuwait   30b
Kuwaiti   kuwaitiano   30e

L

label   etichetta   25a, 25c, 38c
labor shortage   scarsezza di manodopera   38d
labor surplus   eccesso di manodopera   38d
labor union   sindacato   38d, 43a
laboratory   laboratorio   37c
labyrinth, maze   labirinto   3d
lace   pizzo   13c, 25g, 25l
lack   mancare   25a
lack of breath   senza fiato   12b
laconic   laconico   28d
ladder   scala   39a
ladle   mestolo   23c
lady   signora   11a
ladybug   coccinella   15d
lagoon   laguna   13b
lake   lago   13b, 36b
lamb   agnello   15a, 24d
lamp   lampada   23b, 35b
land   terra, atterrare   13b, 32c
landing (plane)   atterraggio   32c
landing (staircase)   pianerottolo   23a
landing gear   carrello   32c
landscape   paesaggio   13b, 28b
lane (traffic)   corsia   33a
Lane reserved   Corsia preferenziale   33b
languages   lingue   37e
languages lyceum   liceo linguistico   37a
lanky, long-legged   slanciato   11a

Laos Laos 30b
Laotian laoziano 30e
lap, stage tappa 27b
laptop computer computer portatile, laptop 19f, 25c, 37b, 38c
large grosso 11a
large bill banconota di grosso taglio 26a
large garbage can bidone 23b
large loan prestito ingente 26b
lark allodola 15b
laryngitis laringite 40a
lasagna lasagne 24b
lascivious lascivo 21a
laser printer stampante laser 25c, 38c, 42b
last scorso, durare 4c
last a long time durare a lungo 4c
last a short time durare poco 4c
last evening ieri sera 4b
last month il mese scorso 4c
last night ieri notte 4b
last year l'anno scorso 4c
late tardi 4c, 8j
late, delayed in ritardo 32b
Latin America America Latina 30b
latitude latitudine 13d
Latium Lazio 30d
laudable lodevole 21a
laugh ridere 21a
laughter risata 21a
launderette lavanderia automatica 25g
laundry biancheria, lavanderia 23b, 25g
laundry basket cesta del bucato 23b
lava lava 13b
law legge 41
law courts palazzo di giustizia 36a
law faculty facoltà di giurisprudenza 37a
lawn prato (erboso) 14a

lawn bowling bocce 27a, 27b
lawn chair sedia a sdraio 23b
lawn mower falciatrice 14a
laws of the marketplace leggi del mercato 26b
lawsuit querela 41
lawyer avvocato 16b, 38a, 41
laxative purga 25h, 40a
lay person, secular laico 11d
layer, stratum strato 13b
layout stesura 3d
lazy pigro 11e
lead piombo 13c
leaf foglia 14a
leaf through sfogliare 25n
lean scarno 11a
lean against appoggiarsi a 3f
leap balzare 3f
leap year anno bisestile 5b
learn imparare, apprendere 22a, 22b, 37f
learning apprendimento 37f
lease contratto d'affitto 23e
leather pelle, cuoio 13c
leather shoes scarpe di cuoio 25m
leave, depart partire 3f, 34
leave of absence congedo 38d
Lebanese libanese 30e
Lebanon Libano 30b
lecture conferenza 17a
left sinistra 3c, 36c
left turn, exit left svolta a sinistra 33a
left-wing di sinistra 43a
leg gamba 12a
leg (chicken, turkey, etc.) coscia 24a
legal legale 41
legal assistance assistenza legale 39b, 44b
legal consultant consulente legale 38a
legal tender corso 26b
legend leggenda 25n, 28d
legislation legislazione 43a
legislative legislativo 43a

legislature   legislatura   43a

leisure   svago, tempo libero   29b

lemon   limone   7a, 14d, 24g

lemonade   limonata   24j

length   lunghezza   3a, 3c

lengthen   allungare   3c, 25l

lens   lente   12d, 25d

Lent   Quaresima   11d

lentil   lenticchia   14e, 24f

Leo   Leone   5d

leopard   leopardo   15a

lesbian   lesbica   44b

lesion   lesione   40a

less   meno   3b

lesson, class   lezione   37f

Let me introduce you to…   Ti (Le) presento…   16b

let off steam   sfogarsi   21a

lethargic   letargico   21a

letter   lettera   18a, 9d

letter carrier   postino (-a)   19e

letter opener   tagliacarte   19d

letterhead   carta intestata   19d, 25c, 38c

lettuce   lattuga   14e, 24f

leukemia   leucemia   40a

level   livello   3b, 3c

Level crossing   Passaggio a livello   33b

level of education   titolo di studio   37f

level-headed   equilibrato   21a

lewd   indecente   21a

liability, loan   ipoteca, responsabilità   26a, 26b

liar   bugiardo   11e

liberal   liberale   43a

liberal party   partito liberale   43a

Liberia   Liberia   30b

Liberian   liberiano   30e

libidinous   libidinoso   21a

Libra   Bilancia   5d

librarian   bibliotecario (-a)   37d, 38a

library   biblioteca   25n, 36a, 37c

Libya   Libia   30b

Libyan   libico   30e

license plate   targa   33c

lie   bugia, dire una bugia   17a

lie down   sdraiarsi   3f

life   vita   11c

life imprisonment   ergastolo   41

life insurance   assicurazione sulla vita   26a

life jacket   salvagente, giubbotto di salvataggio   32c, 34

lift   alzare   3f

lift weights   sollevare pesi   27b

light   luce   6a, 13a, 35b

light (car)   faro   33c

light (weight)   leggero   25g, 25l, 31

light (clear)   chiaro   7b

light blue, sky blue   celeste   7a

light bulb   lampadina   23d, 25b

light music   musica leggera   25j

light signal   segnale luminoso   42a

light, power   luce   23d

light-hearted   allegro   21a

lighter   accendino   25e

lightning (bolt of)   lampo, fulmine   6a

Liguria   Liguria   30d

likable   piacevole   11e

like   piacere   21b

liking   simpatia   21b

lily   giglio   14b

lily of the valley   mughetto   14b

lima bean   fava   14e, 24f

limb   arto   12a

Limited parking   Sosta limitata   33b

line   riga, linea   2b, 19c

line (fishing)   lenza   27a

line (verbal)   battuta   28e

line up   fare la coda   15b

line, verse   verso   25n, 28d

linear algebra   algebra lineare   1g

lined   a righe   3d

lined paper   carta a righe   37b

lotion lozione 25f
louse pidocchio 15d
love amore, amare 11c, 21b
love affair relazione (amorosa) 10b
lover amante 10b
loving amoroso 11e
low forehead fronte bassa 11a
low season bassa stagione 30a, 35a
low-heeled con tacco basso 25m
lower-case character carattere minuscolo 19c
Lucania Basilicata 30d
luggage rack portabagaglio 33c, 35a
lullaby ninna nanna 28c
lump sum somma forfettaria 26b
lunar eclipse eclissi lunare 13a
lunch pranzo 24a, 35a
lunch break pausa mensa 38d
lung polmone 12a
lusty lussurioso 21a
Luxembourg Lussemburgo 30b
Luxembourger lussemburghese 30e
luxury hotel albergo di lusso 35a
lymphatic system sistema linfatico 12a

M

macaroni maccheroni 24b
Macedonia Macedonia 30b
Macedonian macedone 30e
mackerel sgombro 15c
made-to-measure suit abito, vestito su misura 25l
Madonna, Virgin Mary Madonna 11d
Madrid Madrid 30c
madrigal madrigale 28c
magazine rivista 20a, 25n
magic tricks giochi di prestigio 27a

magician prestigiatore (-trice) 27a
magistrate magistrato 41
magnanimity magnanimità 21a
magnanimous magnanimo 21a
magnesium magnesia 13c
magnesium citrate citrato di magnesio 25h, 40a
Magnificent! Magnifico! 16c
magnolia magnolia 14b
magpie gazza 15b
mahogany mogano 13c
maid cameriera 35a
maid-of-honor damigella d'onore 11c
mail posta, spedire 19e
mail delivery distribuzione della posta 19e
mail truck furgone postale 19e
mail withheld for pick-up fermo posta 19e
mailbox cassetta postale, delle lettere 19e, 23a
main principale 8a
main character protagonista 28e
main door portone 23e, 35a
main office segreteria 37c
main role ruolo principale 28e
main story titolo principale 20a
make a call fare una telefonata 18b
make a connection collegare 20b
make an appointment fissare un appuntamento 40a
make bigger aggrandire 3b
make mistakes sbagliare 37f
makeup trucco 12f, 25f, 28e
Malaysia Malaysia 30b
Malaysian malaysiano 30e
male maschio, maschile 11a, 38b
malicious malizioso 11e
malicious gossip maldicenza 17a

malign, speak badly of   malignare
17a

malignant   maligno   40a

malleable   malleabile   21a

mallet   mazza   23d, 25b

Malta   Malta   30b

Maltese   maltese   30e

mammal   mammifero   15a

man   uomo   11a

management   direzione, gestione
38d

management board   comitato
direttivo   38d

manager   direttore (-trice)   26a,
35a, 38d

mandarin orange   mandarino
14d, 24g

mandolin   mandolino   28c

mandolin player   mandolinista
28c

mane   criniera   15a

maniacal   maniaco   21a

manicure   manicure   12f, 25f

manslaughter   omicidio
preterintenzionale   39b

manual   manuale   37b

manure   concime   14a

manuscript   manoscritto   28d

many   molti (-e), tanti (-e)   8h

Many thanks!   Grazie mille!   16c

map   cartina, geografic, mappa
37b

maple   acero   14c

marble   marmo, bilia   13c, 27a

marble sculpture   scultura in
marmo   28b

marbled   marmorizzato   3d

march   marciare   3f

March   marzo   5b

mare   cavalla   15a

margin   margine   3d, 19c, 42b

marigold   calendola   14b

marijuana   marijuana   44c

marionette   marionetta   27a

marital status   stato civile   11c,
11f, 38b

maritime   marittimo   13b

mark, correct   correggere   37f

marker   pennarello   25c, 37b, 38c

market   mercato   38d

market price   prezzo di mercato
26b

market research   ricerche di
mercato (di marketing)   38d

marmalade, jam   marmellata
24c

marmot   marmotta   15a

marriage   matrimonio, sposalizio,
nozze   11c, 11f

marriage counselor   consigliere
(-a) matrimoniale   38a

marriage vow   promessa di
matrimonio   11c

married   coniugato (-a), sposato
(-a)   11c, 11f, 38b

marry   sposare   11c

Mars   Marte   13a

martyr   martire   11d

martyrdom   martirio   11d

Marvelous!   Meraviglioso!   16c

mascara   mascara   12f, 25f

masculine   maschile   8a, 11a

masher   pestello   23c

mask   maschera   27b

masked ball   ballo in maschera
28c

masking tape   nastro isolante
23d, 25b

Mass   Messa   11d

mass   massa   3b

massive   massivo   3b

masterpiece   capolavoro   28b

match   fiammifero   25e

material   stoffa   25g, 25l

maternal   materno   10a

mathematician   matematico (-a)
1f

mathematics   matematica   1g,
37e

matrimonial   matrimoniale   11c

matter   materia   13c

mattress   materasso   23b

mature person   persona matura
11b

mauve   malva   7a

maximum   massimo   3b, 6c

maximum temperature
  temperatura massima   6c
May   maggio   5b
May I help you?   Desideri?
  Desidera?   16c
May I introduce you to…?
  Posso presentarti (presentarLe)…?
  16b
May I speak with…?   Posso
  parlare con.,.?   18b
May I?   È permesso? Posso? Si
  può?   16c
mayor   sindaco   43a
me, to me   mi, me, a me   8g
meadow   prato   14a
meal   pasto   24a
mean   significare   17a
mean-minded   meschino   21a
meaning   significato   17a
measles, red measles   morbillo,
  roseola   40a
measure, size   misura, misurare   3b
measuring tape   metro   3b
meat   carne   24d
mechanic   meccanico (-a)   33a,
  38a
medical checkup   visita di
  controllo   40a
medical examination   esame
  medico   40a
medical faculty   facoltà di
  medicina   37a
medicine   medicina   25h, 37e
medicine chest   armadietto dei
  medicinali   23a
medieval   medioevale   43b
mediocre   mediocre   21a, 21b
mediocrity   mediocrità   21a
Mediterranean   Meditterraneo
  6a, 30c
medium   medio   3b
meet   conoscere   16b
Melanesia   Melanesia   30b
melody   melodia   25j, 28c
melon   melone   14d, 24g
melt   sciogliere   6c
melting point   temperatura del
  ghiaccio fondente   6c

membrane   membrana   12a
memoirs   memorie   25n, 28d
memorize   memorizzare   22b
memory   memoria   22a, 38c,
  42b
memory capacity   capacità di
  memoria   42b
men's clothing store
  abbigliamento maschile   25k
men's shoes   scarpe da uomo
  25m
men's suit   abito, vestito da uomo
  25k
men's watch   orologio da uomo
  25i
mend   rammendare   25g
menopause   menopausa   40a
menstruation   mestruazione   40a
mention   menzionare   17a
menu   menù   38c, 24a, 42c
meow   miagolare   15a
merchandise   merce   25a, 38d
merciful   pietoso   21a
merciless   spietato   21a
Mercury   Mercurio   13a
mercury   mercurio   6c, 13c
merge   fondere   38d
Merge   Confluenza   33b
merit, worth   merito   11e
meritorious   meritevole   11e
Merry Christmas!   Buon Natale!
  5f, 16c, 29c
message   messaggio   35a, 42a,
  42c
metal   metallo   13c
metaphor   metafora   28d
meteor   meteora   13a
meter   metro   3a
meticulous   meticoloso   11e
Mexican   messicano   30e
Mexico   Messico   30b
microphone   microfono   20b
microprocessor   microprocessore
  38c, 42b
microscope   microscopio   13c
microwave   microonda   13c
microwave oven   forno a
  microonde   23b

middle mezzo 3c
middle age mezza età 11b
Middle Ages Medioevo 43b
Middle East Medio Oriente 30b
Middle Easterner mediorientale 30e
middle finger (dito) medio 12a
middleweight peso medio 27b
midge moscerino 15d
midget nano (-a) 11a
midnight mezzanotte 4b
midwife levatrice 38a
migratory bird uccello migratore 15b
Milan Milano 30c
mild mite, tiepido 6a, 24a
mile miglio 3c
military green verde militare 7a
military service servizio militare 11f
milk latte 24h
milk jug brocca del latte 23c
millennium millennio 4b
millimeter millimetro 3a
millionth milionesimo 1b
mincer tritacarne 23c
mind mente 22a
mineral minerale 13c
mineral water acqua minerale 24j
minestrone soup minestrone 24b
minimum minimo 3b, 6c
minimum temperature temperatura minima 6c
minister ministro 11d
ministry ministero 43a
Ministry of Education Ministero della Pubblica Istruzione 37a
minivan pulmino 34
mink visone 15a
mint menta 14e, 24i
minus meno 1e, 1f, 6c
minute minuto 4b
mirror specchio 23a

miscarriage aborto spontaneo 11c, 40a
mischievous malizioso, capriccioso 11e, 21a
miss (a bus) perdere 34
Miss, Ms. Signorina 11f, 16b
missile missile 13a, 44d
missionary missionario (-a) 11d
mist, haze foschia 6a
mistake sbaglio 37f
mistletoe vischio 14b
misunderstanding fraintendimento 17a
mixed salad insalata mista 24a
mocking, derisive beffardo 21a
modal modale 8a
model modello 28b
modem modem 18a, 25c, 38c, 42b
modest modesto 21a
modest hotel albergo modesto 35a
moisturizer crema idratante 25f
molar molare 40b
Moldavia Moldavia 30b
Moldavian moldavo 30e
mole talpa 15a
Molise Molise 30d
mollusk, shellfish mollusco 15c
molotov cocktail bomba molotov 44d
mom mamma 10a
moment momento 4b
Monaco Monaco 30b
monarchist party partito monarchico 43a
monarchy monarchia 43a
monastery monastero 11d
Monday lunedì 5a
money denaro, soldi 26a
Mongolia Mongolia 30b
Mongolian mongolo 30e
monk frate 11d
monkey scimmia 15a

monologue   monologo   28e
monopoly   monopolio   38d
Montenegro   Montenegro   30b
month   mese   4b, 5b
monthly   mensile, mensilmente   4b, 5b
monument   monumento   36a
moo   muggire   15a
mood (emotion)   umore   21a
mood (grammar)   modo   8a
moody   lunatico   21a
moon   luna   5c, 6a, 13a
moonbeam   raggio della luna, lunare   6a, 13a
mop   scopa di stracci   23b
moralistic   moralistico   21a
more   più, di più   3b
Mormon   Mormone   11d
morning   mattina, mattino   4b
Moroccan   marrocchino   30e
Morocco   Marocco   30b
morose   scontroso   11e
mortar   mortaio   23c
mortgage   mutuo   26a
Moscow   Mosca   30c
mosque   moschea   11d
mosquito   zanzara   15d
mother   madre   10a
mother-in-law   suocera   10a
motif   motivo   28d
motion   mozione   43a
motor   motore   32c, 33c
motor scooter   motorino, vespa   34
motorcycle   motocicletta   34
motorcycling   motociclismo   27b
motorway restaurant   autogrill   36b
mound   pedana di lancio   27b
mount   monte   13b
mountain   montagna   13b
mountain boots   scarponi   36b
mountain chain   catena montuosa   13b
mountain climbing   alpinismo   27b, 36b
mouse (computer)   mouse   19f, 25c, 42b

mouse (rodent)   topo   15a
mouth   bocca   12a, 40b
Move   Sposta   42c
move   muovere, muoversi, traslocare   3f, 23f
movement   movimento   3f
movie camera   cinepresa   28a
movie star   stella del cinema   28a
movie theater   cinema   28a
movies   cinema   29b
moving (residence)   trasloco   23f
mow, reap   falciare   14a
Mr.   Signore   11f, 16b
Mrs., Ms.   Signora   11f, 16b
mud, silt   fango   13b
muddy   fangoso   13b
muffler   marmitta   33c
mug   boccale   23c
mugginess   afa   6a
muggy   afoso   6a
mule   mulo   15a
mullet   triglia   15c
multimedia   multimedialità   42b
multinational (company)   multinazionale   38d
multiple   multiplo   1f
multiplication   moltiplicazione   1e
multiplication table   tavola pitagorica   1e
multiplied by   moltiplicato per   1e
multiply   moltiplicare   1e
multiracial society   società multirazziale   44d
mumps   orecchioni   40a
municipal   municipale   43a
mural painting   pittura murale   28b
murder   assassinio, uccidere   39b
murderer   omicida   39b
murmur   mormorare   17a
muscle   muscolo   12a
muscular   muscoloso   11a

museum   museo   36a
mushroom   fungo   14e, 24f
music   musica   25j, 28c, 37e
music stand   portamusica   25j, 28c
musical film   film musicale   28a
musician   musicista   25j, 28c
musicologist   musiologo (-a)   28c
Muslim   Musulmano (-a)   11d
mussel   cozza   15c, 24e
mustache   baffi   11a, 12a
my   mio, mia, miei, mie   8e
My dear John   Mio caro Giovanni   19b
My dear Mary   Mia cara Maria   19b
My name is ...   Mi chiamo ...   11f, 16b
myself   mi   8g
mystery movie   film giallo   28a
mystery, detective genre   giallo   20a, 25n, 28d
mystic   mistico   11d
mysticism   misticismo   11d
myth   mito   11d, 25n, 28d
mythology   mitologia   25n, 28d

N
nail   chiodo, inchiodare   23d, 25b
nail file   lima per unghie   25f
nail polish   smalto   12f, 25f
name   nome   11f, 38b
name day   onomastico   29a
nanny, housekeeper   governante   23f
nape   nuca   12a
napkin   tovagliolo   23c, 24k
Naples   Napoli   30c
narration   narrazione   28d
narrative, fiction   narrativa   25n, 28d
narrator   narratore (-trice)   25n, 28d
narrow   stretto   3b, 3c
narrow-minded   di vedute ristrette   11e

nasturtium   nasturzio   14b
nation   nazione   13d
national   nazionale   13d, 43a
national press   stampa nazionale   20a
national, domestic flight   volo nazionale   32b
nationality   nazionalità   11f, 31, 38b
natural   naturale   13b
natural resources   risorse naturali   44a
nature   natura   13b
naughty, saucy   spinto   21a
nausea   nausea   40a
navigate   navigare   19f, 38c, 42b
near   vicino, presso   3c, 36c, 8j
Near East   Vicino Oriente   30b
nearly   quasi   3c
neat   ordinato   11e
neck   collo   12a
necklace   collana   25i
needle   ago   44c
negative   negativo   1d, 25d, 28b
negligent   negligente   11e
neigh   nitrire   15a
neither...nor   non...né...né   8k
neon   neon   25b
nephew   nipote   10a
Neptune   Nettuno   13a
nerve   nervo   12a
nerve gas   gas nervino   44d
nervous   nervoso   11e
nervous system   sistema nervoso   12a
nest   nido   15b
net (soccer)   porta   27b
net profit   guadagno netto   38d
nettle   ortica   14b
network   network, rete   38c, 42a, 42b
neutron   neutrone   13c
never   non...mai   4c, 8k
New Year   Anno Nuovo   5f
New Year's Day   Capodanno   5f, 29a
New Year's Eve   Vigilia di Capodanno   5f, 29a

New York   New York   30c
New Zealand   Nuova Zelanda
30b
New Zealander   neozelandese
30e
newborn   neonato (-a)   11b, 11c
newlyweds   novelli sposi   11c
newsflash   notizia flash   20b
news item, article, report
cronaca   20a
newspaper   giornale   20a, 25n
newsroom   sala di redazione   20a
newsstand   edicola   25a, 34
Nicaragua   Nicaragua   30b
Nicaraguan   nicaraguense   30e
nickel   nichelio   13c
nickname   soprannome   11f
niece   nipote   10a
Nigeria   Nigeria   30b
Nigerian   nigeriano   30e
night   notte   4b
night work   lavoro notturno   38d
night-dress   camicia da notte   25k
nightingale   usignolo   15b
nine   nove   1a
nineteen   diciannove   1a
ninety   novanta   1a
ninth   nono   1b
nipple   capezzolo   12a
nitrogen   nitrogeno   13c
No!   No!   16c
No entrance   Vietato l'ingresso
33b
No entry   Divieto di accesso   33b
No exit   Vietata l'uscita   33b
No left turn   Divieto di svolta a
sinistra   33b
no more, no longer   non…più
8k
no one   non…nessuno   3b, 8k
No parking   Sosta vietata   33b
No passing   Divieto di sorpasso
33b
No right turn   Divieto di svolta a
destra   33b
No smoking   Vietato fumare   33b
No stopping   Divieto di fermata
32a, 33b

No thoroughfare   Divieto di
transito   33b
No U-turn   Divieto di inversione
a U   33b
No way!   Per carità! Macché!
16c, 21a
nod   fare un cenno   3f
noise   rumore   12c
noisy   rumoroso, chiassoso   12c,
21a
non-carbonated   liscia   24j
non-confidence vote   sfiducia
43a
non-Euclidean geometry
geometria non euclidea   1g
non-teaching personnel
personale non docente   37d
non-transferrable check   assegno
barrato   26a
nonconformist   anticonformista
11e
noon   mezzogiorno   4b
north   nord   3c, 13d, 36c
North America   America del
Nord   30b
North American   nordamericano
30e
North Pole   Polo Nord   13d
north-east   nord-est   3c, 13d
north-west   nord-ovest   3c,
13d
northern   settentrionale   3c, 13d
Norway   Norvegia   30b
Norwegian   norvegese   30e
nose   naso   12a
nostril   narice   12a
nosy   ficcanaso   21a
Not bad!   Non c'`e male!   16a
not even   non…neanche
(nemmeno, neppure)   8k
not really, not quite   non…mica
8k
note (message)   appunto, notare
17a, 37f
note (musical)   nota   20a, 25j,
28c
notebook, workbook   quaderno
37b

nothing   non…nulla, niente   3b, 8k

nothing to declare   niente da dichiarare   31

notice board   tabella avvisi   25c, 38c

noun   nome   8a

novel   romanzo   20a, 25n, 28d

novelist   romanziere (-a)   25n, 28d

novelistic   romanzesco   25n

November   novembre   5b

now   ora, adesso   4c, 17b

nowadays   oggigiorno   4c, 8j

nowhere   da nessuna parte   3c

nth root   ennesima radice   1e

nucleus   nucleo   13c

nude   nudo   28b

number   numero, numerare   1d, 8a, 38b

numeral   numerale   1d

numerical   numerico   1d

nun, sister   suora   11d

nuptial, wedding ring   anello nuziale   25i

nurse   infermiere (-a)   38a, 40a

nursery   vivaio   14a

nursery school   scuola materna   37a

nutcracker   schiaccianoci   23c

nylon   nailon   25g, 25l

O

oak   quercia   14c

oar   remo   27b, 34

oats   avena   14a, 24c

obedient   ubbidiente   21a

obese   obeso   11a

object   complemento, obiettare   8a, 17a

objective lens   obiettivo   25d

oboe   oboe   28c

oboist   oboista   28c

obsequious   ossequioso   21a

obstetrician   ostetrico (-a)   40a

obstinate   ostinato   11e

obtuse   ottuso   2b, 11e

obtuse-angled   ottusangolo   2a

occasional job   lavoro saltuario   38d

occasionally   di tanto in tanto, ogni tanto   4c

occupant, householder · residente   23f

occupation   occupazione   38a

occupational hazard   rischio del mestiere   38d

ocean   oceano   13b

Oceania   Oceania   30b

octagon   ottagono   2a

octahedron   ottaedro   2a

October   ottobre   5b

October first   il primo ottobre   5e

octopus   polipo   15c

oculist   oculista   38a, 40a

odd   dispari   1d

oddball   bizzarro   21a

ode   ode   25n, 28d

of   di   8f

offend   offendere   17a

offer a job   offrire un lavoro   38d

office   ufficio   38d

office (of an instructor)   studio   37c

office hours   orario d'ufficio   38c, 40b

office supplies   forniture per ufficio   25c, 38c

office worker   impiegato (-a)   38a

official paper   carta protocollo   19d

offspring   discendenza   11c

often   spesso   4c

Oh my!   Mamma mia!   21c

oil   olio   24i, 33c

oil painting   pittura a olio   28b

ointment   pomata   25h, 40a

old   vecchio   11b

old age   vecchiaia, terza età   11b

older   maggiore, più vecchio, più grande   11b

older brother   fratello più grande, fratello maggiore   11b

older person   vecchio (-a)   11b
olfactory   olfattivo   12e
olive   oliva   14d, 24f
olive skin   pelle olivastra   11a
olive tree   ulivo, olivo   14c
Olympic games   giochi Olimpici   27b
omelet   frittata   24h
on   su   3c, 8f
on account of   a causa di   8i
on sale   in saldo   25a
on the air   in onda   20b
on time   in orario   32b, 34
on top   in cima   3c
on vacation   in vacanza   36b
once   una volta   4c
once in a while   ogni tanto   4c
Once upon a time…   C'era una volta…   4c
one   uno   1a
one (in general)   si   8h
one billion   un miliardo   1a
one hundred   cento   1a
one hundred and one   centouno   1a
one hundred and two   centodue   1a
one hundred million   cento milioni   1a
one hundred thousand   centomila   1a
one million   un milione   1a
one thousand   mille   1a
one thousand and one   milleuno   1a
One way   Senso unico   33b
One-800 number   numero verde   18b
one-half   metà, mezzo   1c
one-quarter   un quarto   1c
one-third   un terzo   1c
one-way ticket   biglietto di andata   30a
onion   cipolla   14e, 24f
online   online   38c, 42b
online reservation   prenotazione on-line   30a
only   solo   8j

opal   opale   25i
opaque   opaco   7b
Open   Aperto   25a, 33b
open an account   aprire un conto   26a
open up a mortgage   accendere un mutuo   26a
opening time   apertura   25a
opera   opera   25j, 28c
operate   operare   40a
operating room   sala operatoria   40a
operation   intervento chirurgico   40a
operator   centralino   18a
opinion   opinione   22a
opponent   avversario (-a)   27b
opposite   opposto   2b
optic cable   cavo ottico   20b
optic fiber   fibra ottica   20b
optical reader   videolettore, lettore ottico   42a, 42b
optics   ottica   42a
optimist   ottimista   11e
optional subject   materia opzionale   37f
Options   Opzioni   42c
optometrist   optometrista   40a
oral   orale   17a
oral exam   esame orale   37f
orange (fruit)   arancia   14d, 24g
orange (tree)   arancio   14c
orange (color)   arancione   7a
orangeade   aranciata   24j
orbit   orbita, orbitare   3d, 13a
orchestra   orchestra   25j, 28c
orchestra conductor   direttore (-trice) (d'orchestra)   25j, 28c
orchid   orchidea   14b
order   ordine, ordinare, prendere   11d, 17a, 24n
ordinal   ordinale   1d
ordinate   ordinata   2b
oregano   origano   24i
organ   organo   12a, 28c
organic   organico   13c
organist   organista   28c

pantomime   pantomima   28e
pantry   dispensa   23a
pants   pantaloni   25k
pantyhose, tights   collant   25k
papacy   papato   11d
paper   carta   19d, 25c, 37b, 38c
paper cup   bicchiere di carta   24k
parable   parabola   11d
parabola   parabola   2a
parachuting   paracadutismo   27b
parade   parata   27a, 29b
paragraph   capoverso   19c
Paraguay   Paraguay   30b
Paraguayan   paraguaiano   30e
parallel   parallela   2b
parallelepiped   parallelepipedo   2a
parallelogram   parallelogramma   2a
paralysis   paralisi   40a
paramedic   paramedico   40a
parent   genitore (-trice)   10a
parenthesis, bracket   parentesi   19c
Paris   Parigi   30c
parish   parrocchia   11d
parish priest   parroco   11d
parishioner   parrocchiano (-a)   11d
park   parco   36a
parking   parcheggio   33a
parking meter   parchimetro   36a
parliament   parlamento   43a
parody   parodia   25n, 28d
parrot, budgie   pappagallo   15b
parsley   prezzemolo   14e, 24i
part   parte   3b
parted hair   capelli con la riga   scriminatura   11a
partial   parziale   3b
participle   participio   8a
particle   particella   13c
partition, wall   parete   23a
partitive   partitivo   8a

partner   socio (-a)   38a
partnership   partnership   38d
partridge   pernice   15b
party   partito   43a
party, feast   festa   29b
pass   passo, sorpassare, passare   13b, 27b, 33a
pass an exam   superare un esame   37f
pass by   passare davanti   3f
pass near   passare vicino   3f
passenger   passeggero (-a)   32c
passing   approvazione   43a
Passing lane   Corsia di sorpasso   33b
passion   passione   21a
passive   passivo   8a
passport   passaporto   31
passport control   controllo   passaporti   31
password   password   38c, 42c
past   passato   4c, 8a
past absolute   passato remoto   8a
pasta   pasta   24b
Paste   Incolla   42c
pastel   pastello   28b
pastille   pasticca   25h, 40a
pastry shop   pasticceria   24m
paternal   paterno   10a
path   sentiero   14a
pathologist   patologo (-a)   40a
patience   pazienza   21a
patient   paziente   11e, 40a
patio   terrazza   23a
patrol   pattuglia, pattugliare   39b
pattern   modello, modellare   3d
patterned   modellato   3d
paunch   pancia   11a
pavement, sidewalk   marciapiede   36a
pay   paga, pagare   25a, 26a, 38d
pay bail   versare la cauzione   41
pay claim   rivendicazione salariale   38d
pay day   giorno di paga   38d
pay duty   pagare la dogana   31

pay off   saldare   26a
pay off a mortgage   estinguere un mutuo   26a
payment   pagamento   26a
payment on delivery   pagamento a pronta cassa   26a
pea   pisello   14e, 24f
peace   pace   14d, 44d
peach (fruit)   pesca   24g
peach (tree)   pesco   14c
peacock   pavone   15b
peak   vetta   13b
peanut (as sold in the USA)   nocciolina americana   14d, 24g
peanut (in general)   arachide   14d, 24g
pear (fruit)   pera   14d, 24g
pear (tree)   pero   14c
pearl   perla   25i
pearl gray   grigio perla   7a
pebble   ciottolo   13b
pedal   pedale   34
pedestal   piedistallo   28b
pedestrian   pedone   33a
pedestrian crosswalk   passaggio pedonale   33a, 36a
pediatrician   pediatra   40a
peel   sbucciare   24a
peep, peer   sbirciare   12d
pelican   pellicano   15b
pelvis   pelvi   12a
pen   penna   2b, 7b, 19d, 25c
penalty   rigore   27b
penance   penitenza   11d
pencil, crayon   matita   2b, 7b, 25c
pendant   pendente   25i
penguin   pinguino   15b
penicillin   penicillina   25h, 40a
peninsula   penisola   13b
pension, retirement   pensione   38d
pentagon   pentagono   2a
peony   peonia   14b
people   gente   10b
pepper   pepe   14e, 14f, 24i
pepper container   pepiera   23c
per hour   all'ora   3a

per minute   al minuto   3a
per second   al secondo   3a
perceive   percepire   12b
percent   percento   1f
percentage   percentuale   1f
percussion instruments   strumenti a percussione   28c
perfect   perfetto   8a
perfectionist   perfezionista   11e
perfidious   perfido   21a
performance   messa in scena   28e
performer   interprete   25j, 28s
perfume   profumo   12f, 25f
perimeter   perimetro   2b
period (of time)   periodo   43b
period (in a sentence)   punto   19c
periodical   periodico   20a, 25n
peripheral   unità periferica   19f, 38c, 42b
periphery, outskirts   periferia   3d
perjury   falsa testimonianza   39b
permanent memory   memoria fissa   38c, 42b
perpendicular   perpendicolare   2b
person   persona   8a, 10b
personal   personale   8a
personal income tax   imposta sul reddito delle persone fisiche   26b
personal information   dati anagrafici   11f
personal organizer   agenda   38c, 42b
personality   personalità   11e
personality test   test psicologico   38d
perspective, framework   ottica   28d
perspire   sudare   6b
persuade   persuadere   22a, 22b, 41
Peru   Perù   30b
Perugia   Perugia   30c
Peruvian   peruviano   30e

perverted   pervertito   21a
pessimist   pessimista   11e
pest   parassita   14a
pesticide   insetticida   14a
pet   animale domestico   15a
petal   petalo   14a
petroleum   petrolio   13c, 44a
petunia   petunia   14b
pew   banco di chiesa   11d
pharmaceutical   farmaco   25h,
   40a
pharmacist   farmacista   25h,
   38a, 40a
pharmacy, drugstore   farmacia
   25h
pheasant   fagiano   15b
phial   fiala   25h, 40a
philanthropic   filantropico
   21a
philanthropy   filantropia   21a
Philippines   Filippine   30b
philosophy   filosofia   37e
phone bill   bolletta del telefono
   18a
phone book   elenco telefonico
   18a
phone booth   cabina telefonica
   18a
phone call   telefonata   18b
phone card   scheda telefonica
   18a
phone keyboard   tastiera del
   telefono   18a
phone number   numero di
   telefono   11f, 18b
phonetics   fonetica   8a
phosphate   fosfato   13c
photo-sensitive   fotosensibile
   25d
photocopier   fotocopiatrice
   19d, 25c, 38c
photocopy   fotocopia, fotocopiare
   37f
photocopy shop   copisteria   19d
photograph   foto, fotografia
   25d, 28b
photographer   fotografo (-a)
   25d, 28b

photographic shot   ripresa
   fotografica   25d, 28b
phrase   frase   19c
physical   fisico   13c
physical education   educazione
   fisica   37f
physical therapist   fisioterapista
   38a
physics   fisica   13c, 37e
pianist   pianista   28c
piano   pianoforte, piano   28c
pick up one's baggage   ritirare il
   bagaglio   32a
pickpocket   scippatore (-trice)
   39b
picky, fastidious   pignolo   11e
picnic   picnic   29a
piece   pezzo   3b
piece of furniture   mobile   23b
piece work   lavoro a cottimo
   38d
Piedmont   Piemonte   30d
pig   maiale   15a
pile   mucchio, catasta   3b
pilgrim   pellegrino (-a), peregrino
   (-a)   11d
pilgrimage   pellegrinaggio   11d
pill   pillola   25h, 40a
pillow   cuscino   23b, 35b
pillow case   federa   23b
pilot   pilota   38a
pimple   foruncolo   11a, 12a
pinball machine   flipper   27a
pinch   pizzicare   3f
pine   pino   14c
pineapple   ananas   14d, 24g
pink   rosa   7a
pipe   pipa   25e
pirate program   programma
   pirata   42a
Pisa   Pisa   30c
Pisces   Pesci (pl)   5d
pistachio   pistacchio   14d, 24g
pistol   pistola   39b
piston   pistone   33c
pitch   lanciare   27b
pitch black   nero come la pece
   7a

pitcher lanciatore 27b
pitchfork forcone 14a
pizza parlor pizzeria 24l
place posto, luogo 3c, 19c, 38b
place of birth luogo di nascita 11f
plain pianura 13b
plaintiff querelante 41
plane pialla 23d, 25b
plane figure figura piana 2a
planet pianeta 5c, 13a
planner agenda 25c
plant pianta, piantare 14a
plant (manufacturing) stabilimento 38d
plaque placca dentaria 40b
plaster intonaco, ingessatura 13c, 40a
plaster cast fascia gessata 40a
plasterer intonacatore (-trice) 38a
plastic plastica 13c
plastic surgeon chirurgo estetico 40a
plate piatto 24k
plate-rack scolapiatti 23c
platform programma elettorale 43a
platinum platino 13c
platter piatto misto 24a
play (theater) recita, rappresentazione teatrale 20a, 25n
play (an instrument) suonare 27a, 28c
play (a game) giocare 27a
play (action) gioco, azione 27b
play ball (soccer) giocare al pallone 27a
play out of tune stonare 28c
play skipping rope saltare con la corda 27a
player (sports) giocatore (-trice) 27b
player (music) suonatore (-trice) 25j, 28c
playful giocoso 21a

playing card carta da gioco 27a
playoffs, championship campionato 27b
playwright commediografo (-a) 25n
plea supplica, dichiararsi 41
pleasant, nice piacevole, simpatico 11e, 21b
pleasant, friendly face viso simpatico 11a
Please! Per favore! 16c
pleased, content contento 11e, 21a
pleated skirt gonna a pieghe 25k
plebeian plebeo, plebe 43b
pliers, tongs, tweezers pinze, tenaglie 23d, 25b
plot trama 20a, 25n, 28d, 28e
plow aratro, arare 14a
plug spina 23d, 25b
plum prugna, susina 14d, 24g
plumber idraulico 38a
plumbing sistema idraulico 23d
plump pasciuto 11a
pluperfect trapassato 8a
plural plurale 8a
plus più 1e, 1f, 6c
Pluto Plutone 13a
pneumonia polmonite 40a
Po river Po 30c
pocket tasca 25g
pocket calculator calcolatrice tascabile 37b
pocket-picking scippo 39b
poem poesia 20a, 25n
poet poeta (-essa) 25n, 28d
poetics poetica 25n, 28d
poetry poesia 25n
point punto 2b, 27b
point out segnalare 28d
poison gas gas tossico 44d
Poland Polonia 30b
polar bear orso bianco 15a
pole polo 13d
pole vaulting salto con l'asta 27b

police   polizia   39b, 39c
police headquarters
   commissariato   39b
police officer   poliziotto (-a)
   39b
police station   questura   36a, 39b
police van   furgone della polizia
   39b
police officer   carabiniere (-a),
   poliziotto (-a)   33a, 38a
policy (in general)   politica
   43a
Polish   polacco   30e
politeness, courtesy   cortesia
   11e
political science   scienze politiche
   37e
politician   politicante   43a
polka   polca   28c
poll   sondaggio   20b, 43a
pollen   polline   14a
pollute   inquinare   13c
polluted   inquinato   44a
pollution   inquinamento   13c, 44a
polyester   poliestere   25g
polygon   poligono   2a
polyhedron   poliedro   2a
Polynesia   Polinesia   30b
Polynesian   polinesiano   30e
pompous   pomposo   21a, 28d
pontiff   Pontefice   11d
poodle   barboncino   15a
pool   piscina   35a
poor   povero   11e
Poor man! Poor woman!
   Poveretto! Poveretta!   21c
pope   Papa   11d
poplar   pioppo   14c
poppy   papavero   14b
porcelain   porcellana   13c
porch   veranda   23a
porcupine   porcospino   15a
pore   poro   12a
pork   maiale   24d
pornographic magazine   rivista
   pornografica   20a, 25n
pornographic movie   film
   pornografico   28a

pornography   pornografia   44b
portable phone   telefono portatile
   18a
portable radio   radio portatile
   20b
porter   assistente ai bagagli
   32a
portfolio   portafoglio   26a
porthole   oblò   34
portion, helping   porzione   3b,
   24a
portrait   ritratto   28b
Portugal   Portogallo   30b
Portuguese   portoghese   30e
pose   posa   28b
position   posizione   3c
positive   positivo   1d
possessive   possessivo   8a, 11e
post office   ufficio postale   19e
postage   affrancatura   19e
postal box   casella postale
   19e
postal card   cartolina postale   19e
postal check   assegno postale
   19e
postal code   codice postale   19e,
   38b
postal money order   vaglia
   postale   19e
postal package   pacco postale
   19e
postal rate   tariffa postale   19e
poster   cartellone pubblicitario
   20c
posterior   posteriore   4c
pot   pentola, casseruola, tegame
   23c
pot-bellied   panciuto   11a
potassium   potassio   13c
potato   patata   14e, 24f
potato masher   schiacciapatate
   23c
potato peeler   pelapatate   23c
pottery   arte della ceramica   27a
pound   libbra   3a
pour   versare   24a
pouring rain   pioggia torrenziale
   6a

poverty povertà 44b
power potenza, potere 1e, 43a
power brake servofreno 33c
power of attorney procura 41
power steering servosterzo 33c
practice esercitarsi 28c
praise lodare, elogiare 17a, 21a
prawn, shrimp scampo, gambero 15c, 24e
pray pregare 11d, 17a
prayer preghiera 11d, 17a
preach predicare 11d, 17a
preacher predicatore (-trice) 11d
preaching, sermon predica 11d
precede precedere 3f
precious prezioso 25i
precipice precipizio 13b
precise preciso 11e
predicate predicato 8a
prefab casa prefabbricata 23a
preface prefazione 25n, 28d
prefer preferire 21b
Preferences Preferiti 42c
pregnancy gravidanza 11c, 40a
pregnant incinta 11c, 40a
prehistoric preistorico 43b
premature birth parto prematuro 11c
premeditated crime delitto premeditato 39b
premiere showing prima visione 28a
preposition preposizione 8a
prescribe prescrivere 40a
prescription ricetta medica 25h, 40a
present presente 4c, 8a
present perfect passato prossimo 8a
presentable presentabile 21a
presently attualmente 4c
president presidente 43a
president of a university rettore 37d
press stampa 25n

press conference conferenza stampa 20a
press room sala stampa 20a
press agency agenzia di stampa 20a
pressure pressione 13c
pressure cooker, steamer pentola a pressione 23c
presumptuous presuntuoso 11e, 21a
pretentious pretenzioso 11e
pretty carino 11a
price prezzo 24l, 25a, 35a
price list tariffa dei prezzi 25a
price tag etichetta 25a
prickly spinoso, pungente 12e
pride superbia 11d
priest prete 11d
primary school scuola primaria 37a
prime primo 1d
prime minister primo ministro 43a
primrose primula 14b
prince principe 43a
princess principessa 43a
principal preside 37d
print stampare 19f, 38c, 42b, 42c
print (medium) stampa 20a
print run, circulation tiratura 20a
print, mold stampa 28b
printed matter stampe 19e
printer stampante 19d, 25c, 38c, 42b
printing tipografia 20a
prism prisma 2a
prison prigione 41
prisoner detenuto (-a) 39b
private channel canale privato 20b
private detective investigatore privato 39b
private school scuola privata 37a
private television televisione privata 20b

public relations office ufficio
pubbliche relazioni 38d
public school scuola pubblica
37a
public television televisione
pubblica 20b
public transport trasporto
pubblico 34
publish pubblicare 20a, 25n
publisher editore 20a, 25n,
28d
puck disco 27b
pudding budino 24c
pudgy tozzo 11a
Puerto Rican portoricano
30e
Puerto Rico Puerto Rico 30b
pull tirare 3f
pull a tooth estrarre un dente
40b
pulpit pulpito 11d
pulse polso 40a
pump pompa 33c
pumpkin zucca 14e, 24f
punch (paper) perforatrice
19d, 25c, 38c
punch (tool) punzone 25b
punctilious puntiglioso 11e
punctuation punteggiatura
19c
puny smunto 11a
pupil (student) alunno (-a)
37d
pupil (eye) pupilla 12a
puppet theater teatro dei
burrattini 27a
puppy cucciolo, cagnolino 15a
purchase acquisto 25a
pure puro 7a, 11e
purgatory purgatorio 11d
purple, violet viola 7a
purse borsa 31
pus pus 40a
push spingere 3f
push button (on a camera)
scatto 25d
push drugs spacciare droga
39b

put mettere 3f
put a space interlineare 42b
put down posare 3f
put forward avanzare 17a
put into a mailbox imbucare
19e
put on (clothes) mettersi 25l
put on (shoes) mettersi (le
scarpe) 25m
put on makeup truccarsi 12f
put on perfume profumarsi
12f
putrid putrido 12e
puzzle enigma 27a
puzzle section enigmistica
20a, 25n
pyramid piramide 2a
pyramidal piramidale 3d
Pythagorean theorem teorema di
Pitagora 2b

Q

quadrilateral quadrilatero 2a
quadrille, square dance
quadriglia 28c
qualifications Qualifiche 38b
quality qualità 21a
quantity quantità 3b
quarrelsome litigioso 11e
quart quarto 3a
quarter term quadrimestre
37f
quartet quartetto 28c
quartz watch orologio al quarzo
25i
queen regina 43a
question domanda 37f
question mark punto
interrogativo 19c
questioning interrogatorio 39b
queue, lineup fila, coda 25a
quickly velocemente 3f
quiet quieto 11e
Quiet! Silenzio! 16c, 21c
quilt trapunta 23b
quintet quintetto 28c
Quite well! Abbastanza bene!
16a

quotation   citazione, quotazione   26b, 28d

quotation marks   virgolette   19c

quote   citare   28d

quote (stock price)   quotare   26b

quotient   quoziente   1f

R

rabbi   rabbino   11d

rabbit   coniglio   15a

raccoon   procione   15a

race, racing   corsa   27b

racism   razzismo   44b, 44d

racist   razzista   44d

radiation   radiazione   13c, 44a

radiator   radiatore   33c

radio   radio   20b

radio advertising   pubblicità radiofonica   20c

radio broadcasting   radiodiffusione   20b

radio frequency   banda a modulazione di frequenza   20b

radio network   rete radiofonica   20b

radio news   giornale radio   20b

radio station   stazione radio   20b

radio wave   onda radiofonica   20b

radioactive   radioattivo   13c

radioactive waste   rifiuto radioattivo   44a

radiography   radiografia   40a

radiologist   radiologo (-a)   40a

radish   ravanello   14e, 24f

radius   raggio   2a

raft   zattera   34

rag   cencio   25g, 25l

railroad   ferrovia   34

railway crossing   passaggio a livello   36a

rain   pioggia, piovere   6a

rain heavily   piovere a dirotto   6a

raincoat   impermeabile   25k

rainy   piovoso   6a

raise   sollevare   3f

raise one's voice   alzare la voce   17a

raise to a power   elevare alla potenza di   1e

rake   rastrello, rastrellare   14a

ram   montone, ariete   15a

RAM memory   memoria RAM   42b

ramp   rampa   33a

range of products   gamma di prodotti   25a

ransom   riscatto   39b

rap   rap   25j

rape   violenza carnale, violentare   39b

rapist   violentatore   39b

rare   raro   4c

rare (meat)   al sangue   24a

rare thing   mosca bianca   7a

rarely   raramente   4c

rash   eruzione cutanea   40a

raspberry   lampone   14d, 24g

rat   ratto   15a

rate   tariffa, tasso   26a, 33d

rather   piuttosto   8j

ratify   ratificare   43a

ratio, proportion   proporzione   1e

rational   razionale   1d, 11e

rattle   sonaglio   12c

rattlesnake   serpente a sonagli   15c

ravioli   ravioli   24b

razor   rasoio   12f, 25f

reach   raggiungere   3f

read   leggere   20a, 25n, 28d, 37f

read between the lines   leggere tra le righe   17a

reader   lettore (-trice)   25n, 28d

readers   lettori   20a

reading passage   lettura   25n, 28d, 37f

reading book   libro di lettura   37b

real   reale   1d

real-estate agent agente immobiliare 38a
Realism Realismo 28b
realistic realista 11e
Really? Davvero? 16c, 21c
realty tax imposta sugli immobili 26b
ream of paper risma di carta 19d, 25c
reap mietere 14a
reason ragione, ragionare 22a, 22b
reasonable ragionevole 11e
rebellious ribelle 11e
rebus rebus 27a
receipt ricevuta, scontrino, fattura 25a, 35a
receive ricevere 19e
receive benefits ricevere assistenza sociale 44b
receiver destinatario 19e
recent recente 4c
recently recentemente 4c
receptacle recipiente 3e
reception ricezione 42a
recession recessione 26a
recipe ricetta 24n
recipe book libro di ricette 25n
reciprocal reciproco 1d
reckless temerario 11e
recliner sedia a sdraio 23b
recommend raccomandare 17a
record record, primato 27b
recorder registratore 20b
recover rimettersi 40a
recreational activities attività ricreative 27a
rectangle rettangolo 2a
rectangular rettangolare 3d
red rosso 7a
red hair capelli rossi 11a
redness rossore 40a
reduce ridurre 3b
reduced price prezzo ridotto 25a
reduction riduzione 3b
reef banco di scogli 13b
reel mulinello 27a
refer riferire 17a

referee arbitro (-a) 27b
reference book libro di consultazione 25n
references referenze 11f, 38b
referendum referendum 43a
refined raffinato 11e
reflect riflettere 22a, 22b
reflection riflesso, riflessione 12d, 22a
reflexive riflessivo 8a
reform riforma 43a
refrigerator frigorifero 23b
refugee profugo (-a) 44d
refugee camp campo profughi 44d
refund rimborso 25a
Reggio Calabria Reggio Calabria 30c
region regione 13d
regional regionale 43a
register a company immatricolare un'azienda 38d
registered mail posta raccomandata 19e
registration iscrizione 37f
registration fee tassa d'iscrizione 37f
regular regolare 4c, 8a
regular surface mail posta ordinaria 19e
regularly regolarmente 4c
rehearsal prova 28c
reindeer renna 15a
relative (kin) parente 10a
relative (grammar) relativa 8a
relax riposarsi 27a
relaxation riposo 27a, 29b
release on bail rilasciare sotto cauzione 41
relief rilievo, sollievo 3d, 21a, 28b
religion religione 11d
religious religioso 11d
remain rimanere 29b
remarry risposarsi 11c
remember ricordare 22a, 22b
remodeling, renovation rimodernamento 23e

remote control   telecomando   20b

Remove   Rimuovi   42c

Renaissance   Rinascimento   43b

rent   affitto, noleggiare, affittare   33d, 23e

rental   noleggio   33d

rental place   autonoleggio   33d

rented car   macchina, auto noleggiata   34

repair   riparazione   23e

repeat   ripetere   17a, 37f

repetition   ripetizione   17a

reply   risposta, replicare, rispondere   17a, 19e, 42c

report   resoconto, relazione, riferire, riportare   17a

report card   pagella   37f

report, news item, feature   cronaca   20a

report, reporting   servizio   20a

representation (political)   rappresentanza   43a

reproach   rimproverare   17a

reptile   rettile   15c

republic   repubblica   43a

republican party   partito repubblicano   43a

request   richiesta, richiedere   17a

rescue   soccorrere   39a

reservation   prenotazione   24l, 30a, 32a, 35a

reserve   prenotare   35a

reserved   riservato   11e, 24l

reservoir   cisterna   3e

reside   risiedere   11f

residence   residenza, domicilio   11f

residential school   collegio   37a

resin   resina   13c

resistant   resistente   13c

resonate   risuonare   12c

respectful   rispettoso   21a

respiratory system   sistema respiratorio   12a

rest, relax   riposarsi   12b

restaurant (formal)   ristorante   24l

restaurant (informal)   trattoria   24l

restless   irrequieto   21a

restricted   vietato ai minori, minorenni   28a

résumé   Curriculum vitae   38b

resuscitate   rianimare   40a

retail   al dettaglio   25a

retail price   prezzo al dettaglio   25a

retire   andare in pensione   38d

return   tornare, ritornare, restituire   3f, 25a, 29b

return address   indirizzo del mittente   19e

return ticket   biglietto di andata e ritorno   30a

return vehicle conditions   condizioni del veicolo al rientro   33d

Reverend   Reverendo   11f, 16b

review   recensione, recensire, ripasso, ripassare   20a, 28d, 37f

revolt, riot   rivolta   43a

revolution   rivoluzione   43a

rheumatism   reumatismo   40a

rhinoceros   rinoceronte   15a

rhombus   rombo   2a

rhubarb   rabarbaro   14e, 24f

rhythm   ritmo   25j, 28c

rib   costola   12a

rice   riso   24b

rice with vegetables   risotto   24b

rich   ricco   11e

riddle   indovinello   27a

rifle   fucile   39b

right   corretto, destra, retto   2b, 3c, 36c, 37f

right away   subito   4c, 8j

right prism   prisma retto   2a

right to vote   diritto al voto   43a

right to work   diritto al lavoro   43a

right turn, exit right   svolta a destra   33a
right-angled   rettangolo   2a
right-wing   di destra   43a
Rimini   Rimini   30c
ring   anello, suonare   3d, 12c, 18b, 25i
ring finger   (dito) anulare   12a
ring-binder   quaderno ad anelli   19d, 25c
ringed notebook   quaderno a anelli   37b
rinse   sciacquarsi la bocca   40b
ripe   maturo   14a, 24a
rise in prices   rialzo dei prezzi   26b
rite   rito   11d
rival   rivale   27b
river   fiume   13b, 36b
river-bed   alveo   13b
road, roadway, street   strada   36a
road map   mappa stradale   33a
road sign   segnale stradale   33a
roar   ruggire   15a
roast   arrosto   24a
rob   rapinare   39b
robber, burglar   rapinatore (-trice)   39b
robbery, burglary   rapina   39b
robin   pettirosso   15b
robust, strong   robusto   11a
rock   roccia   13b
rock music   musica rock   25j, 28c
rocking chair   sedia a dondolo   23b
Rococo   Rococò   28b
rod   canna da pesca   27a
rodent   roditore   15a
role   ruolo   28e
roll of film   rullino   25d
roller   rullo   23d, 25b
roller skating   pattinaggio a rotelle   27b
Roman   romano   1d
Roman Empire   Impero Romano   43b

romantic   romantico   11e
Romanticism   Romanticismo   28b, 43b
Rome   Roma   30c
roof   tetto   23a
room   camera, stanza   23a
rooster   gallo   15b
root   radice   1e, 14a, 40b
rope   corda   13c, 27b
rosary   rosario   11d
rose   rosa   14b
rosemary   rosmarino   14e, 24i
rosy cheeks   guance rosee   11a
rotten   marcio   14a, 24a
rough   ruvido   11e, 12e, 25g
rough copy, draft   brutta copia   37f
rough skin   pelle ruvida   11a
roughness, rudeness   rudezza   21a
round box   scatola rotonda   3e
round face   viso rotondo   11a
round table   tavola rotonda   37f
row   fila   3d, 28a
rowing, canoeing   canottaggio   27b
royalty   diritto d'autore   28d
rub   strofinare   3f
rubber   gomma   13c
rubber band   elastico   19d, 25c
rubber gloves   guanti di gomma   25h, 40a
ruby   rubino   25i
rude   rude   11e
rug   tappeto   23b
ruin   rovina   43b
ruler   riga   2b, 19d, 25c, 38c
Rumania   Romania   30b
Rumanian   rumeno   30e
rumba   rumba   28c
rumor   diceria, voce   17a
Rumor has it that...   Corre voce che...   17a
run   correre   3f, 12b, 27b
run away   scappare   3f
run into   incontrare   16b
runner   corridore (-trice)   27b
runway   pista   32c

rush hour ora di punta 33a
Russia Russia 30b
Russian russo 30e
rustle frusciare 12c
ruthless spietato 11e

S

sacrament sacramento 11d
sacred sacro 11d
Sacred Scripture Sacra Scrittura 11d
sacrifice sacrificio 11d
sacrilege sacrilegio 11d
sacristan sagrestano 11d
sad triste 11e
safe cassaforte 3e, 26a
safety deposit box cassetta di sicurezza 26a
saffron zafferano 24i
Sagittarius Sagittario 5d
sailing vela 27b
sailor marinaio (-a) 38a
salad insalata 14e, 24a
salad bowl insalatiera 23c
salami sausage salame 24d
sale saldo 25a
sales representative agente commerciale 38a
sales tax IVA 26b
salesman, saleswoman venditore (-trice) 38a
saliva saliva 12a
salmon salmone 15c, 24e
salt sale 13c, 24i
salt container saliera 23c
salt water acqua di mare 13b
salty salato 12e, 24a
salutation saluto epistolare 19c
Salvadoran salvadoregno 30e
sample campione 20c, 25a
San Marino San Marino 30b
sand sabbia 13b
sandal sandalo 25m
sandpaper carta vetrata 23d, 25b
sandwich (bun) panino 24c
sandwich (flat) tramezzino 24c

sap linfa 14c
sapling alberello 14c
sapphire zaffiro 25i
sarcastic sarcastico 11e, 21a
sardine sardina 15c, 24e
Sardinia Sardegna 30d
sardonic sardonico 21a
satellite satellite 13a, 42a
satellite dish antenna parabolica 20b, 42a
satellite television televisione via satellite 20b
satire satira 25n, 28d
satisfaction soddisfazione 21a
satisfied soddisfatto 11e, 21a
Saturday sabato 5a
Saturn Saturno 13a
sauce sugo, salsa 24b
saucepan casseruola 23c
saucer piattino 23c, 24k
Saudi saudita 30e
Saudi Arabia Arabia Saudita 30b
sausage salsiccia 24d
save salvare, risparmiare 26a, 42b, 42c
savings risparmi 26a
savings book libretto di risparmio 26a
saw sega 23d, 25b
saxophone sassofono 28c
saxophonist sassofonista 28c
say, tell dire 17a
scale scala, scaglia, bilancia 13c, 15c, 28c
scalene scaleno 2a
scallop, shell conchiglia 15c
scalp cuoio capelluto 12a
Scandinavia Scandinavia 30b
Scandinavian scandinavo 30e
scanner scanner 19d, 25c
scar cicatrice 40a
scarlet fever scarlattina 40a
scenario, background scenario 28e
scene scena 25n, 28d, 28e
scenery sceneggiatura 28a, 28e
scenic route itinerario panoramico 36b

scented profumato 12e
schedule orario 32b, 34
scheming intrigante 21a
scholarship, grant borsa di studio
  37a
scholarship holder borsista
  37a
school scuola 37a
school bag cartella 37b
school fee, tuition tassa scolastica
  37f
school registration iscrizione a
  scuola 37f
school yard cortile 37c
school year anno scolastico
  5b, 37a
schoolmate compagno (-a) 37d
sciatic nerve nervo sciatico
  12b
science scienza 37e
science fiction fantascienza
  20a, 25n, 28a
sciences faculty facoltà di scienze
  37a
scientific lyceum liceo scientifico
  37a
scientist scienziato (-a) 38a
scissors forbici 19d, 25c
score (musical) spartito 25j,
  28c
score (game) punteggio, segnare
  27b
Scorpio Scorpione 5d
scorpion scorpione 15d
Scotland Scozia 30b
Scottish scozzese 30e
scoundrel scellerato, briccone (-a)
  11e, 21a
scrap iron rottame 13c
scratch graffio 33d
scrawny, skin and bones
  scheletrico 11a
screen schermo 28a, 42b
screw vite, avvitare 23d, 25b
screwdriver cacciavite 23d,
  25b
script copione 28e
scrupulous scrupoloso 21a

scuffle baruffa 39b
sculpt scolpire 28b
sculptor, sculptress scultore
  (-trice) 28b
sculpture scultura 28b
scurvy scorbuto 40a
sea mare 6a, 13b, 36b
sea horse cavalluccio marino
  15c
sea lion otaria, leone marino
  15a
seabed fondo del mare 13b
seafood frutti di mare 24e
seagull gabbiano 15b
seal foca 15a
search ricerca, perquisizione
  19f, 39b, 42b
search warrant mandato di
  perquisizione 39b
seaside area zona balneare 30a
seaside vacation vacanza al mare
  30a
season stagione 5c
seat posto, sellino 32c, 34
seat (political) seggio 43a
seat belt cintura di sicurezza
  32c, 33c
secant secante 2b
second secondo 1b, 4b
second course secondo piatto
  24a
second job, moonlighting
  secondo lavoro 38d
Second World War Seconda
  Guerra Mondiale 43b
second year secondo anno 37a
secondary school scuola
  secondaria 37a
secretary segretario (-a) 37d, 38a
sect setta 11d
section sezione 3c
security services servizi di
  sicurezza 43a
sedative sedativo 25h, 40a
seductive seducente 11a, 11e
see vedere 12d
See you later! A più tardi! 16a
See you soon! A presto! 16a

See you Sunday!   A domenica!
  16a
See you!   Ci vediamo!   16a
seed, sow   seme, seminare   14a
segment   segmento   2b
Select   Seleziona   42c
self-confident, sure   sicuro   11e
self-examination   autopalpazione
  40a
self-learner   privatista   37d
self-sufficient   autosufficiente
  11e
self-taught   autodidatta   37f
sell   vendere   23f, 25a
semester   semestre   37f
semicolon   punto e virgola   19c
seminar, workshop   seminario
  37f
senate   senato   43a
send   spedire   3f, 19e
sender   mittente   19e
Senegal   Senegal   30b
Senegalese   senegalese   30e
senile   senile   11b
senior   anziano (-a)   11b
sense, feel, smell   sentire   12b
sense of smell   olfatto   12e
sensible   sensato   11e, 22a
sensitive   sensibile   11e, 21a
sensitivity   sensibilità   21a
sensuous, sensual   sensuale   21a
Sent mail   Posta inviata   42c
sentence (judgment)   sentenza
  41
sentence (grammar)   frase   8a,
  19c
sentimental   sentimentale   11e
separated   separato (-a)   11f
separation   separazione   11c
September   settembre   5b
September 15   il quindici
  settembre   5e
Serbia   Serbia   30b
Serbian   serbo   30e
serene   sereno   11e
serial, series   programma a
  puntate   20b
serious   serio   11e

serious accident   incidente grave
  39c
sermon   sermone   11d
serve   servire   24n
server   server   19f, 42b
service   servizio   24l, 35a
servile   servizievole   21a
session   sessione   43a
set   insieme   1f
set a record   stabilire un record
  27b
set algebra   algebra degli insiemi
  1g
set of drums   batteria   28c
set the table   apparecchiare   23f
set up a page   impaginare   42b
seven   sette   1a
seventeen   diciassette   1a
seventh   settimo   1b
seventy   settanta   1a
several   parecchio   3b
severe   severo   11e
sew   cucire   25g, 25l, 27a
sewage   acque di scarico   44a
sewage system   fognatura   44a
sewing machine   macchina per
  cucire   23b
sex   sesso   11a, 38b
sextet   sestetto   28c
sexy   sexy   21a
shade, nuance   sfumatura   28b
shadow, shade   ombra   6a
shake   agitare   3f
shake hands   dare la mano,
  stringere la mano   3f, 16a
shake one's head   scuotere la testa
  3f
shaman   sciamano   11d
shamanism   sciamanismo   11d
shame   vergogna   21a
shameful   vergognoso   21a
shameless   svergognato   21a
shampoo   shampoo   12f, 25f,
  35b
shark   squalo, pescecane   15c
shave   farsi la barba   12f
shaving cream   crema da barba
  25f

shawl   mantello   25k

she   lei, ella   8g

shed light on   gettare luce su
13a

sheep   pecora   15a

sheet (of paper)   foglio   19d,
25c

sheet metal   laminato   13c

sheets (bed)   lenzuola   35b

shelf (book)   ripiano, palchetto di
uno scaffale   23b

shell (sea)   conchiglia   15c

shellfish   crostacei   24e

shelter   rifugio   44b

shepherd   pastore (-a)   15a

shift work   turno di lavoro   38d

shin   stinco   12a

shine   brillare   12d

shingle   tegola   23a

shingles   fuoco di Sant'Antonio
40a

shirt   camicia   25k

shoe   scarpa   25m

shoe horn   calzascarpe   25m

shoe repair (shop)   calzolaio
25m

shoe size   numero (di scarpa)
25m

shoe store   negozio di scarpe
25m

shoelace   stringa   25m

shoot, kick   tirare   27b

shoot (fire)   sparare   39b

shoot a movie   girare un film
28a

shooting on location   riprese in
esterni   28a

shop   negozio, fare delle spese
25a

shop for food   fare la spesa   24n

shop window   vetrina   25a

shopkeeper   negoziante   25a

shopping bag   sacchetto della
spesa   23b

short   basso, corto   3b, 11a,
25g, 25l

short (film)   cortometraggio
28a

short coffee   caffè ristretto   24j

short story   novella   25n, 28d

short-sighted   miope   12d

short-story writer   novellista
28d

short-term   a breve scadenza
4c

short-wave   onde corte   20b

shorten   accorciare   3b, 25l

shorts   pantaloncini, pantaloni
corti   25k

shot, kick   tiro   27b

shot (movie)   ripresa
(cinematografica)   28a

shoulder   spalla   12a

shoulder blade   scapola   12a

shout   grido, gridare   17a, 39a

shovel, spade   pala, vang   14a,
25b

show   spettacolo   20b

show-off   sfarzoso   11e

shower   acquazzone, doccia   6a,
23a, 35b

shred   stracciare   19d, 38c

shrewd   perspicace   11e

shriek   squillare   12c

shrimp   gambero   24e

shrine, sanctuary   santuario
11d

Shut up!   Zitto (-a)!   21c

shutter, blind   persiana   23a

shuttle vehicle   navetta   32a

shy, timid   timido   11e

Siberia   Siberia   30b

Siberian   siberiano   30e

Sicily   Sicilia   30d

sick   malato   12b

sick person   ammalato (-a)   40a

sickle   falce   14a

sickly   malaticcio   40a

side   lato   2b

side dish   contorno   24a

side mirror   specchietto   33c

Siena   Siena   30c

sight   vista   12d

sight test   controllo della vista
12d

sign   firmare   11f, 19c, 26a

signal light luce di posizione 33c

signatory, signer firmatario (-a) 26a

signature firma 11f, 19c, 26a, 38b

signs of the zodiac segni dello zodiaco 5d

silence silenzio 17a

silent silenzioso 17a

silhouette sagoma 3d

silk seta 13c

silk worm baco da seta 15d

silly sciocco 11e, 21a

silver argento 7a, 11c, 13c, 25i

silver ring anello d'argento 25i

simple semplice 11e, 22a

simple interest interesse semplice 26a

simultaneous simultaneo 4c

simultaneously simultaneamente 4c

sin peccato, peccare 11d

since da, poiché 4c, 8i

since Monday da lunedì 4c

since yesterday da ieri 4c

sincere sincero 21a

sine seno 2b

Singapore Singapore 30b

Singaporean singaporiano 30e

singer cantante 25j, 28c

single celibe, nubile 38b

single bed camera singola 35a

single-breasted jacket giacca a un petto 25k

singular singolare 8a

sink lavandino 23a

sinner peccatore (-trice) 11d

sinusitis sinusite 40a

siren sirena 39a

sister sorella 10a

sister-in-law cognata 10a

sit down sedersi 3f

sitting (of the house) seduta 43a

six sei 1a

sixteen sedici 1a

sixth sesto 1b

sixty sessanta 1a

size misura 3b

size (of clothes) taglia 25g

skate pattino, pattinare 27b

skateboard skateboard 27a

skater pattinatore (-trice) 27b

skating pattinaggio 27b

skeleton scheletro 12a

sketch schizzo 28b

ski sciare 27b

ski jumping salto 27b

ski resort campo di sci 36b

skier sciatore (-trice) 27b

skiing, ski sci 27b

skin pelle 12a, 24a

skinny magro 11a

skip a class saltare una lezione 37f

skip school, play hooky marinare la scuola 37f

skirt gonna 25k

skit sketch comico 28e

skull cranio 12a

skunk puzzola 15a

sky cielo 6a

slab, block lastra, piastra 13b, 14a

slant eyes occhi a mandorla 11a

slash sbarra obliqua 19c

Slavic slavo 30e

sleep sonno, dormire 12b

sleeping bag sacco a pelo 36b

sleeping coach vagone letto 34

sleeping pill sonnifero 25h, 40a

sleepless night notte bianca 7a

sleet nevischio 6a

sleeve manica 25g, 25l

slice fetta, affettare 3d, 24a, 24n

slide (photograph) diapositiva 37f, 25d, 28b

slide, slip scivolare 3f

sliding door porta scorrevole 23a, 35b

slim, lean snello 11a

sling bendaggio 25h, 40a

slipper pantofola, ciabatta 25m
slippery scivoloso 6a, 12e
slogan slogan 20c
slope pendio 13b
sloppy, disorganized
  disorganizzato 11e
slouch fannullone (-a) 21a
Slovak slovacco 30e
Slovakia Slovacchia 30b
Slovenia Slovenia 30b
Slovenian sloveno 30e
slow lento 3f
slow down rallentare 3f, 33a
slowly lentamente 3f
small, little piccolo 3b, 11a,
  25g, 25l
small bill banconota di piccolo
  taglio 26a
small garden giardinetto 14a
small package pacchetto 25a
small villa, cottage home villino
  23a
small writing pad blocchetto
  25d
smell, odor odore, odorare 12e
smile sorriso, sorridere 11a,
  21a
smoke fumo, fumare 13c, 39a
smoke bomb bomba fumogena
  44d
smooth liscio 12e, 25g, 25l
smug compiaciuto 21a
smuggling contrabbando 39b
snack spuntino 24a
snack bar snack bar 24l
snake serpente 15c
sneeze starnuto, starnutire 40a
snobbish altezzoso 11e
snow neve, nevicare 6a
snow-capped coperto di neve 6a
snowball palla di neve 6a
snowdrop bucaneve 14b
snowflake fiocco di neve 6a
snowman pupazzo di neve 6a
snowstorm bufera di neve 6a
so that affinché, perché 8i
So, so! Così, così! 16a
So? E allora? E con ciò? 9

soap sapone 12f, 25f, 35b
soap bar saponetta 35b
soap-dish portasapone 23b
soap-opera magazine
  fotoromanzo 20a, 25n
soap powder sapone in polvere
  25g
sober sobrio 21a
soccer calcio 27b
soccer ball pallone 27b
soccer player calciatore (-trice)
  27b
sociable socievole 21a
social assistance assistenza,
  previdenza sociale 44b
social worker assistente sociale
  38a
socialism socialismo 43a
socialist party partito socialista
  43a
sociology sociologia 37e
sock calzino 25m
sodium sodio 13c
sodium bicarbonate bicarbonato
  di sodio 25h, 40a
sodium citrate citrato di sodio
  25h
sofa, divan divano 23b
soft soffice 12e
soft drug droga leggera 44c
software software 38c
solar eclipse eclissi solare 13a
solar energy energia solare
  44a
solar system sistema solare 13a
soldier soldato 38a
sole (fish) sogliola 15c, 24e
sole (of a foot) pianta del piede
  12a
sole (of a shoe) suola 25m
solid solido 2a, 13c
solid figure figura solida 2a
solid geometry geometria solida
  1g
solo assolo 28c
soloist solista 28c
solstice solstizio 5c
solution soluzione 1f

solve   risolvere   1f
solve a problem   risolvere un
  problema   22b, 37f
Somalia   Somalia   30b
Somalian   somalo   30e
some   alcuni, alcune, qualche
  3b, 8c, 8h
some of it   ne   3b, 8h
someone   qualcuno   8h
something   qualcosa   8h
somewhere   da qualche parte   3c
son   figlio   10a
son-in-law   genero   10a
song   canzone   25j, 28c
sonnet   sonetto   25n
soon   tra poco   4c
sooner or later   prima o poi   4c
soprano   soprano   28c
sorrow   dolore   21a
soul   anima   11d
sound   suono   12c
sound signal   segnale sonoro
  42a
sound technician   tecnico del
  suono   28a
sound track   colonna sonora
  28a
soup   minestra   24b
soup (thick)   zuppa   24b
sour   amaro   12e, 24a
south   sud   3c, 13d, 36c
South Africa   Sud Africa   30b
South African   sudafricano   30e
South America   America del Sud
  30b
South American   sudamericano
  30e
South Pole   Polo Sud   13d
south-east   sud-est   3c, 13d
south-west   sud-ovest   3c, 13d
southern   meridionale   3c, 13d
sow   scrofa   15a
space   spazio   2b, 3c, 13a
space bar   barra spaziatrice
  19f, 42b
space shuttle   navetta spaziale
  13a
spacious   spazioso   3c

spade   vanga   14a
spaghetti   spaghetti   24b
Spain   Spagna   30b
Spanish   spagnolo   30e
spare wheel   ruota di scorta
  33c
sparkplug   candela   33c
sparkle   scintillare   12d
sparrow   passero   15b
spasm   spasimo   40a
speak, talk   parlare   17a
speak badly of   malignare, parlare
  male di   17a
speaker   cassa acustica, microfono
  18a, 20b
special correspondent   inviato
  speciale   20a
special education teacher
  insegnante di sostegno   37d
specialization course   corso di
  specializzazione   37a
species   specie   14a
speech, talk   discorso   17a, 43a
speech therapist   logopedista
  38a
speech therapy   logopedia   40a
speed   velocità   3a, 33a
Speed limit   Limite di velocità
  33b
speed up   accelerare   33a
speedometer   tachimetro   33c
spell check   controllo
  dell'ortografia   42b
spelling   ortografia   19c
spend (time)   passare, trascorrere
  4c
spendthrift   spilorcio   21a
sphere   sfera   2a
spherical   sferico   3d
spice   spezia   24i
spicy   piccante   12e, 28d, 24a
spider   ragno   15d
spiderweb   ragnatela   15d
spinach   spinaci   14e, 24f
spine   spina dorsale   12a
spiral   spirale   3d
spiral notebook   quaderno a
  spirale   37b

spit sputo 12a
splash spruzzare 12c
spleen milza 12a
splint stecca 39c
spoke raggio 34
sponsor sponsor 20c
sponsoring sponsorizzazione 20c
spontaneity spontaneità 21a
spontaneous spontaneo 21a
spoon cucchiaio 23c, 24k
sporadic sporadico 4c
sporadically sporadicamente 4c
sports car macchina, auto sportiva 34
sports event gara 27b
sports fan tifoso (-a) 27b
sports jacket giacca sportiva 25k
sports program programma di sport 20b
sports reporter cronista sportivo 20a
sporty sportivo 25g, 25l
spot, stain macchia 25g, 25l
spotlights riflettori 28e
spotted macchiato, chiazzato 3d
spouse coniuge, consorte 11c
sprain distorsione, storta 40a
spraying polverizzazione 14a
spread diffondere 3c
spread gossip seminare zizzania 17a
spread out spargere 3c
spreadsheet foglio elettronico 38c, 42b
spring primavera 5c
spring (of a watch) molla 25i
sprinkler spruzzatore 14a
spy spia 44d
spy movie film di spionaggio 28a
spy-hole spioncino 23a
square quadrato 1d, 2a, 3d
square (of a town) piazza 11f, 36a

square box scatola quadrata 3e
square centimeter centimetro quadrato 3a
square kilometer chilometro quadrato 3a
square meter metro quadrato 3a
square millimeter millimetro quadrato 3a
square root radice quadrata 1e
squared al quadrato 1e
squared paper carta a quadretti 37b
squash squash 27b
squat rannicchiarsi 3f
squeal strillare 12c
squid calamaro 15c, 24e
squint strabismo 40a
squirrel scoiattolo 15a
Sri Lanka Sri Lanka 30b
stab pugnalare 39b
stadium stadio 27b
staff, personnel personale 38a
stage palcoscenico 28e
stained-glass window vetrata dipinta, finestra a vetri colorati 23a
stainless steel acciaio inossidabile 13c
staircase, stairwell scale 23e
stairs scale 23a, 35a
stamp francobollo 19e
stamp collecting filatelia 27a
stand up, get up alzarsi 3f
standings classifica 27b
stanza strofa 25n
staple graffa 19d, 25c
stapler cucitrice 19d, 25c
star stella 3d, 5c, 6a, 28e
starch amido 25g
stare fissare 12d
start the car mettere in moto 33a
starting wage stipendio iniziale 38d
state, affirm, maintain asserire 17a
state stato 13d

state of war   stato di guerra
44d

statement   affermazione, verbale
17a, 39b

station   stazione ferroviaria   34

stationery store   cartoleria   25c

statistical   statistico   1f

statistics   statistica   1g, 37e

statue   statua   28b

statute   statuto   43a

Stay still!   Sta' (Stia) fermo (-a)!
16c

stay-at-home job   lavoro a
domicilio   38d

steadfast   costante   21a

steak   bistecca   24a

steal   rubare   39b

steam iron   ferro da stiro   23b

steel   acciaio   13c

steep   ripido   13b

steering wheel   volante   33c

stem   stelo   14a

step   gradino   23a

step forward   fare un passo avanti
3f

stepdaughter   figliastra   10a

stepfather   patrigno   10a

stepmother   matrigna   10a

stepson   figliastro   10a

sticky   appiccicoso   12e

stiff   rigido   12e

stiff neck   torcicollo   40a

stiffness   rigidezza   40a

still, yet, again   ancora   4c, 8j

sting   pungere   15d

stink   puzzo, puzzare   12e

stinky   puzzolente   12e

stir, mix   girare   24a

stitch   punto   25g, 25l, 40a

stock, share   azione   26a

stock corporation   società per
azioni   38d

stock exchange   borsa   36a

stock market   borsa valori   26a

stockbroker   agente di cambio
38a

stockholder   azionista   38d

stocking   calza   25m

stocky   tarchiato   11a

stomach   stomaco   12a

stomachache   mal di stomaco
40a

stone   pietra, sasso, calcolo
13b, 40a

stool   sgabello   23b

stop   fermare, stop   33b, 34

Stop it! That's enough!   Basta!
16c

stopover   scalo   32c

storage room, shed   ripostiglio
14a

storage space   deposito   23a

store   negozio, immagazzinare
24m, 25a, 42b

store chain   catena di negozi
25a

store clerk   commesso (-a)   25a,
38a

store window   vetrina   25a

stork   cicogna   15b

storm   tempesta   6a

story   storia   17a

stove (heating)   stufa   23b

stove (kitchen)   cucina   23b

stove air vent   cappa   23d

stove element   fornello   23b

straight   retta, piatto   2b

straight ahead   diritto (dritto)
36c

straight hair   capelli lisci   11a

straw   paglia   13c, 14a

straw hat   cappello di paglia
25k

strawberry   fragola   14d, 24g

streaked   vergato   3d

streaked hair   capelli striati
11a

street   via, strada   11f, 36a, 38b

street sweeper   netturbino (-a)
38a

strength   forza   11a

stress   stress   40a

stretch   stirare   3f

stretcher   barella   40a

strict   severo   21a

strike   sciopero   38d

striker scioperante 38d
string corda, spago 25c, 25l, 28c, 38c
string bean fagiolino 14e, 24f
string instruments strumenti a corda 28c
stripe, streak striscia 3d
striped a strisce, a righe 25g, 25l
stroke (cerebral) ictus cerebrale 40a
stroke (caress) lisciare 3f
stroll passeggiata, , fare una passeggiata 3f, 29b
strong forte 11a, 11e, 40a
strong desire voglia 21a
stubborn testardo 11e
student studente (-essa) 37d
study studio, studiare 22a, 22b, 37f
stuff roba, farcire 13c, 24a
stumble inciampare, incespicare 3f
Stupendous! Stupendo! 16c
stupid stupido 11e
stuttering balbuziente 11e
style stile 19c, 28d, 42b
stylistics stilistica 25n, 28d
subject materia, soggetto 8a, 37e
subjunctive congiuntivo 8a
subordinate subordinata 8a
subscribe abbonarsi 20a
subscription abbonamento 20a, 42a
subscription fee canone d'abbonamento 42a
subsidiary filiale 38d
substance sostanza 13c
substantive sostantivo 8a
subtitle sottotitolo 28a
subtract sottrarre 1e
subtraction sottrazione 1e
suburb sobborgo, periferia 36b
subway metropolitana 34
subway entrance entrata della metropolitana 34
subway station stazione della metropolitana 34

Sudan Sudan 30b
Sudanese sudanese 30e
sue querelare 41
suede shoes scarpe di camoscio 25m
sufficient sufficiente 3b
sugar zucchero 24i
sugar bowl zuccheriera 23c
suggest suggerire 17a
suit vestito, abito 25k
suitcase valigia 31
sulfur zolfo 13c
sulky scontroso 21a
sullen cupo, tetro 11e, 21a
sum somma 1f
sum up sommare 1f
summarize riassumere 17a
summary riassunto 17a
summer estate 5c
summer vacation vacanze estive 30a
summit cima 13b
summons citazione 41
sun sole 5c, 6a, 13a
sun ray raggio solare 13a
sun tan abbronzatura, tintarella 36b
sundial meridiana 14a
sunstroke colpo di sole 40a
sunbathe prendere sole 6a
sunbeam raggio di sole 6a
Sunday domenica 5a
sunflower girasole 14b
sunglasses occhiali da sole 6a
sunlight luce solare 13a
sunny pieno di sole 6a
sunrise alba 4b
sunset, twilight tramonto 4b
supermarket supermercato 24m
superstitious superstizioso 11e
supplement supplemento 3b
supplementary supplementare 2b
supplies viveri 44d
supply cupboard armadietto delle forniture 38c
suppository supposta 25h, 40a

supreme court   corte di cassazione   41
sure, certain   sicuro   21a
surf   cresta dell'onda   13b
surface   superficie   3c
surfing   surfing   27b
surgeon   chirurgo (-a)   38a, 40a
surgery   chirurgia   40a
surgical appliance   protesi   40a
surname   cognome   11f, 38b
surplus   eccedente   26a
surprise   sorpresa, sorprendere   21a
surprised   sorpreso   21a
survey   sondaggio   38d
surveying   topografia   3d
surveyor   geometra   38a
swab   tampone   40a
swallow   rondine   15b
swamp   palude   13b
swan   cigno   15b
swarm   sciame   15d
swear, avow   giurare   17a
swear, curse   bestemmiare   17a
sweat   sudore, sudare   40a
sweater   maglia, maglione   25k
Sweden   Svezia   30b
Swedish   svedese   30e
sweet   dolce   11e, 12e, 24a
swell   gonfiare   40a
swelling   gonfiore   40a
swim   nuotare   27b
swimmer   nuotatore (-trice)   27b
swimming   nuoto   27b
swimming cap   cuffia   25k
swimming pool   piscina   27b
swimming suit   costume da bagno   25k
swimming trunks   pantaloncini da bagno   25k
swings   altalena   27a
Swiss   svizzero   30e
switch   interruttore   23a, 35b
Switzerland   Svizzera   30b
swollen   gonfio   40a
sword   spada, sciabola   27b

swordfish   pesce spada   15c
symbol   simbolo   1f
symbolic   simbolico   28d
symbolism   simbolismo   28d
symbols table   tavola dei simboli   42b
sympathetic   comprensivo   21a
sympathy   comprensione   21a
symphony   sinfonia   28c, 25j
symposium   simposio   37f
symptom   sintomo   40a
synagogue   sinagoga   11d
synthetic   sintetico   13c
syphilis   sifilide   40a
Syria   Siria   30b
Syrian   siriano   30e
syringe   siringa   40a, 44c
systems analyst   analista di sistemi   38c

T
T-shirt   T-shirt   25k
tab   tabulatore, tabulare   19f, 42b
table   tavolo, tabella   24k, 42c
table lamp   lampada da tavolo   23b
table of contents   indice delle materie   25n, 28d
tablecloth   tovaglia   23c, 24k
tablet   compressa   25h, 40a
tableware   posate   24k
tack   puntina   19d, 25c, 38c
tackle   contrastare   27b
tadpole   girino   15c
tail   coda   15a
tailor   sarto (-a)   25a, 38a
take   prendere   25a
take a trip   fare un viaggio   30a
take attendance   fare l'appello   37f
take off (airplane)   decollo, decollare   32c
take off (clothes)   spogliarsi   25l
take off (shoes)   togliersi (le scarpe)   25m

television reporter   telecronista 20b

television studio   studio televisivo 20b

tell (a story), recount   raccontare 17a

tell a joke   raccontare una barzelletta   17a

teller   cassiere (-a)   26a

teller's window   sportello   26a

temperature   temperatura   6c

template   sagoma   2b

temple   tempio   11d

temporarily   temporaneamente 4c

temporary   temporaneo   4c

temporary work   lavoro temporaneo   38d

ten   dieci   1a

tenacious   tenace   21a

tenant   inquilino (-a)   23e

tender   tenero   11c

tenderness   tenerezza   21a

tendon   tendine   12a

tennis   tennis   27b

tennis court   campo da tennis 27b

tennis player   tennista   27b

tennis racket   racchetta   27b

tennis shoes   scarpe da tennis 25m

tenor   tenore   28c

tense   tempo   8a

tent   tenda   36b

tenth   decimo   1b

terminal   terminal   32a, 38c, 42b

termite   termite   15d

terrace   terrazza, terrazzo   23a

territory   territorio   13d

terrorism   terrorismo   44d

terrorist   terrorista   44d

terse, succinct   lapidario   28d

test   prova   37f

test tube   provetta   13c

test-tube baby   figlio in provetta 11c

testify, vouch   testimoniare 17a, 41

testimony   testimonianza   41

tetanus   tetano   40a

tetrahedron   tetraedro   2a

text   testo   19c, 25n, 28d

textbook   libro di testo   25n, 37b

texture, textile   tessuto   13c

Thai   tailandese   30e

Thailand   Tailandia   30b

thank   ringraziare   17a

Thank God!   Grazie a Dio! 16c

Thank goodness!   Meno male! 21c

Thank you!   Grazie!   16c

thankfulness   gratitudine   21a

thanks to   grazie a   8i

that is to say   cioè, vale a dire 17b, 44e

that, those   quel, quell', quello, quei, quegli, quella   8d

thaw   disgelo, sgelare   6a

the   il, l', lo, i, gli, la, le   8b

The line is busy.   La linea è occupata.   18b

The line is free.   La linea è libera. 18b

The pleasure is mine!   Il piacere è mio!   16b

The sky is clear.   Il cielo è sereno. 6a

The watch is fast.   L'orologio va avanti.   4d

The watch is slow.   L'orologio va indietro.   4d

The weather is foul.   Fa un tempo da cani.   6a

theater   teatro   28e, 29b

theatrical agent   agente teatrale 38a

their, your (pl, pol)   loro   8e

them, to them   li, le, gli loro, a loro   8g

theme   tema (temi, pl)   25n, 28d

themselves   si   8g

then   allora, poi   4c, 8j

theologian   teologo (-a)   11d

theology   teologia   11d

theorem teorema 1f
therapist terapista 40a
therapy terapia 40a
there là, lì 3c, 8j
There's no doubt that… non c'è dubbio che… 44e
therefore allora, dunque, quindi 8i, 17b, 44e
thermal energy energia termica 44a
thermometer termometro 6c, 13c, 25h, 40a
thermostat termostato 6c, 35b
thesis tesi 37f
they loro 8g
thick spesso, fitto 3b
thickness spessore 3b
thief ladro (-a) 39b
thigh coscia 12a
thin, fine fino 3b
think pensare 22b
third terzo 1b
thirst sete 12b
thirteen tredici 1a
thirteenth tredicesimo 1b
thirty trenta 1a
thirty-one trentuno 1a
thirty-third trentatreesimo 1b
thirty-three trentatré 1a
thirty-two trentadue 1a
this, these questo (-a), questi (-e) 8d
thorn spina 14a
thought pensiero 22a
thousandth millesimo 1b
threat minaccia 17a
threaten minacciare 17a
three tre 1a
three hundred trecento 1a
three million tre milioni 1a
three thousand tremila 1a
three-elevenths tre undicesimi 1c
three-twenty-fifths tre venticinquesimi 1c
thresh trebbiare 14a
thriller thriller 25n, 28a
throat gola 12a

through per, attraverso 3c
throw tirare, gettare 3f, 27b
thumb pollice 12a
thunder tuono, tuonare 6a
thunderstorm temporale 6a
Thursday giovedì 5a
Tiber River Tevere 30c
tick zecca 15d
ticket biglietto 27b, 30a, 32a, 34
ticket agent bigliettaio (-a) 32a, 34
ticket machine biglietteria automatica 34
ticket office, counter biglietteria 34
tide marea 13b
tie cravatta 25k
tiger tigre 15a
tight stretto 25g, 25l
tight-fitting aderente 25g, 25l
tighten stringere 25l
till vangare 14a
time (hour) ora 4b
time (in general) tempo 4b
time (occurrence) volta 4b
time difference fuso orario 32c
Time flies! Il tempo vola! 4c
Time is money! Il tempo è denaro! 4c
Time is short! Il tempo stringe! 4c
timetable, schedule orario 4c, 25c
tin latta, stagno 13c
tin box scatola di latta 3e
tincture of iodine tintura di iodio 25h, 39c, 40a
tinfoil stagnola 23c
tint tinta, tingere 7b
tip mancia, (to) dare la mancia 24l
tiptoe camminare in punta di piedi 3f
tire gomma, pneumatico 33c, 34
tired stanco 11e

tiredness, fatigue   fatica   12b

tissue   tessuto   12a

title   titolo   11f, 16b, 25n, 28d

to   a   3c, 8f

to him   lo, lui, gli, a lui   8g

to Sarah's place   da Sara   3c

to someone's place   da   3c

to speak badly of   malignare   17a

to sum up   insomma   17b

to the east   a est   3c, 36c

to the fourth power   alla quarta potenza   1e

to the left   a sinistra   3c, 36c

to the north   a nord   3c, 36c

to the nth power   all'ennesima potenza   1e

to the right   a destra   3c, 36c

to the south   a sud   3c, 36c

to the west   a ovest   3c, 36c

to this day, till now   tutt'oggi   4c

To Whom It May Concern   A Chi di Competenza   19a

toad   rospo   15c

toast   brindisi, brindare   17a, 24n

tobacco   tabacco   25e

tobacconist   tabaccaio   25e

toboggan, slide   slitta   27a

today   oggi   4b, 8j

together   insieme   8j

toilet   toletta, bagno, gabinetto   23a, 32c

toilet (bowl)   gabinetto   23a

toilet paper   carta igienica   23b, 35b

toiletries   articoli da toilette   25f

tolerance   tolleranza   21a

tolerant   tollerante   21a

toll   pedaggio   33b

toll booth   casello (stradale)   33a

tomato   pomodoro   14e, 24f

tomb   tomba   11c

tombstone   lapide   11c

tomorrow   domani   4b, 8j

tomorrow afternoon   domani pomeriggio   4b

tomorrow evening   domani sera   4b

tomorrow morning   domani mattina   4b

tomorrow night   domani notte   4b

ton   tonnellata   3b

tone   tono   25j, 28c

toner   toner   25c

tongue   lingua   12a, 40b

tonic   tonico   25a, 25h, 40a

tonight   stasera, stanotte   4b

tonsillitis   tonsillite   40a

tonsils   tonsille   12a

Too bad!   Peccato!   16c, 21c

too much   troppo   3b

tool   attrezzo   23d, 25b

toolbox   cassetta degli arnesi   3e

tooth   dente   40b

tooth extraction   estrazione   40b

toothache   mal di denti   40b

toothbrush   spazzolino da denti   12f

toothless   sdentato   11a

toothpaste   dentifricio   12f, 40b

toothpick   stuzzicadenti   24k

top   cima   3c

topaz   topazio   25i

topology   topologia   1g

tornado   tornado   6a

torso, trunk   torso   12a

tortuous   tortuoso   3d

total   totale   3b

totalitarian   totalitario   44d

totalitarianism   totalitarismo   44d

touch   tatto, toccare   3f, 12e

touchy, over-sensitive   permaloso   21a

tough   duro   11e

toughness   durezza   11e

tour   giro   30a

tourism   turismo   30a

tourist   turista   30a

tourist information office   ufficio d'informazioni turistiche   36b

tourist place   posto di villeggiatura   36b

tournament   tournée   27b
tourniquet   laccio emostatico   40a
tow the car   rimorchiare la macchina   33a
tow truck   autosoccorso, autorimorchiatore   34
Tow-away zone   Zona rimozione   33b
toward   verso   3c
towel   asciugamano   12f, 23b, 35b
towel rack   portasciugamani   23a
tower   torre   36a
towing   rimorchio   33a
town (hamlet), village   paese   36b
town (market-town)   borgo   36b
town (small city)   cittadina   36b
town council   comune   36b
toxic   tossico   44a
toy   giocattolo   27a
toy box   scatola dei balocchi   3e
toy car   macchinina   27a
toy soldier   soldatino   27a
trace   calcare   28b
track   binario, pista   27b, 34
track and field   atletica leggera   27b
traditional   tradizionale   11e
traffic   traffico   33a
traffic accident   incidente stradale   39c
traffic jam   ingorgo   33a
traffic lights   semaforo   33a
traffic policeman   vigile (-essa)   33a
tragedy   tragedia   20a, 28d
train   treno   27b, 34
train station   stazione ferroviaria   34
trainer, coach   allenatore (-trice)   27b
training   formazione, allenamento   27b, 37f
tranquil, calm, serene   tranquillo   11e

tranquilizer   calmante   25h, 40a
transformer   trasformatore   25b
transistor   transistor   42b
transit   transito   32b
transit passenger   passeggero (-a) in transito   32b
transitive   transitivo   8a
translate   tradurre   17a
translation   traduzione   17a
transmission   trasmissione   42a
transparent   trasparente   7b, 25g, 25l
transplant   trapianto   40a
transport truck   autocarro   34
transportation   trasporto   34
trap   trappola   15a
trapezium   trapezio   2a
Trashed mail   Posta eliminata   42c
travel   viaggiare   30a
travel agency   agenzia di viaggi   30a
travel agent   agente di viaggio   30a
traveler's check   traveler's check   26a
tray   vassoio   23c, 24k, 32c
treasurer   tesoriere (-a)   26b, 43a
treasury   tesoreria   43a
treatise   trattato   25n
tree   albero   14a
Trentino Alto-Adige   Trentino Alto-Adige   30d
trial   processo   41
triangle   triangolo   2a
triangular   triangolare   3d
tributary   affluente   13b
trigonometric   trigonometrico   2b
trigonometry   trigonometria   1g, 2b, 37e
trimester   trimestre   37f
trimmer   potatore (delle piante)   14a
trio   trio   28c
trip, journey   viaggio   30a

triple   triplo   3b

tripod   treppiede   25d, 28b

trombone   trombone   28c

tropic   tropico   13d

Tropic of Cancer   Tropico del Cancro   13d

Tropic of Capricorn   Tropico del Capricorno   13d

tropical   tropicale   6a, 13d

troublemaker   attaccabrighe   21a

trout   trota   15c, 24e

trowel   cazzuola   14a

truce   tregua   44d

truck   camion   34

trumpet   tromba   28c

trumpeter   trombettista   28c

trunk (container)   baule   3e, 33c

trunk (of a tree)   tronco   14a

trust   fiducia, fidarsi (di)   21a

try on   provarsi, provare   25l

tub   tino, vasca   3e

tuba   tuba   28c

Tuesday   martedì   5a

tulip   tulipano   14b

tumor   tumore   40d

tuna   tonno   15c, 24e

tune   aria, accordare   25j, 28c

Tunisia   Tunisia   30b

Tunisian   tunisino   30e

tunnel   galleria, tunnel   33a

turbulence   turbolenza   32c

Turin   Torino   30c

Turkey   Turchia   30b

turkey   tacchino   15b, 24d

Turkish   turco   30e

turn   svolta, girare   3f, 33a

turn around   girarsi   3f

turn left   girare, voltare a sinistra   3f, 33a

turn off   spegnere   20b, 35b

turn on   accendere   20b, 35b

turn right   girare, voltare a destra   3f, 33a

turquoise   turchino   7a

turtle, tortoise   tartaruga   15c

turtledove   tortora   15b

Tuscany   Toscana   30d

tusk   zanna   15a

tweezers   pinzette   25f

twelfth   dodicesimo   1b

twelve   dodici   1a

twenty   venti   1a

twenty-eight   ventotto   1a

twenty-five   venticinque   1a

twenty-four   ventiquattro   1a

twenty-nine   ventinove   1a

twenty-one   ventuno   1a

twenty-seven   ventisette   1a

twenty-six   ventisei   1a

twenty-third   ventitreesimo   1b

twenty-three   ventitré   1a

twenty-two   ventidue   1a

twig   ramoscello   14b

twin   gemello (-a)   10a

twinkle   luccicare   12d

twist   torcere   3f

twisting, winding   avvolgente   3d

two   due   1a

two billion   due miliardi   1a

two copies   doppia copia   19d

two hundred   duecento   1a

two hundred and one   duecentouno   1a

two million   due milioni   1a

two thousand   duemila   1a

two thousand and one   duemilauno   1a

two years ago   due anni fa   4c

two-fifths   due quinti   1c

two-piece suit   costume a due pezzi   25k

two-thirds   due terzi   1c

type in   digitare   38c, 42b

typhoon   tifone   6a

typographical error   errore tipografico   20a

Tyrrenean Sea   Tirreno   30c

U

Uganda   Uganda   30b

Ugandan   ugandese   30e

Ugh!   Uffa!   21c

ugly   brutto   11a, 25l

ulcer   ulcera   40a
ultrasound   ecografia   40a
ultraviolet light   luce ultravioletta
13a
Umbria   Umbria   30d
unacceptable   inaccettabile   21b
unbearable   insopportabile   21a
Unbelievable!   Incredibile!   21c
uncle   zio   10a
unconscious   inconscio   40a
under   sotto   3c
underline   sottolineatura   19c,
42b
underpants, underwear   mutande
25k
underpass   sottopassaggio,
passaggio sotterraneo   33b, 36a
undershirt   canottiera, maglietta
25k
underskirt   sottoveste   25k
understand   capire   22b
undress   spogliarsi   25l
unemployed   disoccupato   38d
unemployment   disoccupazione
38d
unemployment benefits   cassa
integrazione   38d
uneven   disuguale   3d
unfaithful   infedele   21a
unflustered   pacato   21a
unfocussed   sfocato   25d
unfortunately   purtroppo   8j,
21c
ungrateful   ingrato   21a
unhappy   scontento   11e
union member   sindacalista
38d
union negotiation   trattativa
sindacale   38d
United Nations   Nazioni Unite
44d
United States   Stati Uniti   30b
universal suffrage   suffragio
universale   43a
universe   universo   13a
university   università   37a
university chair   cattedra   37a
university degree   laurea   11f

university graduate   laureato (-a)
38b
unknown   incognita   1f
unless   a meno che   44e
unmarried   celibe, nubile   11c,
11f
unpleasant   spiacevole,   21b
unsatisfied   insoddisfatto   11e
unscrew   svitare   23d
unscrupulous   senza scrupoli
21a
untidy   disordinato   11e
until   fino a, finché   4c
until now   finora   8j
unwind   distendersi   27a, 29b
up   su   3c
Update   Aggiorna   42c
uphold, maintain   sostenere
17a
upholsterer   tappezziere (-a)
38a
upholstery   tappezzeria   23b
upper school   scuola superiore
37a
upper-case character   carattere
maiuscolo   19c
upright piano   piano verticale
28c
upset, angry   adirato   21a
Uranus   Urano   13a
urban dweller   urbano (-a)   36a
urinary tract   apparato urinario
12a
urinate   urinare   12b
urine   urina   12b
urologist   urologo (-a)   40a
Uruguay   Uruguay   30b
Uruguayan   uruguaiano   30e
us, to us   ci, noi, a noi   8g
user   utente   19f, 38c, 42b
User name   Nome utente   42c
user-friendly   di facile uso   38c
usher   maschera   28e
usually   di solito   4c
utensil   utensile   23c

V
vacation   vacanza   5f, 29a

vacation in the mountains
   vacanze in montagna   30a
vaccinate   vaccinare   40a
vaccination   vaccino   40a
vacuum cleaner   aspirapolvere
   23b
vagabond   vagabondo   21a
vain   vanitoso   11e
valley   valle   13b
valve   valvola   33c
van   furgone   34
vandal   vandalo (-a)   39b
vandalism   vandalismo   39b
vanilla   vaniglia   24i
vapor   vapore   13c
variable   variabile   1f
varicose vein   vena varicosa   40a
variety program   programma di
   varietà   20b
vase   vaso   23c
vasectomy   vasectomia   40a
veal   vitello   24d
vector   vettore   2b
vegetable garden   orto   14a
vegetables, greens   verdura
   14e, 24f
vegetation   vegetazione   13b
vehicle   veicolo   34
veil   velo   11c
vein   vena   12a
veined, grainy   venato   3d
velvet   velluto   13c
venereal disease   malattia venerea
   40a
Venetia   Veneto   30d
Venezuela   Venezuela   30b
Venezuelan   venezuelano   30e
vengeful   vendicativo   11e
Venice   Venezia   30c
Venus   Venere   13a
verandah   veranda   23a
verb   verbo   8a
verdict   verdetto   41
versatile   versatile   11e
vertex   vertice   2b
vertical   verticale   2b, 3c
Very well!   Molto bene!
   Benissimo!   16a

vest   gilè, panciotto   25k
vestry   sagrestia   11d
Vesuvius   Vesuvio   30c
via satellite   via satellite   20b
vice, bad habit   vizio   11d
victim   vittima   39a
video camera   videocamera,
   cinepresa   25d
video cassette   videocassetta
   20b, 28a
video conference
   videoconferenza   42a
video disc   videodisco   20b, 25d
video game   videogioco   27a,
   42a
video recorder   videoregistratore
   25j
video telephone   videotelefono
   42a
Vienna   Vienna   30c
Vietnam   Vietnam   30b
Vietnamese   vietnamita   30e
view   veduta   35a
viewer   telespettatore (-trice),
   mirino   20b, 25d
vigorous   vigoroso   11a
vileness, baseness   viltà   21a
village   villaggio   36b
vine   vite   14a
vinegar   aceto   24i
vineyard   vigna   14a
viola   viola   28c
viola player   violista   28c
violate a right   violare un diritto
   43a
violence   violenza   39b
violet   viola   14b
violin   violino   28c
violinist   violinista   28c
viper   vipera   15c
viral infection   infezione virale
   40a
virgin wool   lana vergine   13c
Virgo   Vergine   5d
virile   virile   11a
virtual   virtuale   38c, 42b
virtue   virtù   11d
virtuous   virtuoso   11e

waterfall   cascate (cascata)   13b
watermelon   anguria   14d, 24g
wave   onda   13b
wavelength   lunghezza d'onda   42a
wavy, undulating   ondulato   3d
wavy hair   capelli ondulati   11a
wax   cera   23b
wax museum   museo delle cere   28b
we   noi   8g
weak   debole   11a, 11e, 40a
weakness   debolezza   11a
weapon   arma   39b, 44d
wear   indossare   25l
weather   tempo   6a
weather bulletin   bollettino meteorologico   6c
weather conditions   condizioni meteorologiche   6c
weather forecast   previsioni del tempo   6c
weather report   bollettino metereologico   20b
website   sito web   19f, 38c, 42b
wedding   nozze   11c, 29a
wedding dress   abito, vestito da sposa   25k
wedding invitation   partecipazione   11c
wedding suit (men)   abito, vestito da sposo   25k
wedding ring   fede   11c, 25i
Wednesday   mercoledì   5a
weed   erbaccia   14a
week   settimana   4b
weekend   fine settimana   5a
weekly   settimanalmente   4b
weigh   pesare   3b, 25a
weight   peso   3a, 11a, 31
weight lifting   sollevamento pesi   27b
Well done!   Bravo (-a)!   16c
well-built   ben fatto   11a
well-disciplined   disciplinato   21a
well-done   ben cotto   24a

well-mannered   educato   11e
Welsh   gallese   30e
west   ovest   3c, 13d, 36c
western   occidentale   3c, 13d, 30e
wet paint   vernice fresca   23d
whale   balena   15a
What?   Che? Cosa? Che cosa?   9
What a bore! What a drag!   Che noia! Che barba!   16c, 21c
What a fool!   Che sciocco!   16c
What a jam!   Che guaio!   16c
What a mess!   Che pasticcio! Che imbroglio!   16c
What a nice surprise!   Che bella sorpresa!   16c
What a nuisance!   Che seccatura!   16c
What color is it?   Di che colore è?   7a
What day is it?   Che giorno è?   5a
What does it mean?   Che significa? Che vuol dire?   9
What month is it?   Che mese è?   5b
What time is it?   Che ora è?, Che ore sono?   4a
What year is it?   Che anno è?   5e
What's the date?   Quanti ne abbiamo oggi?   5e
What's your name?   Come ti chiami? Come si chiama?   16b
wheel   ruota   33c
wheelchair   sedia a rotelle   40a
when   quando   4c, 9
When were you born?   Quando è (sei) nato (-a)?   5e
where   dove   3c, 9
which (one)   quale   9
while   mentre   4c
whimsical   estroso, capriccioso   11e, 21a
whine   piagnucolare   17a
whipping cream   panna montata   24h

whirlpool   gorgo   13b
whiskey   whiskey   24j
whisper   sussurrare   17a
whistle   fischiare   12c
white   bianco   7a
white-collar worker   impiegato (-a)   38d
Who?   Chi?   9
Who is it?   Chi è?   18b
Who knows?   Chissà?   17b
Who's speaking?   Chi parla?   18b
whole-wheat bread   pane integrale   24c
wholesale   all'ingrosso   25a
wholesale price   prezzo all'ingrosso   25a
whooping cough   pertosse   40a
Why?   Perché?   9
wide   largo   3b, 3c
widow   vedova   11c, 11f
widower   vedovo   11c, 11f
width   larghezza   3a
wife   moglie   10a, 11c
wig, hair piece   parrucca   25f
wild boar   cinghiale   15a
wild rose   rosa canina, rosa selvatica   14b
will   testamento   11c
willow, weeping willow   salice, salice piangente   14c
wilt   appassire   14a
wily, sly   furbo   11e
win   vincita, vincere   27a, 27b
wind (a watch)   caricare   4d, 25i
wind (air)   vento   6a
wind gust   raffica di vento   6a
wind instruments   strumenti a fiato   28c
windbreaker   giacca a vento   25k
window   finestra, finestrino   32c, 38c, 42c
window frame   telaio   23a
window ledge, sill   davanzale   23a
windpipe   trachea   12a

windshield   parabrezza   33c
wine   vino   24j
wine cellar   cantina   23a
wine glass   bicchiere da vino   23c, 24k
wine list   lista dei vini   24l
wine shop   enoteca   24m
wing   ala   15b, 32c
wings (of a stage)   quinte   28e
winner   vincitore (-trice)   27b
winter   inverno   5c
winter vacation   vacanze invernali   30a
wiper   tergicristallo   33c
wire   filo   23d, 25b
wireless   senza fili   42a
wiring   impianto elettrico   23d
wisdom   sapienza   22a
wisdom tooth   dente del giudizio   40b
wise   saggio   11e
wistaria   glicine   14b
with   con   8f
with a drop of alcohol   caffè corretto   24j
with a drop of milk   caffè macchiato   24j
With cordial greetings   Con i più cordiali saluti   19a
with double bed   camera matrimoniale   35a
with espresso coffee   caffè espresso   24j
with friends   presso amici   11f
with ice, on the rocks   col ghiaccio   24j
With kind wishes   Un caro saluto   19a
with one's parents   con i genitori   11f
with sauce   al sugo   24a
with two beds   camera a due letti   35a
withdraw   prelevare   26a
withdrawal   prelevamento   26a
within   entro   4c
within two days   entro due giorni   4c

without   senza   8f
witness   testimone   11c, 41
witty, spirited   spiritoso   11e, 17a
wolf   lupo   15a
woman   donna   11a
women's clothing store   abbigliamento femminile   25k
women's magazine   rivista femminile   20a, 25n
women's shoes   scarpe da donna   25m
women's suit   abito, vestito da donna, tailleur   25I, 25k
wood   legno   13c
wood box   scatola di legno   3e
wooden spoon   cucchiaio di legno   23c
woodpecker   picchio   15b
woods   bosco   13b
wool   lana   13c
woolen   di lana   25l
word   parola   17a
word processing   word processing   19f, 38c
workday   giorno lavorativo   5a
work (labor)   lavoro, lavorare   11f, 38d
work (of art)   opera   28d
work associate   collega   38d
work contract   contratto di lavoro   38d
work experience   esperienze lavorative   11f
work in a bank   lavorare in banca   26a
Work in progress   Lavori in corso   33b
work out   fare ginnastica   27b
workstation   stazione di lavoro   38c, 42b
worksite   cantiere   36a
workday   giorno di lavoro   5a
working hours   orario di lavoro   38d
world   mondo   13a
World Cup   Coppa de Mondo   27b

worm   verme   15d
worried   preoccupato   11e, 21a
worsen, deteriorate   aggravarsi   40a
worship   adorazione, venerazione   11d
worthy   meritorio   21a
wound, injury   ferita   39c, 40a
wrap   incartare   25a
wrapping paper   carta da pacchi   25c
wreath   ghirlanda   11c
wrench   chiave inglese   23d, 25b
wrestle   lottare   27b
wrestler   lottatore (-trice)   27b
wrestling   lotta   27b
wrinkles   rughe   11a
wrist   polso   12a
wristwatch   orologio da polso   4d, 25i
write   scrivere   19e, 28d, 37f
writer   scrittore (-trice)   25n, 28d, 38a
writing   scrittura   25n, 28d
writing desk   scrivania   23b, 37b, 38c
writing pad   blocco   25c
written exam   esame scritto   37f
wrong   sbagliato   37f
wrong number   numero sbagliato   18b
wrongfulness   torto   22a
wrought iron   ferro battuto   13c

X
X-rays   raggi X   39c

Y
Yah! Sure! There!   Ecco!   16c
yawn   sbadigliare   17a
year   anno   4b
yearly   annuo, annuale   4b
yell, scream   urlare   17a
yellow   giallo   7a
yellow pages   pagine gialle   18a
yes   sì   8j

yesterday ieri 4b
yet ancora 4c
yield rendimento, precedenza 26b, 33b
yogurt yogurt 24h
you tu, Lei, voi, ti, te, a te, vi, a voi, 8g
You're welcome! Prego! 16c
young giovane 11b
young lady signorina 11a, 11b
young man giovanotto 11b
young person giovane 11b
younger minore, più piccolo 11b
younger sister sorella più piccola, sorella minore 11b
your tuo, tua, tuoi, tue, vostro (-a), vostri (-e) 8e
yourself ti, si 8g
youth gioventù, giovinezza 11b

youthful giovanile 11a
Yuch! Che schifo! 21a

Z
Zambia Zambia 30b
Zambian zambiano 30e
zealous zelante 11e
zebra zebra 15a
zero zero 1a, 6c
zigzag zigzag 3d
Zionism Sionismo 11d
Zionist Sionista 11d
zipper cerniera 25g
zodiac zodiaco 5d
zone zona 3c, 13d
zoo zoo 15a
zoological zoologico 15a
zoology zoologia 15a, 37e
zoom zoom 25d
zucchini zucchine 14e, 24f

AT A GLANCE Series

Barron's new series gives travelers instant access to the most common idiomatic expressions used during a trip—the kind one needs to know instantly, like "Where can I find a taxi?" and "How much does this cost?"

Organized by situation (arrival, customs, hotel, health, etc.) and containing additional information about pronunciation, grammar, shopping plus special facts about the country, these convenient, pocket-size reference books will be the tourist's most helpful guides.

Special features include a bilingual dictionary section with over 2000 key words, maps of each country and major cities, and helpful phonetic spellings throughout.

Each book paperback, 256 pp., 3 ³/₄" x 6"

ARABIC AT A GLANCE, Wise (0-7641-1248-1) $8.95, Can. $12.50
CHINESE AT A GLANCE, Seligman & Chen (0-7641-1250-1) $8.95, Can. $12.50
FRENCH AT A GLANCE, 3rd, Stein & Wald (0-7641-1254-6) $6.95, Can. $9.95
GERMAN AT A GLANCE, 3rd, Strutz (0-7641-1255-5) $6.95, Can. $9.95
ITALIAN AT A GLANCE, 3rd, Costantino (0-7641-1256-2) $6.95, Can. $9.95
JAPANESE AT A GLANCE, 3rd, Akiyama (0-7641-0320-2) $8.95, Can. $11.95
KOREAN AT A GLANCE, Holt (0-8120-3998-X) $8.95, Can. $11.95
RUSSIAN AT A GLANCE, Beyer (0-7641-1251-1) $8.95, Can. $12.50
SPANISH AT A GLANCE, 3rd, Wald (0-7641-1257-0) $6.95, Can. $9.95

Barron's Educational Series, Inc.
250 Wireless Blvd., Hauppauge, NY 11788
Call toll-free: 1-800-645-3476
In Canada: Georgetown Book Warehouse, 34 Armstrong Ave.
Georgetown, Ont. L7G 4R9, Call toll-free: 1-800-247-7160
Visit our website at: www.barronseduc.com

Books may be purchased at your bookstore, or by mail from Barron's. Enclose check or money order for total amount plus sales tax where applicable and 18% for postage and handling (minimum charge $5.95). Prices subject to change without notice.
Can. $ = Canadian dollars

(#25) R 11/02